Good News

Good News

Social Ethics
and the Press

Clifford G. Christians
University of Illinois

John P. Ferré
University of Louisville

P. Mark Fackler
Wheaton College

New York   Oxford
OXFORD UNIVERSITY PRESS
1993

Oxford University Press

Oxford   New York   Toronto
Delhi   Bombay   Calcutta   Madras   Karachi
Kuala Lumpur   Singapore   Hong Kong   Tokyo
Nairobi   Dar es Salaam   Cape Town
Melbourne   Auckland   Madrid

and associated companies in
Berlin   Ibadan

Library of Congress Cataloging-in-Publication Data
Christians, Clifford G.
Good news : social ethics and the press / Clifford G. Christians,
John P. Ferré, P. Mark Fackler.
p. cm.   Includes bibliographical references and index.
ISBN 0-19-507431-9
ISBN 0-19-508432-2 (pbk.)
1. Journalistic ethics—United States—History—20th century.
2. Foreign news—United States—History—20th century.
3. Journalism—United States—Objectivity.
4. Mass media—United States—Moral and ethical aspects.
5. Mass media—United States—Political aspects—20th century.
I. Ferré, John P.
II. Fackler, Mark. III. Title.
PN4888.P6C47   1993
174'.9097'0973—dc20   92-11131

1 3 5 7 9   8 6 4 2

Printed in the United States of America
on acid-free paper

FOREWORD

Coming as it did after the demise of fascism, the near extinction of communism has been the great happy event of the late twentieth century. However, what the rejoicing champions of old-time capitalism ignore is that their system, too, is very sick. Symptoms of its illness in the United States are the decay of public services (schools, police, roads), the growth of crime and civic apathy, the ballooning of the public debt and trade deficits.

Quite a few Europeans believe that an alternative exists both to the horrors of totalitarianism and to the crippling flaws of jungle individualism. They see the solution in a concept of human society centered on the twin values of freedom and mutuality. In the form of a political option called social democracy, this concept is clearly more developed in Western Europe than elsewhere (as illustrated by the existence of national health services in every country)—maybe because centuries of bloodshed ultimately breed wisdom.

Has this anything to do with media ethics? Certainly.

A foreigner entering the U.S. media scene in the 1980s was amazed by the attention devoted to media ethics in books, reports, periodicals, cover stories, columns, workshops, conferences, college courses, even movies. In contrast, he also observed that the media with the vastest resources on earth (constitutional, human, financial, technological) did a poor job of serving their society. Their inadequacy appeared in such phenomena as their lasting infatuation with the most mediocre president ever elected twice and their relative indifference to the huge savings and loan scandal at home and the tragedies of the Third World abroad—not to speak of the violence in televised entertainment or the absence of documentaries and political debates in prime time on the three major networks. The outside observer was thus led to suspect that ethics was being used partly as an antiseptic, partly as a public-relations ploy, and partly as a means of scapegoating journalists, shifting onto their backs the blame for all the media's misdeeds.

So much has recently been said and written about media ethics in the United States that newspeople could be forgiven for feeling weary of it. There is no need for the commonplace mix of old myths (such as the need for dry factual accuracy and the separation of news from opinion) and recent, even faddish, "no-nos" that one can absorb on the job. But actually there is a crucial need for more scholarship in media ethics—a lot more, but of a different kind.

A few years ago, I attended a week-long ethics seminar at a media institute in the southern United States. Participants discussed one case after another without considering what their own ultimate values, their concept of the universe, humanity, democratic society, and media were or should be. Anyone who has suffered through the uselessness and wrong-headedness of such an exercise becomes intensely aware of a need for deep foundations under ethical thought and action.

Consider the following affirmations: mankind could not survive without solidarity; both the individual and the community matter; communication is essential to human nature; the mission of the media is to provide the public with a means of communication; whatever the media do that may jeopardize the persistence of mankind is unethical, evil. To a European at least, such statements are so obviously true as to look a little silly when strung together.

Yet it seems that much of the media profession, at least in the United States, somehow opposes these notions, sometimes consciously, most often merely in its practice—just as it opposed them in the late 1940s when they were expressed by the Commission on Freedom of the Press. Too many in the profession still take it for granted that human beings are isolated individuals whose rights and appetites are paramount; that society should be ruled only by the forces of the market; that media are nothing but businesses addressing customers; that newspeople know very well what the public needs and wants; that journalists' efficiency should be measured in dollars and cents. Ethics, consequently, is often scorned as the icing on the cake.

The truth, slowly emerging, is that human society cannot improve, cannot function properly, may not even be able to survive, if the media do not do their job well. They must not just give the news and carry advertising, but must assume all their missions as defined by communi-cologists in the United States: provide people with an image of the many aspects of the world that they cannot perceive themselves; serve as a forum where big issues are debated until the needed consensus is reached; teach the culture to all newcomers, children and immigrants, so as to help them become Americans or Spaniards or Swedes; and entertain their audience (a vital function in mass society). For the media, being ethical means fulfilling all these expectations. The media's purpose should be to help cure human society of its ailments: to make it free for all and more happy—as Jefferson implied in the Declaration of Independence. The French sum up this ideal in three words: *liberté, égalité, fraternité.*

All this may sound a little Old Worldish. Admittedly, in Europe, outside of periods like the post–Gulf War crisis in 1991, little attention is paid to media ethics and few media accountability systems are in operation. But Europeans do retain a concept of the media that is much less commercial than in the United States: a public-service concept, especially for broadcasting; and a political-forum concept, especially for the print media. And whatever the world fame of U.S. fact-oriented reporting, investigative journalism, and television entertainment, it is arguable (though arguing it would be anathema in the United States) that European media do a better overall job—which, of course, does not mean that they do a transparently good job.

But media are businesses. A corporation is expected to be profitable, and all its operations are required to be legal. These characteristics leave little room for a firm to be either ethical or unethical. Such terms suggest moral consciousness, which comes only with freedom. The managers of a firm are not free: they are expected to make the business profitable within the bounds of the law. As regards journalists, they are morally responsible only insofar as they are free agents. So most often they are not accountable for the media's worst sin, that of omission. The decision *not* to communicate (the media's most influential act) is usually taken by management for economic or other reasons.

This being said, there are, in my mind, two solutions to the problem, both of which take into account the natural purpose of all businesses. The first involves a change of words: for "ethics" read "quality control." "Quality control" sounds better than "social responsibility" to business ears simply because it involves not expense, but profit—as Japanese car makers have proved. Practically, of course, there is little difference: quality contents (all the important news made understandable and interesting) are ethical contents.

The other solution to the corporate problem lies in the application of collective pressure on management by news workers and customers. Thus production and profits become clearly dependent on ensuring good, hence ethical, service. To that end, media professionals and enlightened citizens, together or separately, should set up and operate media accountability systems. These should have a triple purpose: first, achieve agreement on ethical principles and practical norms; then incite all professionals to respect them; and, most important, unite media and lay people into a powerful social task force.

As I see it, there are three avenues for inciting media professionals to be ethical. The oldest is *external physical pressure,* by laws, police, and courts: these agents of pressure should be used as little as possible but are indispensable to maintain freedom for all. The second avenue is *internal moral pressure* from the individual's conscience: it should be used as much as possible, but it is a weak weapon in these days of big media. The third avenue is, I believe, the most reliable and acceptable: *external moral pres-*

sure, coming from peers and the public, preferably in an institutionalized form, such as media ombudsmen, press councils, critical reviews, and a score of other accountability systems.

Although media accountability systems have proved satisfactory when experimented with (mainly in the United States), they have not multiplied. There are, for instance, fewer than a hundred ombudsmen in the world for tens of thousands of media. A major reason for this underdevelopment is the ideology that often undergirds traditional media ethics: the ideal of rampant individualism and of an unregulated market. This ideology prevents media and media people from being truly ethical.

This erudite, sensible, progressive book does not claim to be presenting a new media ethics. On the contrary, it elegantly traces the genesis and evolution of social ethics over the centuries. To my mind, however, it does offer a new media ethics by championing an alternative philosophical foundation and source of spiritual energy for media ethics. This approach should make media ethics more central, respect by corporations easier to obtain, and means of enforcement—with public participation—more acceptable by professionals.

The extension of parliamentary democracy, the fall of the "Evil Empire" and the spread of free enterprise, media deregulation everywhere, privatization of broadcasting in Western Europe and of all media in former communist states, together with the persistent risk that the human race will destroy itself, make it all the more important, at the end of the twentieth century, that the media do a high-quality job. Quality control, true noncosmetic media ethics, is called for. Such ethics can only be social.

Professeur Claude-Jean Bertrand
Institut français de presse
Université de Paris–2
France

PREFACE

A few years ago, as we worked on this project late into the night at the Christians' house, Cliff's son Paul said his bedtime prayers. "Please help them with whatever it is that they're doing," he asked. The prayer was to the point, suitably ambiguous, and long, long overdue. The reader will have to decide whether this request was fulfilled, but the manuscript is finished now, the publisher's deadline has passed, and we owe our readers an explanation of whatever it is that we have done.

We have written a social ethics of news reporting because precious little normative theory surfaced amid the flood of media criticism and ethics scholarship during the 1970s and 1980s. In those decades, communications media became ever more concentrated and multinational, broadcast networks slashed their news budgets in the face of increased competition from "new" technologies and local newscasts, and public confidence in news reporting continued to slide. As globe-shaking events demanded more sophisticated reporting than ever, both print and electronic media seemed to prefer making a profit to providing substance.

Despite the pronounced need for democratic revision among the institutions and structures of communication, the volumes of moral advice for the news were instead tailored to individual professionals. Media ethics stressed the duties of reporters and editors, downplaying the responsibility they share with the newspapers, broadcast stations, chains, corporations, and conglomerates that employ them. Passion was there, but perspective was not. It was as if the Hutchins Commission's *A Free and Responsible Press,* which had argued forcefully for social responsibility in 1947, needed to be written all over again.

Always on our minds was the way our perspective related to social responsibility theory as articulated in *A Free and Responsible Press* and a decade later in Siebert, Peterson, and Schramm's *Four Theories of the Press.* The pages that follow reveal considerable compatability with the commission's recommendations. We agree that the press should be pluralistic, that it should encourage discussion and debate about pressing social needs, and that moral imperatives arising from the community should matter more than the economic and bureaucratic impulses of media institutions. We feel the same sense of urgency over the potential of organizational imperatives to override the communication needs of a democracy.

There is another resemblance between this book and the Hutchins Commission's 1947 report. Its emphasis on freedom and responsibility parallels the twin concepts central to our moral philosophy: persons and community. Despite the frequency with which free expression is applied to the institutional press, it most often connotes the right of individuals to express themselves, no matter how stupidly or brilliantly. Such freedom is negative. It is the hard-won emancipation from political control that libertarians in the West achieved from the likes of the Privy Council, Stationers Company, and Star Chamber after centuries of political struggle. However much Western culture has distorted their importance, individuals do matter, and the tradition of free expression recognizes that fact.

Responsibility, by contrast, is positive, purposeful, and simultaneously social and personal. Rather than defining the press as free *from* external authority, the concept of social responsibility sees the press as being free *for* social service. It recognizes that individuals live in community, that they rely on others for their very physical and social life. Social responsibility arose as an identifiable moral response to the needs of the news media when entrepreneurs found diminishing room for themselves in the arena of public communication. Start-up costs for daily newspapers had become astronomical, and unused broadcast frequencies were scarce. If there was an invisible hand, then its fingers had been crossed. Thus it was reasonable for those with access to public channels of communication to use them, not in an unrestrained libertarian fashion, but in a manner that would serve their affected publics. This reasoning holds true especially today, when fewer than two dozen corporations control half of the media dispersal in the United States. The recent emphasis on social responsibility has served to remind the media world that democracy and capitalism operate from distinct and often conflicting impulses, that essential political freedoms are often obscured by economic voraciousness.

However important these reminders are, we distinguish our approach from social responsibility because ultimately the latter only modifies libertarianism. Social responsibility may be libertarianism with a conscience, but it is an outgrowth of the same atomistic world view nonetheless. Advocates of social responsibility have been liberal, reformist, accommodating. Lacking an articulate and justified political theory to contradict the autonomous self central to libertarianism, they have hoped that the voluntary efforts of rational individuals would temper the forces of self-interest. This failure to identify an alternative theoretical base usurped the potential power of social responsibility, leaving it preoccupied with the negative freedom of libertarianism, making its social dimensions in the last analysis an exercise in wishful thinking. Social responsibility became subject to sloganeering, empty rhetoric, even cooptation.

The most obvious alternative to libertarianism and its cousin, social responsibility, is a theory of collectivism; but this paradigm is no more compelling to us than are theories rooted in individual autonomy and negative freedom. Collectivism—whether classical Marxism or critical theories of ideological hegemony—assumes that the social order is both definitive and axiomatic. Individualism is a dangerous chimera, beguiling the innocent and disguising the designs of the powerful. Indeed, power becomes collectivism's central concept; theories of collectivism accept the will to power as a defining characteristic of human activity. However, we oppose the reductionism inherent in collectivism; minus the circular argument—assuming what one wishes to prove—we accept the social character of human beings and the importance of power in human relations. But we do not reject selfhood wholesale, and we believe that power can be more productively understood as the empowerment of mutuality. There is too little evidence and clearheaded reasoning to make us tribal Hobbesians.

Distinct from both individualism and collectivism is the integration of person and community into a communitarian whole. We are born one at a time, but never alone. Persons do have rights—the right to live, the right to imagine, the right to communicate, the right to create—and these are rights that communities have no moral rationale for abridging. Although it would be churlish to question them when they are so rarely guaranteed anywhere these days, these rights exist only in relation to community. Just as we draw our sustenance from the community, we have a positive duty to create a social environment in which others can share the same rights equally. This positive duty means not only limiting our physical and social consumption, but also using our creativity to expand the resources that everyone can enjoy.

We situate our ethics of news reporting on this base, anchoring our model in both the history of ideas and the contemporary mind. In the pages that follow, we critique the dominant paradigms, settling on a cultural perspective within which we understand the person and the community. We then explain how this conception illuminates the morality of information, places positive responsibilities on reporters and editors, and redirects the institutions through which they work. Our purpose is to develop a communitarian ethics of the news media that avoids the errors of individualism and collectivism. For the sake of precision, we also distinguish our communitarianism, as necessary, from such related and competing views as Rorty's democratic liberalism, Habermas's communicative ethics, and the relevant theorists of postmodernism. In the process of formulating and applying a communitarian ethics, we encounter important academic debates and intellectual claims that need further elaboration. In order to present as coherent a picture of the whole as possible, most of the scholarly elaborations are reserved for the final chapter. We seek a new philosophical rationale for democratic free expression, appropriate to the late twentieth century; without it we fear that the idea of press freedom will vanish.

We have sought to make this book as clear as possible, illustrating our ideas with concrete cases and simplifying our prose whenever we could without sacrificing nuance. But we set out to write a normative social ethics for the news media, not to write another case book or to engage in casuistry. If our theory-to-example ratio is too high, that is a problem of execution, not of plan.

We have written this social ethics from a shared background in philosophy, theology, and communication theory. Philosophical reflection has guided our theorizing about ethics, society, and the nature of humanness. Theology has taught us that human fulfillment comes from a life of service to others, that the source of being is divine rather than human; indeed, that stewardship of our physical and symbolic resources is obligatory rather than optional. Cultural studies have shown us that communication is not an objective commodity but rather value-saturated symbolic systems through which the diverse dimensions of social life are constructed. The social ethics of news reporting is thus a sensible endeavor for us because it combines philosophical, theological, and cultural approaches to the normative nature of communication. Given the contemporary rupture of the public sphere and the dissolution of the social self, that form of public discourse called news serves as a rich laboratory for constructing a communitarian ethics.

Although we are responsible for the text that follows, we are indebted to a number of persons and agencies that helped us along the way. We have learned much about the values of journalism from the Poynter Institute for Media Studies and the American Press Institute. Insight into the various sections of this book that we dared to unveil over the years came from participants at professional conferences: the Association for Education in Journalism and Mass Communication, the Conference on Ethics and the Professions at the University of Florida, the International Association of Mass Communication Research, the International Communication Association, and the Speech Communication Association. Professors at the University of Missouri's Teaching Workshop on Ethics debated our model constructively. We would still be in the writing stages had it not been for two grants—one from the Donald McGannon Communication Research Center and the other from the University of Louisville College of Arts and Sciences—that provided released time and travel funds for our periodic rendezvous. George Gerbner and Marsha Siefert wrote us a letter for the ages when recommending our manuscript for their Communication and Society series. Em Griffin, Bob Husband,

Robin Lovin, Robert Reid, and Douglas Schuurman commented on portions of this manuscript when we most needed an outside reading. Ted Glasser, Ed Lambeth, and Bob White encouraged us to hasten publication. Jeffrey Ediger and Lori Reed edited the page proofs. Finally, we thank Anita Specht and Diane Tipps for physically preparing the manuscript—draft after draft after draft. All of them helped us with whatever it is that we have done.

Champaign, Ill.   C. G. C.
Louisville, Ky.   J. P. F.
Wheaton, Ill.   P. M. F.
November 1992

CONTENTS

Good News

1

Introduction

The *Chicago Tribune* headline read: "Stray Bullet Kills Young Girl Watching Fireworks." The tragic climax to Janet McClain's life occurred around ten o'clock on a Saturday night, the Fourth of July, in the Albany Park neighborhood of Chicago. She was watching teenagers set off fireworks across the street when someone fired a small-caliber bullet into the crowd at curbside. When Janet slumped over, those closest to her hardly took notice. Was she faint? Tired? Then the bleeding, and frantic people rushed her to a hospital.

Hours later, when doctors had declared Janet dead, police were taking statements, and most of Albany Park was retiring for the night, a reporter asked her family why it had happened; but they could not explain it. Why would a lively youngster in a split second become a rumpled corpse? By what measure of justice is a young girl decimated in Chicago, on a summer holiday, surrounded by friends, celebrating dreams so contradicted in her last violent moments?

In features, editorials, news, and even advertisements, newspapers warn readers that survival in a world of contrary ideals requires caution and vigilance. Smoke too much and cancer will destroy you; fudge too often on tax documents and federal computers will get you; ignore too many parking tickets and the Denver boot will make your car an immovable piece of the streetscape; vote the wrong ticket and lose vital programs; vote no ticket and surrender the franchise altogether. Invariably these warnings involve behaviors readers can control, at least enough to be held accountable under common notions of civic responsibility. But standing on a street corner with friends celebrating a national holiday, and becoming instantly dead for it, is not a case in which the newspaper can offer any caution or explanation, except that the bullet strayed and, by inference, Janet was unlucky.

The puzzling question about this story, buried on page 3 in section 2 of a July 6 edition, is why the newspaper felt obliged to attribute cause at all. Why not head the story "Girl Killed Watching Fireworks" (time and situation) or even the prosaic "Girl's Death Unexplained"? The former

3

headline at least retains the virtue of factuality. And the latter, although it could not claim to exhaust all possible interpretations, at least has the virtue of conveying that the newspaper finds no explanation sufficiently plausible to warrant public announcement.

Neither alternative, however, would answer the question most readers of such a politically indifferent newspaper account would likely cite as their primary reason for taking an interest in the story: How should a common person, naive to the ways of violence, behave on city street corners to enhance the likelihood of surviving friendly celebrations and reduce the likelihood of having one's property snatched, one's dignity stripped, or one's life pointlessly and painfully ended by a stray missile, without adequate elucidation? This book recommends that adequate explanations of the sort that contribute to cultural transformation must find their base in a publicly defensible ethics of news.

On the surface, the Janet McClain story is graphic testimony to the ongoing challenge of urban journalism. Jefferson fashioned his enlightenment function for news in an agricultural nation, and it took the prodigious talents of the University of Chicago's Robert Park and his colleagues early in this century to adapt the press to the demands of covering America's cities. Even to this day, urban minorities complain that they are turned into pathological fragments by the news machine, and financial districts come into sharp relief while neighborhoods languish.

But underneath the metropolitan patina lies the deeper crisis of our public life in recession. As reporters puzzle over the Janet McClains for their readers and viewers, our civic-mindedness seems irretrievably in decline. Serving the public interest has been the press's historic rationale, but big city or village, Independence Day celebrations or endless workdays, the community to be represented is under extraordinary duress. Civic-minded humanitarians have never been a majority; however, in the last few decades, the press's constituency has decisively shifted to a mass audience of atomistic units whose collective attributes it continually monitored as a performance guide. What is the mission of journalism in such a social context?

Responsible journalism gives a "truthful, comprehensive and intelligent account of the day's events in a context which gives them meaning."[1] To the woebegone Hutchins Commission, the world was already too complex; mere chronicle would add to the information overload and achieve no social gain. Sheer facts compiled and collated were insufficient to democratic pluralism, for reasons ably summarized in C. Wright Mills's cryptic term "abstracted empiricism."[2] For news reading and viewing to generate insight, news reports would require more than facts and balance. Thus our appeal takes issue with classical liberalism's perennial solution to the crisis of public discourse: write more copy, publish more pages, expand the so-called marketplace of information. That record of events we call daily journalism needs a framework of meaning that will both discern and validate the truthfulness of the report itself. Such a framework may strike at several levels—sociological to theological—for providing explanation and suggesting ways to structure a more beneficent future. Against the objection that frameworks of meaning (or "plausibility structures," as sociologists have called them) are best left to special-interest journals, we maintain that no explanation of events is possible outside certain assumptions about human nature and social custom, and that these assumptions, in all their color and nuance, are the province of daily journalism as surely as the banner headline is the traditional signal of everyone-pay-attention news.

At a recent convention of newspaper executives in Chicago, the day began with a long anecdotal speech by one of America's most widely published soothsayers. The speech was as bogus as most of the speaker's columns—one person's musings about the future, with astrological data for an evidentiary veneer. The CEOs around at least one attentive breakfast table were asked why such a distinguished group of corporate leaders would surrender the first hour of their working day to such claptrap as this. "It's entertainment," came the reply. On similar grounds, the others present justified this columnist's nationwide sales. Yet imagine the confusion of a neophyte newspaper reader trying to discern the "plausibility structure" of a news story on one page and an astrology column on another. We suggest that the same prospects of confusion and dissonance undermine much news reporting, and that a more self-conscious "framework of meaning" is a step toward a more democratically fecund journalism. Readers want to know what the facts *mean.*

Perhaps Chicagoans are too prone to accept stray-bullet theories of loss of life. In another town, a journalist might be horrified that a life could be so quickly snuffed and insist on more powerful explanations. Could it be that the appearance of stray-bullet theories in a city's newspaper is more a commentary on stray people than projectiles? Where else besides a very large city would the sudden collapse of one of its members be recorded as a cipher? It has been the history of humankind in the face of crime and grief to pursue explanation; ciphers will do for counting cattle in a corral, but not for people in a neighborhood. Journalism is a central means of that pursuit, yet its institutions seem peculiarly framework-shy.

A recent advertisement for the *Columbia Journalism Review* illustrates the press's disinterest in its ideological roots, a glaring weakness in this watershed era. *CJR* quotes an American visitor to Japan who is puzzled by the Shinto religion and says to a Shinto priest, "I've been to your ceremonies and shrines, but I don't get your ideology or theology." The priest pauses to think and apparently responds, "I don't think we have a theology or an ideology. We dance." And *CJR*'s publisher concludes, "This story has something to say to us as journalists. I believe that we too have no theologies, no 'isms.' Our world moves too quickly. . . . There's no time for fixed religions, no dogma. We dance." On the contrary, this book calls for careful reflection about the press's moorings, not merely refinements in reporters' behavior or a happy emotivism in the guise of moral neutrality.

As sound requires harmonics to give it fullness and power, a framework requires an explicit position on the value and end of human life. It might insist that emotional, aesthetic, poetic, or ritualistic considerations be made explicit in ways more common to anthropologists than to news correspondents. A framework will likely concede that all explanations are conditioned by the history of which it is a part, and from which it cannot be independent. An adequate framework requires primarily an account of community—the person in relation to others—and in turn is accountable to a community. Janet McClain episodes cannot be resolved epistemologically; they do not merely raise questions about adequate explanations. The axis is ontological, demanding from us a carefully constituted theory of the human person. Journalism—as with American enterprises generally—has historically taken its orientation from the individual; when McClain's assailant is apprehended, a motive can be fixed—either on the spot or in a courtroom—and the puzzlement dissipates. But we will not know the significance of McClain's life until the matter of personhood finds adequate journalistic foundations. James W. Carey elaborates:

> News is mainly about the doings and sayings of individuals. . . . Groups are usually personified by leaders or representatives who speak or act for them, even when we know this is pretty much a fiction. Edward Kennedy speaks for liberals, Jesse Jackson for blacks, Gloria Steinem for liberated women. Sometimes a composite or a person speaks for a leaderless or amorphous group: "scientists say"; a suicide note from a teenager stands for all unwritten notes. . . . Explanation in American journalism is a kind of long-distance mind reading in which the journalist elucidates the motives, intentions, purposes, and hidden agendas which guide individuals in their actions.[3]

Granting for the sake of argument the dissolution of the public sphere and the urgent necessity of refurbishing a viable communal discourse, journalism's ideological individualism may hide the nuances and hinder an understanding of the structural dynamics that need articulation. Chief among readers' needs is a fuller understanding of what responsible citizenship entails: membership in the school system, the city, the country, the world. Do we have obligations to the Siberian Eskimo or the Dominican cane farmer? If any at all, such obligations seem exceedingly remote. But then, a city dweller's obligation to a neighbor is often remote, too. Journalism should clarify and deepen those connections.

What is an account of community? The great twentieth-century journalist Walter Lippmann borrowed William James's enigmatic depiction of a baby's world as "a great blooming, buzzing confusion" to describe the impossibility of knowing truth *wie es eigentlich gewesen.*[4] When Lippmann noted the blooming buzzingness of the early 1920s, he distinguished news from truth and so underscored the difficulty of doing precision journalism in a libertarian framework. Who can know what facts are, whether facts are true, or how the facts would read if they were stripped of the biases, sloppiness, and ignorance that shields most people from truth? The average Slats Grobnick (columnist Mike Royko's best friend, if he has one) has no chance of sorting out the confusion. Slats does well to maintain enough suspicion to resist the futile interpretations of other half-informed experts. Lippmann urged, as a result of his own troubled sortings, a panel of knowledge-soaked social scientists who could see things rightly because lifetime tenure would keep them above temptations to power or profit—secular monastics whose wisdom would be our authority.

Communitarianism takes a different tack. If the world's confusion has stiffened news reports to bloodless information bytes, communitarian journalism salutes it as a sign of cultural richness, a trove that journalists mine for insights on the ways and means of people bonded by symbol and culture. The "confusion" noted by Lippmann and James is precisely at the interstices of these symbolic webs, where historians, linguists, anthropologists—journalists in disguise—attempt to locate connections from group to group, culture to culture. Bridges are there, we assume. Human beings are not autonomous mental substances linked only by contract to protect person and property. Differences are deep, but commonalities, ambiguous perhaps and distinguished by language and tradition, are more profound still. The *I* knows itself as the *Thou* is known, and not in isolation. An account of community is reporting in which even the formulas employed to capture events in words are fashioned by and for the subject group, a journalism in which describing events is never apart from the "thick description" that permits the buzzing confusion to make itself known, to tell its story.[5] News work conscious of its social and cultural setting is not a panacea, however, and communitarian journalism becomes Orwellian at the point where other institutions so constrain the press that it ceases to bear its own fruit and merely shades another's pasture.

When Culture Suppresses

Donald Woods was a middle-income newspaper editor in East London, South Africa, with a tilt toward the liberal, whose friendship with black activist Stephen Biko changed his life dramatically. (So poignant was the drama that producer Richard Attenborough made a film about it, *Cry*

Freedom, in 1988.) Biko was detained by South African security police in August 1977 and died in custody in September. Police implied that Biko's hunger strike was the cause of death, when in fact he had been beaten senseless and then, under the guise of providing medical solace, driven several hundred miles over rough roads to a "secure" hospital.

When news of Biko's death surfaced, Woods knew, government protestations aside, that he had been killed for political reasons, like many others before him—an intolerable form of control even in a country well known for suppressing human rights. It was also clear to Woods that police were lying about the cause of death; the inquest was stalled. Yet Woods knew the story as no one else, and he was media-connected. He would set the record straight and call government agents to account for the assassination. Wood's columns echoed with fury over the brutality of police fists, the incredulity of Police Minister Kruger, and the injustice of the two-race system. He demanded a public inquest.

A month after Biko's death, security forces pulled Woods from an airport queue; Kruger had placed him under a ban. For five years, Woods was to be prohibited from publishing or entering a publishing house, from being quoted or committing any words to paper, and from speaking or meeting with more than one other person at a time, his immediate family excepted. The ban was South Africa's more passive way of silencing dissent; its laws permitted internal police to quash Biko's voice with blood, then close the files on his case through slow official strangulation. Not only in South Africa was Woods muffled, but house arrest would effectively spike his voice anywhere this side of the moon's Mare Tranquillitatis.

Fire in the heart being what it is, the ban could not quell Woods's intention to tell his friend's story and to expose again—how many times must a story be told—apartheid's evil face. He wrote secretly and privately, under threat of home invasion by security police; the manuscript alone would be a ticket to prison. Friends smuggled pages into England (contrary to Attenborough's version), and Woods planned to apologize for the eventual book by insisting that the publisher had pressed forward on the project without his permission—a lie made necessary to expose worse lies by a government rotting in its triumphalism.

But the ruse was too far-fetched. When acid-laced T-shirts came in the mail, packaged as gifts to his young daughter, Woods and his wife, Wendy, determined that flight to freedom was the only way to get the story out. Disguised as a priest, he slipped into Lesotho in late December—aided by a network of blacks not unlike the underground railroad in America of 120 years earlier, except for the added danger of operating completely outside the law. Wendy and her five children stole across the border separately and discreetly, leaving everything behind. *Biko* was published the next year. And more than a dozen years later, an exiled editor is still speaking and demanding and calling his country to account.

Woods's problem, cast in moral perspective, was the complexity of social institutions that are too intertwined to maintain independent moral vision. His writing even jeopardized blacks, prisoners, his own family, and himself. The bands of a controlled society had pressed tightly at all points, choking off the opportunity to speak though not the courage to do so. Community had collapsed upon itself, the weight of bureaucracy crushing the personal word. Fortunately, by subterfuge other communities were receptive.

In principle, journalists face that same dilemma when publishers and sources hold common club membership, when community becomes so suffocating that Newspeak is the only syntax without pain. Historically, the American press has used its First Amendment leverage to resist government encroachment, but political independence does not keep other wolves from the door. Sometimes from malevolence—but generally from society's sophistications—economic, educational, scientific, and religious institutions coopt the news media's agenda.

The independent voice of the Fourth Estate is axiomatic to the Western press. Since the Reformation defied churchly power and the Enlightenment challenged feudalism, the press has represented—in theory, if not always in fact—the voice of the democratic commoner against the surging currents of state hegemony. The virtues of this independence are symbolized in the language we have developed to explain the institution of the press. A writer-researcher who fulfills this Fourth Estate function we call a journalist. A writer who represents the special interest of one of the other three estates we called in times past a press agent and now a public-relations professional. By this sign we attempt to distinguish between neutral observation and special pleading, between an account born of analytical distance and one born of specific purpose, between relative independence and an explicit agenda.

We recognize that the process of reporting and distributing information is complicated. The line between news reporters and publicists is sometimes as unclear as a foul line in a minor-league ballpark the day after a thunderstorm. Often a feature writer works with material supplied by a PR writer, who reads the newspaper religiously and depends for much of her own picture of the world on the accounts of it shaped by other feature writers and publicists. The same person is often editor, writer, and publicist, especially where communities of interest so intermingle that discrete roles are nearly impossible.

The Woods case speaks of institutional overlap unacceptable to American and European notions of a free press. News stories may begin with doctors, politicians, or generals; but when the story itself is known to carry—intentionally and with predictable consequences—the specific commercial or political interests of the source, we no longer call that report "news." It has become propaganda. And there are far too many quid pro quos in news coverage to assume naïvely that reporters are the people's eyes and ears at all points west of Trieste.

Some news organs take extraordinary measures to avoid blending the roles of reporter and publicist. The unwritten policies of one respected newspaper, for example, alert reporters and their spouses against political involvements and community projects that could be interpreted as conflicts of interest. Since the rule is unwritten, its interpretation in any specific case depends on what the ranking editor feels is right. Declining to write the rule also keeps it out of the hands of plaintiffs who might seek to use the newspaper's policy against itself, so the legal reasoning goes. To what degree the rule generates a journalism of the abstract, a journalism isolated from struggle, a journalism of official sources and official reactions, is a question that keepers of the newsroom culture have every reason to ask and few resources with which to answer. The quest for objectivity carries the risk of requiring value judgments by persons habitually and professionally disconnected from valuative experience.

Perspective and World View

Is objectivity a myth, then, betrayed in practice and subverted by the press's best efforts to frame it in guideline and rule? The problem lies not so much in the virtuous intentions of most journalists to clarify the buzzing confusions, but in the myth's connection to a set of ideas: the classical liberal *Weltanschauung,* a world view with the atomistic self as its centerpiece.

The task of reconstituting the foundations of press theory from Enlightenment individualism to a communitarian base scandalizes the history of journalism because that history has come to turn on the stories of bullishly independent editors whose papers have themselves scandalized status-quo power and provincial mores. It is not enough to call such history Whiggish and revise it with new demographics or social science. The plain truth remains that John Fenno and Benjamin Franklin, Ida Tarbell and Dorothy Day, for all their ironies and contradictions, stood apart from the traditional power of church, market, and government and created by their distance what they considered a new institution.

Reconstituting the basis of press theory also disgraces the working conventions of most journalists. "Get the story first" and "Tell all the truth you know" are tenets that inevitably put journalists at odds with communities that cherish reputation and privacy. The choices here are never transparent, and insisting on a communitarian base will not make them easier.

An editor in Florida puzzles over whether to publish information on divorce proceedings that involve a local judge. Florida's liberal Freedom of Information Act has given the editor access to sheriff's reports of spouse beating and child molestation. But the reports are clearly one-sided and ambiguous. No criminal charges have been brought. Neither the family nor the judge will talk. It appears that some domestic trouble has occurred, but a news story would invariably give a slant that could devastate the judge's career and embarrass his daughter at school. Obvious private solutions are being tried. Yet the editor knows against every measure of community decorum that he must run the story. To withhold publication would deny the courage of independent journalism. To sit on the story might later be regarded as protectionism; it could support the cover-up of other stories; it might cause the electorate to make a less informed judgment on the next circuit court ballot. When the story appears, the troubled family is humiliated publicly. Now the whole town knows—schoolteachers and girl scouts and everybody. Yet the editor keeps his professional integrity intact, knowing that his duty to wrest information from private into public channels has not been thwarted by community sympathies. Sometimes the truth will hurt.

A community-based ethics of the press also runs afoul of the various levels of community, the many duties within each level, and the apparent impossibility of balancing these loyalties within a coherent hierarchy of duties.

An editor in rural Kentucky gets photographs of a local man being forcefully placed under arrest. A scuffle between sheriff's deputies and drunken twenty-year-olds is nothing new in the coal counties. But the editor runs the only paper in his area, he has the only photos of the episode, and he knows the young man's mother as if she were his aunt. She will call, he reasons. She will ask for clemency, for mercy, for compassion, for silence. Not the picture!

He knows the call is coming. He knows about those bonds of family and friendship that work to protect people from undue harm. He knows that townspeople and church members share general commitments to benevolence and forgiveness; that the young man will not be in jail forever; that the town's merchants and repairmen and miners are his readers and advertisers. Will he lose them too over a photo story with as much long-term news value as a profile of the winner of the Baptist sewing bee?

The mother calls; they talk. He publishes the photos and tells the full story of the arrest, not because he calculates that doing so fulfills four duties while skirting only two, but to clear the air of all such calculations. As editor, he considers his first duty to publish news; he believes that all the village loyalties attached to small-town journalism bow to the simple, compelling mission of the newspaper: telling the truth.

On a national and global level, the calculation of community loyalty becomes even more obscure. As early as 1961, UNESCO was attempting to define standards for its well-known Article 19, the right to freedom of opinion and expression contained in the 1948 Universal Declaration of Human Rights. For each 100 people, the 1961 proposal said, a minimum standard for adequate public information is ten copies of a daily newspaper, five radio receivers, and two television sets.

But such measurements of fairness soon gave way to the more qualitative appeal of the MacBride Commission, with its interpretation of "free flow of information" as implying the need for a "new world information order" in which cooperative national policies ensure freedom of information from political and economic forces as well as the responsible use of information for human rights and peace.[6] The response of the American press was firm: the commission's implied dissembling of world news agencies and its tacit approval of state-generated news would lead to unacceptable changes in the patterns of news production. Most U.S. reporters were as little convinced that a Libyan news agency would provide public enlightenment as they were that ten newspapers per 100 people would heighten participatory democracy.

Communitarian journalism at the international level becomes frightful and unwieldy, so it appears. Under savage attack from terrorists and its very existence threatened environmentally, the global order is fragile no matter how noble our intentions. A world community needs more than a prescribed number of news channels or high-sounding metaphors about knowledge distribution. A coal town in Kentucky needs to know whom its police are gang tackling. A precinct in Chicago needs comfort in its grief and relief from its fears. Despite the conundrums and the far-reaching ramifications, community cannot be resuscitated without the leadership of the press. This book will attempt to demonstrate that bringing community to the forefront is impossible without a distinctively new theoretical model to undergird the press's role.

The Model's Four Elements

Imagine a small town surrounded by mountains. A steep and winding road is the only entrance to Dailyville, and many are injured or killed traveling the dangerous route. The good people of the village provide a volunteer ambulance service and maintain an efficient hospital twenty-four hours a day. Then an engineer discovers a likely opening for a short tunnel, and everyone initially applauds the idea. But the local Rockefeller owns a service station along the mountain highway, and the mayor has a prosperous restaurant halfway down. Soon the villagers begin doubting the cost estimates for the new tunnel, and a few reject the idea as too visionary. So to this day, ambulances continue to scream up the road, and medical supplies at the Dailyville hospital are fully stocked. The emergency crews vote badges and honors to one another for a job well done.[7]

Our theory of media ethics proposes to dig a tunnel through the mountain. Instead of Band-aids and antiseptic on the wounds, structural changes are needed in the press's world view, a new occupational norm, and fundamental reforms in the way mass-media institutions hire, involve workers in management decisions, determine their audiences, and engender civic responsibility. Thus we recommend a communitarian model that features the dialogic self, community commitment, civic transformation, and mutuality in organizational culture.

Theories are arenas for struggle. Given that they are not fashioned *de novo,* but in confrontation with the status quo, we consider the problematic to be individual autonomy. Since the Enlightenment in the eighteenth century, the atomistic self has been the West's cultural core and the defining feature of that cultural activity we call reporting. The primary root of the Enlightenment mind was negative freedom—freedom understood as an end in itself. The enduring problem is integrating human freedom with moral order, and the Enlightenment failed to resolve it, stridently insisting on individual autonomy as nonnegotiable.

Conceptually and empirically, individual autonomy characterizes the classical liberal theory of the press. From this viewpoint, the press carries the aura of an autonomous self, floating unconstrained or restricted only in a negative mode by the social order. And formal media ethics, developed within this social and professional context, has imbibed the individualistic spirit as well. Accountability to self became the operating norm; protecting the legitimate boundary lines of other selves was the only social axiom.

Libertarian individualism served a transformative purpose in the seventeenth and eighteenth centuries, but it generates double-talk in contemporary debates about the nature of news; and it contributes no substantive challenges to problems raised by wholesale shifts in the industrial order since the 1890s. A different approach to the media–society relationship is critically needed for grounding a legitimate media ethics, one that wrests individual autonomy out of the core and constrains it along the margins.

Communitarianism is a second constituent in the model, serving as its ground. Emphasizing the collective has been the most obvious reaction to Enlightenment individualism; the integrating norm becomes the social whole rather than individual rights. Communitarianism, however, does not merely synthesize the social theories of atomism and collectivism, but restructures the discourse around the nature of humanity. Our concern is to articulate a normative social ethics that is visionary in character without being merely a variant of classical socialism. And the central feature of human being is community. To the extent that we know the communal, we understand persons. Community is axiologically and ontologically prior to persons; our formulation of this maxim has been shaped most decisively by the tradition of social ethics anchored in Reinhold Niebuhr.[8] We work from a philosophy of culture in which mutuality is the meaning center, and we presume a dialogic communication theory in which the phenomenon of human encounter cannot be reduced without destroying it. In communitarianism, persons have certain inescapable claims on one another that cannot be renounced except at the cost of their humanity. The supreme value of life, an affirmation of unmitigated human dignity, is the foundation of ethics. Universal solidarity is the normative core of the social and moral order.

The theory of media ethics that we advocate—with individual autonomy as its problematic and communitarianism as its ground—makes transformative social change the end. In more formal terms, a communitarian social theory in symbiosis with contemporary media systems gives priority to civic transformation as the press's occupational norm. News, in this perspective, is a narrative construct that enables cultural beings to fulfill their civic tasks. It is a hermeneutic process seeking not profusion of detail, but interpretive insight. Readers and viewers are made literate regarding the sociopolitical text. As a symbolic creation, news identifies the contours of the moral landscape by representing the edge of values along which human community is formed. Print and video news reaches the limits of its symbolic capacity when it serves to revitalize a citizenship shaped by communal norms. Rather than drowning audiences with data and fattening company coffers, communitarian journalism engenders a like-minded world view among a public still inclined toward individual autonomy.

A press devoted to the *telos* of civic transformation aims to liberate the citizenry, inspire acts of conscience, pierce the political fog, and enable the consciousness raising that is essential for constructing a social order through dialogue, mutually, in concert with our universal humanity. Nurturing communitarian citizenship entails, at a minimum, a journalism committed to justice, covenant, and empowerment. Authentic communities are marked by justice; in strong democracies, courageous talk is mobilized into action. Covenant bonds rather than contractual calculations make genuine community possible. In normative communities, citizens are empowered for social transformation, not merely freed from external constraints, as classical liberalism insisted.

The fourth component, the operating principle, is organizational culture characterized by mutuality. Communitarianism insists that mass-media structures make a decisive break with individualistic capitalism or, in more cultural terms, with power pragmatism. As Max Weber recognized early in the twentieth century, the media's bureaucratic structure fundamentally shapes the process of news production; and our ethical models must be sophisticated enough to cut deeply into these systemic forms. In fact, shouldering Weber's challenge, this book insists that unless communitarian standards are integrated into media institutions, reporting cannot redirect its mission toward civic transformation.

A rich notion of accountability will resonate in an organization's consciousness primarily through its discourse, formal and informal. Institutions constitute themselves through language, and therefore such discursive forms as company stories and codes of ethics are powerful resources for defining an institution's moral contours and activating a company's conscience. Moreover, the mutuality principle revolutionizes the workplace. In contrast to contractarian individualism, it insists that authority and decision making be allocated equitably, and that the work environment become humane enough to transform jobs into vocations. Additionally, in the same manner that Heidegger saw technological forms as warring with human freedom, the mass media's technological infrastructure must be radicalized for communitarian motifs to flourish in organizational settings. Our approach makes human values preeminent and scourges the uncritical adaptation to media technologies that has made them formative in conventional notions of newsworthiness—minicams and portable microphones, for example, driving us to concentrate on visually powerful events that themselves begin to define reporting.

This theory of social ethics—grounded in community, aiming for civic transformation, and operating by the principle of mutuality—is normative in character, precisely at the historical point when the status of norms themselves is problematic. Communitarian ethics stands in sharp contrast with descriptive ethics which catalogs practitioner morality, ethics in the analytic tradition, and other nonnormative strategies. These approaches to professional ethics are quiescent and largely coopted. They do not demystify questionable courses or generate critical thinking on the institutional level. However, gaining this intellectual leverage forces us to confront urgent debates about normativity. But only the big questions are worth asking anyhow! Our communitarian model needs to be defended against positions that treat norms as unproblematic and in terms comprehensible to those who have lost their feeling for norms in a technicistic age blind to moral imperatives. In other words, we must explain on what grounds the communitarian version can be justified over against competing mainstream and radical theories.

We recognize that before we can debate the content of universal values, we must recover the potential for normative thinking. Linguists, anthropologists, and social theorists have discovered glimmers of universalism among the splendid diversity of today's cultures and nations. The German philosopher Hans Jonas, for example, embeds an understanding of responsibility within the natural world—parental duty to their offspring. The law of noncontradiction is a universal condition of intelligence. All societies establish taboo rituals at their boundaries and lift up ideals at their epicenter.

Building on the possibility of universal givens, we focus on the irrevocable status of universal human solidarity as a moral imperative. If one understands the nature of history, language, and our personhood as cultural beings, the sacredness of human dignity is inescapable. We experience this universal truth in the second order, but these are cultural inflections of a universal first order nonetheless. And once we enter the first order through universal human solidarity, we recognize that it entails additional proto-norms—justice, stewardship, and reciprocity, for example. We recognize further that universal norms reflect our deepest commitments, our world views, and make it necessary for us to debate and clarify our world views in the public arena. Our goal is not to abolish differences in world views, but to ensure that they contribute constructively to the master norm of universal solidarity.

Through the root metaphor of responsible selves, H. Richard Niebuhr establishes the distinctiveness of our communitarian theory. He releases us from the deontological–teleological debate in ethics by a schematic of persons accountable to one another in community. Given his commitment to language as the matrix of our humanness, Niebuhr's formulation is especially relevant to the lingual enterprise called news. And it is Niebuhr who demonstrates the centrality of normative language for nurturing moral integrity in an age of fragmented lives and alienation. When normative language becomes more fulsome within the press and we recognize it as apodictic to communitarian journalism, then world-view pluralism can finally flourish within the public amphitheater.[9]

Unconditional first foundations are no longer defensible. Yet a credible notion of normativity can be established by attending to Hans Jonas, Michael Polanyi, Thomas Nagel, and others who recognize constitutive norms in culture. In fact, communitarian media ethics contributes to that intellectual tradition as a rich laboratory for articulating a justifiable notion of normativity and for demonstrating that norms are the catalyst for advancing professional ethics as a whole. Without universal norms, our praxis is trapped in the distributive fallacy, with one particular power bloc presuming to speak for the whole.

Given the countless demands on the press of late and the urgency of the hour, propounding a new theory of news media ethics may appear naive and irrelevant. But rather than dismiss theory as the dead hand of scholarship, we are reminded that in the 1920s, when Walter Lippmann was faced with a situation of moral skepticism and collapsing norms similar to today's, he responded with *A Preface to Morals* (1929). His reconstruction carried a theoretical ring, cast as it was from philosophy, history, literature, and sociology. It refused to deal with all the immediate questions that Lippmann confronted in his daily journalism. *A Preface to Morals* sounded a rallying cry for broad explorations beneath the turbulent surface, becoming a best seller with six editions in its first year. Out of this experience and others, he wrote his provocative essay "A Scholar in a Troubled World," in which he located the academic's conscience in uneasy tension between the urgency of affairs and the demand for long-term reflection.[10]

With that inspiration, we present a theory of media ethics in the following chapters. Apparently Louis XIV once appointed himself the Sun god and declared in total arrogance: "After me, the deluge." We do not present this theory in a similar vein as the savior of the land, though we consider it vital for news-media ethics, a pea under the mattress. Lippmann taught us the value of scholarship in hard times.

2

Enlightenment Individualism

The roots of Anglo-American news lie in the Enlightenment. Although definitive in shaping the Western mind until now, the eighteenth century was not a smooth and singular time. The intellectual revolutions of the previous two centuries—the Age of Reason and the Age of Science, as they are often called—exploded into this rough-hewn era.[1] The elite philosophers and scientists of the sixteenth and seventeenth centuries, such as Locke, Bacon, Descartes, and Newton, saturated Enlightenment culture. Immutable laws were presumed to govern both the universe and human reality. Most of the writers and thinkers were popularizers, journalistic types centered largely in France and known as *philosophes:* François Marie Arouet (Voltaire), Jean Jacques Rousseau, Denis Diderot, Baron Holbach, and Antoine Caritat, Marquis de Condorcet.

As the eighteenth century dawned, nine out of ten books appeared in Latin and were available only to the intelligentsia. A century later, in an astonishing transformation of book publishing on the European continent, eight out of ten were printed in the vernacular instead. Knowledge was disseminated on an unprecedented scale; literacy rates doubled and a learned class was born.[2] It was the century of the German geniuses in music—Johann Sebastian Bach, Georg Frederick Handel, Franz Joseph Haydn, and Wolfgang Amadeus Mozart. The American statesmen Benjamin Franklin and Thomas Jefferson were quintessential figures in the movement. Edward Gibbon penned his vitriolic *Decline and Fall of the Roman Empire* during this period. And befitting an age that extolled human centrality, portraiture was adopted by the wealthy class as the preferred form of art.

The Eighteenth-Century Mind

The Enlightenment mind clustered around an extraordinary dichotomy. Typically, historians summarize this split in terms of subject–object, fact–

value, or material–spiritual dualisms. And all three are legitimate interpretations of the cosmology inherited from Galileo, Descartes, and Newton. In fact, the Enlightenment story actually begins in the sixteenth century with the Italian Galileo Galilei (1564–1642), a central figure in the transition from medieval to modern science. Galileo mapped reality in a new way, dividing nature into two famous compartments: primary (matter, motion, mass, mathematics) and secondary (the *meta*physical, *super*natural, values, meaning). In *The Assayer,* Galileo writes, "This great book, the Universe . . . is written in the language of mathematics, and its characters are triangles, circles, and geometric figures."[3] Matter alone mattered to him; he considered all that was nonmaterial, immaterial. He separated out the qualitative as incapable of quantitative certainty. In effect, he suggested two essences: values and meaning, on the one hand; matter and quantity, on the other. His fascination with the Copernican world picture motivated him to promote heliocentricity not as the calculation of astronomers only, but as a wide-ranging truth about the structure of reality.

Within a century, the Englishman Isaac Newton could describe the world in his *Principia Mathematica* (1687) as a lifeless machine composed of mathematical laws and built on uniform natural causes in a closed system. The upper story had been dissolved. All phenomena could be explained as the outcome of an empirical order extending to every detail. Mystery was defined away. Everything except quantity or number was called sophistry and illusion. Principles of mass and gravity extended to the extreme limits of the cosmos, explaining the movement of the farthest planets with the same mathematical laws that described the fall of an apple from a tree. Newton provided mature formulations, raising the mechanistic world view to an axiomatic, independent existence.[4]

Newton proved to be the turning point, not only for the authority of his scientific discoveries (Stephen Hawking described him as a "colossus without parallel in the history of science"),[5] but also for his commitment to the upper story that his own *Principia* ironically eroded. During his lifetime, he wrote 1.3 million words on theology, mastered the writings of the early church fathers—including the extensive fourth-century Athanasian–Arian debate on the nature of God—and was a generous supporter of Anglican church projects around London. Yet among his scientific colleagues, he banned any subject touching religion, insisting that "we are not to introduce divine revelations into philosophy [that is, science], nor philosophical opinions into religion."[6] Newton's loyalties were firmly anchored to scientific method and to transcendent truth, and he resisted warfare between the two. His Enlightenment heirs, however, would abandon the upper story with the same zeal that Newton applied to founding churches in London.

Cartesian Dualism

Within that pattern—from Galileo to the pervasive scheme of Newton—stands the Frenchman René Descartes (1596–1650), who cut the dichotomy squarely into the being of *Homo sapiens*. Lewis Mumford in *Pentagon of Power* ridicules "the crime of Galileo," because his bifurcation allowed the world of value and meaning to start shriveling away.[7] Although Galileo and Newton inspired the Enlightenment as much as anyone, Descartes trod most heavily on a holistic view of reality and ensured that persons also would be swept into the new cosmology. Descartes insisted on the non-contingency of starting points. As Ernst Cassirer observes, for Descartes, reason "is the same for all thinking subjects, all nations, all epochs and all cultures. From the changeability of religious creeds, of moral maxims and convictions, of theoretical opinions and judgments, a firm and lasting element can be extracted which is permanent in itself, and which in this identity and permanence expresses the real essence of reason."[8] Descartes presumed clear and distinct ideas, objective and neutral, apart from anything subjective.

Consider the very conditions under which he wrote *Meditations II* (1642). The Thirty Years' War was spreading social chaos through Europe. The Spanish were ravaging the French provinces and even threatening Paris. But Descartes was in a room in Belgium, on a respite in seclusion. For two years, even his friends could not find him squirreled away and studying mathematics. Tranquility for philosophical speculation mattered so much to him that upon hearing Galileo had been condemned by the Roman Catholic Church, he retracted parallel arguments of his own on natural science.

His *Discourse on Method* (1637) elaborates this objectivism in more detail. Genuine knowledge is built up in a linear fashion, with pure mathematics the least touched by circumstances. "Two plus two equals four" is lucid and testable, and in Descartes' view all genuine knowledge should be as cognitively clean as arithmetic. As Descartes described his method of reason in *Rules for the Direction of the Mind:* "Reduce complex and obscure propositions step by step to simpler ones, and then try to advance by the same gradual process from the . . . very simplest to the knowledge of all the rest. . . . We should not examine what follows, but refrain from a useless task."[9]

By contending, in effect, that one could demonstrate truth only by measurement, Descartes limited his interest to precise, mechanistic, mathematical knowledge of physical reality. As E. F. Schumacher has complained, no one sketched the modern intellectual map more decisively than Descartes, and his philosophical cartography defined out of existence those vast regions that had engaged the intense efforts of earlier cultures and non-Western peoples.[10] Furthermore, based on his idea that the self alone can discern the process of controlling passions and ascertaining truth, Descartes' advocacy of radical skepticism set the stage for "the striking fact about modern Western civilization as against all others: the widespread incidence of unbelief."[11] The modern press could hail a skeptic prince; but no culture survives on skepticism alone, and new orthodoxies would arise to fill the gap.

Individual Autonomy

Neither the subject–object nor fact–value nor material–spiritual split puts the Enlightenment into its sharpest focus, however. Its deepest root was a pervasive individual autonomy. What prevailed was the cult of human personality in all its freedom. Human beings were declared a law unto themselves, set loose from every faith that claims their allegiance. Proudly self-conscious of human autonomy, the Enlightenment mind saw nature as an expansive arena for exploring individual freedom, a field of limitless possibilities in which the sovereignty of human personality was demonstrated by its mastery of the natural order. Release from nature spawned autonomous individuals who considered themselves independent of any authority. The freedom motif—persons understood as ends in themselves—was the deepest driving force, first released by the Renaissance and achieving maturity during the Enlightenment.

Jean Jacques Rousseau was the most outspoken advocate of this radical freedom. Rousseau gave intellectual substance to the notion of free self-determination of the human personality as the highest good. He contended that freedom embodied in human beings justifies itself as the final aim. "I long for a time," he wrote, "when freed from the fetters of the body, I shall be myself, at one with myself . . . when I myself shall suffice for my own happiness."[12] Although such unbridled liberty took root with Pico de Mirandolla's "Oration on the Dignity of Man" in the Renaissance, the Swiss Rousseau provided its most mature version. In *Emile* (1762), for instance, Rousseau contended that civilization's artificial controls demean humanity and make us vicious,[13] whereas free in a state of nature the "noble savage" lives in harmony and peace. Joseph de Maistre observed that, for Rousseau, asking why people born free were nevertheless everywhere in chains was like asking why sheep born carnivorous everywhere nibbled grass.[14] What we observe empirically does not invalidate our own true nature. Liberty is the inalienable ingredient that makes humans human, even though under so-called normal conditions its sacred frontiers are desecrated. Rousseau represented the romantic wing of the Enlightenment, revolting against its rationalism; he won a wide following well into the nineteenth century for advocating immanent and emergent values rather than transcendent and given ones. While admitting that humans were finite and limited, he nonetheless promoted a limitless freedom—not just disengagement from God or the church, but freedom from culture and freedom from any authority. Even among those with a less pastoral vision, autonomy became the core of human being and the center of the universe.

Obviously, one can finally arrive at autonomous individuals by starting with the subject–object dualism. In constructing the world view of the Enlightenment, the prestige of natural science—then typically called "natural philosophy"—played a key role in setting people free. Achievements in mathematics, physics, and astronomy allowed humans to dominate nature, which had formerly dominated them. In Cartesian terms, the scientific method enabled the human race to be "masters and possessors of nature." Science provided living evidence that by applying reason to nature and human beings in fairly obvious ways, people could learn how to live progressively happier lives. Crime and insanity, for example, no longer needed repressive theological explanations, but were deemed capable of mundane empirical solutions. If the problems are characterized as primarily epistemological, one tends to restrict the post-Enlightenment alternatives to epistemology. The burning issue then becomes how we can know—and all kinds of subjectivity models or phenomenology or contemporary hermeneutics are directed precisely to overcoming the scientistic notion of lawlike abstractions and operational definitions through fixed procedures.

Likewise, one can get to the autonomous self by casting the question in terms of a radical discontinuity between hard facts and subjective values. The Enlightenment did push values to the fringe by insisting on a sharp disjunction between knowledge of what is and what ought to be. Enlightenment materialism in all its forms isolated reason from faith, knowledge from belief. As Robert Hooke insisted three centuries ago, when he helped found London's Royal Society: "This Society will eschew any discussion of religion, rhetoric, morals, and politics." With factuality gaining a stranglehold on the Enlightenment mind, those regions of human interest that implied "oughts," constraints, and imperatives simply ceased to appear. Certainly, those who see the Enlightenment as separating facts and values have identified a cardinal difficulty. The realm of spirit became a matter of faith and intuition, rather than truth. The spiritual world contained no binding force, but was left to speculation by the divines, many of whom shared the Enlightenment belief that their pursuit was ephemeral.

But the Enlightenment doctrine of individual autonomy created the greatest mischief. Individual autonomy stands as the centerpiece, bequeathing to us the universal problem of integrating human freedom with moral order. This perennial question appears on the human agenda in various forms: the individual's place in a social system, constraint and emancipation, determinism and free will, order and anarchy, individualism and mass society, dynamic socialization and stultifying institutions.

Several individualistic philosophies acted in concert to undergird the Enlightenment with a theory of human nature presumed as unproblematic. Examples can be drawn from France, Germany, and England.

Consider, for instance, the radically individualistic character of Descartes' landmark declaration, "Cogito, ergo sum." In his *Meditations Concerning First Philosophy* (1641), Descartes seeks an absolute proof that I exist. What concerns him is distinguishing fact from illusion. Is my nightmare or daily routine the reality? I fall asleep and dream of an igloo at high noon. I wake up and it is midnight in New York City. Presuming that I pass the most strenuous tests of skepticism, it is still true that I must perceive in either case. Whether dreaming appearances or negotiating the real world, my own mind is necessary. Therefore, my thinking capacity is indubitable, even if I doubt everything. I think, therefore I am.

Gottfried Wilhelm Leibniz was the foremost philosopher and mathematician to initiate the Enlightenment in Germany. Although he opposed French skepticism, his notion of windowless monads resonated well with Enlightenment individualism as a whole. Leibniz defined monads as the essence of substance, the ultimate real constituents of the universe. As the fountainhead of reality, these unique and pure substances exist in their own right as independent beings. Each monad is characterized by an inner activity, a mental or spiritual force. Inasmuch as monads are self-contained, none can lose force or gain substance outside itself. Moreover, each monad is a living and perpetual mirror of the others, since all are microcosms, containing within themselves the entire universe.[15]

John Locke's most important British predecessor, Thomas Hobbes, contributed the individualist theory of egoistic selves. In his view, human will is a physical force that gives the human species the same natural right as other animals to kill or be killed. Hobbes constructed in essence a selfish system of ethics in which power prevails; the right to harm or subdue for self-preservation is relinquished only by mutual agreement in a social compact.

Whatever the theory's specific formulation, the nexus of human freedom and moral order remains a classic concern for the philosophical mind. And in struggling with the complexities and conundrums of this relationship, the Enlightenment, in effect, refused to sacrifice personal freedom. Its tactic was not resolution—even though the problem had a particular urgency in the eighteenth century—but categorically insisting on individual autonomy. Given the oppressiveness of political and ecclesiastical systems, such an uncompromising stance for autonomy at this juncture is understandable. The Enlightenment began and ended with the assumption that human liberty ought to be cut away from the moral order, never integrated meaningfully with it. Because this motif has dominated the democratic West until now, our ethical theory, to be successfully counter-Enlightenment, must take a radical stance precisely at this point.

Robert Bellah and his circle—working in the tradition of Alexis de Tocqueville's monumental *Democracy in America*—recognize the irrevocable significance of integrating individual freedom with moral order. While democracy, in their view, operates with a "first language" that is utilitarian and individualistic, Bellah and his coauthors seek to recover a "second language" now almost lost in our cultural memory—that is, forms of moral discourse that anchor the self and society, and provide a sense of calling for our jobs, leisure, and politics: "We are concerned that [our] individualism may have grown cancerous—that it may be destroying those social integuments that Tocqueville saw as moderating its more destructive potentialities, that it may be threatening the survival of freedom itself."[16] Tocqueville was a Catholic who believed that liberty needed religion to mitigate its excesses. Bellah and his colleagues conclude that our most urgent task at present is recovering "the insights of the older biblical and republican traditions."[17] However, these authors do not seek to revive religious institutions per se. They are concerned with a different problem— how we can make moral sense of our lives rather than pursue the unencumbered self. In this appeal, they read the Enlightenment problematic correctly and reaffirm that unordered liberty becomes license.

Individual autonomy is the dominating theme in the world view of modernity. According to Thomas Luckmann, we have bestowed "a sacred status upon the individual by articulating his autonomy.... 'Ultimate' significance is found by the typical individual in modern industrial societies primarily in the 'private sphere.' "[18] While the twentieth-century West retains a common-sense appeal to ontic, moral, legal, and social responsibility, the very notion of responsible action tends to languish as either mere appearance or an archaic survival from a prescientific age. The authenticity of responsibility has become a problem of first-order magnitude.

In Christopher Lasch's historical overview, individualism of the Enlightenment kind has gone to seed. In modern culture we see the world as a mirror, "whereas rugged individualists saw it as an empty wilderness to be shaped in their own design."[19] The acquisitive person of the nineteenth century accumulated for the future, but the narcissist now demands immediate gratification and lives with inner emptiness, in a state of restless, perpetually unsatisfied desire. Self-made persons emerged from the Enlightenment stream as the archetypes of the human dream. Social mobility was predicated on individual initiative alone, exercised through "habits of industry, sobriety, moderation, self-discipline, and avoidance of debt."[20]

But self-preservation has replaced self-improvement as our existential goal. The West is overcome today "not by the sense of endless possibility but by the banality of the social order [it has] exacted" in the name of fulfillment.[21] In this sense, narcissism has more in common with self-hatred than with self-admiration. The ideology of intimacy conceals a despair of finding it. Life together is not a struggle for social change but for self-realization. Our current unseemly self-absorption renders public life impossible and simultaneously hollows out our personal sphere as well.

When the Enlightenment gave birth to a distinctive self, separated from nature and from culture, the very possibility of understanding basic human questions was erased in principle. Such is the conclusion Alasdair MacIntyre correctly draws in his influential book *After Virtue*. He makes it obvious that modernity has been unable to negotiate moral criteria or to understand the nature of community and moral judgment because its ethos is so individualistic. The integral substance of morality has been eclipsed at the starting point. Modern liberal individualism leaves our ethical discourse in grave disorder. MacIntyre accurately perceives that such individualistic paradigms as the emotivist self, autonomism in morality, and fictions like natural rights can have little comprehension of morality and only scanty wisdom about it. For MacIntyre, the teaching, acquisition, and exercise of morality can occur in a contemporary version of the Aristotelian tradition only if we construct "local forms of community within which civility and the intellectual and moral life can be sustained through the new dark ages which are already upon us."[22]

Libertarian Press Theory

Intellectually and sociologically, individual autonomy characterizes the classical liberal theory of the press. Obviously, the liberal press is an institution based on a complex pattern of ideas, but its centerpiece is the same autonomous self that controlled the Enlightenment mind.

Although the classical liberal theory of the press was largely a product of Enlightenment doctrines of humankind and society, liberalism's individualistic philosophy combines several elements developed during earlier historical periods. In Greco-Roman thought, Leucippus and Democritus advanced a universe of indivisible and indestructible atoms; the Sophists—especially Protagoras and Gorgias—made humans the masters of their own fate. A Christian theology of persons blossoming during the Renaissance and the Reformation endowed each human being with dignity as God's creation, each with a soul worth saving and each living potentially in personal relationship with the divine. In addition, the astrophysical world view of the seventeenth-century Age of Science provided an analogue for human

individuals as irreducible, self-sufficient entities. If atoms are the fundamental building blocks of all matter, as physical reality testified, then are
not individuals the essential units of society? The Enlightenment contributed immeasurably to the acceptance and diffusion of the classical liberal
self: "When the [seventeenth century] began, the authoritarian order
seemed secure; when it ended, the Crown was subordinate to Parliament,
and liberalism was in the ascendancy. The eighteenth century provided the
laboratories in which the tenets of liberalism were put to a practical test."[23]
One such test was "the transfer of the press from authoritarian to libertarian
principles."[24]

In political theory, John Locke's conception of government as the consent of sovereign individuals captured the Enlightenment mind. And it was
his commitment to the sacred self that most forcefully elaborated both
Enlightenment doctrine and the classical liberal theory of the press. In
fact, Locke's *Essay Concerning Human Understanding* (1690) was so influential that it is sometimes credited with singlehandedly ushering in the
Enlightenment era. His monograph reached the streets and domiciles; it
appeared in more editions than did the philosophical classics of Bacon,
Berkeley, Descartes, Hegel, Hobbes, Kant, Leibniz, or Spinoza. As Newton's writings did for the physical world, Locke's *Essay* captured the public
imagination. Locke's picture of humanity and government appeared as
eighteen arguments against licensing before the English House of Com-
mons in 1694. It provided ringing phrases for the American Declaration
of Independence and the substance of the Constitution. In Anglo-American
press theory, free expression as a natural right is a vital proposition derived
from Locke and popularized in eighteenth-century England and America
through *Cato's Letters* (essays published by the British journalists John
Trenchard and Thomas Gordon).

In Lockean terms, the self is an independent mental substance with no
specified relation whatsoever to other mental substances; the individual
and society stand in natural opposition. With the individual philosophically
intact, in Locke's *Two Treatises of Government* (1690) society becomes an
aggregate of the self-seeking automatons that compose it, and government
an artifice instituted by mutual agreement for protecting individual liberty,
life, and property. The well-being of individuals ultimately justifies society
and government. And in Thomas Jefferson's adaptation of Locke, a free
press is a tool for safeguarding civil liberties when they are threatened by
government encroachment: "This formidable censor of public function-
aries, by arraigning them at the tribunal of public opinion produces reform
peaceably, which otherwise must be done by revolution."[25]

Certainly, any theory of the press is largely shaped by the environment—social, economic, cultural, intellectual—in which it exists. Thus the
press's basic concept in England and America since the eighteenth century

has been the idea of a rational, moral, and autonomous self as having reality and meaning in relation to a transcendent order of reason and moral law; in this scheme, the self is limited in the exercise of its will only by right reason and individual conscience. The notion of the atomic self acted like a magnet, drawing together the main elements of classical liberal press theory: the doctrine of the self-righting process, the right of individual publishers to be free of government control, and the philosophy of natural law. Classical liberals saw the press as a social force that, like the autonomous self, somehow floated independently of the historical order and freed people from the tyranny of ignorance and superstition. As summarized by Harry Girvetz: "Social institutions are created by the fiat of self-contained individuals; they are instruments, even expedients, which the individual can employ or discard without fundamentally altering his own nature."[26]

Negative Liberty

Inherent in the classical liberal theory of freedom, therefore, is a negative conception that equates liberty with freedom from external and arbitrary restraint:

> The fundamental sense of freedom is freedom from chains, from imprisonment, from enslavement by others. The rest is extension of this sense, or else metaphor. To strive to be free is to seek to remove obstacles; to struggle for personal freedom is to seek to curb interference, exploitation, enslavement by men whose ends are theirs, not one's own. Freedom . . . is co-terminous with the absence of bullying or domination.[27]

Nobody may compel me to be happy in his own way, argued Kant; paternalism is the greatest despotism imaginable.

While warning of constraints in general, libertarianism focused on government intervention; the concept of negative liberty was directed primarily against despotism. Negative liberty was "conceived as the answer to the question, 'How much am I to be governed?' "[28] Locke and Mill in England; Burke, Tocqueville, and Benjamin Constant in France; and Jefferson and Paine in the United States addressed different issues regarding political liberty, but all argued against government control on the grounds that we violate or degrade human nature if the private sphere is not unalterably preserved.

The idea that individuals must be left free to achieve their own self-appointed goals derives in part from the "expressivist turn" of the Romantic era, which Charles Taylor locates within the Enlightenment's discovery of the internalized self.[29] To argue that individuals ought to be free to pursue whatever goals the commonweal can tolerate is to express not merely a political preference, but an ontological a priori. As Leibniz set the stage for the radical individuation that Herder applied to nations, the unique self was considered accountable only to itself to actualize the goal that it alone had chosen. This presumption reigned uncritically because nature was seen to pursue its inexorable destiny in that fashion, and the deity of the Deist also conducts business unfettered. Taylor observes that individual differences became both sign and proof that each person had an original path to tread, that differences in persons were not only between good and criminal minds, but between smart and dim-witted minds as well. In such a context, government fulfills its duty when it protects those original paths from the excesses and consequent injustices that would impede an individual's quest, *de minimis*. Government may not take the cancer-causing tobacco from your purse or pocket, for example, but it may legitimately clean the air by restricting tobacco use in public forums. This is government of negative freedom.

Certainly, freedoms are useless if the political, religious, or economic situation deprives individuals of their liberty. Nevertheless, negative liberty refuses to identify freedom with conditions for fulfilling it. Nothing may be allowed to downgrade the meaning and value of freedom: "In their zeal to create social and economic conditions in which freedom is of genuine value, men tend to forget freedom itself."[30] While material security, sufficient health, accurate knowledge, and a believable justice system are crucial for creating the conditions for freedom, libertarians admit in principle, pursuing them does not guarantee liberty. Indeed, Dostoevsky's *The Brothers Karamazov* illustrates that providing the conditions for freedom can actually deny freedom. The cold lessons of history indicate that the negative liberty of noninterference, as a rule, leaves more paths open to pursue than does freedom defined any other way. According to libertarianism, identifying freedom with its conditions or extending it to include other desirable ends, such as equality and justice, leads to theoretical confusion and irrational action. The crucial sense of freedom is the absence of obstructions along the roads that individuals choose to walk; in the libertarian world view, this emphasis must not be lost even though some use it to oppress or to exercise undue privilege. From a libertarian perspective, freedom is the opportunity for action rather than action itself; the compelling urgency of the latter should not obscure the nonnegotiable character of the former.

Freedom of expression, in particular, came to be seen as a natural right essential to the preservation of individual autonomy. According to libertarianism, freedom of the press is a personal and universal prerogative to publish one's views freely, a natural right belonging to anyone who cares or has the wherewithal to establish a newspaper, magazine, or broadcasting station. Tyrants may abridge the rights granted to people at birth, but no one can eradicate them totally. They belong to the same divine scheme of things as do the unchanging physical laws controlling the universe. Censorship is therefore intolerable, an attempt to abrogate a natural law by which society operates. "For Constant, Mill, Tocqueville, and the liberal tradition to which they belong... no power, but only rights, can be regarded as absolute."[31] On every short list of absolute rights was free speech.

The discovery of what Charles Taylor calls the articulate self was concurrent with new expectations for diversifying the public forum and the new political philosophy that bore no animus—in theory at least—toward contrary opinions. The seeds of this idea had been sown centuries earlier and flowered with the Romantics. If one surrenders the notion that truth is external, whether in ideas (Plato) or God (Augustine), and adopts the Romantic thesis that the "inexhaustible domain is properly within," it is but a small step to insist that the mind must be fostered and fed, not censored. Life takes on the impoverishment of utilitarian mechanics if humans cannot freely examine even that which they never fully comprehend. "This concept of an inexhaustible inner domain is the correlative of the power of expressive self-articulation."[32] One could no more ask human beings to stop expressing thoughts of the mind than one could expect a bird to stop flying. To censor was to behave in radical contradiction to human nature.

What appeared in libertarian philosophy as a natural right was at least equally balanced in real life by self-interest. As the mission of the press and possible regulations were debated in eighteenth- and nineteenth-century America, owners and publishers showed as much concern with threats to their profitability as with interference in the freedom of expression. In his *Legacy of Suppression,* Leonard Levy persuasively argues that those who adopted the state and federal constitutions and the Bill of Rights did not believe wholesale in free expression, but consented to it as a political tool. The rising commercial classes in England and America during the eighteenth and nineteenth centuries found libertarian ideals compatible with their socioeconomic ascendancy.

Freedom of the press became integral to a democratic society. In Supreme Court Justice Felix Frankfurter's famous words, "Freedom of the press... is not an end in itself but a means to the end of a free society."[33] Through an expedient combination of principle and political factionalism, press freedom triumphed in the legislature and the courts and was enshrined in the Bill of Rights. As Theodore Peterson reminds us, when the framers of the Constitution added an amendment protecting the liberty of the press, "they had no intention of binding the publisher to certain responsibilities in exchange for his freedom."[34] In the Enlightenment climate, freedom of the press was regarded as nearly absolute, a right subject only to individual reason and conscience and to the minimal postpublication restraints of a free society composed of autonomous individuals possessing similar and equal rights. Thus, as Charles Beard argued correctly, "in its origin, freedom of the press had little or nothing to do with truth-telling. . . . Freedom of the press means the right to be just or unjust, partisan or non-partisan, true or false, in news column or editorial column."[35] In libertarian perspective, the small minority who abuse freedom will be exposed by those who find it profitable to discredit them. For this reason, requiring responsibilities in exchange for freedom is unnecessary; most people assume them, and the rest can cause no substantial harm.

In legal terms, the negative principle took the form of Sir William Blackstone's "no previous restraint" doctrine, which was his definition of press freedom. Lord Mansfield, chief justice of the King's Bench in England from 1750 to 1790, articulated the principle against government censorship, and Blackstone incorporated it into his influential commentaries. In this sense, individuals enjoyed freedom of the press insofar as they were free from any prohibitions before publication. As Peterson has put it, "It was enough to remove all but a minimum of restrictions on the press; for if the press were unhampered, it would feed information and ideas into the marketplace, and from their interchange truth would emerge triumphant."[36]

Individual autonomy's most pointed expression in the press is unconditional freedom for individual practitioners. Sociologically speaking, a fierce independence, freedom from external controls, an insistence on rights, and cries of censorship at any hint of regulation are conventions carved into the culture of media professionals. In Thomas Jefferson's vision of democracy, "Where the press is free, all is safe." The information system must stand untouched, says traditional theory, or society cannot be served effectively. That Jeffersonian flame burns hotly yet today. Self-imposed regulations, internal constraints through morally enlightened practitioners—these voluntary curbs most newspeople will accept. Ombudsman Richard Harwood notes the "ethical and professional anarchy" of the "standards for our trade," using hyperbole to emphasize his belief that "all but the mentally infirm are aware that we have no common standards in the news business."[37] But newspapers and broadcasting stations directly controlled by the government are inconceivable, even loathsome. Protecting one's independence is the press's first order of business, according to this view. A few government regulations may be tolerated reluctantly, but the free-press doctrine is considered the very lifeblood of an effective news system. News organs such as the Qatari daily *Gulf Times,* which can raise issues but never question the emir ("The ruler represents an example of unity and integrity"), are considered the crux of the problem and an impediment to genuine progress.[38]

Twentieth-Century Emphases

Already in the nineteenth century, chilly winds began blowing on libertarian ideology, and they have become a hurricane in the twentieth. The
revolution in politics from elitist democracy to mass democracy, the economic shifts from an agrarian economy to an urban–industrial system, and
Darwinian fluidity at odds with Newtonian fixity combined to challenge
severely the libertarian world view. However, a body of classical liberal
ideas still survives in recognizable form. Political philosophers Robert Nozick and Frederich Hayek, for example, defend the foundations of liberty
by seeking to roll back the bloated contemporary state. In their view,
individual initiative and unfettered competition in a free market are the
time-honored means to achieve legitimate social goals without arbitrary
force. The wherewithal to pursue one's chosen ends depends on the right
to property and to full personal control over accumulated resources.[39]
Nozick insists that liberal politics can prosper only when a "minimal state"
is nonintrusive and nondirective. The state is no more than a "night watch-
man," restricting its role "to protecting all its citizens against violence,
theft, and fraud, and to the enforcement of contracts."[40] For Hayek, democracy is not an end in itself but only a "utilitarian device" to safeguard
the highest political end, liberty.[41] How can radically different aspirations
otherwise be accommodated?

> Wittgenstein, Elizabeth Taylor, Bertrand Russell, Thomas Merton, . . .
> Thoreau, Casey Stengel, the Lubavitcher Rebbe, Picasso, Moses, Ein-
> stein, Hugh Hefner, Socrates, Henry Ford, Baba Ram Dass, Gandhi, Sir
> Edmund Hillary, . . . Buddha, Frank Sinatra, Columbus, Freud, Ayn
> Rand, Thomas Jefferson, . . . Emma Goldman, Peter Kropotkin, you, and
> your parents. Is there really only one kind of life which is best for each
> of these people?[42]

An economically viable press in this laissez-faire and libertarian framework
will generate an abundance of information, reflecting a free society's
diversity.

Moreover, typical readings of the First Amendment presume a libertarian past. They thereby continue to influence our thinking about the
American mass-communication system. Although pure libertarian theory
is inextricable from the composite of ideas that it has always been, the
Supreme Court until recently has included justices (notably Hugo Black
and William O. Douglas) who were absolutists regarding the First Amendment. Their liberalism read "no law" in the First Amendment to mean
that all statutory restrictions were unconstitutional. In a sense, they were
the most conservative of jurists, refusing any compromise with demonstra-
bly hurtful speech, provided that speech was somehow distinguishable from

illegal behavior. As a corrective for the repression of free speech during World War I, the absolutist doctrine served an important goal.

But compromise always typified the Court's majority. Highly regarded legal scholars like Alexander Meikeljohn, Oliver Wendell Holmes, and Louis Brandeis have not so much rejected libertarianism as qualified it in restricted areas. For example, governments operating under libertarian theory have permitted minimal restrictions on defamation, invasion of privacy, obscenity, and sedition, while maintaining the principle that all possible viewpoints deserve to be published. Of course, some factions of the press and legal theory currently stand at odds with the motif of individual autonomy and negative freedom, but, on the whole, dominant press values and public policy measures are in concert with it.

Academic Media Ethics

Individual autonomy, we have argued, has been the primary feature of the Western social environment since the Enlightenment and the animating force in the culture of the news profession as well. The history of formal journalism ethics, developed as it was within this professional and social context, also imbibed the individualistic spirit. A complete account of academic work in journalism ethics would delineate the concern for journalism's status as compared with that of law and medicine, shifts from a craft orientation to professional training, and the influence of scientific naturalism on reporters' commitment to objective facts. But our purpose in this section is to examine the role of individual autonomy in the structure, decision making, and ethics of the press; the focus here is on sovereign individualism. We will include the other relevant factors in the story only to the degree that they impinge on individual autonomy.[43]

Systematic ethical studies of journalism in the United States originated during the industrious 1920s, when five major works rose together from America's heartland: Nelson Crawford's *The Ethics of Journalism,* Leon Flint's *The Conscience of the Newspaper,* William Gibbons's *Newspaper Ethics,* Paul Douglass's *The Newspaper and Responsibility,*[44] and Albert Henning's *Ethics and Practices in Journalism.* None recognized another in quotation or argument, yet a remarkable similarity appeared among them. The distinguished educators who wrote these early books did not allow ethics instruction to languish along the fringes, but did the serious work of developing a solid academic foundation for it. They linked themselves to the long tradition of systematic work in ethics, seen as a scholarly enterprise since Xenocrates included ethics as a division of the Platonic Academy in 339 B.C. These textbook authors carved out much of the structure that continues to dominate media-ethics instruction—case studies, free-standing courses, explicit pedagogical aims, and so forth.

Of greatest importance for our purposes here, this 1920s literature shared a kindred definitional framework. These writers understood the subject matter of ethics to be moral responsibility as exercised within one's professional community, a maxim generated largely from the authors' small-town and church experience. As Henning conceived it, ethics was constructed from the basic principles of "right action toward one's fellows."[45] They emphasized standards of right and wrong *relationships*—surely duties among colleagues, but also advertisers and publishers, and to the public. A nonfunctional approach dominated, in which passion for righteousness, duty, communal welfare, trust, decency, and honesty of purpose was a common exhortation signaling a deep connection with others. Reporters were exhorted not to "betray trust," but to live by a "nobility of purpose that exalts" and to own up to their moral obligation to "serve well and faithfully."[46] Professional behavior was considered morally appropriate to the degree that it enhanced mutually appreciative understanding and promoted joint control and influence. The need for human bonds was assumed more than self-consciously articulated, but it was a strong undercurrent nevertheless. These early academicians knew that codes and courses in ethics can be fruitful only when social bonds are firm, that precepts are finally sustained only among those with common values, with shared culture. Although it took the greater profundity of John Dewey to articulate the issues clearly in *Individualism Old and New,* these writers did not discuss right action in terms of abstract principles, but as virtue embedded in social connections.

Many in this first generation of journalism educators concerned with ethics were inspired by a particular brand of progressivism linked to the moralistic perspective of the small town (a tradition, as Richard Hofstader notes, inherited largely from rural evangelical Protestantism).[47] Their writings were grounded in the values and attachments typical of the Progressive era. They sharply opposed any sort of partisanship, rejected talk of crime, scandal, and sex as repulsive, and sought a "higher" tone and reputation for their craft. With the founding of the *Journalism Bulletin* (1924) as the voice of collegiate journalism educators, and its successor *Journalism Quarterly* (1927), the progressive voice was given expression. These journals reverberated for a decade with outraged cries against sensationalism, demands for university training in ethics, and earnest appeals for codes of professional responsibility.

Against practitioners or their colleagues who were tempted to sell the press to the highest bidder, those who fostered ethics instruction in the 1920s spoke with one voice about the press as an instrument of public service. Nelson Crawford's second chapter, "Journalism as a Profession," echoed Jefferson, Lippmann, and Herodotus regarding "the tradition of public accountability and public service."[48] And Flint quoted what he labeled the finest words ever uttered by an editor: "We think of this newspaper as if it were a person, an intelligent, courageous, well-bred gentleman, giving the best that is in him to his employer, the public."[49]

William Gibbons's *Newspaper Ethics* illustrates an identical individualism, tempered with a dogged sense of public obligation. "Underlying all," Gibbons concluded in his Foreword, " . . . is the fundamental wish to be of service to society. The newspaper is a public servant and its conscientious editor acknowledges obligations that reach beyond the bounds of the counting room."[50] In Chapter 1 he dismissed the debate whether journalism was a trade or a profession by pointing to a more fundamental issue: "As a public institution, the public welfare, not private gain" should be the newspaper's "chief concern."[51] In Chapters 4 ("The Newspaper and the Public"), 7 ("The Newspaper's Responsibility"), and 8 ("The Newspaper in a Democracy"), Gibbons delineated a social-responsibility theory of the press, with every major doctrine equivalent to those later propounded by the Hutchins Commission in 1947. In a manner identical to Hutchins, Gibbons made the danger of big-business commercialism a prominent theme throughout these chapters, and economics the entire focus of Chapter 5. In the same way that the Hutchins Commission anchored its report in democratic political theory, Gibbons argued from the political science literature:

> Since democratic government rests upon and requires the exercise of a well-informed and sensible opinion by the great bulk of the citizens, when the materials for the formation of such an opinion are so artfully supplied as to prevent citizens from judging fairly the merits of the question, opinion is artificially created instead of being allowed to grow in a natural way, and a wrong is done to democracy.[52]

The Hutchins Commission insisted that news should be presented in a context that gave it meaning, and contextual reporting was likewise the cornerstone of Gibbons's argument when confronting issues like confidentiality, accuracy, crime reporting, and fair trial.

The five books mentioned above constitute a considerable achievement for one decade, although a cynic could reduce the public-service appeals to rhetorical flourishes. The leaders in ethics who wrote them gave instructional issues their due and articulated the press's mission in the face of an often uncooperative university not committed to journalism education as a whole. These books also confronted the remnants of Horace Greeley's spirit among practitioners. (Greeley insisting that graduates "overcome the handicap of a college education" before he would hire them.) They established a rationale for teaching courses in ethics that is a permanent legacy, and the substance of their public-service appeals rivaled in quality anything that has appeared since. Their thinking about the press was classical liberal theory; therefore, their frame of reference was consistently individual behavior and negative freedom, yet encased in and ameliorated by a deep sense of communal duty.

After Crawford's *Ethics of Journalism* was published in 1932, the term "ethics" and its cognates disappear from book titles for forty years. That fact symbolizes the end of a short-lived era. The flurry of academic activity in the 1920s—expansion of curricula, founding of societies such as Sigma Delta Chi and Theta Sigma Phi, and adopting codes of ethics—could not prevent the demise of ethics as "moral responsibility to my fellows." As documented by William C. McWilliams, *Gemeinschaft* failed to root itself deeply within the journalism vocation, even as it floundered in the Progressive era as a whole.[53] It could not thrive; press freedom meant autonomy from all constraints—and professionalism implied loyalty to the ideal of objectivity rather than service to the local community. Lacking a communal core, the communal trappings eventually collapsed, too.

The ethical framework of these first-generation educators was altered by their concern for professionalism and their quest for recognition. The fox in the chicken coop was professional status, often heralded as the best approach to improving journalism's dignity. Lawrence Murphy of the University of Illinois, for example—the *Bulletin*'s and *Quarterly*'s first editor—was committed to codes of ethics and scholarly organizations that promoted ethics prominently. A committee he chaired for the Illinois Press Association in the 1920s recommended a "Professional Certification Plan," similar to a CPA for accountants. In Murphy's scheme, journalists guilty of violating the ethics code could have their license revoked by a journalistic review board. However, helping journalism attain the respectability of medicine and law preoccupied Murphy the most. An extended argument for professionalism—its benefits, its meaning, and how to achieve it—dominated the *Bulletin*'s and *Quarterly*'s articles and editorials during his editorship (1924–1929). As John Dewey recognized in the 1920s, the demise of local, integrated, close-knit communities resulted to some degree from the creation of an elite group of experts and professionals, isolated from the public.[54] In that sense, Murphy's insistence on garnering an elevated position for journalism practitioners simultaneously eroded the communal framework for ethics that he presumed. Certainly he did not lament the trend toward professionalization or worry, as Emile Durkheim did, about the shift from community to specialized vocations. Professional culture began orienting journalistic values more powerfully than did practitioners who identified with the public.

Into the vacuum moved the understanding of news ethics that has dominated until today. Reporters' morality became equivalent to an objective—

that is, unbiased—reporting of facts. The seeds of this definition existed already in Henning, although he continually highlighted the "shared experience" motif of the 1920s. The growth of omnibus newspapers in the 1830s and of networks and national news-gathering associations in the 1890s brought into the media's structure the virtue of impartially transmitting pure information. By the 1930s, news conventions had rejected political partisanship and bias of all forms because they restricted readership and audience. To report as much uncensored information about as many events as quickly as possible, from a nonpartisan, "facts-only" point of view, became the supreme goal.

The natural sciences provided another impetus for objectivity. Advances in physical science became the applauded ideal as educators promoted its methods and principles. Empiricism in the social sciences tended to endorse specific standards of behavior in the news profession, emphasizing brute facts and unflinching neutrality. In fact, even behind the appeals for professional duty were individualistic definitions of reporters and society, with objectivity the preponderant ideal. Grove Patterson, for example, makes an impassioned plea in his Don R. Mellet Memorial Fund lecture that individual newspersons demonstrate moral leadership in improving democratic life, and the cornerstone of their responsibility he viewed as objective reporting and unslanted facts.[55]

This phenomenon has been described as the development of a new social role, that of the professional communicator. While reporter independence retains its supreme value in journalism culture, the ideology of objectivity, when fused with large-scale media technologies, actually created a corps of technical writers linking geographically disparate entities. The ethnicity, occupation, social class, and local affiliations enabled by face-to-face interaction were replaced by mass-mediated forms of communication. Reporters, magazine editors, and radio announcers became brokers in information symbols, identified not with particular communities but with generalized language that modulated this national mosaic into a political functionary.[56]

A countervailing trend emerged shortly after World War II. Over against journalistic norms of skilled efficiency and independence, media critics encouraged professional communicators to adopt a more active and creative role, to survey the social system and recommend ways of correlating its parts. The 1947 Report of the Commission on Freedom of the Press is the most famous statement of this period, through the term "social responsibility" deliberately shifting the issues away from the individual and freedom toward their opposites. The report forthrightly denied the premise of neutral observation—that events themselves control content—and emphasized instead the observer's interpretation, participation, and analysis.

The supreme ethical standards were seen as relevance and thoroughness, a reporting not merely of facts but the truth behind them "in a context which gives them meaning."[57]

It is ironic that the impetus for this privately funded commission came directly from the center of concern for individual autonomy that we have cited as the Enlightenment's chief legacy to the modern press. The story of Henry Luce's contacting Robert Hutchins and their subsequent assembling of Lasswell, Merriam, Niebuhr, Hocking, and other world-class intellects is well known. Equally common is the knowledge of Luce's bitter disappointment with the results of the commission and of his stunning judgment—"a gentleman's C and nothing more"—on the scholarship that shaped the commission's findings. At the politically superficial level, one could imagine that Luce was offended when his commissioners voted him into an observer's role, a seat that Luce quickly vacated, preferring to leave the commission to its own devices rather than tend the gallery while debate raged on the floor. At a deeper ideological level, the commission was breaking fresh ground (not surprising, given its composition), shedding the freight of individual autonomy and groping toward a press theory with more at stake than mere negative freedom. Well might Luce have winced at Hocking's talk about a "co-agent state" or Hutchins's growing interest in "the great conversation" and its implications for news coverage. Visions of Will Hays's astute sense of civic constituents, and the commission's apparent appreciation of Hays's strategy on film content, would have sent most able-minded Enlightenment editors into a frenzy. On the one hand stood Roosevelt's New Deal, anxious to assert federal authority over private realms; on the other was the world's grievous experience with European and Pacific autocracy, against which spirit the Enlightenment had once opened freedom's gates. Yet for all its intellectual linkage to the liberalism of Locke, Milton, and Mill, the Hutchins Commission was a dawn's early light that a new framework of press theory was needed for an uncharted era of international and domestic needs. The democracy of self-contained selves was emerging from the 1940s as the democracy of interdependent communities, and the press could not fail to see, note, and assist the adjustment. Both Hutchins and Luce observed the changes, with polar opposite responses.

This alternative voice resurrected, in effect, the 1920s concern for ethics as communal duty. It sounded a note that continues, though muted, until today. Social responsibility was included as one of the *Four Theories of the Press,* published in 1956. J. Edward Gerald wrote a book on news and society titled *The Social Responsibility of the Press* in 1963, although he focuses almost exclusively on individual performance. The third edition of *Responsibility in Mass Communication* (1980) is also structured around the social-responsibility notion, contending that the theory demands freedom for the press from government and business constraints in order that it can serve society through the principles of fairness and truthtelling.

However, social-responsibility doctrine has always been relegated to the fringes of journalism education and the newsroom. Nearly fifty years after the Hutchins Commission report, news personnel generally remain hostile to its focus on the public good and on broad-based reporting about significant issues of the day. In one notable recent case, an editor retiring from the *San Francisco Examiner* after five decades in journalism said, upon receiving a distinguished achievement award from the University of Southern California, "We tell [readers] about the socioeconomic implications of a debate in Botswana when they really want to know what the guy next door sold his house for. We feed them quiche and Evian water; they want hamburgers and a Coke."[58] Indeed, Theodore Peterson has argued that social responsibility largely survives as a slogan about the public's right to know.[59] Principles based on this perspective remain undefined and its theoretical sophistication limited.

In terms of journalism theory and practice on the whole, attachment to professional skill and the kind of knowledge defined by the social sciences led journalism ethics away from its 1920s orientation, in which direct personal knowledge and long-term understandings of local life established the boundaries of fairness. The community motif could not survive with the same impact in the new configurations of the social sciences and the professions, especially as journalism educators increasingly sought separation from the public through appeals to professionalization and expert status. The Progressives found their values difficult to maintain in the shifting tides of the twentieth century. Sophisticated coteries of journalists held on to the promise of their profession as an ethereal amalgamation removed from changing local custom and attitudes. Obligation to a professional community did not, however, advance the work on ethics. In such an environment, ethical standards developed in line with the social values of professional journalists. But this newer form of social organization jettisoned the genuine community background.[60]

Empathetic understanding of social life and culture gave way to knowledge attainable through scientific inquiry. Social science promised an objective view of human nature that shifted the focus to statistical analysis and detachment. People were defined as consumers and audiences. Human values were of interest not because of their meaning for members of a locality or tradition, but for the information they provided the sales strategists. The community became the market. Demographics grouped people together on the basis of little more than common consumption patterns. Market analysis made such consumption communities objectively real to the practitioner. Market-research organizations used ever more sophisticated quantitative techniques to establish themselves as necessary contributors to the journalism process. Pockets of resistance occasionally appeared in journalism's intellectual and vocational life, but progressive thought generally had started with the attempt to resurrect the local and communal, and ended with an enthusiastic acceptance of the professional statistical model that undermined it. The *Gesellschaft* of news practitioners replaced the public community as the salient form of social order in the news enterprise. Practitioners perceived themselves as bound together through the work methods they shared and the status to which they aspired. Ethics was not something attributed to the values of the public they supposedly served, but had become proper conduct within the journalism federation itself.

Thus the ethics of individualism and independence that took shape during the formative 1920s and 1930s was firmly in place by the 1950s. Although ameliorated by the community consciousness of the 1920s and questioned by the Hutchins Commission in 1947, an ethics of individual rights and personal decision making in terms of a day-by-day orientation began controlling the agenda. And journalism ethics is still characterized by the same individualistic assumptions.

Those who have done descriptive ethics tend to reflect the libertarian individualism that dominates the newsroom. John Hulteng's *The Messenger's Motives,* Bruce Swain's *Reporters' Ethics,* Norman Isaacs's *Untended Gates,* Gene Goodwin's *Groping for Ethics in Journalism,* William Rivers and Cleve Mathews's *Ethics for the Media,* Conrad Fink's *Media Ethics,* Philip Meyer's *Ethical Journalism,* and Tom Goldstein's *The News at Any Cost* define ethics in terms of a reporter's personal convictions, conundrums, and choices. These books are saturated with illustrations of the actual moral behavior of news reporters, and occasionally of advertisers or public-relations professionals. Their aim is to describe systematically the way ethical decision making actually functions among media practitioners. In a widely circulated document carrying a professional emphasis to the extreme, *Drawing the Line* is a compilation of thirty-one case studies written by editors who describe their most difficult ethical dilemmas.[61]

Goodwin does his homework by interviewing 150 journalists and media critics, and including nearly all the relevant literature and ethics codes in his research. Meyer uses sophisticated statistical techniques to survey staff members at 300 newspapers across the United States. As a genre, the descriptive ethics literature has moved us beyond our impressions and has documented the important shifts under way in what journalists perceive as ethical issues. These volumes do sound alarms against inappropriate actions, maintaining a realistic flavor throughout but insisting that journalists fulfill their roles as citizens and human beings. Goldstein, a veteran reporter himself, is, in fact, a vigorous critic at times. All the books noted above offer down-to-earth advice and repeatedly call for more competence and detailed operating standards. However, they do not see their purpose as extending beyond an illumination and a critique of personal behavior, professional morality, and the values actually employed by practitioners as they make decisions. They presume a classical liberal or neoliberal paradigm.

Stephen Klaidman and Tom Beauchamp's title, *The Virtuous Journalist,* highlights its practitioner focus; a review aptly captures the book's thrust as "The Good Journalist Doing Well."[62] The authors begin with journalistic independence, but argue against absolutist versions of negative freedom. They advise readers that although they employ virtue language in headings and titles, "we do not mean to imply that virtues can or should replace rights and duties." They adopt a "reasonable reader" model as the standard that reporters and editors ought to use for making news judgments. While the authors articulate basic moral concepts in order to prevent "purely subjective preferences," the ethical framework throughout is on practitioner decision making and behavior.[63]

In the most prominent modern attempt to construct a philosophical media ethics, over his career John Merrill had defended an individualistic approach on theoretical grounds. He published his influential *The Imperative of Freedom* in 1974, promoting an uncompromising autonomy in the neo-Lockean mold and citing Friedrich Hayek and Robert Nozick, among others, as important contemporary catalysts. He warned strongly against the collectivist tendencies of social-responsibility doctrine, condemning it as an "incipient authoritarianism creeping into American society" under a beneficent disguise.[64] Upon the 1990 republication of *The Imperative of Freedom,* Merrill summarized his argument: "The underlying spirit of libertarianism is found throughout; if I were to rewrite the book today, this libertarianism might be muted somewhat to reflect a greater concern with journalistic ethics. However, I maintain that freedom must be prior to, and is essential to, any consideration of ethics."[65]

In his latest monograph, *The Dialectic in Journalism,* Merrill integrates freedom with responsibility; responsible freedom, he calls it, "a moderated and socially concerned use of journalistic freedom."[66] The foundation for his "organic unification of opposites" is the dialectical tradition from Heraclitus (sixth-century B.C. Greece) to Georg W. F. Hegel (nineteenth-century Germany).[67] In the existential moment, Merrill challenges practitioners to reconcile classical and neoliberal antinomies, positive and negative freedom, duty and consequences, altruism and egoism, the people's right to know and journalistic autonomy, absolutism and situationalism. Reporters will deviate from basic maxims "when reason dictates another course or when projected or anticipated consequences warrant the desertion of these rules."[68] While he realizes that "absolute positions and ideologies are not realistic or helpful," the paradigm case is still "the journalist facing an increasingly complex world" and engaged in "a personal . . . struggle for freedom and authenticity."[69]

The lessons learned from this brief history of academic media ethics are obvious. Anglo-American culture, one of its institutions (the press), and communication ethics have all been dominated by identical assumptions. They have become a set of concentric circles, woven into a whole by similar social, economic, political, and intellectual constraints. The result is a largely quiescent ethics, echoing the conventions in place rather than resisting or contradicting them.

Only on occasion have the scholars of media ethics made any effort to restrain the profession's accommodation to the atomistic, technological, and industrial imperatives that characterize the culture at large. In *Committed Journalism,* Edmund Lambeth considers the "works of Mill and Locke, and liberalism itself . . . towering contributions" vital to democratic life yet today.[70] He celebrates the "enduring contribution of classical liberalism and of a free press," such as protecting free inquiry.[71] But his very title is a calculated attempt to distance himself from unbridled journalistic objectivity and individual autonomy. His social philosophy is sufficiently broad to incorporate the community emphases of Alasdair MacIntyre, Robert Bellah, and Glenn Tinder. As a student of ethical theory, Lambeth constructs an integrated system of five principles operating like a Rubik cube, together challenging the journalistic enterprise to reform and diligent stewardship. However, on balance, mass-media ethics has failed to develop persuasive critical reflection about journalism's collective culture and institutional structure, and thus tends to reinforce the status quo.

Deficiencies in Individual Autonomy

An impressive amount of intellectual effort in the last two decades has been devoted to a sharper understanding of liberalism—its philosophical premises and institutional forms. In that analysis, the impotence and deficiencies of individual autonomy have become obvious, and can be illustrated almost at random in terms of the press and society at large. Regarding theory, the culture of individualism binds the press to an increasingly suspect type of free expression based on the views of John Stuart Mill. Thomas Scanlon notes that although individual autonomy is appealing in many ways, it is a "notoriously vague and slippery notion."[72] Mill's argument and its variants must invoke freedom from coercion—a constraint, for example, against undue government encroachment. Certainly, autonomy can be useful in political argument, in the sense that a citizen's "actual ability to exercise independent rational judgment" must be built in at the outset. The concept of negative liberty, therefore, can give "theoretical form to the intuition that freedom of expression is based on considerations that cannot simply be outweighed by competing interests in the manner that 'clear and present danger' or 'pure balancing' theories of the First Amendment would allow."[73]

However, for all its importance in political matters, a theory of free expression anchored in individual rights cannot resolve certain fundamental disagreements that have arisen in Anglo-American history. For instance, to what extent should public policy be based on a balancing of competing goals or on absolute principles, or are both essential components of a complete theory impossible to integrate given the actions of the courts and Congress? To what extent should defenders of free expression appeal to long-term benefits as legitimately outweighing severe short-run costs? Is the theoretical base of free expression singular or multiple and diverse? "To what extent does the doctrine rest on natural moral principles and to what extent is it an artificial creation of particular political institutions?"[74] In terms of the last question, Mill's defense of "the liberty of thought and expression" relies on general moral grounds, independent of specific laws or governments. However, debates over the new world information order have made it obvious that freedom of expression is not independent in this sense, but involves both natural and artificial elements.

Moreover, Mill's kind of free expression no longer exhausts the relevant concerns. In commercial speech, what direction does it provide regarding false or deceptive advertising, the regulation of cigarette or liquor commercials on television, restrictions on classified ads for employment, and meanwhile full First Amendment protection for that form of commercial speech we call *Consumer Reports?* If we are to endorse the generalization that commercial speech as a category must be guarded less stringently than political speech, or that false or deceptive religious communication is less harmful than advertising, in what sense does appealing to individual rights yield the relevant distinctions? Or on what Millian grounds should pornography or obscenity receive less than complete First Amendment protection? If they ought to be fully protected, then how does one confront the interests of a broad spectrum who do not wish to be exposed to material they define as offensive? Claiming individual rights stakes out a territory for a particular few without establishing an articulate social policy. Or, to note an example directly within mass media's news function, how can the theory of free expression that is native to libertarianism separate out among competing interests in the debate over the deregulation of broadcasting? How does it explicitly contradict racism and sexism in the news enterprise? Perhaps no theory of free expression can break the dilemmas cleanly; however, driven by the absence of restraint, libertarianism does not set a comprehensive framework but merely endorses the individual interests of media owners.

There is another angle of vision. The main philosophical role of a theory of expression is to answer its apparent irrationality. Why maintain immunity for a class of acts that yields as consequences "harms which would normally be sufficient to justify the imposition of legal sanctions"?[75] Confronting that issue requires an adequate delineation of the protected class itself, and an account of the nature and grounds of the privilege entailed. At the foundational level, in other words, an adequate theory must measure "the nature and importance of audience and participant interests and, especially, . . . what constitutes a sufficiently equal distribution of the means to their satisfaction" when disagreements arise over maximum freedom versus tolerable cost.[76]

Meanwhile, political theorists in the legacy of Joseph Schumpeter actually redefine democracy to accommodate it more directly to the ethos of efficiency. Rather than abandon liberal democratic theory in the mid-twentieth century, Schumpeter developed a revised model on the presumption that democracy ought to be understood as a mechanism for directing governmental functions.[77] As long as procedures for free elections, free speech, and free assembly, for example, are maintained, the system operationally avoids tyranny. Schumpeter reconstructs a liberal democratic theory that orients free expression to mature technological industrialism by insisting on a standardized process of political participation (documented by flow charts, graphs, and computer printouts). As an alternative to unpredictable and emotional public debate over human betterment and social justice, Schumpeter's thesis closes a neat circle: the scientific frame of mind perceives reality within an impersonal, mechanical framework, permitting and abetting the creation of a social and economic technology requiring predictable, standardized human components, which modern philosophy, sociology, and political science assert are the only kind of human components that exist in any case.[78] To Schumpeter's formulation, individual autonomy and negative freedom provide no counterpoint.

These weaknesses on the theoretical level preclude any further wholesale commitment to free expression grounded in individual autonomy. Obviously, our intention is not to subvert or undervalue the significance of the free-expression doctrine, but to ensure that it is adequately justified. Autonomy as a ground has served a valiant historical purpose in guaranteeing that on matters of thought and discussion the peasant counts equally with the king. Rights and liberties were a potent bulwark against tyranny; they inspired strategies of resistance. However, the best in legal, historical, philosophical, and political scholarship turns us at this stage toward a theory that assumes positive freedom, toward an elliptical construction in which justified moral rules constrain the production of valued consequences. A singular theory designed to legitimize negative freedom does not give a satisfactory place to considerations of distributive justice, for example, at least in the theoretical sphere. Although individual rights and liberties ought surely to be respected, the philosophical task at this stage is to assign them their proper density, not allowing these weights to be determined by the existing social configurations or by an aggregate of personal preferences.

> Autonomy should be a moral good, not a moral obsession. It is *a* value, not *the* value. If . . . it rests on the conviction that there can be no common understanding of morality, only private likely stories, then it has lost the saving tension it competitively needs with other moral goods. . . . I am told that I have the right to fashion my own moral life and shape my own moral goals. But how do I go about doing that? . . . My autonomy, I have discovered, is an inarticulate bore, good as a bodyguard against moral bullies, but useless and vapid as a friendly, wise, and insightful companion.[79]

Libertarian individualism proved to be a revolutionary concept in the seventeenth and eighteenth centuries. The Enlightenment philosophy of the press was written in blood against tyrants who controlled the news in the name of divine prerogatives. But "the Enlightenment belief in a purely autonomous consciousness has been as torn apart as Pentheus in the *Bacchae*."[80] It currently generates confusion about the news media's rationale and mission, and excludes the substantive issues from our media-ethics agenda. The press needs a more radical notion of the media–society–ethics relationship at this critical juncture in history. Thoughtful members of the news profession realize that the great issues of the information age demand more intricacies than journalistic morality in the democratic liberal tradition has provided. However, if we reach into journalism's intellectual treasury, we come up empty-handed. We now live, in principle, in a postliberal age, and our historic commonplaces are epistemologically bankrupt. The human sciences carved out a privileged role for *Homo sapiens* from the mid-seventeenth through the eighteenth century. However, at today's watershed moment, such an "archeology of knowledge" is disappearing "like a face drawn in sand at the edge of the sea."[81]

Normative Social Ethics

Collectivism has been the most obvious alternative to Enlightenment individualism. Instead of an atomistic model that insists on individual rights and liberties as the ultimate concern, collectivism is a holistic paradigm in which the integrating norm is the entire social organism.

> The organism is conceived as a harmonious balancing of differences; and
> since the time factor—as growth, development or becoming—is the es-
> sence of life, the full form of the organic is represented as a dynamic
> equilibrium of functions maintained through a progressive differentiation
> of elements within the whole. . . . The unity of the organism is a unity of
> functions.[82]

According to this view, originating with Hegel, what is real to society's
members can be real only in relation to the whole, because above the
political affairs of humankind stands *Geist,* the subjective absolute.[83]
Within the social philosophy of collectivism, the classical left has achieved
the greatest specificity and preeminence by locating power in capitalist
societies within the modes and relations of production. The good society
is marked by collective property ownership and equal political power.[84]

Communitarian democracy is a third social theory. It does not merely
synthesize collectivism and individualism, but fundamentally reconcep-
tualizes the issues and conclusions.[85] This book maintains that a communitarian social philosophy ought to undergird media ethics.

Rights Versus the Common Good

Communitarianism contends that a liberal politics of rights rests on un-
supportable foundations and should be given up for a "politics of the
common good."[86] If individual needs and desires are both the source and
the outcome of justice, then the latter becomes "little more than a way
station on the road to self-determination."[87] Amy Gutmann reduces Michael Sandel's argument in this regard to three propositions, personally
finding each of the steps suspect:

> (1) To accept a politics based on rights entails believing that justice should
> have absolute priority over . . . our conception of the common good. (2)
> To accept [such a] priority . . . entails believing that our identities can be
> established prior to the good. . . . (3) Since our identities are constituted
> by our conception of the good, justice cannot be prior. Therefore, we
> cannot consistently believe in the politics of rights.[88]

In other words, claims to rights and notions of justice cannot exist "independently of specific forms of political association which by definition
imply a conception of the good." Therefore, obviously, ahistorical individual rights can never have priority; appealing to them tends to justify
selfishness and buys the freedom to be ourselves at too dear a price.[89]

For communitarians, political liberalism's triad of rights, entitlements,
and procedural justice constricts the moral domain and begs the substantive
questions.[90] Under the guise of neutrality, it actually privileges a particular
social order.[91] Liberalism lives on the mistaken assumption that our per-

sonal identity exists independently of socially given ends; it confuses an aggregate of individual goods with the common good. It has no conceptual apparatus for coping with the intolerance that flourishes among fragmented selves devoid of settled roots and established traditions. Critics of liberalism generally reject its "temerity . . . when faced with the task of establishing fundamental values."[92] When rights language prevails among jostling rights bearers, "the winner takes all and the loser has to get out of town. The conversation is over."[93]

Analysts of social change, both left and right, believe that social movements grow out of detachment from traditional structures. On the one hand, Western political theory is committed to categories that "occlude understanding of the communal wellspring of democratic social struggles."[94] It makes a radical division between private and public, between settled historical communities bound by traditional beliefs and the arenas of progress and reform. On the other hand, in leftist political perspective, social movements such as trade unions presume that the highest level of consciousness is that of "deracinated individuals" who have outgrown their "older beliefs" and are "able to rationally calculate 'objective interests.' "[95] Ironically, socialists agree with the right in presuming that local cultures are inherently conservative. Scorning traditions as the dead hand of the past, socialist movements have historically focused on the processes of industrial production at the expense of local communities. The values of community life and folkways are seen in monochromatic terms and dismissed as opiates.[96]

In contrast with these positions, a communitarian world view holds that social institutions reproduce "the bonds of historical memory and cultures" and thereby "serve as the arenas where people can distinguish themselves from elite definitions of who they are, can gain the skills and mutual regard necessary to act as a force for change."[97] Rootedness in time and space, if sustained self-critically, prevents "a rootless and anomic form of individualism easily manipulated by the state."[98] As Michael Sandel observes, "Where libertarian liberals defend the private economy and egalitarian liberals defend the welfare state, communitarians worry about the concentration of power in both the corporate economy and the bureaucratic state."[99]

Obviously, socialist critics share those worries; but unlike them, communitarians are simultaneously concerned for "the erosion of those intermediate forms of community that have at times sustained a more vital public life."[100] Moral agents need a context within which to assess what is valuable, and values are nurtured in particular settings. We can ascertain what is worth preserving only from specific social situations in which human identity and interests are shaped.[101] Thus communitarians emphasize democratization; the politics of community must be reconstituted in order to gain control "over the runaway megastructures of modern capital and technology."[102]

Because doctrines of the press are a subset of these larger sociophilosophical issues, the erosion in our culture necessitates a more formidable press ethics than one that essentially assumes a continuity with the Enlightenment legacy. Thus we propose a normative social ethics of the news media that articulates a necessary relationship between the press and society founded on principal judgments and commensurate with the social theory that we have labeled communitarian democracy.[103]

The communications enterprise is a dominant social institution in the electronic global age. A normative social ethics grounded in a theory of person-in-community thus provides a moral framework that is isomorphic with the complicated structure of contemporary media technologies. Hans Jonas correctly insists on a brawny, long-range ethics commensurate with the extent of contemporary power.[104] Information networks on a global scale cannot be served by a minuscule ethics. Social ethics addresses most meaningfully the mass media as a social institution, always keeping the issues lodged in large political and cultural movements. It wrestles forthrightly with organizational structures and probes directly into substantive questions about economics, management and bureaucracy, ideological politics, allocation of resources, collective alienation, the press's raison d'être, and distributive justice—without opting for a complete dissolution of the political order. As so definitively established by Aristotle, moral issues are inevitably political in their implications, and fundamental political issues are moral. This is substantive ethics in which the central questions are simultaneously social and moral in nature.

Clearly, a host of existential matters must be solved, but if news-media ethics is to be done on a grander scale than heretofore, we must develop a body of stimulating concepts by which to facilitate the discourse. Conceptual clarity at the theoretical frontier is the catalyst for advancing the field, the north star by which we set our course. Obviously, it is foolish to look for a quick fix and unacceptable to hide under fancy nomenclature. A theory anchored in social ethics is a disinfectant for our moldy conventions. As in ancient buildings, it can square up the lines like a cornerstone.

Our experience with the foundational 1920s offers a poignant reminder of the high stakes at hand. In terms of an educational rationale for media ethics, the 1980s advanced little beyond the productive 1920s. However, the one glaring weakness of the 1920s remains: its failure to integrate theory fruitfully into ethics instruction and research. Granted, news-media scholars of the 1920s felt no special urgency to work the theoretical trenches; they lived off a combination of ecclesiastical culture, small-town moorings, progressive values, and a steadfast commitment to libertarian press theory. However, if writers in this formative decade did not have to concentrate

on epistemology, the current challenges to community and liberalism demand theoretical sophistication for the very survival of media ethics. Without theory in the 1990s, the 1980s will have accomplished little more than
momentarily resurrecting the achievements of Henning, Gibbons, Crawford, and Flint. It is a sobering historical fact that the disposition toward
community in general, and work on news-media ethics in particular, van-
ished quickly as professionalism and scientific naturalism shunted them
aside in the 1930s. The current opportunities of a vital field could likewise
turn to ashes through intellectual neglect.

3

Communitarian Ethics

The horror occurred early one October morning at Bluewater Lake, New Mexico. Michael Volkman had scarcely left his five-year-old daughter, Sage, asleep in a camper to go fishing with his son when they heard barking dogs and saw smoke rising from the campsite. They ran back to find their camper burning. Moments before it exploded, Volkman pulled out his lifeless daughter. He administered CPR, and Sage resumed breathing. She was flown to the burn center at the University of New Mexico Hospital and two weeks later was transferred to the Shriners Burns Institute in Galveston. Third- and fourth-degree burns covered almost half of Sage's body. Her taut, melted skin would not permit her to stretch her limbs fully or to close her mouth. She could not walk or feed herself. Her fingers were gone, and her left eye was nearly blinded. No longer the pretty green-eyed girl with a broad smile, Sage needed massive skin grafts and physical therapy.

For some primordial reason, fire is always news, and fire that causes harm to humans usually becomes a lead story. Sage's tale was no exception. Both Albuquerque newspapers, the morning *Journal* and the afternoon *Tribune,* ran stories about Sage from the time of the accident through various stages of her therapy. Sage's parents wanted the publicity to raise money for her therapy and to prepare the community for Sage when she eventually reentered public life. Each newspaper complied, but they diverged in their use of photographs.

The *Journal* ran three stories about Sage shortly after the fire and accompanied them with a school photo of Sage before the accident. The *Journal* followed these stories with another on her treatment, this time printing a photograph of Sage wearing a mask and another of Sage's family. When Sage returned to Albuquerque, the *Journal* printed another story, this one with Sage covered by her Jobst suit and mask. The next article carried no photograph at all, although a file picture of Sage before the fire was printed in later editions. Section editor Dan Ritchey thought that "[i]t seemed dishonest to write stories about the child being accepted while saying the child's face is too gruesome to run in the newspaper,"[1] but editor

Jerry Crawford's judgment prevailed. Crawford drew a line between "our responsibility to our readers and helping this little girl," a line that reflected state editor Bruce Daniels's distinction between "arresting photographs and pornography."[2] The *Journal* judged explicit photographs of Sage to be offensive.

The afternoon *Tribune,* which has about one-third the circulation of its morning rival, thought otherwise. When Sage was first injured, the *Tribune* printed a few city briefs. Then it decided to publish a pictorial essay in a special tabloid section without advertisements. The cover carried a photograph of Sage without her mask, being held by her smiling mother. Inside, the essay began with a photo of Sage in therapy alongside her earlier school portrait. The pictures accompanied this letter:

> Dear Readers:
>
> We wanted this article written to make our daughter Sage's adjustment to her new life as easy as possible.
>
> We should like you to be aware of her struggle from when she was first burned and almost through death's door to her return to us as a 6-year-old girl with feelings who sees life in terms of Barbie dolls and her Brownie troop.
>
> When you come upon Sage unexpectedly in a store or restaurant, your first reaction may be one of sadness.
>
> But if you do run into her, we hope you will see her as we do—as a brave little girl.
>
> Thank you.
>
> From Sage's family: Michael, Denise and Avery Volkman.
>
> P.S. We would like you to share these thoughts with your children.[3]

The rest of the twelve-page tabloid told the story of Sage's life before and after the accident through photographs, diary entries by Sage's mother, and quotations from Sage and the rest of the family. The most disturbing picture shows Sage and her mother after her daily bath. Sage is naked and crying; her mother, concerned and resolved, gazes at her and holds what remains of her hand.

Unlike the *Journal,* the *Tribune* ran a full array of revealing pictures. Managing editor Jack McElroy said, "The question never arose of not publishing the photographs."[4]

What accounts for the different decisions? Neither paper claimed greater objectivity; both ran factual, deliberative stories of social value. Both cooperated with the Volkmans' desire to alert and educate the public and to ask for donations to the Sage Volkman Fund. Yet the papers reached different conclusions, and each claims to have made the better choice, even in retrospect.

Their disagreement reflects the different processes of decision making that the newspapers followed. The *Journal* spurned graphic photographs in large measure because of the way it defined the moral problem. By asking whether it should print explicit pictures of Sage, the paper created a dichotomy between pleasantness and gruesomeness that it could use to judge the suitability of the photographs. Time after time, editors rejected submissions as "much too graphic" or even "gruesome." Clearly, the *Journal* was operating by the values of decorum and restraint: when in doubt, do not take the risk. Its overriding principle—avoid offending the public— gave its decision-making process a conservative bent. In this way, the newspaper believed that it would best serve its readers.

In that the *Journal* deliberated according to a set of articulated values and principles, its decision can be considered ethical. However, even though both papers were purposeful and consistent, and thus ethical in the minimal sense of the term, both could not have chosen correctly. The *Tribune* printed what the *Journal* rejected on moral grounds; unless we are willing to accept the crudest form of moral relativism—discussed in greater detail below—then one decision had to be preferable. Neither choice may have been unethical, but given that their decisions were made about the same case, surely one was more ethical than the other. To say otherwise is to propose that any choice is acceptable as long as it is made carefully. This suggestion could be true only if process were the sole arbiter of moral insight; in such a case, a newspaper would be obliged to discrim- inate good and bad process on the meaning of the term "careful," which seems to imply, in this context, something more than "we gave thought to it" or "we followed our hunch." "Careful" at least suggests that the decision did not ignore morally substantive contrary claims, did not ride roughshod over established traditions, and did not naively bring about unnecessary harm. And to make any of these claims is to beg the question of process: in a paper's attempt to show "carefulness," it has already invoked moral ideas and claims that stand apart from process and judge its goodness. If process is the only concern, the paper is clearly left with an ethics of efficiency which Jacques Ellul has justly condemned as inimical to freedom.

Charles Taylor speaks to the *Journal*'s concerns in his recent study of the self in modernity. He understands that all humans feel an "urgent and powerful cluster of demands" that we recognize as moral concern for life, integrity, and the well-being of others. These he cites as "uncommonly deep and universal." On the one hand, demands of this sort seem like instincts such as one's reaction to chocolate or aversion to food infested with maggots, our preference to conduct our business dry rather than rain- drenched and to avoid the feeling of embarrassment. Such elemental de- mands explain much daily behavior. Even from our perspective as instruc- tors in higher education, classroom behavior shows many of these proclivities and aversions. On the other hand, prohibitions on killing and lying seem to involve claims "about the nature and status of human beings."

On this side, a moral reaction affirms some ontological account of the self. It says something about the nature of personhood and the shape of meaningful human life. On this dimension, Taylor calls for "strong evaluation," discriminations of right and wrong that do not depend for validity on individual inclinations or choices, "but rather stand independent of these and offer standards by which they can be judged."[5]

Taylor calls for normative ethical decisions in an era when professional values ("Don't publish gruesome photos which may offend readers' sensitivities" for instance) have been neutralized by the Enlightenment's fact–value dichotomy. Strong evaluation seeks to recover moral decision making from mere "careful process" and link it to a fuller account of the way life is lived. Strong evaluation, in Taylor's description, would insist that the *Tribune* and the *Journal* cannot both be right, though both could be wrong and neither may have as fully justified a moral course as some third alternative. But the *Journal* cannot dismiss its coverage on hunches or on editors' visceral responses; this story calls for more reasoning than that.

Rather than defining the problem as whether to use graphic photographs, the Albuquerque *Tribune* defined it in terms of adequately communicating the story of Sage. This latter definition deliberates the process more than it seeks absolute distinctions. The *Tribune* strove to make its message both powerful and acceptable. It operated on the values of adventure and sympathy—adventure in the sense that communication is more a practice of unfolding opportunity than an occasion for acceptance or rejection in the sense of the Golden Rule. In fact, much of editor Tim Gallagher's enthusiasm for Sage's story came from his childhood experiences as the brother of a boy with Down's syndrome who was gawked at whenever he left the house. The values of adventure and sympathy led the newspaper to serve its readers creatively as it also sought to help Sage's acceptance by the community and to raise funds for her long-term therapy.

The divergent portrayals of Sage Volkman raise significant questions regarding moral decision making in news gathering and reporting. Is there guidance for ethical reasoning other than the vague and relativistic maxim to be true to yourself? And what is wrong with relativism? What makes one decision better than another? How does one know what is morally good or right? Is there reason to be sympathetic to Sage? Why not simply assert that a fire occurred in which certain combustibles were chemically reconstituted, including certain portions and surfaces of a little girl? Why not report just the brute facts of nature? Only after answering these questions can one begin to perceive how news ought to be reported.

In Chapter 2 we explained that the moral legacy of contemporary journalism is the myth of individual autonomy and its concomitant ideal of negative freedom. The problems permitted by this Enlightenment inheritance are legion; the freedom to report early election results before voting polls have closed is but one example. The press's position on individualism and negative freedom is close to absolute. Whenever challenged, the press thrusts the First Amendment forward as a fetish to ward off the spirits of responsibility. The First Amendment is an effective talisman because the culture at large, and not just the press, is so infused with Enlightenment individualism that the culturally situated distinction between inwardness (the self) and outwardness (newspaper reports of other selves) is not perceived as a construct at all, but as an unquestionable given.[6] However, challenges to the press's irresponsibility from a critical public continue unabated, not simply when the press appears to wield power without responsibility but, more important, because the power of Enlightenment individualism to explain the mission of the press is becoming more noticeably deficient.

Even when the press behaves admirably, as in the case of Sage Volkman, Enlightenment individualism lurks nearby. The individualism and freedom of American journalism would explain the coverage as entirely voluntary, meaning that the press had no responsibility toward the girl. Instead, according to this conception, the coverage reflected the free choices of individual newspapers. Had they chosen not to cover the accident, their newspapers would have been no less moral because the sole responsibility is to act freely and alone. As John Merrill writes, "[R]esponsibility as individually defined . . . is the valid [theory], the meaningful one for our society, and . . . any other concept of press responsibility would be incongruent with our ideology, our constitution, our tradition, and our concern for a pluralistic society."[7] It is even conceivable that some journalists would accuse both Albuquerque newspapers of boosterism, which somehow conflicts with their ideal of independence, not to mention objectivity. It is the same spirit of autonomy that makes balanced coverage of such blockbuster debates as the right to abortion virtually impossible. Press critic David Shaw has convincingly demonstrated that most media outlets have chosen not to represent the interests of fetal life, quite apart from how readership divides on the question and with smugness about the difficult ongoing issues concerning public policy. It is as though, in Shaw's analysis, a million Sages did not exist.[8] Thus we must be careful even in our praise not to overstate the press's performance.

Articulating an alternative to Enlightenment individualism that both coheres with human being as we can best understand it and provides a groundwork for the moral imperatives of journalism requires more than praising particular deeds of the news media or decrying their misdeeds. Although case studies can illustrate particular concepts in the process of moral reasoning, too often they serve as the sort of casuistry that leads to perpetual arguments and finger pointing and at best to slight adjustments in policies and practices here and there. Instead, a grounded normative alternative to individual autonomy must articulate the desirable goals of news reporting and address the means by which stories are gathered and presented. This task falls within the realm of applied ethics, a reflexive process between principles from theoretical ethics and the social context of news reporting.[9] To counter Enlightenment individualism successfully, a normative ethics of news reporting must insist that both community and personhood are central to the nature of human being; that our account of what constitutes human existence will necessarily influence beliefs about the proper conduct of democratic government; and that the media stand in a vital position—at the center of those webs of meaning by which people understand and transform culture.

The Incredibility of Ethical Relativism

As Paul Tillich taught us, the most compelling foundation for ethics is ontology, in our case with a particular focus on the ontological status of human being.[10] Thus we propose to specify the essential moral characteristics of human life. One viable alternative to our normative position is deriving moral precepts from a social system or custom. This foundation, however, is tentative; it always begs the ultimate questions about the justification for a specific social system or custom, even if its conclusions or principles are valid. John Rawls, for instance, bases his influential theory of justice on democratic political theory. It is not clear whether his "veil of ignorance" applies to nondemocratic societies—unless, of course, it could be proved that democracy best elicits human dignity. If it could, then there would be no need for Rawls to base his approach on democracy as such; it would serve him better to rely on conclusions reached from a notion of human dignity.[11] Custom is similarly a shaky ground for ethics, for if we follow the conventions of one culture, no matter how apparently honorable, we must suspend them in other cultures; or if we should be fortunate enough to discover universal moral practices, we would have to recognize that they are sociological rather than normative. For normative principles, we must look to the nature of our humanity. What enhances it is good, and what denigrates or destroys it is not.

How do we discover the essential characteristics of human beings? If the desire for objectivity is embedded in this question, then the task is hopeless, for the social sciences, humanities, and natural sciences are conditioned by presuppositions, as scholarship in the philosophy of science has demonstrated conclusively ever since Thomas Kuhn explained the role of paradigms in *The Structure of Scientific Revolutions*.[12] No understanding of human being can be objective in the popular sense. Instead, the goal is verisimilitude, or "intelligent recognition," the illumination of human experience and ethical decision making in a way that is recognizable across boundaries of class and culture.[13] In order to deal with the realization of human potential, focusing on both means and ends, a justified ethics will explicitly draw from value-laden philosophies of the human condition.

It could not be otherwise. A justified ethics will acknowledge its value base as it resonates with the character of human experience. The hope for justification lies not in the search for objectivity, but rather in explicitly recognizing every human endeavor as value-laden. Therefore, insisting that epistemologies are value-laden is not to confess ethical relativism.

Relativism is untenable partly for sociological reasons. Whatever their differences, journalists, like members of other professional groups, have much in common. This is Deni Elliott's argument, which she illustrates with the following scenario based on Janet Cooke's Pulitzer Prize–winning hoax that led to Cooke's resignation from the *Washington Post:*

> Editor Ben called Reporter Janet into his office. "You lied in our news columns, Janet," said Ben, "You fabricated that 8-year-old drug addict." Janet readily agreed that Ben was right. "Well, I don't think we should mislead our readers, but if you think it's O.K., then that's fine with me," the editor said.
>
> Later, Ben met with editors from other newspapers at an ASNE conference. He told them about the exchange he had with Janet. The editors listened attentively and finally one said, "Well, Ben, we do our best to publish accurate stories at my shop, but if you think it's O.K. to print lies, that's up to you." The other editors nodded in agreement.
>
> Some time later, in early spring, one Pulitzer Prize judge stopped another. The first said, "Did you know that we gave a Pulitzer for a fabricated story?" The second answered, "Oh, the one about the 8-year-old drug addict? Great story, wasn't it? Remember, we're here to judge stories, not the ethical standards of the reporters."[14]

Using the absurdity of this scenario, Elliott discusses three nonnegotiable principles of journalism, those that define it as a profession and guide its practices.

The first is that news reports should be accurate, balanced, relevant, and complete. Not all stories may meet these criteria, but journalists do not question them. In fact, journalists base their moral judgments about stories precisely on this yardstick. Janet Cooke was judged to be blameworthy because she fabricated a story; she defied the principle of accuracy; she lied. Judgment is swift and decisive because journalists, at least in the West, assume that truthtelling is a moral universal.[15]

Second, journalists share the principle that reporting should avoid harm—what philosophers call the principle of nonmaleficence. As Elliott points out, without this precept journalists would not care whether they harmed others or not, and this is clearly not the case. Journalism-ethics textbooks are full of cases that discuss the conflict between telling the truth and harming people. Should rape victims be named in news accounts? Should juveniles be named in crime stories? How should broadcasters report acts of terrorism? These questions would not be raised if each horn of the dilemma, telling the truth on one side and avoiding harm on the other, were not accepted as a universal duty.

The third maxim for journalists, according to Elliott, is to report information that viewers and readers need to know. In fact, this principle often solves cases in which there is a dilemma between truthtelling and nonmaleficence. Although reports of Senator Gary Hart's extramarital relationship with Donna Rice ruined his chance to receive the Democratic nomination for the presidency in 1988, journalists decided that it was more important to inform voters about Hart's character and judgment than to protect his reputation.[16] The need-to-know principle tipped the balance in favor of truthtelling over nonmaleficence. In the summer of 1991, when the National Archives released tape recordings made of White House conversations during the Nixon era, the former president's reputation was dealt another blow. On the tapes, Richard Nixon expressed his concern about the supposed power of American Jews. Twenty years after words are uttered in a private office, does the public still need to know? Yes, and so a new version of Richard Nixon—the president as anti-Semite—is added to a reputation that many people blame the media for destroying. Public need to know? Yes, the attitudes of those whose words turn public events are the public's business. This same reasoning led the Dallas *Times-Herald* to print the name of a former Soviet spy turned double agent, despite the man's threat of suicide if his name were made public. According to the *Times-Herald,* "From time to time, newspapers receive threats about stories from people attempting to protect their identities. In our judgment, if a story is newsworthy and supported by the facts it is our policy to publish. In this instance it was decided that the story could not be suppressed, even in the face of Mr. Rees' threats."[17]

Reporters debate among themselves whether particular stories are accurate, balanced, relevant, and complete, whether harm could have been avoided under particular circumstances, and when the public's right to know outweighs the principle of nonmaleficence. However, they do not dispute the underlying normative principles of truthtelling, nonmaleficence, or the public's right to know. Elliott calls these principles "universal, normative, and definitional."[18] Similarly, Thomas Cooper's study of more than 100 media-ethics codes from around the world concluded that non-Western media systems also reflect a commitment to truthtelling and responsibility to prevent harm.[19]

These standards are universal, but they are broad and clearly subject to interpretation. Their ambiguity, however, does not invalidate their claim to universality; rather, it suggests that journalists live in a world of plurality, not relativism. Unlike relativism, pluralism allows for a variety of values, but according to a scale of acceptable norms. Relativism would refuse to enforce any norm on any journalist who does not personally espouse it; lying and harm seeking could then be viewed as justifiable on utilitarian grounds, acceptable means to the greater happiness of the group whose well-being the reporter values. Relativism is the scenario in which value judgments are entirely open to a cost–benefit analysis, with anyone's analysis counting as adequate for the argument as the next person's. Relativism casts each dilemma into a gain–loss format, all the while begging the question of what constitutes happiness itself. Cultural pluralism encourages a range of moral options based on justifications derived from responsible versions of how reality is constructed, what human nature entails, and why certain penultimates are obligatory, given the full range of human relations.

Charles Taylor warns that this pursuit of "moral ontology"—claims of oughtness based on claims of how reality is constructed—poses some of the most difficult questions facing the modern era. The largely implicit ontologies that lie behind a journalist's commitment to truthtelling remain subjects rarely discussed, Taylor insists, often because of the "tentative, searching, uncertain nature of many of our moral beliefs" themselves. Many journalists, skeptics by profession, resist a theistic explanation (that persons are created in God's image) but discount as well the "naturalist's attempt to deny ontology altogether." These undecideds "concur that through their moral beliefs they acknowledge some ground in human nature or the human predicament which makes human beings fit objects of respect, but they confess that they cannot subscribe with complete conviction to any particular definition of . . . an essentially modern predicament."[20] Cultural pluralism accepts change as both obligatory (holding that moral life is a process) and radical (conceiving new expressions of justice and love, for example). Mutuality as an operative principle in cultural pluralism recognizes the interdependency and accountability of persons, the inviolability of personhood, the essential nature of relationship in our understanding of the self.

Herbert Gans corroborates Elliott's thesis concerning universal principles in journalism. In *Deciding What's News,* Gans points out that American broadcast and print journalists share eight clusters of values that derive from turn-of-the-century progressivism: altruistic democracy, ethnocentrism, individualism, moderatism, national leadership, responsible capitalism, small-town pastoralism, and social order. Altruistic democracy, the belief that government should serve the public interest, leads reporters to scrutinize the honesty, efficiency, and dedication of politicians and the cooperation of citizens in activities such as racial desegregation and political participation. Ethnocentrism describes the domestic emphasis of the news and its American slant in foreign reports. Whether reporting on political, social, or economic news, the press tends to emphasize individual heroes and villains rather than groups or impersonal processes. Journalists also prefer moderates, labeling true believers as extremists, reactionaries, or radicals. And the news media value the president, the person responsible for maintaining the social order as embodied in elite individuals and elite institutions. Their belief in responsible capitalism means that businesspersons should compete for the best profits but not at the expense of workers or consumers. Small-town pastoralism refers to journalists' distrust of corrupted cities and distaste for the ennui of suburbs, and their romantic image of small towns where, they believe, individuality and harmony can thrive. Taken together, these values determine not only what is reported, but how news stories are cast.[21]

The observations of Elliott and Gans are descriptive; they illustrate the values and perspectives that journalists, at least Western or American journalists, share. Obviously, we must be wary of overgeneralization because our ability to observe is always incomplete. However, the available evidence does indicate that news reporters hold a litany of ethical principles and enduring values in common, and this knowledge indicates that news reporters in fact do not behave normlessly. But *is* does not imply *ought*. If news reporters ought to adhere to a moral framework, it is not because doing so is accepted practice, or because of newsroom socialization, or because of the threat of institutional sanctions. Rather, an ethics of news reporting, if it is to be something other than etiquette or social custom, rests on an application of moral universals. The task of dispelling relativism may draw on sociological observations for illustration, but it must rely on compelling philosophy along the lines of what Hadley Arkes provides in his recent book, *First Things*.[22]

Discussing the idea of moral universals seems out of step today, a throwback to an oppressive medieval Catholicism or to periods of political intolerance such as France's Reign of Terror. Moral universals appear to have little intellectual support except for a problematic natural-law theology or a philosophical foundationalism currently on the defensive. Today's sophisticate takes pride in championing diversity and pluralism, trotting out ethnographies such as Colin Turnbull's *The Mountain People* to show that different cultures have different moralities and that to argue otherwise foists one's intentions on others in an act of moral or ideological imperialism.

This viewpoint is both facile and contradictory, however. It is facile because it confuses *is* (moralities conflict) with *ought* (*vive la différence*); it is contradictory because moral relativism itself becomes a normative universal. Enlightened intellectuals obfuscate the issue further by insisting on moral relativism on the one hand, and by opposing such atrocities as wage-slavery capitalism or Middle Eastern genocide on the other. Relativists would universally oppose Ku Klux Klan rule in the South or gang rule in Los Angeles, and they never defend Hitler's New Order. Television dramas sent willy-nilly into foreign markets, precisely to salvage profits not yet reaped domestically, require for moral justification what Richard Posner calls the Pareto superiority principle, a version of the utilitarian calculus that proposes moral worth if at least one person is better off under Plan A than Plan B, and no one is worse off.[23] But Posner is quick to note that the Pareto solution is "apparent rather than real," since measuring relative utilities is impossible. However bankrupt a relative calculation of convenience or conviction may be, its rejection need not lead to abject intolerance. There are moral universals, but only a handful of them. Plenty of room remains for tolerance, respect, and even admiration of cultural differences.

Ethical relativism is the belief that because moral judgments vary across cultures and historical periods, all moral systems are equally good, even if they are antithetical.[24] Ethical relativism may be open-minded and tolerant, but it pushes diversity beyond the limits of reason and fact. To believe that ethics is the code of the majority would allow the majority to tyrannize the minority. Without a normative basis for moral decision making, relativists frequently accept a utilitarianism that seeks a least noxious resolution for the distribution of limited goods and resources. However, relativism is the most conservative of moral strategies, because it seeks stability with established mores and has no reason to consider counterclaims from outside the group (unless, of course, those claims work effectively to enhance long-range dominance in return for short-range concessions). Unable to argue on the basis of justice or love, groups on the periphery—or groups clearly oppressed—have little recourse but to establish themselves as the central power and then commence with a new set of assertions in accord with their own traditions and cost–benefit analysis. An ethical relativist would have to accept the Nazi death camps or Stalinist pogroms as logical extensions of the beliefs, grounded in social and historical contexts, of those in control. "Live and let live" becomes horribly ironic. Relativism assumes that standards require agreement for their validity, that moral principles are socially appropriate only to the degree that they are universal in practice. As Arkes points out, the sharpest arguments over moral relativism in this country occurred in the Lincoln–Douglas debates, with Lincoln insisting that slavery was wrong for all humans everywhere because it conflicts with the nature of human being and Douglas arguing that slavery was acceptable wherever it was the will of the local majority.[25] Slavery was for Douglas a political rather than a moral question, morality being judged according to relativism as nothing more than majority rule in Sunday dress.

Edward A. Purcell explains the impact of modern relativism as a function of the acceptance of Darwinist principles in the social sciences during the 1880s, especially in the works of William Graham Sumner. But other academic fields also rushed to the new scientific ground: Oliver Wendell Holmes, Jr., in law, Harold Lasswell in political theory, Ruth Benedict in anthropology, Alfred Korzybski in semantics, Rudolph Carnap in philosophy, and Eric Temple Bell in mathematics. John Dewey plays a central role in Purcell's account, as the father of the now common perception that anything to the right or left of mainstream relativism leads inexorably to political authoritarianism. Absolutist philosophies of all stripes were logically analogous to feudal oligarchy, and historically coincidental. Nazism was explained as a triumph, if not the last gasp, of absolutist theory (absolutist in the sense of claims to moral universality based on metaphysical constructs about the nature of reality). Purcell writes, "By the early forties philosophical naturalists, regardless of their other disagreements, were almost unanimous in maintaining that theoretical absolutism of any kind was the logical concomitant of totalitarianism. Allow an absolutism into social or political theory, and any *Führer* or *Duce* had a perfect rationale for action."[26] Richard Rorty carries on that tradition in the 1990s: contingency for normativity; irony for truth; solidarity for mutuality. The language of moral norms and moral claims is a syntax now on a different galaxy: people do not talk that way anymore, and the eradication of such categories is all the better.[27]

However, drawing on observations stemming back to Aristotle, Arkes explains why certain moral principles are both universal and categorical—apply, in other words, to everyone under all conditions. He first observes that human beings in all societies think in terms of right and wrong, good and bad. Although prescriptions and proscriptions may vary, moral thinking as such is part of the human condition. Second, human communities, whether families, tribes, or states, are built on moral rules. Whatever else they might be, human communities are moral associations. Third, moral statements are always cast as universals, binding for others as well as oneself. Human beings judge between acts that are justified and unjustified, and they are free not only to reflect on standards of behavior, but also to choose between courses of action. Arkes points out that human freedom in the moral sense of the term means that people can act contrary to moral universals without suffering recriminations from the laws of physics for doing so. Similarly, people are not held responsible for acts that they cannot affect, nor are their actions reasonably judged apart from the motives that guided them.[28] Humans are moral beings, and morality always makes universal and categorical claims. Relativism is thus untenable: Can a court of reasonable persons unashamedly defend slavery as a reasonable practice?[29]

Arthur Dyck presses the point further. He recognizes that individuals or groups evaluate moral situations differently and change their judgments of what is morally acceptable. However, disagreement does not necessarily imply ambiguity, as the old debate over the roundness or flatness of the earth illustrates. Dyck demonstrates how moral dissimilarities between cultures often result from differences in interpreting nonethical terms. Infanticide, for instance, was practiced in cultures which proscribed the killing of innocent persons, just as we do, but which believed that personhood did not begin until a few days after birth. To bring the illustration closer to home, the abortion debate centers on the issue of when life begins. Both pro-choice and pro-life advocates insist that murder is wrong; they disagree over the relevant biological information, including what information is applicable in determining priorities of rights: the woman's privacy versus the fetus's viability. Dyck makes a strong case for the universality of certain moral principles, arguing that ambiguity stems from interpretation rather than from what he calls the "right- and wrong-making characteristics" of moral principles themselves.[30] "Similarly," Elliott observes, "many of the ethical conflicts in journalism come down to a lack of clarity in how terms are used rather than real disagreement about how to judge right and wrong."[31]

Robert Fullinwider reminds us that moral relativists do not threaten our social order as much as the anxious often assume. Certainly, a sophisticated, conceptually vigorous ethical relativism exists from Protagoras to Gilbert Harman, but it is hard to find generally. Most of our relativism is epiphenomenal, as Fullinwider observes correctly, long in cultural fashion as resistance to detestable authority or insensitive judgmentalism. "Do your own thing" and "respect differences" actually serve in everyday life within a moral framework (as minimal claims about tolerance). Similarly to Elliott's observations about the journalism profession, insisting on tolerance arises from an arsenal of moral commitment rather than seriously undermining it. Fullinwider calls for expanding our repertoire, for providing a deeper and broader discourse that enables us to exercise more profoundly our powers of moral discrimination. As we develop "more refined and complex views of rules, rule-systems, and authority . . . and come upon useful and clarifying distinctions," we will no longer need to "invoke the protective devices of relativism."[32] In that spirit, the following section constructs a communitarian ethics of mutuality.

Mutuality

Human beings are social, though independent; they exist spatiotemporally as persons in community. Given the paradoxical character of this relationship, moralists and social philosophers have often emphasized one characteristic over the other. The Enlightenment's monadic self and privatized experience persist for this very reason; we appear to think and decide and act with a large degree of independence. Yet we are every bit communal; hence the tradition of radical socialism, which views humans fundamentally in terms of the tribe or state. Communitarian ethics accounts for both traits, but weaves them together in extraordinarily complicated ways and separates them only for purposes of analysis. It takes seriously Max Scheler's "phenomenon of fellow-feeling," in which our self-identity is considered so intertwined with our awareness of others that we grasp our own distinctiveness only gradually. Emotional identification is primordial, involuntary; we often know the feelings and thoughts of others better than our own.[33] Humans are aware of the co-givenness of values prior to their personal givenness.[34] The intellectual challenge is to eschew every remnant of dualism in construing the individual and society connection. Hans Jonas says, "In the inextricable interweaving of human affairs as of all things, it is nowise unavoidable that my action will affect the fate of others; and thus any staking of my very own is always a staking also of something that belongs to others and to which I have properly no right."[35]

Comprehending the nature of the self is vital, but stopping there or reducing groups to collections of automatons reenacts Enlightenment worship at the altar of individual autonomy. Certainly, with Immanuel Kant we can say that persons should be treated as ends in themselves, never as means to an end. But human beings are simultaneously communal, and their community must be encouraged as emphatically as their personhood. In Aristotelian terms, the *polis* is prior to its members. Social systems precede their occupants and continue after them. Indeed, Socrates argued playfully that he could not be responsible for ruining the *polis* or free to save it because the *polis* educated him. At the deepest level of the self, human beings personally treasure the moral commitments and existential meanings that they share communally. As Alfred Schutz contends, selves are not fashioned out of thin air. We are born into a sociocultural universe whose values (regarding gender, race, and age, for example) are either presumed or negotiated. That persons make this historically given world believable does not demean them or render this world less real. It merely testifies that human identity is constituted organically, that persons depend on and live through the social realm.[36]

Martin Buber

For Martin Buber, existence in its authentic form is communication; normative life is dialogic. Dialogue is another name for a morally appropriate act; a moral will rests on the freedom of other selves. Genuine dialogue is to our humanness what blood is to the body: when the flow of blood ceases or becomes diseased, the body dies; when dialogue stops, love disappears, and hate and resentment are born. Buber calls the dialogic relation a primal notion in his famous lines, "In the beginning is the relation" and "The relation is the cradle of actual life."[37] He intends that ontologically, as a category of being. Relationships, not individuals, have primacy. "The one primary word is the combination I–Thou."[38] This irreducible anthropological phenomenon—the relational reality, the in-between, the reciprocal bond, the interpersonal—cannot be decomposed into simpler elements without destroying it. A singular self existing outside others, unique and distinct, pursuing an isolated destiny across time—such claims rupture reality and preclude human development. Thou–I, the person, grows through interaction with others and not through isolated introspection. Fulfillment does not result from being unencumbered.[39]

Buber sweeps epistemology into his anthropology. He declares that we have understood reality when we have gotten inside the self-in-relation, that we ourselves live humanly when we accept others with unconditional positive regard. "The inmost growth of the self is accomplished . . . in the relation between one and the other, that is, pre-eminently in the mutuality of the making present . . . together with the mutuality of acceptance, of affirmation and confirmation."[40] Liberal promises of progressive improvement have failed to deliver; only remnants of wistfulness remain. Through the experience of mutuality, Buber seeks to recover a vigorous form of hope that trusts social life without denying its tragic character.

Buber was born in Sigmund Freud's Vienna, yet his widely acclaimed classic, *I and Thou* (*Ich und Du*), offers a sharp contrast to Freud's internal states—*Ich* and *Es* and *Uber-Ich*. Buber speaks not of internal parts, but of human relationships. Our personhood, in Buber's view, is shaped within two modalities of human relation. Persons are knowable only in I–Thou relationships; the I–It modality reveals only ephemeral appearances. In the first, we are involved with our whole being, and our uniqueness is open to the particularity of others. In the second, we dehumanize, depersonalize the other, and in the process dehumanize ourselves. Apprehending the real otherness of persons is the crux of morality. The I–It relationship prospers only when I–Thouness is allowed to recede. Over against the I–It pattern stands Buber's dialogue, where a flood of unalloyed openness brings persons into being.

Monologic communication (the I–It relation) is in the imperative mood—a directive system whether as cybernetics, mainline stimulus–response communication theory, or demagoguery and propaganda. Norbert Wiener, inventor of cybernetics, in his curiously titled book *The Human Use of Human Beings* was already taking pains in 1954 to emphasize that one version of monologic media—"the electrical theory of messages"—is intrinsically and irresistibly a theory and program of control. He had a

vivid premonition of the disastrous results if modern culture were to become dominated by one-way, machine-based communication media.

Attempts to take Wiener's warning seriously and ameliorate the tyranny
of mass-media technologies have not been notably successful. And over
against monologic views held uncritically, Buber speaks compellingly of
restoring dialogic communication as humankind's primary need today: "In
sick ages it happens that the I–It world, no longer irrigated and fertilized
by the living currents of the You world, severed and stagnant becomes a
gigantic swamp phantom and overcomes man."[41] He resists the naïveté of
pasting ethical principles onto a form of communication intrinsically de-
basing; Buber offers in dialogic theory a revolutionary alternative that goes
to the root and rethinks the issues from the ground up and the inside out.[42]

John Macmurray

Buber himself was not interested in developing a systematic metaphysics
for his seminal ideas practically expressed. The *shtetl* communities of Has-
idic Judaism gave him an experiential context for mutual bonding with a
"living Center" and with others.[43] The Scottish philosopher John Macmurray develops Buber's ruminations into "one of the clearest and most
comprehensive philosophical systems which starts from and returns to the
ontological primacy of persons-in-relation."[44] Macmurray's first book, *Interpreting the Universe* (1933), introduced the philosophical essentials, but
in the Gifford Lectures delivered at the University of Glasgow in 1953 and
1954, he elaborated comprehensively the communitarian perspective.[45] He
proposes a dialogic view of human existence, not just of mind and discourse
or of one culture to other cultures. "To be" equals "to be with/for others."

Macmurray situates his communitarian social philosophy in the history
of ideas, determined to demonstrate that the mutuality of persons differs
qualitatively from mechanical and organic ways of symbolizing reality. But
he concentrates on providing a rationale for three propositions entailed by
communitarian theory: all meaningful knowledge is for the sake of action;
all befitting action is for the sake of community building; and ultimate
reality is fundamentally personal.

First, we know ourselves primarily as agents in relation to and deriv-
atively as thinkers withdrawn from action. Only by overcoming the traditional dualisms between thinker and agent, mind and body, reason and
will, can being be conceived as "the mutuality of personal relationship."[46]
Praxis is the inclusive term; thought arises out of action and returns to
action for its incarnation and verification. Rather than focusing on the
states of being, humans are in the process of becoming something. When
action goes askew, I figure out what went wrong and what solution is most
coherent. Like a hiker lost in the woods, I withdraw temporarily from the

trail and consult a map, but my conclusions need to be tested by resuming the journey. Action determines whether our conceptual map is correct. During this reflection, the self acts in terms of the larger pattern of action—in this case, finding a destination. Acting, that is, precedes and follows reflective reprieves. "Philosophy is necessarily theoretical, and must aim at theoretical strictness. [But] it does not follow that we must theorize from the standpoint of theory."[47] Thus rather than dismissing the idea of rationality, Macmurray reclaims and reconstructs it into an inclusive understanding of the action self. He combines thinking and acting in a rhythmic way that differs radically from the traditional notion of thinking, which excludes acting.[48] Macmurray searches for a comprehensive concept that does full justice to a unified humanness and centers on agency: "As an ideal limit of personal being, [action] is the concept of an unlimited rational being, in which all the capacities of the Self are in full and unrestricted employment."[49]

Second, all meaningful action is for the sake of friendship. In Sartre, to realize my freedom I must negate rather than confirm the other. For Macmurray, my whole being cannot experience uniqueness except in openness to the uniqueness of others. Action, to be meaningful, must be for community building; the bonding of persons is the epicenter of cultural formation, its constitutive ambience. Given the primacy of relationship, unless I use my freedom to help others flourish, I deny my own well-being. Because fulfillment as persons is never achieved in isolation, but only in relation, our encounter inheres in our beingness. In order to maintain our existence, we are committed to the mutual existence of the others with whom our person is interconnected. Persons are distinguished from nonpersons by their consciousness of intentional action, but it is consciousness of the other and not primarily self-awareness. Our communality, in other words, is both absolute (without it we are not human at all) and relative (always beyond our present achievement as the goal of our existence).[50] There is no sheer being; the relational is indigenous to our humanness. Therefore, our being is either coming into mutuality or betraying it; no neutral territory exists between static integers. The personal and communal may be integrative without being completely integrated. The empirical self exists on several different levels simultaneously.

Although our deepest intentions—the dynamics of our essence—are relational, our everyday psychological motivations (that domain within one's conscious control) are an admixture of love and fear. Child responsiveness to parents demonstrates bonding as intrinsically human,[51] but our space–time existence entangles us in disjunction and the impersonal. Thus our choice of action is necessarily a moral choice. Without others there is no possibility of action, except in such extreme cases as the proverbial marooning on a desert island. And no action can be right if its enactment would destroy the very conditions for morality itself. Choices are morally appropriate only if my self-freedom allows the possibility of another's freedom. "Since the relation of persons is constitutive for their existence as persons, . . . morally right action is [one] which intends community."[52]

On this point, Macmurray shows the departure of the mutuality model from the model of human existence that Taylor attributes to Augustine. For Taylor, Augustine commandeered Plato's notion of the ideal and changed the direction of anthropology: truth as inwardness. Taylor calls this turn "radical reflexivity" and insists that Descartes owes his "cogito" to the prior work of Augustine, "because Augustine was the first to make the first-person standpoint fundamental to our search for the truth." From the idea of "memoria"—a deeply personal and pervasive implicit understanding of the reasonableness of the external world and the truthfulness of the world of ideas—comes Taylor's judgment that Augustine reached for the ultimate mystery "in the intimacy of self-presence."[53] Thus Augustine introduced "the inwardness of radical reflexivity and bequeathed it to the Western tradition of thought."[54] We are indebted to Augustine for providing ontological vision to our common notion of the self. We now recognize selfhood as a possession as natural as having heads or arms. We consider "inner depths the way we have hearts or livers, as a matter of hard, interpretation-free fact."[55] It was never Augustine's notion that persons exist in isolation from other selves or from a personal God. But his ontology needs Macmurray's explicit intersubjective connections in order to be acceptably wholistic.

Third, MacMurray cuts personal being into the very heart of the universe. Ultimate reality is accessible to us only in relation as a Thou, as an object. Macmurray self-consciously uses biblical symbols and intends his model to be congruent with Judeo-Christian theism. When he argues that human relationships need their ground and inspiration in absolute Personality, he himself chooses the religions of the Bible as exemplars that God acts intentionally in order to realize community.[56] If the divine cosmic epicenter is not personal and living communally, there is no root in being to separate persons from mere organisms. We understand the logic of divine–human mutuality through experience, and in their relationship with a "supreme and universal Agent," the "universal community of persons" discovers the normative pattern of liberating mutuality.[57]

Thus MacMurray provides one example of how to meet J. B. Lotz's challenge: "Ontology must be rescued from submersion in things by being thought out entirely from the viewpoint of person and thus of Being. . . . Ontology is truly itself only when it is personal and persons are truly themselves only as ontological."[58]

Seeing how this communal motif operates in the daily life of journalism is an enormously complicated task. Human activities, whether personal, social, or institutional, promote a state of relatively liberated personhood. How might this observation apply to the news industry? Such a moral commitment recognizes that information is a social necessity: "People . . . cannot be expected to do what is morally right and correct unless they have the knowledge needed to make a particular decision."[59] There would be a conscious effort to present information useful not only to the relatively wealthy for whom advertisers use news and entertainment as bait, but also to the disenfranchised, to those in whom advertisers rarely take an interest. Recent changes in the freedom to advertise both confound and underscore this point. Manufacturers of fashion apparel, automobiles, and beverages are surely focused on selling an image, not necessarily a product. Stuart Ewen insists that such advertising, without explicitly saying so, offers "to lift the viewer out of his or her life and place him or her in a utopian netherworld where there are no conflicts, no needs unmet."[60] The majority of televised commercials meet Ewen's objection. But public-interest groups, and not the vehicles of media, have succeeded in the last fifteen years in securing the right to advertise goods that clearly benefit lower economic strata.

Precisely this social good was at the heart of the Supreme Court's decision to permit the free public advertisement of pharmaceutical products.[61] As long as trade associations could shield consumer pricing information as competitiveness unbefitting the profession, the elderly and those on fixed incomes would inevitably spend a larger share of their resources on a decreasing purchase of health. Media are the beneficiaries of such legal challenges much more often than they are the initiators of policy change, their own vested interests obscuring public view.

The concept of liberated personhood also redefines what news is and changes how news is reported. The goal would no longer be an ever-elusive objectivity, but rather telling true stories that promote economic, political, and social emancipation. Michael Schudson cites the chief responsibility of journalism as providing "the materials that allow political communication to take place"; and he exclaims, "[H]ow can we have a responsible journalism when the news media are intent primarily and sometimes exclusively on making money, not providing service?" Schudson's abrupt question turns on the argument that stewardship supersedes autonomy in the hierarchy of journalism's responsibilities.[62]

Paul Tournier places the emphasis of this moral imperative on the self. Tournier's perspective is psychiatric, but it has broader applications. Tournier offers four primary characteristics of persons: they are unique, despite their images and appearances; they are knowable only through dialogue (scientific observation can reveal only the self's image or appearance); persons communicate rather than merely associate; and they are creative rather than physically or psychically routine and mechanical.[63]

Any discussion of community risks conceptual ambiguity because the
term is so elastic. Community may serve as a call for bygone agrarianism
(Dorothy and Toto on their Kansas farm) or as a euphemism for state
control (Winston and Julia in Oceania). Community sometimes has racial
meaning (the black community), professional meaning (the medical community), or religious meaning (the Jewish community). When we speak
of the community of Davenport, community is local; the global village
represents something international. Community is a truly user-friendly
concept, subject to almost any meaning. As Richard P. Hiskes says,
"Community has always been a rather murky political concept, not because
it defies all definitions given, but because it seems to collect them."[64] Gary
Gumpert's speculation also hits the mark: "[T]here is little agreement over
what is meant by the term, perhaps because the acceptance of a particular
definition suggests a social perspective that implies not only a style of living,
but also responsibility and obligation to others."[65]

Wendell Berry

No essayist speaks more powerfully about the contours of community, and
the need for revival of genuine community, than Wendell Berry. For him,
community is a constant theme, and rural community is his passion. In
"The Work of Local Culture," he observes that an old bucket left outdoors
for years does for nature what human communities must do actively and
thoughtfully: "collect leaves and stories, and turn them to account." Here
may be modern literature's finest metaphor for the media. But Berry is
not naïve. Relationships can be ugly; acrimony is as likely as harmony.
Berry links the liability insurers to the demise of mutuality: "A good
community . . . insures itself by trust, by good faith and good will, by mutual
help." Critics who dismiss such pastoralism as Luddite myth must reckon
with Berry's admission that community is no guarantee of happiness, only
our best chance at being able to endure unhappiness: "Community life is
tragic . . . because it involves unremittingly the need to survive mortality,
partiality, and evil. . . . No community can survive that cannot survive the
worst."[66] Flannery O'Connor's short stories illustrate this point profoundly.[67]

However, not just any group of people is a bona fide community in an
ethical sense, and not every bona fide community is actually good. Berry
insists that a good community is "common experience and common effort
on a common ground to which one willingly belongs."[68] But that is not
enough. Persons form associations out of an innate need, and many of
them promote mutual health and growth. Those formed for the purpose
of destroying or diminishing human life and property—groups, in other

words, formed to exploit either members or outsiders—cannot be considered communities in a normative sense. Nor can the likes of William Faulkner's fictional communities, which Berry points out are doomed by slavery and greed.[69] Because a moral community is a condition for personhood, a group is not ipso facto good, and no community can excuse inhumane behavior.

A moral community demonstrates more than mere interdependence; it is characterized by mutuality, a will-to-community, a genuine concern for the other apart from immediate self-interest. According to Derek McKiernan, "[C]ommunity is marked by immediate social relations that have organically emerged, are democratically organized, in which the self-identity of each member is fused with the identity of the collective and which coheres around a value or set of values."[70] In this way a community is distinct from a public, a collection of persons who do not meet face-to-face but who share political needs nevertheless.[71] Communities themselves belong to a larger public. Indeed, they will thrive only in a larger area that, at minimum, values tolerance; at the maximum, community requires love. "Only love can do it," Wendell Berry writes.[72] "If one has faith to move mountains, but no love, the effect is nothing," Paul announced to early Christians at Corinth.

Clarifying the nature of this other-centered orientation is no small task in building an understanding of community. Pious wishing and romantic dreaming are as obviously immaterial to our concerns as intellectualizing love into an abstraction that may be surveyed and codified, as Pitirim Sorokin attempted to do.[73] The Christian tradition captures our intended meaning in the term *agape,* a description of the love of divine being toward humans as an act of beneficient will. Taylor cites this love—and human participation in it—as the only answer to Nietzschean nihilism. Can humans realize the fullness of their humanity? Nietzsche surely believes so, once the ethic of benevolence has been eliminated. "Only if there is such a thing as *agape,* or one of the secular claimants to its succession, is Nietzsche wrong."[74]

One begins to understand the distinctions when self-serving dictators take the lives of their own people by treachery and brutality, as did Iraq's Saddam Hussein against the northern Kurds and China's ruling octogenarians against students in Tiananmen Square. In one sense, further discussion of the Nietzchean alternative is foreclosed for all but academic, and hence politically irrelevant, purposes in the face of these manifestations of the *Übermensch*. If such events do not persuade humans of the need to recover the good community, then all the pages written on altruism and agape—mutuality—are so much lost forest and nothing more. This discussion itself, if Nietzsche is correct, must be interpreted as intellectual treachery—authors' subtle attempt to impose their will on readers in the guise of moralism and harmony. Yet choosing mutuality is not the same as understanding its dimensions.

Self and Society

The conceptual silt begins to settle as we filter intellectual history to clarify the primary ways in which the relationship between self and community has been understood. As Frank Kirkpatrick explains in *Community: A Trinity of Models,* three distinct models of the self in community have emerged since the Renaissance: atomistic, organic, and mutual.[75] Although Thomas Hobbes is usually associated with atomism, Friedrich Hegel with organicism, and Martin Buber with mutuality, the models have not been restricted to any one thinker or historical epoch. Indeed, incarnations of these enduring conceptions of human nature and its fulfillment can be seen in the flesh and blood of contemporary life.

Atomism. We traced the historical roots of the atomistic model in Chapter 2. Various versions of it still permeate thinking in the United States through the stalwart individualism of its ideals—Horatio Alger entrepreneurship and Lone Ranger justice. This model calls to mind independent atoms contracting rationally with one another for the terms of their bonds. Human beings are individual, isolated, and self-interested; they cooperate solely to protect their own interests, particularly their property. Collective life is little more than the voluntary association of free agents, a way for individuals to pursue their self-interests with minimal interference from others. The atomistic model conceives of morality as the powerful agreeing to adjust power among themselves, agreements in which the powerless take no part.

In the atomistic model, society is highlighted by the fundamental separateness of persons; the gaps between them are bridged voluntarily and rationally, never out of recognition that humans must live with and for other persons. The atomistic model admirably underscores the uniqueness of persons who are valuable as such and who need not qualify for acceptance and respect on the basis of merit. Atomism's failure is its profound lack of appreciation for the wholeness of reality. It fundamentally rejects the notion of interrelatedness. In fact, the reductionist temper of atomism regards the language of "wholeness" as a religious and metaphysical misconception.[76] Atomism understands several elements well, but it has no sense of ecology.

The folklore of the press as watchdog is one clear application of atomism to the world of news reporting. Here the press considers itself staunchly independent: apart from government and unconstrained by business. Harking back to the early nineteenth century, when Edmund Burke and Thomas B. Macaulay first referred to the reporters' gallery of the English Parliament as the "fourth estate," this folklore had become established by the Gilded Age. Joseph Pulitzer said, for instance, that his *St. Louis Post-Dispatch* would "serve no party but the people; be no organ of Republicanism, but the organ of truth; will follow no causes but its conclusions; will not support the Administration, but criticize it; will oppose all frauds and shams wherever and whatever they are; will advocate principles and ideals rather than prejudices and partisanship."[77] Much as later journalists would report the Watergate scandal and the Iran-Contra affair, watchdogs during the Gilded Age exposed the corruption of New York's Boss Tweed and Standard Oil's John D. Rockefeller.

According to Timothy Gleason, the press developed the watchdog concept during the nineteenth century, when U.S. courts accepted "good motives" and "justifiable ends" as common-law defenses in cases of libel and contempt. The watchdog concept provided such a justifiable end, a rationale designed to afford the press extraordinary legal protection.[78] Belief in the watchdog function of the press assumes that reporters are independent agents whose social contract, the First Amendment, grants them professional freedom in exchange for the exposure of misdeeds in government and business. Never mind that the press thereby participates in policymaking or that journalists themselves work for businesses; these observations pale in the glow of a heroic guardian press.

Organicism. The atomistic model of human association emphasizes persons at the expense of society; the organic model reverses the emphasis, stressing society's importance and downplaying the self. This model conceives of society as a complex organism with interdependent organs related to one another functionally. Organicism not only overcomes the extreme individualism of the atomistic paradigm by denying the myth of monadic independence and isolation, but also serves as an alternative to contractual notions of community. According to the organic model, society is greater than the sum total of the individuals it comprises. Indeed, in the same way that human beings are more than a collection of organs, so society is more than a collection of citizens. The whole is primary; persons are secondary. Unfortunately, by denying personal uniqueness and the irreducibility of persons' relation to one another, the organic model in principle permits political totalitarianism because the systemic whole matters more than its parts.

The difference between the atomistic and organic models comes into focus with Martin Linsky's three-year study of how the press affects policymaking in Washington. Linsky's research examines the interconnectedness among the press, government, and society, albeit without totalitarian implications. (For that, one might turn to the all-for-one, one-for-all rationale of the press in the People's Republic of China.) Linsky denies the existence of an independent press, at least on the federal level. In the same way that luminaries such as Walter Lippmann and George Will have advised those they covered, or as newspapers have lobbied Congress for favorable legislation, the press as an institution is not so much a watchdog over government as an active participant in the process of governmental policymaking.

Linsky's example of the Love Canal episode illustrates this process. In December 1979 the Department of Justice, acting on behalf of the Environmental Protection Agency, filed a $124.5 million lawsuit against Hooker Chemical, the city and the Board of Education of Niagara Falls, New York, and the Niagara County Health Department for an end to disposing of toxic chemicals in the Love Canal area, for restoring the site, and, if need be, for relocating residents. Government lawyers also commissioned a preliminary study of possible genetic damage among Love Canal residents; evidence of birth defects or cancer would prompt a fuller scientific inquiry, one complete with a control group. Around May 1, 1980, the preliminary study revealed that twelve of the thirty-six Love Canal residents examined showed evidence of chromosomal damage. A full investigation was in order.

On Friday, May 16, the EPA decided to inform the Love Canal residents of the test results immediately and to hold a press conference the next day. However, someone leaked the results of the preliminary study to the *New York Times* before the press conference. On Sunday, network television and the *Times* highlighted the story; and on Monday, Love Canal residents held two EPA officials hostage for several hours. Two days later, the EPA promised to relocate 710 families from the Love Canal area. Shortly thereafter, the review of the preliminary study was completed. As did subsequent studies, it concluded that there was an "inadequate basis for any scientific or medical inferences from the data (even of a tentative or preliminary nature) concerning exposure to mutagenic substances because of residence in Love Canal." According to the review, the EPA's decision and the public's hysteria had been premature.

Press coverage hastened the government's decision to move Love Canal residents, thereby undercutting the EPA's original deliberation. The press affected both policy choice and the policymaking process; its reporting hastened decision making and pushed it up the bureaucracy. The press did not determine policy, but it did influence the odds of particular choices being made. Linsky's analysis of the Love Canal episode supports the central tenet of the organic model of community: that social institutions are interdependent. As Linsky concludes, "[A]ll of this means that journalists must satisfy us, all of us in government and out, that their decisions are being made in a thoughtful and reasoned process that takes into consideration the consequences of those decisions for the institutions and process of government and for specific individuals and policies as well."[79]

Mutuality. The atomistic model of community cannot accommodate the wholeness of social life, and the organic matrix cannot accommodate the irreducible self. However, the mutuality model accepts both personhood and social interdependence as givens. The atomistic and organic forms of association are necessary but insufficient conditions for mutuality, because mutuality defines community in terms of distinct persons who find fulfillment by living for one another. The parts are not subsumed by the whole, but neither are the parts paramount. Mutuality differs qualitatively from the social contracts of individuals seeking their own self-realization.

Mutuality recognizes the value of other people, not just for self-enhancement, but in terms of what they themselves are. Social relations are not merely for individual ends, but are fundamentally an end in themselves. Human community is intentionally inclusive. An act is morally right when compelled by the intention to maintain the community of persons; it is wrong if driven by self-centeredness.

Relationships are not merely functions that serve a higher good. The mutuality model accepts interdependence as a matter of fact. Community is a matter of intention—the intention to live for others. The concept of persons in relation is primary; the focus is neither on the persons nor on the community as such, but rather on the interaction, the in-between, the commitment to the well-being of the whole. The human encounter must be understood ontologically, as a category of being. This irreducible anthropological phenomenon—the relational reality, the reciprocal bond, the person as interpersonal—cannot be decomposed into simpler elements without destroying it.

The University of Iowa study of libel and the press illustrates the mutual model of community. Randall Bezanson, Gilbert Cranberg, and John Soloski were interested in nonlitigatory methods of resolving libel disputes. The cost of libel litigation chills controversial news coverage, and the judicial process is so slow that genuinely aggrieved parties are not vindicated until years after the defamation is first printed or broadcast. Because understanding defamation and the responses to it in legal terms serves mainly to fan the flames of litigiousness, these scholars reconceptualized the problem and their results are apropos to the model of mutuality.

They focused their attention on the question: What leads people to sue for libel? This query is especially poignant given the fact that plaintiffs ultimately win only 10 percent of libel cases. Since their odds of winning are so low, what—other than the encouragement of lawyers paid on a fee basis—would lead them to sue the press for libel? To resolve this puzzle, the Iowa scholars examined the entire litigation process, beginning with the offending story and ending with the legal resolution. They discovered that when plaintiffs ask for a retraction, correction, or apology, the media, reluctant to admit mistakes, usually refuse. James Gannon, editor of the *Des Moines Register,* commented:

> Somebody calls and gets bounced from one person to another—you know, four or five different people in the newsroom—and finally ends up with someone who's on deadline and irritated and saying, "Well, that's just the way we do it, buddy! That's our policy" and, you know, bang, or something like that. And I've had these horror stories told to me—people who have gone through this, and they feel they just don't get a hearing, a real hearing, and they don't get a courteous response. . . . I think in general newspapers do a pretty bad job of responding to complaints from the public.[80]

It is then that the plaintiffs contact a lawyer. Angered by the way that the media treated them, they decide to sue in order to punish the media and to restore their reputations, not to win large settlements or awards.

The authors of the Iowa study conclude that alternatives to libel litigation exist in newsrooms already: reporters must be more genuinely responsive to complaints from outsiders. According to the authors, "The manner in which media publishers deal with plaintiffs following publication unnecessarily fosters litigation. The media, therefore, have some self-examination to do."[81] The authors also suggest systemic changes that would discourage frivolous suits and speed the process of legitimate ones. Seen in light of the model of mutuality, the Iowa study emphasizes real dialogue (a sign of mutuality) and recognizes both individual interests and the commonweal. Bezanson, Cranberg, and Soloski avoid pitting the press against the public (atomism) or denying legitimate individual claims (organicism). The press and the public would benefit by such responsiveness.

This conclusion may provide guidance in cases beyond libel. The issue of whether to report a rape victim's name is but one example. Those who favor naming the victim argue that plaintiffs as well as defendants should be named as a matter of course in all stories about crimes, including rape. It is unfair, they say, to name the accused, who have not yet had their day in court, while keeping accusers hidden from public view. Opponents of this position argue that rape is a special case, that naming the victim further victimizes her by exposing her to public speculation and even to ridicule and derision. Furthermore, if rape victims believe that they will be named in the news, they will probably become even more reluctant to report the crime in the first place. According to this viewpoint, naming the victim will hinder exposing this crime—an effect with dire social consequences.

Although the *Des Moines Register* has a policy against naming the victims of rape, in 1990 it ran a front-page series for five consecutive days detailing the experiences of Nancy Ziegenmeyer from the time she was abducted and raped to the day Bobby Lee Smith was convicted of the crime. A year later, the *Courier-Journal Magazine* in Louisville broke its policy and told the story of Cindy McDonald, who was raped by her former boyfriend, Michael Ray Barnes. What both reports have in common is the victim's permission. Both newspapers had firm policies, but both were willing to listen to the concerns of courageous individuals. Ziegenmeyer said, "I'm going to do my damnedest to keep it from happening to another woman."[82] McDonald expressed a similar sense of mission:

> I tried to talk at first to the nurses I worked with at the hospital. I thought they'd be interested. One asked how could I be so open about rape. Why would I expose myself to so much pain? They said, "You'll ruin your reputation."
>
> Well, nothing is 100-proof in life. You can't guarantee it won't happen to you. If I could, I'd go into schools and teach those kids about rape, educate the males and females both."[83]

In most sensitive cases, openness and dialogue are hallmarks of morally responsive news reporting.

The idea of community has definite implications for the structure of the press. It has been clear for some time that media conglomerates and chains usurp community control. More than fifty years ago, John C. Bennett wrote, "The organs of public opinion—the newspapers most obviously, but also to some degree our institutions and churches—are controlled by a climate created by the class interests of those who have most economic power. One result of this concentration of economic power is that it tends to undermine political democracy without destroying its forms."[84]

Whatever specific applications result from the commitment to person-hood-in-community, all parties in the community should be able to participate in the news process. The news media, then as now, typically serve groups with a desirable demographic profile and ignore the rest. This bias effectively excludes, politically and socially, people who are undesirable as markets.[85] The inclusiveness of community clearly implies institutional and intellectual restructuring.

Types of Ethical Thinking

Mutuality as a model of community serves effectively as the ground of moral decision making because it is universal, categorical, and normative. In other words, mutuality not only crosses social and historical boundaries, but also provides us with moral purpose and not merely a moral description. Mutuality explains that human beings, to be truly human, are best understood as persons-in-relation who live simultaneously for others and for themselves. Neither persons nor their communities are paramount; their relationship is. Applying the model of persons in community to the various problems of news reporting—choosing the right action in specific situations—requires that we turn our attention to methods of moral decision making. Mutuality provides the rationale for moral decisions, but it does not easily translate into moral judgment. On what basis can we conclude that some behavior is right? For the answer, we must examine the three broad types of ethical thinking: ethics of consequence, virtue, and duty.

Consequentialism

Perhaps the most common type of moral decision making in the United States is consequentialism. Philosophers refer to consequentialist thinking as teleological ethics, from the Greek word *telos,* meaning "goal." It is no wonder that goal-oriented thinking is used so widely to solve moral dilemmas: it reflects the can-do practicality that we assume helped make the United States economically and politically powerful. Consequentialism asks what goals I want to reach, and defines moral behavior as whatever leads to those goals. In popular language, the ends justify the means. Consequentialism thinks in terms of the effects of behavior or policy and not in terms of the rightness or wrongness of acts themselves.

The most popular form of consequentialism is utilitarianism, as articulated by Jeremy Bentham. He formulated the method of moral decision making in terms of calculating the greatest amount of happiness for the greatest number of people. Morality became a type of mathematics for Bentham, and its practicality has been immensely attractive.

Here is how the principle of utility works: a local car dealer is rumored to be "hiding" half of his inventory across the state line at the end of the year, when the tax assessor is scheduled to visit to determine how much tax the dealer owes on the cars that he has in stock. Should the newspaper assign a business reporter to the story, or should the reporter be kept at her desk rewriting press releases from local businesses concerning promotions, awards, productivity, and new hires? The principle of utility would probably conclude that the reporter should pursue the story of the shifty car dealer. People would benefit more from the car dealer's proper payment of taxes than from the publicity of local businesses and their employees. This conclusion assumes, of course, that the newspaper confirmed the rumor and that the state collected back taxes and charged penalties, or that fully researched newspaper reports would dissuade other car dealers from similar tax-cheating strategies, even if no penalties or repayments were required of the original dealer.

Despite its immediate appeal, utilitarianism breaks down because predictions of consequences are never precise, not to mention the dubious nature of the best-laid plans. Perhaps the newspaper's investigation, followed by state prosecution, would come up empty-handed; perhaps boosterism would attract more business to the community. But then again, perhaps not. Future effects can hardly be banked on, or even completely reckoned. As Arkes points out, "[W]e are still experiencing the extended consequences of Caesar crossing the Rubicon."[86] At best, consequentialism can provide what appears to be a reasonable course of action. However, it cannot ensure the rightness of any course of action until all the results are in—and often they never are.

Furthermore, although maximizing pleasure and minimizing pain are attractive goals for social behavior, they do not capture the range of moral activity. The consequences of decisions and behavior are important, but consequentialism used as the *modus operandi* of moral decision making oversimplifies by ignoring significant features of moral contexts. Reporter-source confidentiality, for instance, has been an important issue in recent years. Sometimes reporters claim privilege to hide questionable practices, but often they do so to ward off an overly intrusive state. If pleasure were the essence of moral behavior, as utilitarians claim, then journalists would often be foolish, if not plain wrong, to go to jail instead of revealing their sources to a nosy judge. Ethical behavior sometimes requires sacrifice and even suffering.

Unfortunately, journalism ethics has a long history of effects thinking. In the 1890s, for instance, when newspapers were roundly criticized for pandering and sensationalizing and even lying, the criticism typically took the course of arguing that such news reports caused crimes and all sorts of debauchery.[87] Anthony Comstock, the nineteenth-century crusader against mail fraud and salacious literature, claimed that sensational newspapers made crime look attractive to teenagers. He even specified the newspaper-induced crimes for which scores of New York City teenagers were arrested during one month: "7 for arson, 49 for burglary, 2 for counterfeiting, 9 for felonious assault, 1 for forgery, 5 for grand larceny, 16 for highway robbery, 1 for housebreaking, 9 for attempted murder, 12 for murder, 2 for perjury, 28 for petit larceny, 8 for attempting to commit suicide, and 7 for drunkenness."[88] Obviously, such effects could never be proved, so the criticism was uncompelling.

Frederic Wertham's *Seduction of the Innocent* met a similar fate in 1954, and the long list of studies on the effects of television and video games is filled with conditions and provisionals, none of them able to bear the weight of policy. When the Attorney General's Commission on Pornography sought in 1986 to strengthen its recommendations for enforcement of existing obscenity laws (and close legal escape hatches in child-pornography prosecutions), it appealed to research that clearly indicated the influence of pornographic depictions on desensitizing their audience to actual human suffering.[89] The research and the recommendations provoked a firestorm of charges of censorship of the popular arts. The "effects tradition" research that has been most resilient over the last two decades is the Cultural Indicators project headed by George Gerbner and associates, but this project has never led to policy change.[90] Moral guidelines for media based on predictable consequences are tenuous at best.

Virtue

In the past decade, moral thinking has shifted away from consequentialism and toward a renaissance of virtue. Rather than judging decisions by the way they play themselves out, the ethics of virtue considers moral behavior in terms of the sort of persons who make decisions and the way behavior shapes character.[91] Wendell Berry captures the nature of virtue ethics in his novel *Remembering:* "That he is who he is and no one else is the result of a long choosing, chosen and chosen again."[92] Virtue requires that we be conscientious and morally perceptive—in other words, that we persist in moral behavior until it becomes second nature, habitual, common, the definition of our character—and that we learn strong empathy, so that we not only understand how we affect others but feel it.

This approach, first developed systematically by Aristotle, focuses more on motivation than on behavior as such, and serves as a corrective to the frequent predicament of consequentialists in approving an act that had desirable effects but was done for self-serving reasons. Commercial-television programmers sometimes broadcast shows like "Roots" that are instructive, but they do so primarily to generate profits from advertising revenue, not for the purpose of historically accurate enlightenment. Praise for such programming would be misplaced by consequentialists, who would judge the act rather than the motive; virtue thinkers would correctly applaud those creators and producers of the programming whose work on the project was motivated by a social conscience.

Journalists are familiar with the ethics of character portrayed in *The Front Page.*[93] The film criticizes news reporters, not because of the bad effects of their writing or because of the duties they defy, but because of the type of people they are. Hildy Johnson, the central character, is a veteran reporter for the Chicago *Morning Post* who is well on his way to becoming a quintessential journalist like his editor—an "unprincipled man," according to Hildy's future mother-in-law. Although he promises his fiancée to "cut out drinking and swearing and everything connected with the newspaper business" (failing to mention the disrespect, lying, and laziness rife among city hall reporters), he is lured away from going to New York to marry her by a breaking story of the escape of a death-row inmate. Hildy even goes so far as to bribe a source with $260 of the wedding money that his fiancée had entrusted to him. In disgust, his fiancée calls Hildy "a rotten, selfish animal without any feeling," to which Hildy replies, "I'm a newspaperman!" At the end of the film, Hildy's editor passes along to him a watch inscribed "To the best newspaperman I know." Through caricature, *The Front Page* judges character and, by implication, virtue.

Virtue ethics, however, can have an overwrought view of what personal motivation is able to accomplish. Some critics of broadcasting have suggested that the industry could be morally overhauled by training virtuous people to work in all phases of television. Motivated by good intentions, they would transform broadcasting gradually as they reached a critical mass. However, this position is weak when it highlights personal motivation while ignoring systemic, structural constraints. The most virtuous broadcasters in the world would have minimal impact on an industry as long as the structure of its institutions remains intact. No doubt the practice of piety makes people pious, as the practice of truthtelling makes for honest people, but institutional and systemic structures reduce the choices of virtuous people and therefore limit their impact.

Duty

A more compelling means of moral decision making is an ethics of duty. Claiming that behaviors are duties is to say that a dutiful act itself fosters an integration of personhood and community. Duty does not wait until the jury of effects is in, nor does duty apply exclusively to individuals. Duty does not distinguish between means and ends. Duty is incorporated—or acted out—in specific behaviors or policies by the community. Duty recognizes that certain types of behavior as such keep us human, that the human community requires dutiful actions to keep it a human community. Truthtelling is one such behavior; only crises may provide the exceptional occasions when we are justified in lying, because lies violate human community and empower the liar at the expense of the person who is duped. Lying operates in the I–It modality and thus renders liars as well as their victims subhuman.

It should be obvious that a communitarian ethics of duty differs categorically from Kant's deontological version. H. Richard Niebuhr argued for the responsible self as a root metaphor—that is, an expression that opens up our way of being in the world. The self is dynamic, in his view; our personhood is manifest in the action of answering. The responsible self interacts with the entire spatiotemporal context, but our "relation to other selves is primary: we respond to responders; . . . the self [is] in dialogue with community."[94] Since Aristotle's day, one traditional metaphor of moral being has been "man-the-maker"—fashioning our selfhood in terms of ends discerned. In contrast, Kant's "man-the-citizen" lives according to formal laws that must be obeyed. Niebuhr's third alternative replaces the agencies of realization and obedience with a dialogical self *(Homo dialogicus)* dwelling in responsive relations.[95] The motivating question for him is neither "what is my goal" nor "what is the law," but "what is fitting" in terms of a responsible fit within the total "circumambience of life."[96]

Arthur Dyck elaborates on the concept of communal duty through an inflection on W. D. Ross. Such self-evident obligations as promise-keeping, gratitude, making reparations, beneficence, and justice are not merely characteristics of morality that humans recognize implicitly or explicitly; they are required for communities to exist cooperatively and to flourish. Dyck refers to Ross's prima facie duties as "moral requisites for community."[97]

All prima facie duties are not applicable to each circumstance a community faces. Gratitude, for instance, hardly applies to the decision a city must make about requiring its cable-TV franchise to include a community-access channel; justice and beneficence would. As this example suggests, we must be careful to discern which duties apply to the context at hand. Whatever has a direct bearing on the performance of prima facie duties is a relevant contextual factor in moral decision making. As Karen Lebacqz says, "[M]oral decision-making is always an interplay between the act of discernment, the actual situation, and certain general moral duties."[98]

Dyck describes these prima facie duties as "right- and wrong-making characteristics of actions"; they are rules of thumb applied discriminantly to any particular context. In other words, prima facie duties refer to the types of behavior that promote human communities. Although the duties are exceptionless as statements of what right and wrong mean, they are meant to be applied cautiously in particular circumstances; the rash application of any one duty as a hard-and-fast rule may deny the application of another, overriding duty. We are all familiar with the Kantian absurdity—never lie, even when telling the truth may lead to murder—or the Tarasoff case, in which the psychiatrist kept the confidence of a patient who confessed his plans for murder. Moral dilemmas arise whenever two or more duties would lead to different decisions. We act rightly when we follow prima facie duties and when we judge between conflicting duties on the basis of upholding or enhancing our personhood within the nurturing community.

It should be noted that two of the prima facie duties, beneficence and nonmaleficence, involve consequences. The ethics of duty, however, does not depend on consequentialist reasoning, even though potential effects sometimes matter. A reporter has a prima facie duty to keep a promise of confidences made to a source (although such promises should be made prudently); but in a crisis her duty of nonmaleficence might override her promise of confidentiality if, for instance, she was privy to the knowledge of a plan of terrorism on the source's part. Whenever consequences matter, they are always tied to the duty to lift relationships to the plane of I–Thouness in contrast to antihuman impulses and structures that pull toward I–Itness.

All the prima facie duties apply to news reporting; professionals are not exempt because of their status as news reporters. Veteran reporters are obliged toward beneficence just as lawyers, physicians, or plumbers ought to be beneficent. However, because of their role in information services, reporters' duty to tell the truth takes on greater proportions. In the standard example, a reporter who arrives first at the scene of a car accident is obliged to render whatever first aid she can; however, once an ambulance crew is on hand, the reporter can gather as much information as possible as long as she is unobtrusive. Her primary moral duty is to treat other human beings with dignity and care; her secondary duty is toward the reading public.

Had cases such as that of WHMA-TV in Anniston, Alabama, not arisen, this discussion of duty and role would probably be taken for granted. However, when two WHMA reporters videotaped an unemployed roofer dousing himself with lighter fluid, striking three matches, and burning until he had second- and third-degree burns over half of his body, they exaggerated their professional duty to observe and report events. Professional responsibilities to inform the public did not override their duty of beneficence.[99]

The Persian Gulf war of 1991 gave more subtle and broad-based dimensions to this kind of dilemma. Like the serendipitous Anniston case, Gulf coverage focused on one individual—his mind, history, intentions, character, and power—who was dousing not himself but his region of the world with the volatile fumes of militarism. When Kuwait was overrun in August 1990, the U.S. military presence in the area was clearly vulnerable. Forces built up rapidly, while news personnel still in Baghdad pursued the Saddam Hussein story as best they could. Meanwhile, U. S. officials organized press pools and scheduled briefings, all designed to propagate the need for the imminent shooting war and to control its coverage in the interests of the military. Did the American press have a duty to keep the early secret of U.S. military weakness in the region, lest Hussein's army advance into Saudi Arabia? Did the press understand that its repetitious visuals of Marines practicing amphibious landings were militarily strategic and diversionary? Did the media shield U.S. television viewers from the awfulness of war, its human tragedy—surely the terror of Hussein's front-line ragtag soldiers—in preference to burned-out trucks and Patriot antimissile missiles scoring hits in the sky?

The full verdict is still not in, but we advance the view that in the Gulf, as in early reporting on Vietnam, the press rendered a strongly nationalistic version of events to the exclusion of genuinely humane coverage. We grant and applaud the coverage of the bombing of civilian areas in Iraq; it is important that citizens of one nation know the hurt and pain of fellow human beings in another. We grant and applaud the necessity of not reporting on secret military missions, provided those missions are not suicidal and not more destructive of the declared enemy than just-war theory permits. (A secret mission to drop nuclear bombs in Baghdad warrants headlines; to penetrate enemy lines to better engage military forces warrants secrecy.) We grant and applaud the discontinuance of live television coverage of Scud landings in Israel—information that would have given target data to Hussein's launchers and bring further grief to noncombatants. We worry, however, that field-coverage heroics placed journalists at risk unnecessarily, and that the media's admiration for the generals created a tone in most of the reporting that was altogether too fascinated with the power of military technology and indifferent to oppositional and even allied points of view. Indeed, Iraq and Kuwait and all their problems of public health and economic devastation created by the war—those are yesterday's stories. With the end of dramatic footage, the U.S. media retrenched to cover the first inconsequential months of intraparty squabbling about who will carry the banner in a national election. News too quickly follows the gaming instinct, while nameless people suffer.

What is most distinctive about the press or any other social institution is its power to define reality. The public expects the press, although trusting it begrudgingly, to produce full and accurate reports of matters of social importance. But the question of power is central. The press reports the news that it considers important, and by doing so it interprets the political, economic, and cultural domains for the public. Lebacqz subtitles her book "the paradox of power" because professions have authority—the power to define reality. The fact that professionals often lack the power to exercise their authority does not deny that a profession is powerful in the aggregate. Reporters who follow their prima facie duties to persons and community often find themselves powerless as individuals to reshape the press so that it responds in harmony with communal prerogatives. Therefore, fundamental reordering of the press's mission, conventions, and structures is required.

Epilogue

Let us return to Sage Volkman in Albuquerque. Having rejected ethical relativism on the grounds of its intellectual and moral paucity, we learned that we can discriminate between the ethics of the two newspapers' policies. The basis of discrimination rests on community, understood in terms of mutuality. Because community is made possible—not to mention enhanced—when prima facie duties are practiced, we can use these duties to evaluate the decisions and to suggest a direction for media policy to take. In that both the *Journal* and the *Tribune* reported Sage's story, both told the truth and promoted beneficence. However, the *Tribune* used a visual sensitivity that helped prepare the community for Sage's reentry and reintegration. The *Tribune* in this case was more morally perceptive, recognizing the fuller dimensions of community in the present situation. We now turn our attention in Chapter 4 to applying this communitarian ethical framework to a more elaborate understanding of news reporting, and in Chapter 5 to redefining the media's organizational culture.

4

Civic Transformation

The little-known history of the black antebellum press is now coming to light with the publication of manuscripts, correspondence, and speeches from those editors and fugitives who make up the opposite side of the "great editors" story. Samuel Ringgold Ward, the second son of slave parents who escaped the South in 1820, founded the *True American* in 1847, and two years later, the *Impartial Citizen* in Syracuse, New York. He was a Congregationalist minister and popular speaker for the American and Foreign Anti-Slavery Society when he joined a plot in 1851 to rescue a fugitive slave from the custody of federal officers. That foiled attempt to obstruct formal justice led to his own flight to Canada, where he published the *Provincial Freeman,* and he later toured England raising funds for the abolitionist cause. In Canada in 1851, Ward urged readers of Henry Bibb's *Voice of the Fugitive* to a "universal agitation, by the press and the tongue, in church and at the polls" to "rid our beloved adopted country of this infernal curse," slavery.[1]

Patchwork or Fundamental Change?

The stories of Ward and Bibb and the indomitable Mary Ann Shadd Cary are not unlike that of Donald Woods. Different times and places, different races and political settings, yet the key is the common difficulty in their telling, the risk of advancing an unpopular idea, the failure of mainstream journalism to provide all the news the public needs. Repressive social structures had coopted the free marketplace of ideas lauded since the Puritan Revolution in seventeenth-century England.[2]

Yet this media failure is too easy a target for such a common dart. The economics of news require that editors select only a part of the world's wonder for each daily edition or broadcast; the daily news is always silent on someone's important concerns. Preachments to reporters to think more boldly, provide more tough news (or even good news), challenge city hall powerbrokers, ask the piercing questions, identify news sources, probe the back alleys and the dusty roads—these are perennial. We raise here not merely a challenge to stiffen editorial courage or cultivate more trustworthy sources, praiseworthy as these adjustments could be. Professionalism, hard work, and agonizing judgment calls already lie behind every creditable newspaper and broadcast station. Mostly underpaid and overworked, journalists race to get the story right and fast, to beat the constant pressure, to find a second confirmation when phone calls go unanswered. Fine-tuning the skills and sensibilities of candidates for employment in the democratic press is the commendable task of journalism schools and professional organizations and institutes. These grand efforts are accomplished with considerable devotion to the ideals of liberal democracy; it is not our task to recommend here some missing piece that magically completes the jigsaw puzzle and efficiently turns rough-edged elements into a smoothly honest, grimly fair news operation.

Neither is technology per se the issue. Faster typesetting, satellite hookups, desktop-publishing equipment, and upgraded circulation systems obviously have their role in swiftly distributing public information; but technical solutions are no more final than the UNESCO news sheet quota of the 1960s. Improved media technologies seldom narrow the gap between information elites and cultural illiterates. Jacques Ellul argues persuasively that technology (the hardware) is a function of technicism (a mindset), which transforms cultures into a slag of information without ears to hear. Technological inventions usually disguise accelerating rigidities of human mind and will in the costume of a comic narrator whose pointless story never ends, the information equivalent of Homer's Sisyphus or all-night rock and roll.

Nor is it enough to cry, "Small is beautiful!" and reposition a Los Angeles news team to a base in Texarkana. Certainly, newspaper and network bureaus are prone to converge on major population centers and miss the lesser drama of Boise's library board. But who is served by merely turning tables and assigning reporters to the little lettuce in the nation's daily menu? Even where sophisticated news teams might turn up a good story, an institutional culture seems to dictate against certain forms of coverage. The Mobil Corporation is hardly a backwoods institution, yet it too claims a story: "Network news departments exercise total control of the agenda of issues, and who may speak to the public. . . . This network control, with no system or forum for rebuttal, has resulted in a narrow and selective discussion of major public issues—and the systematic exclusion or distortion of many viewpoints."[3]

Are journalists obliged to tell the Mobil story, or the black fugitive story, or any story? Professional newspeople accept the obligation to be truthful in reporting, even fair; once a story breaks, obligations seem to follow like sidebands on a frequency. But who sets the agenda? Reporters constantly question the prior decisions of media gatekeepers to cover, wrap, or rush. Sometimes, of course, coverage is said to be "obligatory" because an event has obvious national or local news value, or because a given journal has so defined itself that failure to report would violate the purpose of the entire enterprise. Chicago's perennial city council wars will not be top-of-the-fold in the Lubbock *Avalanche-Journal,* and so the many-tiered voices of American journalism carry on their discordant commentaries. Yet as long as there is news of public record, general-interest journalism, *broad*cast news in the original sense of the word—indeed, as long as public interest has any meaning at all—multiplying the number of voices or channels is not in itself the apex of achievement.

Rethinking the Press's Mission

Public-affairs reporting grounded in a communitarian ethics requires that decisions about news coverage be driven by community norms, not by markets or mechanical efficiency. We do not dispute profitmaking, only the idea of profit as the determinative goal. Modernizing our instruments is mandatory; we resist only the technological imperative. As Jürgen Habermas complains, entrance into the national community has mushroomed since the nineteenth century as requirements for citizenship have become less restrictive. But nearly universal access occurs at the historical moment when the public arena has lost its vitality.[4] The press abetted this impoverishment by serving primarily as a vehicle of expert transmission rather than a network of vernacular discussion—a journalism modeled on information rather than a "journalism of conversation. . . . Talk about the public continues, of course, but no one any longer knows what they are talking about. A definition of the public and public life is smuggled in, but it is not subject to critical scrutiny. . . . The term has simply gone dead."[5] Journalism's twentieth-century transformation into an industrialized news business reconceived the public as "a market, united by little more than its demographic profile and a shared propensity to consume news."[6] The public will only begin "to reawaken when they are addressed as a conversational partner and are encouraged to join the talk rather than sit passively as spectators before a discussion conducted by journalists and experts."[7]

Obviously, publishers and broadcasters face dilemmas here. Too often the report on midlife health is juxtaposed in radical contradiction with advertisements evoking Wild West cigarette satisfaction. We speak here, however, about norms that drive a newspaper or broadcast station, and insist that justice, covenant, and empowerment take precedence. Is a minority story consistently overlooked, perpetrating a "culture of silence" with an effect similar to apartheid's ban? Is a new minority created by a systematic bias when a group that opposes a newspaper's dominant ide-ology finds itself shut out, not by race or gender but by ideas? Markets or instrumental wizardry often impose criteria that an ethics of community would not condone. Is a policy question too hot to handle, as Daniel Boorstin suggests in describing the feeble editors of Wyoming bowing to big ranchers and their mercenary armies?[8] Not persons as means to ends, even profitable ends or increased proficiency, but people whose humanness depends on a viable community—nurturing the community story is the keynote of responsible journalism. Facilitating a thorough understanding of public life is the press's beacon. The press has bigger fish to fry than merely improving technology and streamlining performance, important as those advances may be. The issue is whether reporting serves to activate the *polis*. "Journalism only makes sense in relation to the public and public life. Therefore, the fundamental problem in journalism is to reconstitute the public, to bring it back into existence."[9]

A Community Experiment

The *Columbus Ledger-Enquirer* recently made a major effort to revitalize public discussion in western Georgia.[10] It commissioned a poll of the 175,000 residents, seeking to establish the crucial issues the community faced. Influential citizens filled in long questionnaires, and a newspaper team conducted indepth interviews with residents across the socioeconomic spectrum. The final report, "Columbus Beyond 2000," identified the key problems: faltering schools, inadequate transportation, low wages, meager night life, and elitism in city politics. The *Ledger-Enquirer* published the report in daily installments.

The series provoked precious little public action, and the executive editor wanted the process to move forward. He leaped across "the chasm that normally separates journalism from community" and hosted, at the newspaper's expense, a six-hour town meeting "to turn up the public heat."[11] Other assemblies, events, and task forces—including a town meet-ing for 400 teenagers—kept up the momentum. The newspaper served as a community bulletin board, its executive editor joined a thirteen-member steering committee, and several staff members participated on various levels. Using the metaphor "a tribal fire," the newspaper encouraged cit-izens to retell the region's history and celebrate its heroes.

> As it expanded, the citizens' movement (United Beyond 2000) remained a concern of the *Ledger-Enquirer,* but not its creature. . . . What Swift and his staffers did, in effect, was reconstrue the newspaper's relationship to discussion in the public sphere. . . . Not a confrontation between politicians and reporters, but face-to-face talk among local citizens became the news-paper's aim. . . . The proper location for this discussion was assumed to

be the community itself, rather than the halls of government. . . . The *Ledger-Enquirer*'s project presents a clear instance of journalism re-imagining its public functions. . . . It is public not only because it involved the community in open discussion, but because it began something new, interrupting the automatism of economic growth to give citizens a chance to consider, in public, what they wanted to make of their city."[12]

H. Richard Niebuhr recognizes that language is the marrow of community. Persons are displayed, made accessible, nurtured, and integrated into social units through symbol, myth, and metaphor.[13] Words for him are concrete forms of life, whose meaning derives from an interpretive, historical context that humans themselves supply. Symbolic forms are social, not "isolated ejaculations, separate and therefore meaningless sounds."[14] Our constitutive relations as human beings are linguistic. Through "continuing discourse" we experience what Niebuhr calls "compresence"; we exist "in encounter, in challenge and in response."[15]

In the Lockean problem of communication, in contrast, mental life is individual, ahistorical, and asocial, and therefore language passes through an open field between isolated integers to "excite in the hearer exactly the same idea they stand for in the mind of the speaker."[16] The invisible individual "makes words stand for what ideas he pleases";[17] for Locke, the inner sanctum of the individual mind, self-enclosed and incommunicado, generates meaning and must be protected from unwarranted intrusion. But the dangers of an Orwellian 1984, in which Big Brother leaves no private hiding place, creates a conundrum for the Lockean tradition. In order to share consciousness, we must not "fill one another's heads with noise and sounds, but . . . lay before one another [our] ideas, which is the end of discourse and language."[18] One aspect of the Enlightenment project, therefore, was to guarantee unfettered communication in order to streamline information and increase clarity. But while seeking to enhance the possibility of understanding through an abundance of communication, we violently intrude on that sacred arena of personal meaning that ought to remain opaque so as to protect one's individuality.

Niebuhr's linguistic community destroys the Lockean dichotomy. From his perspective, language is the matrix of humanity; it is not privately nurtured and made problematic as it enters the public sphere. Niebuhr holds form and content together; concepts are not isolated from their representations; he weaves the social and individual dimensions of language into a unified whole. Niebuhr ransoms us from Locke's unproductive question, "How can private and isolated minds engage one another?" Through the social nature of language and self-definition as irrefragibly grammatical, Niebuhr integrates message and community, reporting and communal formation. In the process, he contradicts the Enlightenment imperative for news—the transmission of objective, unencumbered, and fulsome data—making news instead a semiotic agent of community formation.

To be more precise, when the axis of the press's content is shifted from individual autonomy to communitarianism, its mission is fundamentally reoriented. In this reformulation, the goal of reporting becomes civic transformation. Operating within a communitarian world view itself, the news media seek to engender a like-minded philosophy among the public. A revitalized citizenship shaped by community norms becomes the press's aim—not merely readers and audiences provided with data, but morally literate persons.

Both classical and neoliberal theory have defined the press's goal as informing its readership and audience; the enlightenment function, this goal is commonly called. Assuming that humans are rational animals, the press advances society's interests by feeding an individual's capacity to reason and make decisions:

> Man as a thinking organism is capable of organizing the world around him. Although men frequently do not exercise their God-given powers of reason in solving human problems, in the long run they tend, by the aggregate of their individual decisions, to advance the cause of civilization. Man differs from lower animals in his ability to think, to remember, to utilize his experience, and to arrive at conclusions. Because of this unique ability, man is unique. He is the prime unit of civilization as well as its mover. . . . Although the path to truth might lie through a morass of argument and dispute, that which lay at the end of the path was definite, provable, and acceptable to rational men.[19]

Thus Thomas Jefferson maintained that the press—despite its errors and vituperation—is vital for educating individual citizens: "No experiment can be more interesting than that we are now trying, . . . the fact that man may be governed by reason and truth. Our first object should therefore be, to leave open to him all avenues to truth. The most effective hitherto found is the freedom of the press."[20]

Orthopraxy, Not Orthodoxy

In the liberal legacy, the underlying purpose of the news media has been to discover truth, to present evidence on which decisions can be based, to provide a bounteous fare—true, half-true, and false—that the public molds into a coherent body of knowledge. Under the rubric of information, broadcasting primarily signals events as they unfold, the newspaper provides more details and a wider range of stories, magazine journalism gives a meaningful context, and documentaries and books supply a full-bodied portrait. In traditional liberal philosophy, education in the schools plus information in the news equals informed public opinion, which the government exists to implement. Of late, mice nibble around the edges, but the vital information principle stays righteously on course. We characteristically suppose that the day's raw intelligence is democracy's lifeline; and for supplying that material, we assign the press a strategic role.

However, from the perspective of communitarian ethics, the enlightenment function is too static and narrow, a half-truth at best. The press's goal is not a luminous cranium, but surefootedness. The aim is not orthodoxy per se but orthopraxy—that is, not merely correct doctrine, but proper action. The belief that knowledge piles up brick by brick rests on Cartesian myth; in fact, the recent spate of studies on news production confirms vividly that no news reports emerge pure. With Aristotle, *theoria* and praxis, contemplation and practical wisdom, can be distinguished as moments in our historical situation; however, the Enlightenment erroneously sequestered each of them.[21] Noam Chomsky reminds us that concepts do not live in splendid isolation, and to the degree that we presume so, they are coopted by powerful interests to benefit themselves.[22] Getting one's head straight does not automatically generate intelligent social activism. As Jay Rosen concludes in a gloss on Hannah Arendt, "The public realm should not be equated with a civics classroom. . . . The case of the *Ledger-Enquirer* is thus important because it shows journalists exchanging behavior for action and encouraging citizens to do the same."[23]

Seeing human organisms whole and inescapably communal entails John Macmurray's action self, summarized in Chapter 3. Critical consciousness results from dialectical reflection and involvement, from an ongoing process of deepened thinking by intensified action, and vice versa. This type of cerebral work is not architectonic, but issue and polity oriented. The question is what we need to improve our present society and how such transformation can be accomplished. Although cast in his own idiom, Marx raised the enduring question: How can we not merely understand the world, but change it? Obviously, action that is ill-informed becomes futile and self-defeating; information atrophies unless it vivifies human needs. Thus the press's mission is not civic intelligence but transformation.

At this historic moment, the demands on a free press have never been greater. In a complicated world, itself made possible by global media technology, the news enterprise is central. While the restructuring of Eastern Europe and the former Soviet Union are the most dramatic shifts at present, the need to fashion a new world order is obvious everywhere. For the press to fulfill its social responsibility as the Enlightenment Age crumbles around us, we must continue to irrigate it, to reestablish its rationale. The classroom and newsroom must keep battling the particulars: declining readership, economic viability for broadcasting, the disinterest of young adults in newspapers, minority ownership, and visual literacy. Meanwhile, a long view of the press's mission has become ever more indispensable.[24] The enlightenment function is too tame, too easily pirated, and no longer epistemologically credible. As a substitute, a tough-minded civic transformation inspires us to think big while working close to the bone of everyday journalism. Oriana Fallaci warns that "journalism is an extraordinary and terrible privilege."[25]

This *telos* of communitarian journalism has distinctive features: justice, covenant, and empowerment. Authentic social orders are marked by justice; communities are delightful only when justice reigns. Covenant bonds rather than contractual arrangements make genuine community possible. In contrast to the negative freedom of classical liberalism, normative communities empower citizens for social transformation. Therefore, that narrative form commonly called news ought to facilitate justice, covenant, and empowerment in order that civic transformation become a characteristic feature of strongly democratic nations.[26]

News: The Justice Story

The argument for justice over against the canons of individualism makes sense only in a framework where acquisitiveness is dislodged as a chief end of human life. There is no point in bashing the media with a justice stick if, in fact, prosperity is the destination to which persons rightly aspire.

A community-based ethic of the press does not require that each news organization assume sufficient insight to articulate precisely the overarching purpose of human life, and certainly not that all newsrooms everywhere come to univocal agreement on what that *telos* might be; rather, the point is that persons have an end and a direction and that society's end cannot be acquisitiveness. If it were, journalism could rightly team with the state in a leviathan beyond Hobbes's most chilling image—a seamless web of structure and authority preserving a semblance of order amid the passion to acquire. Ayn Rand has become the patron saint of a world view devoted to acquisition in its most sophisticated forms, and strains of her objectivism echo in the pronouncements of some media managers. "I make news," declared James Gordon Bennett, Jr. "I feel I owe no responsibility to the people who purchase my publications. . . . The only responsibility I have is to myself, and if to my own self I am true, then my readers will have been served as well," said the publisher of *Coronet* in response to advocates of social responsibility.[27] Journalism consistent with this understanding of social order would find little reason to abstain from propaganda in its purest form, Ellul's subtleties discounted as unnecessary and tangential.

Axiological alternatives to rampant individualism contest the Hobbes–Rand continuum. Catechists in the Calvinist tradition confess that the chief end of persons is to "glorify God and enjoy him forever." Jews recall that the older covenant requires the doing of justice and showing of mercy, the "walking humbly with thy God." In an ancient Latin American prayer: "O God, to those who hunger give bread; and to us who have bread give the hunger for justice." Other theological and philosophical traditions render similar readings. Virtually none urges the confessor to solidify individual wealth or power, to achieve domination, or, in Nietzschean terms, to become the *Übermensch*. Always the thrust of moral reasoning is to tame the torrent of greed, to ease the torment of self devoted to self. "He who finds his life will lose it" is a warning repeated across moral traditions, wherever cultures have matured beyond the conception of self typified since the Enlightenment by disconnected automatons. When Leibniz argued for windowless monads as *Urstoff,* he created a world of fundamental discontinuity; the Hobbes–Rand tradition provides journalists with a convenient rationale for undergirding such a universe. Where persons are bonded, however, accountability washes over these sandy dikes and narcissism surrenders to justice as the press's normative end.

In his ontological ethics, Paul Tillich contends that the only unconditional imperative "is the demand to become actually what one is essentially and therefore potentially."[28] Although he believes that central features of the human condition hold true despite particular historical and cultural differences, he agonizes over the contradiction between the essential unity of our communal being and the empirical alienation of human beings. Therefore, he defines the overriding ethical imperative as reunion of the separated.[29] Justice entails "a clear, radical, unequivocal commitment to the poorest, the weakest, and the most abused members of the human family."[30] Justice rejects privilege and insists on repairing social, economic, and political inequities.

In Tillich's view, justice for the oppressed stands as the centerpiece of a socially responsible press. The litmus test of whether the news profession operates justly over the long term is its advocacy for those abused or ignored by established power. Communitarian ethics holds the reporter's feet to the fires of injustice and suffering, not because this responsibility exhausts all the daily obligations of stations and newspapers, but because it is a meaning-center of the news operation nonetheless. Is the press a voice for the unemployed, food-stamp recipients, Appalachian miners, the urban poor, Hispanics in rural shacks, the elderly, women discriminated against in hiring and promotion, ethnic minorities with no future in North America's downsizing economy? Does the news profession respond to the stirring vision in which justice flows down like a mighty stream? In a day when the powerless have few alternatives, a press bound by distributive justice will serve as a megaphone for those who cry for fairness, relief, and recognition.[31]

Introducing the language of *telos,* purpose, and ultimate ends of human life raises immediately one of the most serious professional dilemmas faced by members of the press, a step into public morality feared more than libel suits and subpoenas to testify, a leap that seems to serve journalists the dirge of professional suicide. Ethical commitments are considered privately honorable, but extending them beyond the personal domain into public discourse is commonly regarded as regressive and illegitimate. "Shield from public view whatever private convictions that might illuminate the moral imagination" seems to be a nearly universal newsroom commitment.

Journalists understood well the caveat of the Allentown, Pennsylvania, city official concerning the popularity of *I Love You to Death.* This motion picture set in his city romanticizes a relationship in which the wife tries repeatedly to murder and to contract the murder of her spouse, only to remarry after serving a prison sentence. The official obviously felt that Allentown's real character was skewed by the film when he ventured, "I have no respect for people who try to murder other people. But that is merely my personal view." Privatizing moral conviction leads to a public vacuum in which all moral claims are indicted as personal predilection or bias. Justice is an empty term in such a culture. How can professional journalists bridge the widening gap between legitimate private commitments and shrill calls for public justice dismissed as political rhetoric or interest-group lobbying?

Communitarian journalism asks of voices in the public square that rewards of wealth and power not be determinative, that choices of story coverage and advocacy not hinge on outcomes that advance individual gratification, that egoism as a formal moral system surrender to a more penetrating vision. A press nurtured by communitarian ethics requires more of itself than fair treatment of events deemed worthy of coverage. Under the notion that justice itself—and not merely haphazard public enlightenment—is a *telos* of the press, the news-media system stands under obligation to tell the stories that justice requires.

Hocking's Intersubjectivity

Long before his name entered media circles through Hutchins Commission proceedings, William Ernest Hocking insisted on the duty to speak as a cardinal human obligation. The mind cannot know itself or assign meaning to the chaos of percepts that constitute the everyday world apart from framing its thoughts in a common language. Nor can a social order—even a minimal order of two minds—exist apart from this peculiarly human symbol-making activity. Because reality clearly presents persons with requirements for self-knowledge, meaning, and social organization, the obligation persists to expedite those requirements with participatory eagerness. Lethargic silence or, more commonly, the mere acceptance of a symbolic reality without creative investment in forming it, is a refusal to respond humanly to the reality within which we live. And failing to be what we are is a fundamental moral lapse.[32] Even the purposely silent—like Merton's Trappists and other sects—retain virtue in their renunciation of the primal duty only because their silence itself speaks prophetically. The virtue of silence depends on the duty to speak and would, in a mostly quiescent and subdued culture, be immoral in itself. And to silence other persons pragmatically—whether through political, economic, or social means—is at least equally reprehensible, because it denies a central feature of their humanity.[33]

Hocking's intellectual journey underscores the importance he placed on persons-in-relation. At age thirteen, he became convinced of human animality through reading Herbert Spencer's *First Principles,* but he abandoned the Hobbes–Rand tradition after his study of William James's *Principles of Psychology* at the Iowa State College of Agriculture. During graduate study at Harvard, Hocking found a middle ground between James's utility model of community and the idealism of Josiah Royce. Biographer Leroy Rouner credits James as the mentor who opened Hocking to central concerns for the self and one's relation to the world, to other selves, and to God.[34] Confronted with his era's rampant empiricism, Hocking sought a recovery of classical politics as a wisdom-seeking discipline, a "realism of the Absolute," as he termed it. He rejected a narrow view of persons in which one's "very ideas and ideals vary with the chemistry in the blood, and therefore are devoid of authority."[35]

Basic to Hocking's theories of communication is his view of persons. For Hocking, the self is distinctive yet interdependent, the creative source of ideas and standards, of imagination and belief—"intersubjectivity," he called it. There is no "public conscience" apart from the minds of persons composing the public. Bind those minds, Hocking warned with an eye to the forces of irrationalism and totalitarianism, "and all the mental and moral life of the public is stopped at its source."[36] Yet the power of human imagining cannot really be halted. Curtailed or encumbered it may be, but the mind still seeks the meaning of its existence. A mind situated in repressive environments may find it hazardous to express thoughts, but the mind that fails to communicate has dehumanized itself by denying its one ultimate duty and ignoring its one ultimate right: "Thought, of the inner germination, to get into the open, and to work its way to power. This is the incompressible atom of individual and social life."[37]

Hocking had the good fortune to take that idea—the duty to speak—into the newsroom when he wrote *The Framework of Principle* for the Commission on Freedom of the Press in 1947.[38] "The utterance of opinion is not merely the announcement of an 'I think'. . . . It is a social force and intended to be such," Hocking wrote, with echoes of the writings of Max Lerner and, earlier still, John Milton.[39] The moral rightness of the "force of speech" was immediately apparent to Hocking in its effect of changing the arena of social conflict from settings of actual violence to the colloquy of opposing ideas, the final forum of progress. The simple truth of Hocking's argument is apparent to anyone who has even the remotest contact with events of the last thirty years. From the 1968 demonstrations at the Democratic National Convention to the "rebellion" in 1973 at the Pine Ridge Reservation to the gay rights demonstrations of recent decades, the goal was clearly to air ideas otherwise smothered in conserving categories, and the means were news media, both electronic and printed. Alan Parker's 1988 film *Mississippi Burning* took considerable liberty with the story of three civil rights workers killed in 1964, but the movie ventilated a national steam room just after America's first serious black presidential candidate put energy and passion into an otherwise turgid political race. NBC's documentary "Kent State" gave viewers reason to doubt the virtues of militarism and official suppression of speech. In 1989, PBS's "Ethics in America" series helped the nation think anew about cost–benefit calculations and community duties.

Hocking had already assured the radicals of his day that the "force of speech" would not spare them the "anger, contempt, suffering" or loss of some followers that results when ideas create new social distinctions and parties divide. But physical harm was "not an integral part of the argument" and could be avoided in a justice-seeking society, he concluded—at least in principle. The colloquy, a sufficient arena for matching wits and intellectual force, takes from violence its bloody terror and gives to media their essential role.[40] Ringgold Ward was not devoted, after all, to the extermination of Caucasian races or the perpetuation of racial war, but to the idea of the franchise, of equal treatment under law, of color-blind opportunity. Hocking would not be surprised that Ward's agenda has achieved considerable popular support since 1850, only chagrined at the cost in lives and personal agonies. Media more open to the names and stories on the fringes of their narrow vision might have spared the culture from at least some of its "stray" events—violence as grievous as Janet McClain's Fourth of July and nearly as hard to explain.

The Courage of Moral Resolve

Hindsight allows contempt for the nineteenth-century editors of powerful northern papers who, unwilling to tell the slaves' story, created the need for the African-American press of Ringgold Ward and his compatriots. The same contempt indicts the silence of journalism North and South, a silence still pervasive into the 1950s and middle 1960s and in some places,

not just South Africa, into the 1990s. Yet some courageous journalists—
Elijah Lovejoy, William Lloyd Garrison, and others—broke the silence at
great personal cost because justice fired their consciences. In Lovejoy's
case, the popular history of his gunfight at the riverside warehouse obscures
an important chapter in the story of communitarian journalism.

The young editor of the Alton *Observer* was killed by a mob on the
night of November 7, 1837, and the last of his four printing presses destroyed. A proslavery mob wrecked his first press in St. Louis, and his
second was thrown into the Mississippi nearly as soon as it arrived across
the river in a "free state." During a night raid a third was demolished;
Lovejoy barely escaped being tarred and feathered. Yet the editor had
determined in good faith to keep on publishing, and at the Upper Alton
Presbyterian Church to keep on preaching. Or were his promises in good
faith at all? Did Elijah Lovejoy actually break his promise to the people
of Alton when he persisted in pressing for an end to black slavery?

The popular record has Lovejoy escaping the slave soil of Missouri after
his religious newspaper there had contested the execution by fire of the
free black and riverboat porter Francis L. McIntosh in April 1836. Mc-
Intosh did not have the privilege of a court trial, of course; the execution
was accomplished by a gang of vigilantes operating outside official authority
but with the state's tacit approval. To Lovejoy, this death-squad style of
justice was reprehensible and, in an older type of patriotism, unfit for a
civilized democracy. The fact that Lovejoy's office, press, and home were
attacked following his exposé no doubt helped persuade him to find safer
lodgings across the river. Even his fellow ministers advised that he not
tempt the demons of public opinion by raking the ashes of McIntosh's pyre.

Upon his arrival in Alton, a progressive town trying to win valuable
river commerce from St. Louis, Lovejoy allegedly promised in a speech
to area businessmen that he would remain silent on slavery in exchange
for their blessings and financial backing.[41] But Lovejoy guaranteed to the
Alton businessmen only that he was no formal abolitionist. No one could
have doubted that he stood opposed to slavery; it was the radicalism of a
Garrison that the Alton merchants wished to suppress. (Lovejoy helped
found the Illinois Antislavery Society.) A more precise account of the
fateful meeting records Lovejoy as saying, "I am not, and never was in
full fellowship with the abolitionists. But gentlemen, as long as I am an
American citizen . . . I shall hold myself at liberty to speak, to write, and
to publish whatever I please on any subject, being amenable to the laws
of my country for the same."[42]

Had Lovejoy forsworn his hatred of slavery to the middle-of-the-road
moralism of Alton buyers and boat owners, and prospered as an editor
utterly responsive to a local community's economy-minded will, he would
serve as a model puppet of the status-quoism that communitarian jour-

nalism resists. Rather, we hear in that old Puritan defense the passion for justice, a commitment to wider obligations in deference to self, and a carelessness of personal consequences. "I shall hold myself at liberty," he said, poignantly alert to the same notion that Hocking called the duty to speak, and insistent on situating his appeal in the tradition of relative freedom that, a generation earlier, had been codified in the national constitution. "Amenable to the laws of my country," he claimed, not as one governed solely by conscience, much less by acquisitiveness, but thoroughly linked to an ideal held imperfectly by free-soilers, by democrats, and by the church which had ordained him and in which his own conversion from cultural to personal faith had been effected. "Whatever I please in any subject," he asserted, directly rejecting the culture of silence that would keep a slave's story hidden but a boat's cargo public. Apparently, Lovejoy's problem in Alton was not a broken covenant with its leaders, but his stiff-necked refusal to consort with its apostles of acquisition. He recognized clearly that unless justice marks our social life, our collective existence actually perpetuates a cancerous dehumanization.

Investigative journalism is a running record of the strategic potential of framing the news narrative in terms of justice. The Charlotte *Observer*'s series on brown lung disease scrutinized the textile industry and government for failed air cleanup efforts. An estimated 18,000 Carolinians were disabled with byssinosis, the reporters claimed, and this after thirteen years of evidence linking cotton dust to the disease. The series was filled with cases of disabled (and now deceased) workers who tried in vain to get help from the South Carolina Industrial Commission or to settle affairs for their families in the face of premature death. That the paper told the story does not itself solve the problem, but the telling becomes an event of vindication and a release for the energy of reform.[43]

Benjamin Barber has written poignantly that "the heart of strong democracy is talk."[44] Not the aggressive, adversarial speech common in law courts and admired by liberal democrats, the speech that trades on free-market analogies and reduces talk to persuasion, but discourse that entails the empathy of active listening and creative change. Barber distinguishes strong democracy from mainline liberal democracy by precisely this quality of talk: its passionate embrace of stories not one's own in order to achieve a deeper insight into the core of what humanness means, then to move in a natural continuum from talk to action and back to talk again. Mere jabbering—or even scientific logistics of the kind used by large law firms in pretrial defenses before mock juries—does not achieve the commonweal here. Talk radio may fashion a rhetoric of quantity that embraces intimidation, as the 1988 movie by that name deftly exposed. But talk that calls for listening, mutuality, affiliation, and action builds and rebuilds just community.

Strong talk presupposes courage born of mutuality. In 1989 George
Bush urged the American nation to declare war on illegal drugs. Previously,
Ronald Reagan had relegated the antidrug crusade to his wife, who articulated the hapless "Just Say NO" campaign with results as exciting as an
airport stump speech. Under the Bush program, in contrast, funds were
assigned and a drug czar appointed. Shipments and warehouses were uncovered and middlemen prosecuted. South American drug kingpins were
indicted in U.S. courts. The only fatalities in the U.S. phase of these
initiatives were the addicts and street peddlers who succumbed to the risks
of the habit itself. In Colombia, however, nearly a dozen journalists as
well as several judges and police officials and politicans were assassinated.
Several hundred journalists were threatened with violence in the drug
cartel's attempt to prevent the Medellín newspapers from reporting on the
interdiction crusade.

This kind of pressure generates interesting case material for journalism
conferences and classes; but on reflection, one cannot explain the perseverance of editors and reporters under such duress apart from a conviction
that the common good, the welfare of neighbor as well as brother and self,
rests on the refusal to succumb to silence in the face of terrorist adversaries.
Chin to chin against an iron jaw, journalists still argue for the justice that
human fulfillment requires. They may do so in much the same way that
Reinhold Niebuhr applauded Gandhi's nonviolent resistance as "a type of
coercion which offers the largest opportunities for the harmonious relationship with the moral and rational factors in social life,"[45] an unchar-
acteristically wooden way of urging that human solidarity not be violated
when the fruits of human fallibility must be challenged. Promoting justice
is the mediated equivalent of strong talk that wrenches a society's structural
goals loose from unquenchable acquisitiveness.

No matter how reflective our action or how articulate our political
strategies, civic transformation needs a comprehensive vision to orient us
and keep us from losing our way. "When architects design buildings, they
begin with an image of forms and lights and shadows to which they give
increasing articulation. Is there any such image for us here?"[46] Communitarian ethics suggests that there is—the prophet Isaiah's vision of "justice
making its home in the wilderness and righteousness dwelling in the grass-
lands."[47] Justice incorporates covenant and empowerment into a harmonious whole; community life is fundamentally flawed without it.

News: The Making of Covenant

Notions of community are changing rapidly. Robert Nisbet traces the emergence of a political clerisy in the 1920s in response to lessons learned in

the Great War. John Dewey, Charles Beard, Charles Merriam, Lewis Mumford, Walter Lippmann, and others were galvanized by the war experience to generate a postwar national community trading on the energies of combat but focusing on peacetime progress. The publication of Dewey's *Individualism Old and New* in 1930 captured the prevailing feeling that small groups of intimates—churches, families, neighborhoods—that had defined "society" throughout the nineteenth century were all but moribund. The "present condition" required a strenuous transformation from these static and traditional hierarchies, with their informal codes and simple obligations,[48] to a "Great Community," which would achieve genuine equality across race and gender, molding all the while a new conception of the individual-in-relation. The urgings were not Hegelian directly, since Dewey had left Hegel; not pragmatic entirely, since the dew of pastoral Vermont was still more appealing than the steaming asphalt of Chicago or New York; but definitely national, truly secular, vibrantly progressive, and consistently organizational. The Great Community would render individualism a fleeting relic from an age come and gone thanks to science.

Instead, the Great Depression and the Second Great War did in the Great Community. Intermediate groups have risen, fueled by widespread suspicions of bureaucracy and second-thought conservatism, growing despite historians' predictions that such a resurgence was impossible given the absence of a feudal era in America's past. Nisbet suggests that, in view of such unprecedented changes, *In pluribus unum* would be an appropriate revision of the national motto: let no voice be silenced, but many speak to the benefit of all. Daniel Boorstin, on the same theme, recommends *E pluribus plura* as a more appropriate signification of democracy's many faces.[49]

Yet communitarian journalism insists on this fundamental distinction: the "many voices" are not the cacophony of liberalism's marketplace, or the pulsating organicism of national movements inspired by monochromatic visions of progress, but the open and activist forum of democratic pluralism. Gone are days, if ever they were, when self-made publishers could indulge their bigotries and dismiss their critics with admonitions to start another newspaper, if you like and if you dare. Broadcasters faced the truth about limited resources when Herbert Hoover's voluntary radio conferences gave way to legislation regulating this exploding new marketplace of wireless entertainment. Even in the current post–Fairness Doctrine mood of broadcast deregulation, the government assigns frequencies and powers, and competing applications are seldom successful. In newspaper publishing, it is absurd to propose serious competition to established corporations. If a *Times* or a *Tribune* does not swallow the hapless entrepreneur, the open jaws of the "Gannettoids" are as hungry for prey as a cub reporter on a first stakeout.[50] Breaking into the record or movie production and distribution business is increasingly an enterprise restricted to corporations able to drop millions without a quiver. In the face of these economic realities, genuine projection of a "representative picture of the constituent groups in the society"—a Hutchins Commission ideal validated time and again since its articulation—is imperative for a media system based on the mutuality of community.

For the press to highlight covenantal bonds is not a decolonizing, denuding enterprise. Democratic pluralism shuns the shapeless melting-pot metaphor of Dewey's Great Community. Ukrainians speak to concerns in a manner different from the Zulu, to be sure. Covenant does not obscure these differences. Political *unum* and cultural *pluribus* are not mutually exclusive, at least in principle. Communitarian pluralism goes beyond a news hole proportionate to the demographics of a region. It recognizes the need to respect a minority of an isolated tribe, to favor the interests of those with least clout. When pluralism aggressively champions the differences within a framework of human solidarity, true covenant has the ground to spread its roots. Yet given the culture of silence that screens too many persons of varied ethnicity, an obligation to promote and explore the hidden people is the "affirmative-action" duty of a press jealous for covenant. Media channels seldom take the inarticulate and cloutless to the top of the page, yet in rare instances, a hero arises like a faint star against a full moon.

When Dorothy Day began hawking tabloids for a penny in New York City's Union Square on May Day 1933, the Nazi tempest was brewing in Germany, Stalin was building an impressive military and autocratic state, and radical protesters in New York and elsewhere increasingly called for new measures to achieve what the New Deal could not.[51]

Day's *Catholic Worker* was to be a silence breaker of prophetic proportions. When demonstrators greeted Day with protestation and amazement ("Religion in Union Square! It is preposterous!"), Day claimed that she was offering a voice for the worker, the unionist, the unemployed—a voice found neither in the religious press of her day nor in the big dailies, and atypical of the church whose name she invoked. How could such passion arise?

In the Day home in California, young Dorothy had only a meager form of religion. Her father was a journalist uninterested in nurturing his soul; her mother tended to Episcopalian quietude. Yet seasoned with two years in Greenwich Village, an abortion, a broken marriage, and political disillusionment, Day converted firmly when her first child was born.

The church her new home, French philosopher Peter Maurin became her mentor. His personalism insisted that true faith meant living in covenant bonds, seeking the values of other-mindedness, and assuming personal care for social change, even if such a strategy would generate a revolution of nearly imperceptible steps and barely visible changes. Of journalism, Maurin wrote in one of his poetically styled "Easy Essays,"

> To tell everybody
> that a man died
> leaving two million dollars
> may be journalism
> but it is not
> good journalism.
> But to tell everybody
> that a man died
> leaving two million dollars
> because he did not know
> how to take them with him
> by giving them to the poor
> for Christ's sake
> during his lifetime
> is good journalism.
>
>   . . .
>
> The news is the occasion
> for the journalist
> to convey his thinking
> to unthinking people.
> Nothing can be done
> without public opinion,
> and the opinion of thinking people
> who know how
> to transmit their thinking
> to unthinking people.[52]

Day adopted Maurin's advocacy model for her *Catholic Worker*. Until her death in 1980, she wrote and edited a version of Catholic personalism that extolled the small efforts of unknown people who sought to make a difference, with little worry over the impersonal movements that hung in the Greenwich Village air and touched few with their abstractions and innuendoes. She never permitted the paper to become an institution—no paid ads, no foundation grants, no renewal notices to subscribers, no bequests, and no tax breaks because the Catholic Worker movement was not a legal entity. "You don't need to be incorporated to wash a man's feet," she wrote in 1944.[53] Family was Day's metaphor for the *Worker* community: "We address ourselves to families, who have all the woes of insecurity, sin, sickness, and death, side by side with all the joys of family." The *Worker* would model in its own drafty "newsroom" the communitarian ideals of its columns.[54]

Dorothy Day's *Worker* gave immigrant factory workers and second-generation laborers a name—an active name, a name to encourage the small achievements of sharing and perseverance that marked a worker's rounds of family, neighborhood, job, and church. Day enhanced community by calling its accented, mixed members to covenant responsibility and some sacrifice for benefiting the whole. In an era when popular media stigmatized Italians, Slavs, Africans, and Orientals for deviousness and moral backwardness, Day's paper pointed to their positive contributions.[55] It was not banal sentimentality that overlooked the clannishness and exclusivity of the workers' narrow subcultures. It was a new name that resisted stereotypes and focused on persons able and excellent in nonconformist ways. When she died, *Time* reported that among the mourners in the humble New York parish hall where she had regularly worshipped was a drifter in tears who said, "That fine lady gave me love." Few other journalists have left such a legacy.[56]

Current staffers at the *Catholic Worker* label the Maurin–Day legacy "personalist anarchism." As a theory of social action, they consider it neither Marxist nor liberal, but see it as forging a prophetic community at odds with today's large-scale bureaucratic order. For editor Katherine Temple, the *Catholic Worker* attempts to fulfill Jacques Ellul's vision: "The emergence of social, political, intellectual, artistic bodies, associations, interest groups or economic or [religious] groups totally independent of the state, yet capable of opposing it."[57] Over against a depersonalized and technological world, human covenant—rather than a quaint form of retreat—is the animating spirit of the *Catholic Worker*'s self-conscious, radical personalism.[58]

Rather than appealing to the rights language of contract, those who, like Day, have insight into true community emphasize the emotive, mutual indebtedness of covenant commitment. Rather than taking a functional view of social life as an external exchange of goods and services, communities driven by covenant stress empathy and trusting vulnerability. Instead of a mere collective held together by self-interest, covenant communities are committed to the steadfast nurturing of partnership.[59]

In the mid-1980s, when reporter Ron Allen (then of WCVB in Boston) began planning a series at the renowned Bridgewater State Hospital, he confronted a history of bureaucratic sidestepping and uncustomary state censorship. *Titicut Follies,* a documentary made by Fred Wiseman in 1967, was the first extensive look inside the maximum-security hospital, and that motion picture had been banned from general viewing by the Massachusetts Supreme Court. But five unexplained suicides inside the hospital in 1987 (later judged to have been preventable) were enough to open the doors to Allen, albeit under stringent conditions of privacy concerns and patient rights.[60] Once inside, Allen's team, treading lightly through a labyrinth of bureaucracy, caught the stark world of the criminally insane in its cruel truth: Jimmy Slavin, the killer of his own son, in remorse intends to blind himself by staring at the sun; a homicidal psychopath placidly works with a butcher knife in the hospital kitchen; a deranged orphan gets in trouble with the law and lands at Bridgewater for reasons neither he nor the state could explain (and who, through the broadcast, was recognized by a sister and reintroduced to his family after twenty-five years). Such stories, told with compassion and honesty, earned Allen and WCVB a Peabody Award; they serve as choice examples of communitarian journalism at major market levels. Meanwhile, the courts have yet to lift the ban on Wiseman's documentary.

New York City dock workers would probably take little interest in the news that Robert Left Hand Bull and Clifford Broken Leg were two of a half-dozen tribal council representatives who could not make last May's Rosebud Sioux meetings. Boston realtors would give short shrift to the solid-waste cleanup, reported during that meeting, at Antelope Dump on Sioux lands. Phoenix bankers and the Head Start program at the Pine Ridge Reservation likely as not have few interests in common and normally would not exchange prodigious amounts of information. Yet readers of the *Lakota Times* ("Serving the Lakota Nation and All Indian Country") had access to these items and more, some of crime and some of illnesses and hospitalizations. It is a serious paper with a serious purpose, telling stories that help to keep a distinctive community linked, legitimizing the community's sense of history and struggle. The *Lakota Times* receives no extended treatment in histories of American journalism, and this paper monopolizes no one's territory. Yet it is a clear example of the idea that ethically sound reporting matters greatly as a vehicle of transformative citizenship.

Radicals within the Soviet hierarchy used fax, telephone, and videotape to globalize their vigil during the short-lived but ominous military coup attempt in 1991. Could the Russian president know that crowds outside his barricaded office complex were only a hint of the wider world community supporting his bold denial of the generals' demands? Isolated geographically, Boris Yeltsin persevered, emerging to respond to questions from U.S. admirers on ABC only days after resuming control, on a program reminiscent of America's colonial (and mythic) past: the "National Town Meeting."

Rural Inuits outside Nome, Alaska, had been divided by the Bering Strait from their ethnic relatives for eight decades, until first satellite interlinks on the Siberian side, and then exchange flights to render the image personal, built bridges over the sea and across national fences.

An ethics of the press anchored in such civic transformations presupposes human dignity and seeks interdependence. It admits irrational prejudices but honors the possibility of peaceful change in a context of empathy and mutuality. "Love suffers long and is kind, love hopes all things" is ancient wisdom. But to press the covenantal principle too far into media ethics might resemble a lecture in herbal healing at a surgeons' convention or an operetta as entertainment at a Marine boot camp. The call for journalists to "love one another" makes a rough fit with the Hildy Johnson *Front Page* stereotype. Yet the principle reiterates the simple idea that a neighbor's good takes precedence over personal gain; inviolate is the commitment to render selfless service to those within one's sphere of influence.

Difficult though mutuality may be in terms of newsroom culture, it strikes communitarians as unavoidably crucial. How will journalists displace self-gratification with other-mindedness if not by some compelling option that projects others' needs as equal to or greater than one's own? In Paulo Freire's terms, why take the dialogic seriously apart from a radical reorientation, an upheaval of gigantic narrative proportions, that finally accepts another "story" as worth hearing? Freire critiques the banking method—the deposit of truth into the minds of listeners by learned authorities—as the epistemological opposite of communitarian journalism.[61] The banking method plays on old and fanciful "bullet" themes of persuasion and on new, ingenious, and elitist theories of social change. The dialogic mode is less moved to persuade than to understand.

Except through a covenantal commitment, the press will not participate credibly in the "browning" of America. By the mid-twenty-first century, "the average U.S. resident, as defined by Census statistics, will trace his or her descent to Africa, Asia, the Hispanic world, the Pacific Islands, Arabia—almost anywhere but white Europe."[62] In New York State, 40 percent of schoolchildren already belong to a non-Caucasian ethnic group, and the proportion will reach 50 percent by the end of the decade. "In San Jose [California] bearers of the Vietnamese surname Nguyen outnumber the Joneses in the telephone directory fourteen columns to eight."[63] Fifteen hundred small stores in Detroit are owned by a subculture of Chaldean Christians with Iraqi roots. In the next century, the United States will no longer represent Europe in miniature, but the world. Compared with prior generations of immigrants, language and ethnic identity are increasingly nonnegotiable. Legislative drives to make English the sole official language, racial conflict on college campuses and in ghettoes and suburbs, school curricula, immigration policy, affirmative-action programs, workers' compensation for resident aliens—those are issues of immense cultural complexity, central to citizenship, as America becomes a majority nonwhite society. The mutuality principle sees beyond the melting pot and embraces the merits of multiracialism; it dedicates the news enterprise to soothing fears in the national soul and challenges the public to thrive on cultural diversity.

In his call to valuative pluralism, Richard Neuhaus follows MacIntyre's reading of Enlightenment dualism to argue that moral values, embedded in ontological categories and inextricably manifest in faith communities, have been quashed by a monolithic appeal to rationalism in a former era and to pragmatism more recently, the driving ideologies of American corporatism.[64] In the process of searching for a national common ground, norms have surrendered to efficiencies, values to programs. The recovery Neuhaus urges is a vigorous appeal to communities knitted together by a covenantal vision. He seeks authoritative public discourse—narratives powerfully representing communal norms and expressing the impulse to an ever-widening human embrace. Our entreaty here is to incorporate media institutions in that task. The "presentation and clarification of the goals and values of a society"[65] assumes enough trust between persons to identify their values and target their application—sufficient trust to learn and relearn, to listen long and speak with caution—in concert with the rest of the wayward world.

News: The Empowerment Story

The duty to speak, the responsibility to name, the right to hold opinion publicly, personally, commonly—on these foundations a communitarian press ethics distinguishes itself from the mainstream contractarian version.

Since his first exposure to the English-speaking world in 1968, Paulo Freire has argued for "naming the world" as the opening wedge into meaningful social change. Day achieved this for subsistence laborers and the urban poor. Ringgold Ward sought no less when he pointed out the immorality of the Fugitive Slave Act. Elijah Lovejoy's troubles with drenched type fonts and night raiders began when he refused to let a boat porter's lynching recede from memory; naming that event made of personal tragedy an episode of historical record.

To name the world, in Freire's terms, is to transform it from objective, untouchable otherness into a reality that the speaker has begun to adopt and transform. Claude Lévi-Strauss notes the astounding numbers of names employed by technologically primitive tribes in the use and nurture of their botanical environment. The Subanun people in the southern Philippines have several hundred names for plants and fauna; plant names used by their neighbors the Hanunoo approach 2,000, including 45 types of edible mushrooms; indeed, 93 percent of the total number of native plants are named, active agents in Hanunoo culture.[66] Clearly, the distinctions borne on these many names make mushrooms a more lively commodity to the Hanunoo than to most Chicagoans. Yet Freire's interest is not finally botany but society, the cultural structures that names build, maintain, and ultimately threaten and remake. For Freire, to label the world is to transform it, and thereby to engage in the process of liberating stewardship.[67]

Obviously, our remarkable human creativity in naming can become a wonderful subterfuge. An all-news radio station (which as a generic name is itself a subterfuge) has presumptuously called its weathercast "Weather Command." How such feeble predictions about precipitation and temperature—all without the slightest possibility that the meteorologist's intervention can alter even a degree of temperature or a dewdrop—can be thought to warrant the name "command" is a semantic monstrosity impossible to justify (unless we assume that nature is doing the commanding, in which case a more honest forecaster would call her slot "Weather as Commanded"). Chicago's notorious Cabrini-Green public-housing complex bears the name of the first American citizen to be canonized, the Italian-born Frances Xavier Cabrini, who founded sixty-seven mission houses in the United States, Europe, and Latin America—the "saint of the immigrants" she was called. Yet there exists a wide discrepancy between a pious Catholic order and the mores of this spoiled and violent, hapless and broken near–North Side tenement. Naming is not the whole task, but a unique human capacity and a necessary step to fundamental social realignment.

Freire insists that through literacy and social activism, the oppressed learn to name their world, not to dominate it as feudalists in their castles or cotton merchants on their verandas, but to take responsibility for it. Hegemony in this sense is not a term of authoritarianism; it points to the exercise of human skillfulness to achieve social justice in complex environments resistant to change. Freire finds no virtue in the illiteracy of Brazilian farmers, though their inability to read does have a certain economic payoff for those in control; it tends to keep farmers at their plows instead of at political rallies or writing desks. There is arguable functional efficiency in a group of isolated coffee workers selling their time or crops at prices told to them by the literate and learned. But such functional efficiency is more akin to the final purpose of a four-cycle engine than that of a human being. Freire insists that farmers read and speak in order to liberate themselves from an oppressive situation—to begin the vocation of bean growing and not just to grow beans.

"The question, from my point of view," writes Freire, "is not just to take power but to reinvent power, that is, to create a different kind of power."[68] The dominant understanding of power is interventionist, aiming at mastery or control. In Freire's alternative, power is relational; it is characterized by mutuality rather than sovereignty. Empowered persons, in his perspective, are not distant and dominant, but are given their maximum humanity—power akin to that of Alcoholics Anonymous, in which vulnerablity and exchange within a community enables persons to establish a sense of purpose and direction. Freire's reinvented power rejects the paternalistic, elitist view that the oppressed are powerless and must wait passively until the revolution is handed to them.

"Only through communication can human life hold meaning" is Freire's imperative to literacy.[69] Naming one's world, even a peasant world, helps human beings struggle toward the governance of work, the distribution of produce, the training of young workers, and the strategic transformation of the worksite. Through critical consciousness humanity prospers: family is established as a first circle of intimacy; faith is cherished as a window to the transcendent; creativity is substituted for numbing regimentation; celebration is evoked at the task accomplished and the future yet to be.

Did naming the world ever lead to such utopian visions? Surely, naming is a constant task, as justice is a dynamic quest and covenant is a searching ideal. But naming moves a person from periphery to center, from respondent to activist, from *paisano* to co-worker. Naming is the human way of affirming the moral dimension of all we do, and good names are always, in Freire's vision, community enterprises. In the 1940s when racism was strong and widespread, many newspapers omitted the titles "Mr.," "Mrs.," and "Miss" in front of the last names of African-Americans—a not-so-subtle tactic to suggest that the respect due our fellow sojourners did not accrue to people of color. Yet those same papers had to use first names to distinguish the genders. Enoch Waters reports that some southern black parents began naming their children "Attorney," "Doctor," "General," "President," and, most mischievous of all, "Mister."[70]

Empowerment deflates the impulse to control into a readiness to serve. In a personal–mutual world, individuals do not aspire to hegemony over subjects, but to cooperation with peers. Power is a force for other-minded energies, not self-directed felicitousness. The will to power is expressed in promoting the highest aspirations of a group's service to the public, just as the duty to speak is enveloped in the responsibility to seek truth. Empowerment tolerates falsehood as the essential elbow room of experimental discourse, but never as an intentional means to an end. Empowerment allows for inequities and compromise when the end of the process assumes the franchise for those on the periphery. Contrary to classical liberal instincts, wealth does not make communitarian reporting easier; thickness of newsprint does not signify representative coverage.

Michael Walzer describes the danger of statelessness—the vulnerable social condition of nonmembership—in his study of distributive justice. Although such persons are usually still permitted some access to markets, they are unprotected in an arena that tends to exploit weakness and respect strength. With no guaranteed social place, they are always liable to expulsion. This was the cruelty of the Japanese-American relocation camps ordered by federal law in 1942, as surely as it was the plight of Kuwaitis when Iraq plundered their country in 1990.[71]

"Statelessness is a condition of infinite danger."[72] We might add that gaining membership is a problem of infinite complexity. When the Supreme Court gave blacks full membership in public education in 1954 by guar-

anteeing protection in the quest for equal participation, White Citizens
Councils sprouted throughout the South. Highway billboards urged
"Never! Impeach Earl Warren!" Congressional committees charged the
civil rights movement with communism. FBI agents increased surveillance
of alleged conspirators. The president winced at a Supreme Court that he
felt had exceeded the public's willingness to cooperate. And newspapers
around the country, including the powerful Hearst chain, trumpeted the
Court's ruling as an ominous portent of socialistic upheaval.

Empowerment assumes the benefits and protections of membership.
Media that empower far exceed the Rawlsian ethic of mutual aid, which
requires that in a chance meeting of strangers, providing help is morally
obligatory if an emergency exists and if the risks of giving aid are minimal.
By contrast, empowerment media strive to force the meeting of strangers
and push the provision of aid as risks accelerate. In 1954 the Court, reading
public opinion, postponed implementation of its ruling for one year, hoping
for a calmer transition. But not until 1960 did the *New York Times* urge
the country to heed the rising voices of Martin Luther King, Jr., and the
Southern Christian Leadership Conference. The risks of opening membership to strangers should be a journalist's primary occupational hazard.
Membership is a highly symbolic process; the media ought to show aggressive leadership in using their inventories of such symbols.

Benjamin Harris began the journalism enterprise in this country with
four small pages, all of which would not constitute half the words of the
Wall Street Journal's editorial page. Between Harris and the satellite blips
sending copy to regional printing plants are 300 years of risk taking and
struggle. What compels such risks, in the face of perilously favorable odds
that words offensive to those in power will bring about substantive evils
which no Congress can prevent?

Robert Bellah's probe into the American middle-class soul begins with
case studies of individuals who acknowledge their need to find enduring
values, but when asked finally why they converted from hedonist or radical
or careerist into caring father or social service worker, each cited reasons
not markedly different from those which had motivated them before their
conversion: "I feel better doing life this way." For all their soul searching
and priority shifting, typical middle-class Americans, in Bellah's view, still
have no better reason for their actions than an enlightened egoism. Good
is still that which serves the self well, his subjects affirm. Such a thinly
veiled egoism provides no explanation for the risk taking that generates
empowered communities.[73]

Multiple Layers

When James Carey bemoans the paucity of public language and a public
vision, he trades on Dewey's notions of the need to develop a viable public

philosophy, urging the placement of public justice at the center of our culture's institutional agendas. Schools, universities, park boards, county planning commissions, churches, utility watchdog groups, newspapers (the list is endless) have no common need to do one another's work or to negotiate one another's professional standards. But at the center of their purposes should be some common vision of an inclusive, cooperative society, a vision that throughout the modern century has been tepid, splintered, and inarticulate. Solutions are beyond simple adjustments in policy or style, code or conduct.[74]

An accident story in the DuPage, Illinois, *Daily Journal* concerned two women in their early twenties killed in a head-on crash along a four-lane highway when a drunken driver, a man with sixteen prior traffic citations, crossed the center line and struck their oncoming vehicle. He survived, stood trial on numerous counts, and was eventually sentenced to three years of confinement, with release time every weekday to pursue his work in Chicago. He spent evenings and weekends in the DuPage County jail.

After some public uproar over the lightness of the sentence, the issue faded. News stories went on to other topics and the courts to other cases—that is, until the mother of one of the victims, still grieving and outraged over the judge's ruling, tracked the offender to an office party in a tavern, a clear violation of his work-release agreement. She found the man sprawled on a tabletop. Jubilant with revenge, she summoned authorities and called the newspaper. Police packed the besotted felon off to more permanent confinement, and the *Journal* ran a large photo of the mother holding a picture of her deceased daughter along with a story of her sleuthing and the man's apprehension. But tucked into the story in the third column, twelfth paragraph (after a review of the crime and the man's past traffic record) was a statement from the defense attorney about the mother's harassment of his client's family and her constant shadowing of his every step, as if she were daring him to make his eventual mistake. The attorney intended to file suit against the mother.

How is an editor to build out of this series of tragedies a story that will distinguish public good from public evil and empower readers to serve the good? The editor may rightly oppose drunken driving as a menace to public safety. She may favor sympathy with the accident victims and their families. She may join the outrage, temporary though it was, against a lenient judge. But just as easily, she could pursue the perpetrator's story—victimization by alcohol, carelessness with tragic consequences, peer influence at an office party, an irate mother whose dead-of-night phone calls and constant scrutiny made a terrible situation even more grievous, and now a family with severely reduced means while the convict serves the remainder of his sentence in the TV lounge of a crowded jail. Which version enables citizens to engage responsibly in social transformation?

When the multiple layers are woven together with finesse and psychological savvy, the result is the equivalent in news to Shakespeare in British literature. "In Ricky's Wake" by *Washington Post* reporter Walt Harrington is one such classic, a Sunday magazine feature about Ruth and Bucky Jenkins, "suspended somewhere between despair and redemption" after their son killed himself at twenty-two.[75] One night Ricky had put on clean clothes and a gold necklace, gone to the shed behind the house, started his motorcycle, and poisoned himself with carbon monoxide sometime before morning.

A pregnant girlfriend, broken windows, addiction to model airplane glue, a water fountain rigged to drench Sister Claire, the neighbor's car stolen for a joy ride stuck axle-deep in a mud field, sleepless at night, bouncing from job to job—Ricky nearly sent his parents to their grave before he went himself. His father was a fireman; Ricky set a field aflame. "Ricky gained control by making others lose it; chaos was his upper hand," but on that Saturday night in June,

> Ricky wanted to be free of his imagined worthlessness . . . and he wanted his parents to be free of him. But they are not. Ricky wasn't only the cause of his family's troubles, but also their reflection. . . . How to take responsibility but not blame? That is what Ricky's parents are struggling to do. They haven't yet found redemption. But God knows, they're trying.[76]

Now, three years later, for this *Washington Post* reporter, Ricky's suicide meant long, wrenching conversations with the Jenkinses and their daughters Janet and Linda—and dissecting the involvements of an endless list of teachers, counselors, law officials, and friends. Walt Harrington had softly burrowed his way into Ricky's circle, and the family welcomed him into their psyches. To Mrs. Jenkins, for a year Ricky's suicide "was like an elephant sitting on my chest."[77] Mr. Jenkins was still taking little consolation and giving none. He kept a stiff upper lip at work, but often he could be found at night sobbing in the shed—that monument to a father's guilt. He had almost torn down the house looking for a suicide note, and came to be reconciled with a mysterious marking in the family Bible: "I surrender my will to the wisdom of a loving God."

And out of Harrington's sensitive hearing comes forth a Pulitzer-quality drama, a liberating word that disinfects some of the open wounds while enabling Ricky's family to work through the hard lessons learned at the cost of a renegade son. Harrington's details were honed in the sunshine; he even read the story out loud to the family to test its ambience and accuracy before its publication. Readers fight back tears as they situate themselves in the family pathos. Our preoccupation is not a beleaguered family or a contrary son, but the universal human struggle with guilt in the deepest recesses of our being. As we reach into the mysteries and power of intimacy, when ought we accept responsibility but not the blame? Whether a family is devastated by suicide or not, has revengeful children or not, lives traumatically or serenely, is insecure or brash, works the assembly line or the penthouse—Harrington crafts Ricky into Sartre's universal singular, and we wrestle through the drama with our own version of coming to peace with guilt.

News media concerned to tell empowerment stories that multiply themselves by empowering others surely need a public ethic that transcends the rhetorical circle of individual happiness and egoistic fulfillment. Public storytellers must know the good as much as they need a language to describe the bad, at least for response to be beneficent rather than destructive.

Reporting and Evil

However, the good–bad distinction appears to many journalists and other social observers like medieval monastic justice, false dichotomies built on visions of angels and demons in a tug-of-war over souls, with Gehenna the mudpit between them. Much of this reaction is explained by our clumsiness at labeling the bad. We are permitted in the public forum to debate error, mistake, repression, sublimation, sometimes fault, less often guilt, but not evil. Images of gargoyles and Dante's purgatorial swamps send the word "evil" onto the same kill list as terms like "very," "sources said," and "yesterday." Evil as a category of action, as an explanatory term or a descriptive label, is an anachronism in a world skeptical of final judgments and judgment calls.

Psychiatrist M. Scott Peck has placed the term "evil" back on the agenda of mental healers with his case-study reader *People of the Lie*.[78] Peck speaks of evil in terms of the inability of persons to comprehend, when told plainly and even forcefully, the self-destructive and other-destructive nature of their motives and actions. In each of the book's compelling narratives, psychiatric art failed to bring healing because, Peck claims, patients refused to confront their insistence on hurting themselves and those around them: they had a fix on evil. Peck's next book, another best seller and equally controversial, was his call to take genuine community—an extension of the growing self in league with others—to international levels of relations and transtribal bondings.[79]

News media are less concerned with the deeply personal movements of psychotherapy than with the entrenched, sometimes institutionalized efforts of cities, counties, political parties, aldermanic wards, and school systems to self-destruct through a failure of empowering dialogue. Yet trading on Peck's central insight, how is a newspaper to explain, other than in terms of evil, the silent factories across the industrial Midwest, jaded labor–management disputes, the necessity of prison reform, tax fraud and

investor fraud, carelessly high amounts of sugar and saturated fats in pro-
cessed meals, fast-food containers that stimulate the greenhouse effect,
and widespread resistance to reform in child-marketed kidvid? News coverage itself must do its own internal analysis: blanket insistence on standing
by a story when all indicators point to shoddy reporting or tainted sources;
prodding the grief-stricken when a dozen less intrusive angles would serve
the public's need for information; cooperation with public-relations writers
until news columns, especially in consumer sections, are nearly indistin-
guishable from paid advertising. News media are not pristine, and they are
too often unwilling to face the judgment of public or professional peers
that their actions and motives are sometimes (wrenching term, odd sound)
evil.

Columnist Roger Rosenblatt contends that these wider panaceas are
not the domain of newspapers. Reporters need a *story,* he insists, "something shapely and elegant. Poverty is disorderly, anticlimactic and endless.
If one wants truth about the poor, one must look where the ball is not.
The poor are poor all the time."[80] There is no story in poverty, according
to this expert, unless a poor person marches on Washington or starts a
tenement fire. We note the fallacy of this position, its inherent elitism, and
its retreat from all but the most indiscriminable "facts" of a news story.
Communitarian journalism struggles for the "larger truth" that Rosenblatt
assigns, perhaps, only to books or sermons or learned lectures. But people
are much keener than this view of journalism's role credits them, and truth
is more complicated—transformation more integral—than the "quite small
elements of information" that Rosenblatt regards as the domain of the
press.

Psychotherapeutic healing, Peck insists, requires that patients trust the
therapist, creating at times a temporary paternalism but, more happily, a
sympathetic submission to the medical and moral advice of the healing
"other." Until such trust is established, the patient seeking analysis is half-
analyst herself, still caught in a solipsism that resists the harsh judgment
of reality and refuses to confront evil. Analogies of this kind of trust in a
media setting are nearly incomprehensible. The heroes in the journalism
hall of fame have "independent entrepreneur" etched across their name-
plates. The demise of the National News Council, the refusal to enforce
professional codes, the aggressive dismissal of international initiatives to
correct ethnocentric news flow—journalism's fierce independence is in bold
italicized Roman.

Yet a communitarian ethics suggests that news media, for all their
Fourth Estate independence, are not alone in the world and should not
behave as if they were. The discovery of values and their maintenance in
social experience are not the monopoly of a press baron, a media company,
or an industry isolated from peers. "Evil," and therefore "good," reenters

the journalism vocabulary at just the point where community eclipses individualism as a baseline ethical concept. Edward R. Murrow intuitively understood that viewers must be nudged toward responsible action. When he produced the classic documentary of migrant farm workers, "Harvest of Shame," tears flowed in the screening room after the first exhibition. The sorrowful song at the end tore into every conscience in the room. But Murrow did not seek pity; he wanted knowledgeable response. So he reworked the final scenes and concluded: "Is it possible we think too much in terms of Christmas baskets and not in terms of eliminating poverty? . . . The people you have seen have the strength to harvest your fruit and vegetables. They do not have the strength to influence legislation. Maybe we do. Good night and good luck."[81] Murrow acted on Aristotle's dictum regarding tragedy, that great art does not end with pity or fear but "effects proper purgation." He knew that to hold up injustice as a spectacle is to trivialize it, even though the response is not derision but lament. He sought empowered viewers.

News as Social Narrative

Elijah Lovejoy's Alton *Observer,* Dorothy Day's *Catholic Worker,* and Edward R. Murrow's "Harvest of Shame" represent a revisionist definition of news. To them and their like-minded colleagues over the past century, all committed to nurturing civic transformation, news is a narrative genre more akin to public storytelling than to transmitting signals through space. They understand that cultivating a critical consciousness involves an interpretive process far more complex than the five-W format. Communitarian ethics is shaped in terms of ethically justified textual representations.[82] In that spirit, the vice president of the Oakland *Tribune* contends:

> When I trained to become a reporter during the middle 1960s, the definition of "news" was that which was new, strange, picturesque or unexpected. That definition endures, but it did not prepare me to research and write stories about why hospital costs rose faster than the consumer price index or what in Jimmy Carter's manner made voters question his suitability to be president. The skills of weighing information and weaving facts together into a coherent pattern, with appropriate shadings and emphasis, need to become a primary focus. . . . What happens when the issue is toxic pollution or product liability or unfair insurance rates, and no legal brief helps define the discussion? . . . The reporter usually resorts to a "he said/she said" discussion, in which big crimes and little ones can easily appear the same. Such imprecision leads to stories that are not all wrong, but not quite true. . . . Reporters with *working principles to use on stories* may have to work harder, but they will serve the public better. . . . [83]

Stories are symbolic frameworks that organize human experience. Narration gives order to social life by inducing others to participate with us in its meaning. Through stories we constitute ways of living in common. In Walter Fisher's terms, humans are narrative beings who have an inherent awareness of discursive coherence (whether or not a story hangs together) and of narrative fidelity (whether or not a story rings true). From childhood days, humans pursue this narrative logic. Stories that exhibit these attributes—coherence and fidelity—entice us to join with others who share them.[84] Anthropologist Renato Rosaldo discusses these qualities in terms of narrative force:

> Cultural depth does not always equal cultural elaboration. Think simply of the speaker who is filibustering. The language used can sound elaborate as it heaps word on word, but surely it is not deep. Depth should be separated from the presence or absence of elaboration. By the same token, one-line explanations can be vacuous or pithy. The concept of force calls attention to an enduring intensity of human conduct that can occur with or without the dense elaboration conventionally associated with cultural depth.[85]

Narratives are linguistic forms through which we think, argue, persuade, display convictions, and establish our identity. They contain in a nutshell the meaning of our theories and beliefs. "Not only men and women of affairs but also ordinary people tell themselves stories about who they are, what they care about, and how they hope to realize their aspirations."[86] "I have learned from Zimbabwe and Zambia," writes Michael Traber, "that storytelling is fundamental to human life and at the very heart of communication, both interpersonal and technically mediated. Descartes' dictum, 'Cogito, ergo sum,' would, in Africa, have to be changed to 'I am a storyteller and I sing and dance, therefore I am.' "[87]

Hannah Arendt was recognized at her death in 1975 as one of the finest social philosophers of the twentieth century. Her books *The Human Condition* and *On Revolution* are classics, and her essay "Thinking and Moral Considerations" is priceless. She is well known to the public through her reporting on the Eichmann trial for the *New Yorker*. Shaped by her battles with totalitarian Nazism, Arendt has understood more keenly than most the formative role of narrative in the public sphere. The civic arena, in her view, is a unique human domain forged out of dialogue and persuasion. Democratic polity cannot rest on authoritarian claims to truth or on a tyrant's dominating will. Everyday practice must be participatory for a state to be regarded as democratic in any substantive sense. Citizenship requires practical wisdom—that is, the consensus of multiple perspectives achieved by communication. Judging is inherently a social act driven by a common-sense desire to exchange opinions with others in our locale about recommended courses of action. Forging creative results is the litmus test, of course; the public theater, in a normative sense, is action space for taking initiatives.[88] Thus Arendt enthusiastically ties narrative and public philosophy together. Storytelling "cuts through abstractions and other obscurities," enables us "to think creatively and imaginatively" about "the endless details of . . . a disorderly world," and in the process transforms "essentially private experience into a shared and therefore public reality."[89]

The stories surrounding Nelson Mandela's twenty-six years in prison, Paul Revere's ride, the Selma march, the demolition of the Berlin Wall, and the "velvet revolution" in Czechoslovakia were fodder for political revolution. When a Salman Rushdie novel satirized a beloved Muslim story, his life was put under siege. As the foundational story of communism crumbled, the long-suppressed ethnic stories among the Armenians, Ukrainians, and Azerbaijanis reasserted themselves. The memories embodied in collective narratives are particularly precious to the displaced—Palestinians, Armenians, Kurds, and Misquito Indians, for example. In contrast, word and image bites of mayors cutting ribbons and heads of state waving from airplane stairs are pseudostories that do not engender common commitments.[90] Public indifference to the frivolous character of such stories indicates in itself that great storytellers—as opposed to mere image makers— probe deeply into our belief systems and shape the social landscape.

Stanley Hauerwas's theological ethics trades on the insight that stories constitute a community's moral framework. In *A Community of Character,* for example, Hauerwas responds to Alasdair MacIntyre's doleful conclusion at the end of *After Virtue*: "What matters at this stage is the construction of local forms of community within which civility and the moral life can be sustained through the dark ages which are already upon us."[91] Thus the axis of Hauerwas's book is appropriate forms of community, grounded in stories of substantive morality and not merely in formal rules of proper procedure. For him, moral power is inseparably connected to a body of language given us as a legacy; the legacy moves us toward a moral horizon, and thereby holds the whims of autonomous individualism at bay.[92]

Communities are woven together by narratives that mediate their common understanding of good and evil. Stories stitch together "the seamless web of culture that shapes who we are, how we live, whom we love or hate or kill . . . and how long we shall survive."[93] Everyone has general views on the meaning of life and death, of happiness and of reward. People may be wrong about their deepest beliefs or may not articulate them imaginatively.[94] But, as Dewey says in negative terms, "One thing a person knows better than anybody else, and that is where the shoe pinches on his own feet."[95] Communities are constituted by a set of values that specify their members' roles and aspirations. "A community is at bottom an ethical construction."[96]

Community Norms

Kant's rationalistic ethics used the universalizability test: What would a moral agent will to be a maxim for all, without contradiction? Instead of that ahistorical and individualistic procedure, narrative ethics asks: "What norms or institutions would the members of an ideal or real communication community agree to as representing their common interests after engaging in a special kind of argumentation or conversation?"[97] Citizens do not engage in a "silent thought-experiment" but in "argumentative praxis"; community members participate in an "intersubjective procedure" in which they mutually search for "principles of action" that together they recognize as valid.[98] The moral intuition behind both Kantian universalizability and communal norms is the ancient Golden Rule, "Do unto others what you would have them do to you." In other words, we are enjoined to invert perspectives, to judge from another's point of view. In communicative ethics, "such reversibility is essential to the ties of reciprocity that bind human communities together."[99] Under modern conditions, linkages with significant others must increasingly be exercised through such mediated forms of communication as the press.

Is freedom the goal of public life? Not quite, argues Hauerwas. Liberation is a by-product of "participation in a truthful polity capable of forming virtuous people" who collectively express a "diversity of gifts and virtues."[100] Is the goal market-driven enterprise? Enlightenment? Dialogue? Rescue from the jihad? In large part, the press shapes our public discourse and communal visions, and does so rightly when it enables citizens to act transformatively out of truthful narratives. Stories may be good or bad, even when they ring true and seem coherent to the faithful. Narratives may not be dialogically formed, in other words, but represent a brutal reign of terror. Idi Amin punctuated his stories with mutilated bodies along the sidewalks. Jim Jones's fellowship chanted and danced to a common grave. Christopher Columbus discovery stories mask inhumanity and exploitation. Thus communitarian ethics challenges those storytellers whom we call reporters to specialize in truthful narratives about justice, covenant, and empowerment. "The narrative of news, whether broadcast or print, can be viewed as a total verbal order resting on a variety of master codes. . . . All stories by nature, including journalistic ones . . . have some principle for assigning significance to an event present in them."[101] When the mission of news is not simply enlightenment but proactive citizenship, the predominant codes will be social justice, communal bonding, and participatory politics.

The relationship of language to reality is much more complex than common sense assumes. Words do not merely transmit preexisting ideas and mirror real-world entities directly; but neither is language a random compilation of symbols. John Hartley provides a useful metaphor:

> Neither news nor language [is a] transparent window on the world. They are both more like maps of the world. A map differs from the terrain it indicates in very obvious ways, without ceasing to maintain a relationship which allows us to recognize the terrain through it. But in order to find our way with a map we have to understand its own distinct codes, conventions, signs and symbols. A map organizes, selects, and renders coherent the innumerable sense impressions we might experience on the ground.[102]

Language abstracts, just as a map does. Both maps and language collapse some elements together, enhance the importance of others, and ignore some dimensions entirely. Given that language recapitulates, the symbols we use create what we view as reality. In discussing the nature of language in the context of AIDS, for example, Paula Treichler argues that "[w]e cannot . . . look 'through' language to determine what AIDS 'really' is. Rather, we must explore the site where such determinations *really* occur and intervene at the point where meaning is created: in language."[103]

Again, to quote Hartley's argument about news, "It is not the *event* which is reported that determines the form, content, meaning or 'truth' of the news, but rather the *news* that determines what it is that the event means: its meaning results from the features of the sign-system and the context in which it is uttered and received."[104] The language of news, like a road map, not only differs from what it describes, but also alters how we perceive the description. Language does not merely reflect reality from the outside; recomposing events into narrative ensures that humans can comprehend a reality at all.

Those conversant with Western thought will recognize the historic importance of the shift toward reporting as social narrative and toward ethical reflection on that way of understanding the news media.[105] The argument can be summarized like this: Enlightenment epistemology, inspired by Descartes, generated an unavailing search for a secure foundation, for clear and distinct axioms unencumbered by context. Richard Rorty vilifies this dominant scheme as "the quest for certainty over the quest for wisdom." Philosophers assumed the mandate "either to attain the rigor of the mathematician or the physicist, or to explain the appearance of rigor in these fields, rather than to help people attain peace of mind. Science, rather than living, became philosophy's subject, and epistemology its center."[106] Rorty labels this epistemological system "foundationalism," although "objectivism" is a more typical name for the amalgam of practices and commitments that have prevailed for three centuries in Western thought as a whole.

The attacks on this misguided view of human knowledge originated with the counter-Enlightenment; continued with American pragmatism, critical theory in the Frankfurt school, hermeneutics, and Ludwig Wittgenstein's linguistic philosophy; and has persisted to our own day, when the phenomenal interest in Rorty, Kuhn, and interpretive research generally symbolizes a crisis in correspondence views of truth. Institutional structures remain caught in Enlightenment inertia, but in principle the tide has turned toward restricting objectivism to the territory of mathematics, physics, and the natural sciences. In reporting, objectivity has become increasingly controversial as the working press's professional standard, although it will remain entrenched in our ordinary practices of news production and dissemination until a convincing alternative mission for the press is formulated.

The Janet Cooke scandal sparked piecemeal debate over the boundary between fact and fiction in news. It spawned renewed interest in the power of investigative reporting. The "New Journalism" took it on the chin and may be out for the count (although, as David Eason argues, "Jimmy's World" is not actually representative of the literary journalism genre[107]). Isolated problems were debated—the fact that both Cooke and her editor were black, the *Washington Post*'s hiring policy, guidelines for using sources, and so forth. But in general the conventionalists rallied around a nostalgic view of a credible, long-standing enterprise betrayed in this instance by a reporter whom Benjamin Bradlee dismissed as a pathological liar.[108] No systematic, full-scale examination of the press's mission occurred in terms of the problematic status of objectivist thinking.

The press, under continuing Enlightenment tutelage, maintains representational accuracy as its *telos*, with adjustments in detail but not in principle. We still assume, though without the enthusiasm of earlier decades, that news corresponds to reality and is bound ideally to neutral algorithms. Practitioners counsel one another to make the best possible attempt at value-free reporting, even though that goal is never perfectly attainable. By analogy, we are told, a surgeon who cannot ensure an operating room pure of bacteria does not use a kitchen table and a butcher knife. Objectivity, for example, is still the centerpiece of the Society of Professional Journalists, Sigma Delta Chi Code of Ethics, and most reporters equate ethics with impartiality.[109]

Objectivity as Pathology

Objectivity is not only impossible, but scarcely desirable. Fact cannot be separated from value; detached observation is unattainable. Human objectivity is an oxymoron. "There is no Archimedean point from which to remove oneself from the mutual conditioning of social relations and human knowledge."[110] To be human is, in part, to value; thus the quest for systematic disinterest and disengagement is more akin to pathology than to quality understanding. It signifies moral indifference and disguises the observer's motivations under the prestige of the white lab coat. It denies the fact that even "the choice of what we want to know is primarily political and ethical,"[111] thereby keeping control of the public agenda in the hands of professionals and corporations, away from those social groups that threaten, if empowered, to change the structure of social, political, and economic decision making. While the consequences of using narrative conventions require ongoing scrutiny, news is most ideologically influential when journalists nurture the supposition that its practice is value-free.

But rather than maintaining a façade of objectivism—reporters as impersonal transmitters of facts—communitarian ethics compels all of us—journalist and news consumer—toward a rich concept of truthful narrative. Instead of being regarded as an information enterprise trapped in epistemology, truth is thereby relocated in the moral sphere. Regrettably, the few serious struggles over truth in the last centuries have been transmogrified into epistemological discourse. The ethical question of how we should live has typically floundered on debates over whether it is cognitively meaningful, which itself has succumbed to philosophical relativity. Do-gooders are relegated to the fringes to guard moral scraps. Rorty understands the significant stakes here, defining truth not as privileged representations of reality, but as—in William James's phrase—"what is better for us to believe."[112] Since Walter Lippmann distinguished news and truth in the 1920s, the epistemology of news has been critiqued and debated, but truthtelling still has not received its due. The point is that truth belongs in the moral sphere and therefore should become the province of ethics scholarship, especially when the dominant scheme has reached a historical crossroads.

When truth is articulated in terms of the moral order, we can mold its elastic meaning around the context, motives, and presuppositions involved. As Dietrich Bonhoeffer contends, telling the truth depends on the quality of discernment that keeps penultimates from gaining ultimacy.[113] A truthful account, in other words, strikes gold, gets at "the core, the essence, the nub, the heart of the matter."[114] In Anthony Giddens's phrase, it entails "discursive penetration."[115] This is a normative framework of a radically different kind, one that fundamentally reorders the press's professional culture.

Obviously, once knowledge becomes separated from foundations and commensurability and is released from epistemological objectivism, guidelines must be sought somewhere. News as social narrative turns not to subjectivism and romanticism, but to interpretive studies for its orientation and specificity. We are not arguing that careful, well-honed techniques be abandoned for impressionism and idle rumor. Forsaking the quest for precision journalism does not mean imprecision, but precision of a fundamentally different sort. To replace news gathering rooted in empiricism, rigorous qualitative procedures must be followed instead. Fiction and fabrication are not now acceptable as substitutes for fact and accuracy. Reporters aiming for critical consciousness among the public will seek what might be called "interpretive sufficiency." They will polish their research and writing skills in terms of sophisticated qualitative strategies. In composing their reading of events, the news media selectively form a coherent translation—coherence being a pattern in all narration. (Accounts that are merely unconnected listings are incoherent—that is, not comprehensible.) Explicit appeal to the interpretive approach will ensure the story's completeness, rather than crudely tailoring events into a cosmetic cohesion.

While "interpretive sufficiency," in some form, has long served as a trademark of distinguished journalism, it should now become an everyday imperative. The examples from international news are endless. ABC News has provided extensive coverage of the trade union movement in Poland. In his research on its reporting over seventeen months (August 1980 through December 1981), Kevin Carragee concludes that ABC overemphasized Lech Walesa, the Roman Catholic Church, and repressive Soviet communism—the discrete, the visual, and the familiar—at the expense of the complex social and historical roots of the Solidarity movement. In spite of its massive detail, "the network's account offer[ed] little or no examination of the working class origins of Solidarity, its ability to transcend previous divisions within Polish society, its heterogeneous political orientations, and its relationship to socialism."[116] And how are reporters to cover the staggering complexities of another nation's historic realignment in the heart of Eastern Europe—Czechoslovakia? Behind the orderly façade of the "velvet revolution" is a deeply divided country—politically (with Czech and Slovak contingents able to cancel out each other), economically (free-marketeers, various kinds of privatizers, conservative pragmatists), and culturally (urban and rural, authoritative and participatory, religious and secular, traditional and modern). In effect, with interpretive sufficiency we raise the ante, weaving it into our expectation of ordinary press performance. Superficiality is the enemy of communitarian journalism, as it has always been for thinking professionals, although technical efficiency—that is, stenographic reporting—in the liberal press tends to obscure the dangers of reductionism.

Since the days of Giambattista Vico (1688–1744) in Italy and Wilhelm Dilthey (1833–1911) in Germany, the counter-Enlightenment tradition has sustained an alternative view of concept and theory formation, and of human knowing generally.[117] In this perspective, theories must be grounded historically and biographically, so that they represent complex culture adequately. The concepts of social science are not derived from a free-floating and abstruse mathematics, but resonate with the experience, attitudes, definitions, and language of the people actually being studied. Journalists trained in counter-Enlightenment research identify with social meanings in their role as participants and formulate seminal conclusions about them as observers. Such historians of reporting as James W. Carey lament an escalating professionalism that wrenches journalism from its civic moorings and recasts it as a scientized culture remote from everyday life. The genius of qualitative studies is to confront that sequestering head-on; it enables us to work the backyards and sidewalks, but with *savior-faire* and competence. The same mutuality principle that distinguishes communitarian journalism animates qualitative data collection as well.

Through disciplined abstractions (John Lofland), ethnomethodology, contextualization, thick description (Clifford Geertz), coherent frames of reference (Alfred Schutz), case studies, naturalistic observation, and other research practices, reporters can stake out a claim to interpretive sufficiency and assume responsibility for their efforts.[118] Semiotic scholars from Ferdinand de Saussure to Roland Barthes and Umberto Eco help to distinguish textual signifiers such as icons, social myths, and connotations. Through critical research, reporters come to grips with the complex ways ethnographers insert themselves into the interpretive process. A rich literature has been developed on constructing the life histories of ordinary people.[119] In a fundamental sense, qualitative approaches are a temperament of mind—"the sociological imagination," C. Wright Mills called it—rather than merely a series of techniques for handling the telephone, minicam, or interview pad. However, while the creative process always remains central, tough-minded standards and valid procedures can be taught and learned. We accept the maxim that any investigation—journalistic or academic—imprisoned within itself and therefore self-validating is irresponsible. The public nature of reporting demands that our strategies be clear and available for scrutiny. Qualitative methods help make journalism accountable; and in the hands of conscientious veterans, they can turn a concrete experience of justice, covenant, or empowerment into enduring probes of the body politic.

Veteran reporter Richard Critchfield is a serious student of participant-observation methodology. He shares with anthropologist Oscar Lewis a commitment to indigenous cultures, and self-consciously uses village-reporting strategies that rival the best of the social sciences. For his exceptional Vietnam coverage, Critchfield received the Overseas Press Club Award in 1965. He is convinced to this day that "our defeat was not a failure of power but a failure of knowledge"—a negligence, among other things, "to learn enough about the ordinary Vietnamese peasant out in his

village and about his Confucian culture." By our inability to understand
the South Vietnamese, "we let them down."[120] Reporting for the *Christian
Science Monitor,* the *Economist* of London, and the *Washington Star,*
Critchfield's village studies have become classics: Creole fishermen and
octopus divers in Mauritius, Bedouin shepherds on the Iran–Iraq border,
a Moroccan village below the Atlas Mountains, tenant farmers near Zam-
boanga on Mindanao Island in the southern Philippines, and Tibetan ref-
ugees in the Pokhra-Jomoson Himalayan region.[121] And in two books, he
reports on domestic culture: *Those Days: An American Album* (1987) and
Trees, Why Do You Wait? America's Changing Rural Culture (1991).

> Village reporting forces the reporter to look at problems, not in terms of
> the politics of the surface, as reporters habitually do, but in terms of
> technological and cultural trends beneath the surface. . . . My work has
> convinced me that the place to go if you want to understand the assas-
> sination of Indira Gandhi, which changed the course of Indian history, is
> to a Sikh Punjab village. . . . Village life, I have come to believe, is not
> only vital in itself, but the basis of all civilized behavior, including our
> own.[122]

Enlightenment individualism underscored the rights of the humble singular in a social order dominated by monarchical privilege and brute force.
But it simultaneously isolated facts from values. Communitarian ethics fills
the vacuum that the eighteenth century created with this rupture; it draws
us toward commitments impossible under the old regime. The contemporary age, supercharged with information, has become fragmented by
linguistic games. The poststructuralists contend that relationships between
signifier and signified are no longer trustworthy. Forms of representation
flash through our experience like a remote control grazing cable television.
For Jacques Derrida, modern discourse is an arbitrary system of differences, of oppositions and conventions; language is an unending series of
significations allowing "reified dogmas" and "official political codes" to
govern human existence.[123] Communitarian ethics likewise laments the
inauthenticity and power mongering of today's mass-mediated narratives.
But is deconstruction our exclusive option? Only academic totalitarianism
plucks from the dark sky those stars by which humans of various rank and
culture claim to navigate their journey. In a gloss on Rorty, the Enlightenment dream that liberalism can be rationalized or scientized has failed,
but we must maintain the expectancy that it can be poeticized.[124] While
deploring the unconscionable abuse and neglect, the glimmers of hope
since Samuel Ringgold Ward compel us to continue calling for narratives
that nurture civic transformation.[125]

5

Organizational Culture

A hundred sins belong to journalists alone. Sexist and racist comments are wrong. Exploiting the privacy of grief-stricken parents is inexcusable. Misquoting a speech or incorrectly identifying a police officer is wretched practice. If individual reporters "are ignorant, naive, lazy, sloppy, cowardly, vain, over-ambitious, prejudiced, dishonest, greedy—whatever professional faults derive from such failings are their own. Some of them will soon be fired by a watchful editor."[1] These personal failures send shock waves through the news craft as a whole. Female and black journalists were stung by the Janet Cooke caper. A legal counsel who provides incompetent or shady advice besmirches other lawyers assigned to news organizations. Jingoistic sportswriters degrade their colleagues. Unfortunately, others suffer for the malfeasance of a few.

But a preoccupation with individual shortcomings diverts our attention in news media ethics from institutional accountability. Claude-Jean Bertrand of the University of Paris properly condemns individualistic ethics as "largely irrelevant"—in fact, as "perhaps unwittingly . . . a cover-up for what is most seriously wrong about American media." Or, stated in different terms, "can anyone, even for a second, dream of comparing them [individual violations] with corporate behavior" and with media policy that create serious vacuums in coverage and long-term distortions in our news judgment?[2]

A reporter who stereotypes an urban resident is unethical. On the other hand, "consider the hundreds of media companies which for years ignored disease and famine in Africa because they would not spend the money to maintain correspondents in that part of the world and because their only purpose . . . is not to serve but to please customers, who happen not to be interested in the Third World."[3]

Journalists who fail to find a second source and then lie about it to their supervisors are acting immorally; but what about a local television station that opts for increased revenues rather than an additional reporter to cover local affairs? Reporters who accept freebies violate a commonly accepted convention; but what of local media that omit important disclosures about the area's biggest employer or their heavy advertisers?

The communitarian model is a social ethics that cuts deeply into organizational structures and processes. As a distinctive alternative to descriptive ethics rooted in individual autonomy, communitarianism escapes Bertrand's complaint. It enables us to examine meticulously the degree to which institutions are accountable. A theory of persons-in-community does not obliterate specific human choices, obviously; but it recognizes that—except for a rare freelancer or independent—journalists are members of an institutional framework. A nontrivial ethics, therefore, centers primarily on media accountability systems.

The communitarian journalism developed in this chapter assumes a generic institutional mosaic. Organizational culture has identifiable features, whether the particular forms are commercial corporations, a public-broadcasting unit, individually owned local newspapers, or multinational conglomerates such as Capital Cities Communications. Of course, a television station operated by a state university on a nonprofit basis differs enormously from the New York Times Corporation, with profits of $160 million annually, gross revenues over $100 billion, a menagerie of weeklies, magazines, two dozen daily newspapers, broadcast outlets, a cable system, and investments in three Canadian newsprint companies. A convincing social ethics ought to specify the distinctive features among such a range of media institutions while also identifying the commonalities of organizational forms. Otherwise one is led to such facile conclusions as "Colossal media are inherently evil and micro media righteous," or "Public media are naturally sound and commercial media unacceptable," or "Inkpot and feather media are appropriate and technological sophistication, by definition, is inappropriate." As explained below, large-scale bureaucracies create urgent ethical conundrums, but our concern across the board is an organizational culture integrated by mutuality and oriented in its policies, workplace environment, and infrastructure toward the goal of civic transformation. Media systems as lighthouse and power plant are but two examples of institutional forms shaped by communitarian principles.

Two Models

The lighthouse paradigm situates the public's voice in a vehicle of common expression for purposes of exposition, persuasion, humor, bonding, economic redistribution, and group survival. The *Lakota Times,* which provides specialized information for the Native American "family," is an illustration. Hundreds of magazines published in the First and Third Worlds serve similar functions of collective identity and prophetic expression to the wider culture. The *Provincial Freeman* reminded American abolitionists of the heart of their cause. The sixteenth-century Marprelate tracts challenged established church authority in Britain, all the while generating profound instincts for political and theological discourse among a disparate, passionate network of people who looked to an open future and saw distant change in a long stream of words.[4] Like an offshore lighthouse, newspapers or broadcast stations shaped by communitarianism call attention to peripheral and otherwise hidden stories; from their small island the beam nurtures pluralism, by serving the common interests of all through the special interests of a few.

In the lighthouse model, media access encourages the silent to speak; in mutual service a single voice becomes the glint of resolution made courageous in company. The widespread use of videotape by amateur newspeople is now credited with raising First World consciousness concerning the *intifada* movement in the areas occupied by Israel. Audiocassettes, Polaroid photos, and handwritten diaries brought from Tiananmen Square into the countryside and beyond China's borders prevented a government hammerlock on this revolutionary news event. Such pluralism is a hundred flowers blooming, a thousand points of light, Ivan Illich's "tools of conviviality," a region brought to alert over shoreline spoliation or city council patronage. *McClure's* was no friend of big business as the Rockefeller family engineered its new public image in the 1900s. The *Christian Century* was dismissed as "curious" when it called for a Disinterested Party to challenge a political system hellbent on polarized special interests. But such campaigns are an essential part of a pluralist cacophony. They empower by peeling away the assumptions of majoritarian efficiency, by coalescing new minorities in a dynamic reconfiguration of the just and the good.

The power plant, our second institutional paradigm, reflects changes that reshaped American mass media in the nineteenth century. Like a central generating plant dispersing energy to light a million bulbs, a paper or station in the communitarian mode becomes a public forum for the widest spectrum of debate about civic transformation. Multicultural news replaces a mythologized unicultural news as the major media recognize the diversities of their coverage zone. Like the highly politicized and segmented news sheets that gave way to the all-purpose newspaper in the nineteenth century, sponsored broadcast programming surrendered to network-produced entertainment sandwiched by advertisements in the twentieth. Instead of presenting partisan news, large-circulation media printed the news most relevant to the widest appetites of major consumer segments. Regional and national coverage edged out local reporting.

But community newspapers filled the vacuum, and large media saw enough of their clientele spin off to begin—aggressively in the last fifteen years—recovering the pluralism they had lost, by printing and broadcasting local news once again. And then some of the best news organizations brought on both liberal and conservative editorialists. Even the alleged lightweight of national media, Gannett's *USA Today,* typically runs opposing viewpoints on the editorial page. The public square where politicians once bellowed high and fluent oratory has become in exemplary cases a page of heat and light read on a subway or in a waiting room. The accents of a city's people shape the front page and enable them to wrestle with issues of social justice on their home turf.

Tremors of this power-plant paradigm are felt in Milton's spirited call to "set open" the temple of Janus with his two controvertible faces in a free marketplace of ideas.[5] It embraces Holmes's dissent in *Abrams,* his stirring plea "to believe even more than they believe the very foundations of their own conduct that the ultimate good desired is better reached by free trade in ideas."[6] It finds expression in the Supreme Court's "preferred position" theory of the First Amendment, under which government prior restraint must bear the "heavy burden" of demonstrating some compelling national interest before speech may be legally proscribed. It echoes the New Testament's assurance that "the truth shall set you free." It took prophetic form in the 1960s when courageous television crews ensured that the Bull Connors terrorizing the land were shamed into silence by Martin Luther King's eloquent appeal for justice to roll down like a mighty river.

And on occasion, an independent producer breaks into gargantuan media structures and exploits them as an antiestablishment tool. In such unpredictable fashion, for example, American moviegoers were rocked with *Roger and Me,* a "hit" documentary that told the story of auto workers in Flint, Michigan. Warner Films was a complicitor with Michael Moore in putting corporate leaders at the viewers' mercy; executives emerged cinematically who worried over the fate of investors but were relatively indifferent to the devastating consequences of plant closings on local mortgage companies, real-estate values, schools, and the families who depended on General Motors paychecks. Roger Smith, then the president of GM, could not have received a more scathing public rebuke had all the nation's news correspondents descended on Detroit in frontal assault. A first-time filmmaker's artistry—and tenacity—told the story, albeit clumsily and with artistic license. Sometimes even contrary to company policy or against their better judgment, newspapers, magazines, radio, and local television force disclosure, forge consent, publicize a group's aspirations, and move talk around the public square like a thread weaving through fabric.

While disputants compete in the paradigm of the power plant, its spirit is not a relativist potpourri of many vegetables in simmering stew. Nor is it the skepticism which insists that only questions are important, never their answer. When Dietrich Bonhoeffer refused to sign on as a Nazi propagandist in 1940—or even to petition for an exemption—the Reich Chamber of Literature forbade him to publish any kind of written work.[7] We rightly regard Bonhoeffer's stubbornness as courage, but quickly err in believing any "signing on" to be inherently restrictive and irresponsible, as if adhering to a string of words not followed by a question mark is to relinquish intellectual freedom. Promoting alternative views on op-ed pages does not imply that no truth is worth commitment. This paradigm is not the journalistic equivalent of moral skepticism. Its epistemology allows for growth and change as a full range of activist voices sound their appeals and extol their allegiances to audiences of equally active listener-respondents.

Communitarianism is the precise opposite of the philosophy behind a two-page advertisement in *Time*'s right-to-die issue. Through Maharishi's Master Plan, the ad promises, any national government can conduct its business "with the same silent perfection with which the government of nature governs the universe." Unfortunately for these mystics, silence does not address and resolve public problems such as health-care delivery, sewage treatment, or property taxes that force many older citizens to abandon their homes. It should come as no surprise that the Master Plan, unworkable in the abstract, depends on a "coherence-creating group . . . which will enliven the unified field in national consciousness."[8] Our argument is that sound, not silence, creates democratic pluralism, that a full range of opinion outstrips the machinations of a silent elite. Accordingly, Adrienne Rich notes that "vital texts" have begun to turn the wordless, negated experience of women into an affirmation "pursued in language."[9]

Public policy notwithstanding, our sense of purposefulness—the "meaning of our lives," as a previous era might have phrased it—achieves some clarity and escapes the Nietzschean loss of the "whole horizon" only through speaking and listening. Charles Taylor reminds us that "we find the sense of life through articulating it."[10] Neither silence nor regimented doctrine assures the self that within human reach are commitments based on secure responses to the "whys" of existence. The quest for meaning does not require a vigorous, pluralistic press; but such a press fosters the questions and vents the answers in such a fashion as to prevent the mind from collapsing on its private doubts.

Reformers question which paradigm—narrowcasting or broadcasting, lighthouse or power plant—represents organizational accountability. Which achieves genuine pluralism? Which provides a product geared to relatively powerless classes of people while respecting the rights of those who already use and control information media? Which arises from a workplace marked by mutuality? Which paradigm provides constructions of reality and cultural self-awareness that the institution itself can embrace as accurate, fair, and forceful? Which avoids paternalism? Which guards against the colonization of opinion?

No organization achieves either intimacy or an effective working style without enabling the pathos of dependency, identity, power, and inclusion to percolate through the system. Certainly, media institutions at the center of the reforming process ought to be self-conscious about the dynamics by which groups within the organization generate a culture. This self-awareness should lead to the aggressive maturation of either the lighthouse or the power-plant model. But like institutions generally, the press seldom follows a prescribed outline. The challenge is to understand how organizations change, how they process reform, and why mutuality offers the reformer a theoretical advance with procedural implications.

The Oakland *Tribune* has eliminated gender and race discrimination in its hiring practices. The Berkshire *Eagle* investigates consumer complaints against local automobile dealers even though it suffers huge losses in advertising revenue. Since the days of Edward R. Murrow's "Harvest of Shame," public and commercial television have periodically invested heavily in news features on social injustice. How can such instances of institutional integrity become the rule rather than the exception? Outlined below is a series of important commitments that arise out of communitarian ethics—first establishing corporate entities as moral agents bound to mutuality, and then rewriting the institution's discourse, organizing its workplace, and diffusing its bureaucracy accordingly.

Corporate Moral Agency

Morally speaking, media organizations are unusual entities:

> A judge once bemoaned that they have "no pants to kick or soul to damn," and concluded, "by God, they ought to have both." Unlike a real person, the corporation has no conscience to keep it awake all night, no emotions for the psychiatrist to analyze, and no body to be thrown into jail. It is a *persona ficta,* and its fictional nature, coupled with remarkable down-to-earth power, makes it a thoroughly puzzling object of moral understanding.[11]

Obviously, institutions are more than impersonal machines. They do resemble a complicated package of gears, engines, and levers; but like people, corporations write contracts, meet deadlines, take precautions, act incompetently, issue reports, pay taxes, own property, and incur financial liability.

But is an opposite view sustainable? Are organizations equivalent to the persons who embody them? Since corporations act intentionally, the moral-person theory concludes, "Corporations can be full-fledged moral persons and have whatever privileges, rights, and duties as are, in the normal course of affairs, accorded to moral persons."[12] However, while it is plausible to draw suggestive parallels between corporations and persons, no one argues that institutions should register for the draft or should be entitled to Social Security benefits. As Thomas Donaldson concludes, "Can corporations have a right to worship as they please? To pursue happiness? [They] fail to qualify as moral persons . . . in any literal sense of that term."[13]

The solution to the machine–person dichotomy is the rational-agent model, which considers the corporation a moral agent, but not a moral person. Institutions use moral reasoning in their organizational decision making, but that does not entail their having all dimensions of personal morality, such as pleasure and guilt. Kenneth Goodpaster and John Matthews establish the moral-agency argument by asking whether a corporation has a conscience. They begin by explaining that responsibility has three meanings. One is causal; an example is Joseph Pulitzer's responsibility for creating the School of Journalism at Columbia University. Another meaning associates rules with social roles: lawyers are responsible to their clients and reporters to their sources. The third involves decision making that assumes persons to be trustworthy and reliable. Goodpaster and Matthews focus on this third notion of responsibility as the locus of moral reasoning.[14]

The two traits of moral reasoning are rationality and respect, rationality referring to the capacity for clear deliberation and careful implementation of decisions, and respect entailing empathy for others. Those individuals who exercise rationality and respect are morally responsible. By analogy, or extension, those institutions whose planning, policy, and performance are based on rationality and respect can also be said to be morally responsible. That is, moral responsibility is the province of corporations as well as individuals. Because corporations are able to exercise rationality and respect, they are, like individual persons, moral agents accountable for their actions.

Corporate decisions arise from a loose combination of internal power centers, although they are normally coordinated by a leadership team and formalized by standard operating procedures. Moreover, in order to qualify as moral decision making above the level of machine operations, the process must involve a capacity for structuring the very policies that guide rational action. Obviously, some institutions are so thoroughly fragmented or so imprisoned by technicalities that they are analogous to sick or insane persons who cannot tell right from wrong. But in the very definition of institutional structure is the capacity for recognizable, rational agency that never functions perfectly but meets Goodpaster and Matthews's criteria and therefore confers accountability. Institutions assume the burdens and benefits of morality and develop something akin to consciences.[15] As moral agents, they resemble formally the legal notion that corporations are artificial persons, or juristic beings, created as such by the law in order to assign responsibility to corporate activity.[16]

Objections to this view typically locate ethics in a system outside the institution. Milton Friedman, for instance, argues that businesses are responsible only for making profits and obeying laws. Given the sanctity of voluntary agreements—in this case, between management and the stockholders who own the company—employers are duty-bound to maximize earnings. The common good will result not from conscious corporate policies—corporations are ill-designed for achieving social justice anyhow—but through the checks and balances of unbridled competition in the marketplace.[17] John Kenneth Galbraith takes a different systemic stance by arguing that the locus of ethics resides in laws and governmental policies. Whether through the invisible hand of corporate competition or through deliberate regulation by government, both approaches situate ethics exterior to businesses themselves.

Despite the importance of the marketplace and the government, economic theories that locate ethics outside the corporation exaggerate the differences between individuals and institutions, and they permit a double standard between one's private and nine-to-five values and behavior. Many of the current popular portraits of journalists are like Charles Dickinson's novel, *Rumor Has It;*[18] they reflect a gentle-at-home, cutthroat-at-work dichotomy, a Jekyll and Hyde split made right because each style of behavior is viewed as appropriate to the setting. Furthermore, an institution cannot choose not to establish policies with ethical bearings because all activity has moral dimensions. As Goodpaster and Matthews observe, "The issue in the end is not whether corporations (and other organizations) should be 'unleashed' to exert moral force in our society but rather how critically and self-consciously they should choose to do so."[19]

Of course, defending a meaningful sense of corporate moral agency involves complicated issues in organizational theory. The dominant tradition has been functionalist in character. With a positivist epistemology and a determinist view of human nature, functionalism has employed elegant statistical strategies for understanding organizational processes. Prediction and control of projected outcomes are sought by carefully calibrating the relevant variables and testing all conceivable hypotheses. Mainstream functionalism seeks that technical knowledge which enables institutions to operate efficiently, and success depends on creating organizational models that generate measurable effects stipulated by managers and consultants.

However, functionalism generally presumes a linear theory of communication, which our dialogic approach discredits as reductionistic and unsophisticated.[20] The emphasis in communitarian ethics on mutuality and empowerment is radically opposed to the prediction and control motifs in mainstream organizational theory and research. And the Enlightenment underpinnings of the latter are at odds with the communitarian model.

Therefore, in order to specify the logic and content of institutional accountability in terms of communitarian ethics, we adopt an organizational-culture framework instead.[21]

Organizations are cultures in the sense that their members engage in producing a shared organizational reality. Through organizational symbolism—myths, awards, stories, rites, policy statements, logos, legends, architecture—an institution's practice is made "intersubjectively meaningful."[22] While traditional research investigates sending and receiving networks to make information flows more effective, communication in the cultural paradigm emphasizes the construction and reproduction of symbolic meaning systems. "Thus communication is not just another organizational activity that occurs inside an organization; rather it *creates* and *recreates* the social structure that makes organization."[23] Organizations, therefore, manifest human consciousness. They are visible expressions of world views, organized understandings "of what constitutes adequate knowledge and legitimate activity."[24] And the metaphors for interpreting these shared beliefs derive from the humanities rather than the natural sciences—that is, "more and more from the contrivances of cultural performance than from those of physical manipulation—from theater, painting, grammar, literature, law, play."[25]

This position is dubbed "cultural purism," since organizations are viewed as cultures having no independent existence outside the shared meaning systems that constitute them.[26] But many of the evocations of culture in the organizational literature have not made a decisive break with functionalism, and culture becomes an instrument of manipulation.[27] Given the current unrest in the human sciences and today's turbulent economic conditions, culture has gained notoriety in *Business Week, Fortune,* and popular trade books as a tool of aggressive management. Through ceremonies, parties, and executive-led rallies, corporate loyalty is supposedly fostered, office drudgery masked, absenteeism reduced, and disgruntled employees pacified. Symbolic devices, in other words, offer tantalizing possibilities for mobilizing the organization's membership.

These petite versions of cultural pragmatism are as foreign to our communitarian model as is functionalism. However, what emerges in the following discussion is not middle-of-the-road cultural purism, either. As Dennis Mumby argues correctly, cultural strategies tend "by and large to be descriptive, often lacking a critical element." The "deep structures of power that define and solidify" organizations are typically ignored. In that light, what unfolds in the paragraphs below is "a perspective on organizations that stays true to the cultural approach (with its focus on interpretive practices), but that broadens its scope to recognize the pervasive effect of ideology and power on the production of organizational realities."[28]

Thus organizational discourse not only is reenacted in naturalistic settings, but is viewed as representing various disputes over terrain and authority among units of the organization. The workplace is not merely cast up in symbolic form, but is the site for fundamental human struggles over the meaning of vocation. And the institutional infrastructure—particularly its technological dimension—is stitched into the conceptual whole. It cannot be ignored in a cultural analysis or dispatched to political economists. However, in order to formulate his critical edge, Mumby appeals to contemporary social thought—Habermas, Althusser, and Giddens, for example. In contrast, our critical posture—with its emancipatory and transformative impulses—derives from a normative communitarianism centered in mutuality.

Cultural theorists are fond of bandying about this apocryphal artifact from baseball: "Three umpires disagreed about the task of calling balls and strikes. The first one said, 'I calls them as they is.' The second one said, 'I calls them as I sees them.' The third and cleverest umpire said, 'They ain't nothin' till I calls them.' "[29] The shrewd third umpire recognizes that language plays a critical role in creating reality. Calling a strike does not merely label an objective event; the umpire's naming connects a player's action with that overall pattern of meanings known as baseball. J. B. Thompson is correct in saying that interpretive theory has highlighted the symbolic construction of sociohistorical reality, while neglecting the role of language in repression, deformation, subterfuge, and distortion.[30] Yet ideological masking is impossible except on the presumption that humans continually enact and re-create their realities just like umpires do. This is what we mean by time-and-space existence, and institutions create themselves in similar fashion. In that sense, organizations, by definition, are also intermeshed value systems accountable as moral agents. Dominant power interests do not bring organizations into being *de novo,* but coerce, filter, and redirect an inescapable process for antihuman ends. Stuart Hall makes the same distinction from a different direction: "It does not follow that because all practices are . . . inscribed by ideology, all practices are *nothing but* ideology."[31] Thus Goodpaster and Matthews are correct in insisting on an accountable motif for institutions, defined by what they call reason and respect. It would be nonsense for umpires to deny accountability for their decisions, and likewise for humans in everyday life—and for corporations.

Organizational Discourse

A rich notion of accountability will resonate in an organization's consciousness only through its discourse. Presuming that institutions constitute their reality through language, narrative forms enable organizations to structure themselves almost *ad infinitum*—toward laissez-faire freedom, collegiality, profit, responsibility, innovation, quality products, public service, civic transformation, or whatever. Because organizational language legitimates particular philosophies of life while excluding others, discourse systems are a primary resource for ensuring that media institutions become compatible with communitarianism. Three discursive forms—company stories, codes of ethics, and self-criticism—are especially powerful vehicles for defining an institution's moral contours.

Company Stories

The narratives that dominate institutional memory encapsulate a company's value system and create its pattern of ethical compliance or deviance. Such moral dramas encapsulate organizational culture. They "punctuate and sequence events in such a way as to privilege a certain interpretation of the world"; they represent "a signification system" that accents "certain meaning formations and hence interests over others."[32] And such narratives are always moral dramas—they make a point, they interpret events in terms of a moral imperative, they animate an ideal. "Where narrativity is present, we can be sure that morality or a moralizing impulse is present too."[33]

Imagine how the legend of David Begelman circulates around the hallways and banquet rooms of Columbia Pictures. Begelman served as a successful senior executive vice president at Columbia whose latest project, the Spielberg blockbuster *Close Encounters of the Third Kind,* was reaping huge dividends. Begelman was riding the crest, yet for reasons he later explained as "neurotic displays of self-destructiveness," he sought a financial windfall through forgery and overbilling. Hoist on his own petard, Begelman took a leave of absence, repaid his debt to Columbia, and weathered a state's attorney's investigation.

Meanwhile, in Columbia's boardroom, drama of a moral kind was unfolding over how the company should treat its rehabilitated colleague. Company president Alan Hirschfield took a legalistic approach. "Corporate officers who intentionally hurt the company must be released."[34] But firing a mogul who dipped for relatively small change—and that after his apology and repayment—seemed indecent and inhumane to board member Herbert Allen. "This is not a moral issue," he said. "It's a story of a breakdown. And since when is a breakdown immoral? After three months of investigation, I don't think we found one fact that Begelman materially hurt the shareholders of this company." Still another board member, and the company's largest single shareholder, echoed the caring theme when he said, "If I thought Begelman was a thief, I wouldn't have him around Columbia. We're not defending a thief but a sick man who did some stupid things . . . who had psychological problems that have now been corrected."

All the while, Hirschfield maintained, "The whole business showed a lack of respect for authority, for values, for the company. It was 'public be damned, shareholders be damned, S.E.C. be damned.' " Hirschfield obviously considered a recovery of values through law to be the correct corporate response, but in an ironic Shakespearean twist, he was ousted by a board that could not abide his hard line, and Begelman was retained in a new position and at a higher salary. The conflict of values was resolved well enough to allow this organizational event to be represented in oral form among employees in the coffee shop and on ritual occasions such as Begelman's retirement.

Obviously, the board attempted to fix the meaning around compassion—a company's willingness to forgive personnel who apologize and make restitution. But even as it moralized the Begelman story in terms of corporate humanity, the board reaffirmed its ideology of profit. Begelman was cast in heroic proportions as the genius for blockbuster cinema. The moral of the story was that Columbia protects money-making executives, not employees on every level. This company narrative masked incompetent board supervision, a greedy financial climate, and ethical callousness.

However, organizational narrative is a complicated phenomenon. As Paul Ricoeur has contended, all discourse systems carry a "surplus of meaning."[35] Cynical workers, as a matter of fact, might tell the Begelman story in conjunction with its opposite—for example, how a custodian was fired without notice or hearing on suspicion of stealing the company's pencils. Any analysis, to be exhaustive, must recount all the social contexts in which organizational narratives are told. Our point here is that although all forms of signification have multiple meanings, leaders who shape organizational reality in terms of their own agendas understand the powerful character of a company's discourse.

A classic story out of another communications company, IBM, illustrates further that narratives are as central to understanding organizational life as are its products, employee files, or bank accounts. Apparently a young female security guard once stopped Thomas Watson, Jr., IBM's chairman, from entering a security room without proper identification. Watson silenced his entourage of white-shirted engineers and waited patiently at the doorway until an aide returned with a badge.

The story crystallizes IBM's commitment to rules: no one is above company policies. The story is easier to remember than arid corporate directives. This moral drama has impact because of the immense disproportion in social status between the actors. And in its retelling, it exalts Watson's heroic gentlemanliness rather than exposing him as the lawgiver who extracts strict obedience to maximize efficiency and to maintain IBM's core rules about company secrecy in a technological race with competitors for its market share. Meanwhile, the male-dominated corporate structure remains intact and unexamined.[36]

Regrettably, rather than these moral dramas enabling critical self-reflection, empirical studies indicate that typically the company's intention coalesces with employee understanding. Given the concurrence-seeking tendency that social psychologist Irving Janis identified in *Victims of Group Think,* organizational narrative ordinarily becomes framed in similar terms from top to bottom. In principle, all linguistic constructions have multiple meanings, but in cohesive cultures they tend to fall into a unified semantic field. Organization members retell the narratives with pride and commitment. Jacques Ellul despairs that the propagandized generally welcome it. And Antonio Gramsci argues that hegemony succeeds because subordinates actively reiterate the world view of elites.

Codes of Ethics

Codes of ethics serve a systematic purpose in creating an organizational conscience. Self-regulation has long stood as the only control mechanism forthrightly defended within the news enterprise itself. And the press's fixation on negative freedom continues to hinder it from intelligently considering all inside mechanisms for increasing responsibility. But, with reservations, various broadcasting and newspaper companies are now adopting codes at a mushrooming pace—though frequently for the misguided reason that they supposedly enhance press credibility. Too often, codes serve as a public-relations tool, like paint over bad plaster. And a few companies still refuse to put implicit codes into print, ostensibly because they want to foreclose the possibility of plaintiffs using those codes as evidence of negligence; intrinsically there is resistance to the democratizing impulse that would likely result from published guidelines.

Although a code of ethics alone cannot improve corporate conduct, M. Cash Mathews insists that it can be an effective component in a broad strategy to institutionalize ethical behavior.[37] This broad strategy requires wholesale institutional commitment; a code of ethics that is ancillary will be as useful as a sixth toe or a second appendix. One structural modification would be a company ethics committee, a sort of collective ombudsperson, with authority to examine all corporate operations. It would be composed of professionals representing all sectors of the organization: editors, reporters, photographers, clerical staff, advertising salespersons. In order to help gain breadth and critique, it is also imperative that moral philosophers be included from outside the company. Both the *Philadelphia Inquirer* and the *Louisville Courier-Journal* have experimented successfully with ethics coaches.

Such a task force could establish a binding code of ethics integral to daily corporate practice, arrange periodic ethics workshops, grapple with the ethical issues that employees raise, and reward those employees who contribute positively to the corporate culture. As Mathews suggests, the ethics committee would not only help to resolve ethical quandaries but also participate in corporate planning. In this way, ethics would be built into the institution, not just added as window dressing or afterthought. It would bring a company squarely to the point, raised by Taylor, that a moral framework is a condition of community. The supposition that otherwise responsible people can do without an explicit framework, and merely select from moral options on a case-by-case basis, Taylor regards as a denial of the possibility of individual identity. Are media corporations situated in a culture wherein they play a shaper's role? Then to deny a moral framework is to be both incomprehensible and pathological.[38]

A powerful company ethics committee could never be formed without the support of an upper management that is receptive to change. That is precisely Mathews's point: "Unless senior management supports the concern with ethics, there are not likely to be any organizational changes. Therefore, when outside professionals or consultants are used to hold ongoing workshops or to revise the written code of ethics, senior management needs to be fully supportive."[39] Codes of ethics are not rules to foist on the rank and file, with exemptions for the boardroom. An organization can self-consciously develop a code of ethics in which all parties participate and which—meeting the criterion of mutuality—is as binding on editors and publishers as on reporters. The mutuality model necessarily involves all workers in the interpretation and articulation of the professional values that govern their work. Just as codes of ethics are not handed down, enforcement of codes is not the lonely role of top managers exerting judicial power over their juniors. Codes are also not static documents with the unchanging sacredness of the Decalogue; revisions and reconsiderations become part of a media company's commitment to the future—a corporate investment in self-critical, responsible reporting.

Some great newspapers and broadcast units oppose written codes; others embrace them in elaborate detail. The former recognize the dynamic of rapidly changing moral contexts (and the persistent threat that codes can become effective tools for plaintiffs); the latter understand written codes as signifiers of shared culture.

On balance, the mutuality principle accords best with written codes of ethics and procedures regularly reviewed in a process open to everyone with an interest. Communities with explicit functions cannot be maintained unless they attach specific rebukes for failure to meet obligations. People cannot legitimately be called to account without a visible process that applies agreed-on principles to determine innocence or guilt. Written codes force corporate leaders to declare and explain themselves, and allow fair negotiation of claims. Surprises are less frequent and quixotic, enforcement more foreseeable, if codes are taken from the inscrutable reserves of managers' psyches and placed parsimoniously into a document that all can read and criticize. In the best settings, the document becomes a symbol of mutual trust born of the difficult process of repartee in a demanding profession noted for its suspicion of group coverup and collusion.

Even in small shops, written codes have the effect of building a tradition of respect for professional norms and even-handed fairness in dealing with unfriendly news and outside wolves. Editors of community newspapers from the Carolinas to Prudhoe Bay accept calls and requests that challenge news judgment and seek special treatment. Written codes of ethics provide moral continuity from call to call. Written codes widely discussed in a community make the arm-twisting of county politicos less of an embarrassment on either end of the phone call; the document serves as a third party around which discussion can proceed and, on occasion, a principled exception can be formulated. For Adolf Hitler, Idi Amin, and Al Capone, the case is shut. Ordinarily, the corporate conscience refuses to tolerate outright lies, breaking and entering, and physical assault. But frequently, the moral dimension is not obvious or the choices tragic. Everyday journalism in a complicated world often leaves newspeople with a forked tongue or a double mind. Media institutions are not an amalgamation of individuals making unfettered decisions; presuming autonomous action case by case inevitably results in minimalism. Modulating their responses in concert through a communal process sustained over time enables journalists to maintain a sense of center and periphery when concrete moral judgments must be made. Stations and papers that struggle through ongoing ethics committees with issues regarding coverage of suicides or rape victims, for example, guarantee higher-level responses at the crisis moment than when individual practitioners shoot from the hip.

Editors at the Minneapolis *Star-Tribune,* through reporter Lori Sturdevant, had committed the paper to concealing the name of the public-relations specialist who passed along a largely irrelevant tidbit of information on the Democratic Farmer Labor party's candidate for lieutenant governor. The promise of confidentiality had been made without knowledge that Dan Cohen, the PR man, was a paid Republican adviser. Now the informant's political motives were clear, and under other conditions would be included in the story. No corporate policy covered this twist of events. Do the editors overrule the reporter's confidentiality pledge, or stay with a promise that amounts to a tacit admission of being fooled by a media-slick pro? The *Star-Tribune* decision is widely known, and still strongly debated. Yet through the costly litigation that followed (Cohen sued for breach of contract), the policy at this major newspaper grew clearer, sharper, and more morally certain: promises made will be kept. This was good news to future news sources who otherwise could hardly hope to predict what might become of an agreement as it passed up and down the paper's hierarchy. Moreover, promises will be made with the presumption of good-faith disclosure on the part of sources and with the approval of management. This was good news for reporters, whose integrity is injured whenever their pledge is compromised post facto, and who should not conduct the business of news gathering as autonomous investigators unattached to a corporate mission. A codeless dilemma, mishandled and costly, has given birth to a codified corporate resolution that honors the veracity of oral agreements in the best tradition of the courageous Fourth Estate.

The issue is not codes or no codes, but the type of codes news organizations adopt. Hortatory codes insisting that journalists tell the truth, promote justice, act honorably, and keep faith with their readers are vacuous rhetoric. Only explicit, practical, itemized, and carefully nuanced codes establish a company mystique while decreasing quandaries and resisting flagrant misjudgments. The *Washington Post,* for example, is uncompromising about plagiarism: "Attribution of material from other newspapers and other media must be total. Plagiarism is one of journalism's unforgivable sins." The *Louisville Courier-Journal* refuses all advertisements that "attack, criticize, or cast reflection on any individual, race, religion or institution." CBS has explicit news standards for covering "Demonstrations, Riots, and Other Civil Disturbances." The Society of Professional Journalists/Sigma Delta Chi code has helped make freebies outmoded: "Nothing of value shall be accepted." The *Roanoke* [Virginia] *Times–World News* has exacting guidelines regarding anonymous sources.

However, even when institutional codes are generated through democratic participation and are contoured with finesse, conceiving of them as rules is counterproductive. This traditional perspective is entrenched in the functionalism paradigm; we tend to think that a panoply of guidelines improves a company's productivity if obeyed automatically. In fact, professional ethics generally adheres to mainstream organizational theory, conceiving of ethics in rule-oriented terms. When facing ethical dilemmas, we tend to believe, right action depends on following prescriptions.

However, as Karen Labacqz has convincingly argued, situation ethics has put all such rule morality in jeopardy. Rules are never independent of particulars. "Rules take situations seriously and definitions of situations already incorporate moral notions."[40] And organizational-culture theory also refuses to reduce linguistic structures (well-polished ethical tenets, for example) to information strings in the imperative mood. Instead, codes of ethics crafted in mutuality are understood to stimulate the moral imagination. Codes keep supple the organizational conscience. They do not merely represent organizational values, but constitute them. Since Aristotle, discernment has been recognized as the axis around which morality revolves. Ethical codes orient our discernment constructively, but that relationship is something other than a fail-safe, mechanistic rule system. Since the formulations of Lawrence Kohlberg and Carol Gilligan, rules have been seen as merely conventional means of doing and conceiving ethics.[41] Moral-development literature insists that persons seeking wholeness and maturity rise above the implicit utilitarianism of rule-keeping to develop the conscience of virtuous persons (thus does Aristotle emerge in modern ethical theory). To follow rules blindly is to surrender moral impulse; to achieve consensual guidelines based on the common reflections of informed conscience, alert to appropriate tradition and animated by the hope for others' happiness, is to find the echo of the ancients in the preachments of contemporary theory.

Media Criticism

During the 1940s, George Seldes's newsletter *In fact* provided the first regular media criticism by an insider.[42] A. J. Liebling's articles on "The Wayward Press" for the *New Yorker* were shrewd and witty; they set the standard for internal critique.[43] Irving F. Stone became a legend by attacking the feeble ways in which the news media cover politics. Their veteran status has made some contemporary journalists respected critics as well: James Reston, Nicholas von Hoffman, Garry Wills, Tom Wicker, and increasingly Walter Cronkite in attacking Lawrence Tisch's stewardship of CBS News. David Shaw of the *Los Angeles Times* is an example of full-time media critics employed by newspapers and TV stations. "Sixty Minutes" has on occasion savaged its own network and its competitors for gaffes or negligence or counterproductive policies. *Lies of our Times* represents an ambitious monthly attempt to correct the record. Periodicals of politics and opinion—*The Nation, National Review, The New Republic, Harper's,* and *The Atlantic*—are sometimes concerned with the press's structure and performance. However, when judged in terms of the importance of prophetic discourse, self-criticism is languid. Magazines snipe at newspapers, and a few newspapers shoot back; both expose the hypocrisies and warts of mainstream television. Anecdotal criticism usually seems unfair and merely invites counter-examples.

Journalism reviews as a genre are designed to provide less erratic and bolder media criticism. They bring underreported and omitted news to public consciousness and undermine convenient mythologies. Some flourished in the 1960s, dying of exhaustion after the Vietnam war. The *Chicago Journalism Review* emerged in the aftermath of the violent 1968 Democratic National Convention. According to reporter Ron Dorfman, "When the convention was over and the national press had left town, local editors proceeded, deliberately and shamelessly, to rewrite history in an effort to patch up Chicago's reputation as 'the city that works.' "[44] Outraged reporters organized their rebuttal by initiating the *Chicago Journalism Review* (1968–1975), stimulating similar efforts, staffed by working journalists, across the United States: *Philadelphia Journalism Review* (1971–1974), *Hawaii Journalism Review* (1971–1973), *Review of Southern California Journalism* (1971–1975), *Buncombe: A Review of Baltimore Journalism* (1977), and *The Unsatisfied Man: A Review of Colorado Journalism* (1970–1974).[45] Two originated with universities: the *Montana Journalism Review* (1958–1979) and the *Columbia Journalism Review* (founded in 1961). The *St. Louis Journalism Review* resulted from one man's vision, in the tradition of single-editor reviews (Seldes, Liebling, and Stone). When he launched it in 1970, Charles L. Klotzer understood the media's power in controlling what the people know and influencing social reform.

> Collaborating with reporters to establish a watchdog over the media would not only establish peer review of the print and broadcast industry, but would also propel social consciousness and responsibility into the heart of decision-making. . . . Traditionally, reporters do all their grumbling to each other, lamenting the sins of their editors or colleagues. With *SJR,* they could express themselves publicly or, if necessary, anonymously, and know that their comments will be circulated and read not only by their peers, but also by the public at large.[46]

Columbia Journalism Review is currently the most distinguished veteran, second only to *Editor & Publisher* in the percentage of readership among news professionals (56 percent to 63 percent, respectively). The *Washington Journalism Review* boasts a comparatively high readership also (43 percent), while the *Nieman Reports* is more respected than diligently read.[47] But none of these survivors has gained as broad a public audience as *MORE* (1971–1978) had. Of the forty or more reviews extant in the 1960s and 1970s, nearly all have disappeared, victims of volunteer staffs, a shortage of funds, and opposition from the mainstream press.

Signifying forms, such as moral dramas, codes of ethics, and professional critiques, have penultimate status (in Dietrich Bonhoeffer's sense). They inspire our moral awareness—or, in institutional language, they activate the company's conscience. But without a normative foundation, narratives, codes, and professional critiques are ingrained with daily pressures or encumbered by economic interests. They are surface-level formulations whose longevity and legitimacy presuppose deeper philosophical justification. The nearly intractable problem with moral dramas involves imbuing them with a critical dimension so that they empower rather than oppress.[48] When codes of ethics are issued by fiat and exempt upper management from their restrictions, they are not emancipatory either. But even participatory codes do not automatically guarantee ethical enlightenment. Media criticism risks being little more than arrogant posturing or self-serving moralism.

A finely honed normative ethics with cognitive substance remains a nonnegotiable priority. And the academy need not play an exclusive role. Reflective ombudspersons, news councils (national, state, and local), philosophically inclined and well-read news directors, research centers, and ethical specialists in newsrooms—these options prevent organizational culture from turning in on itself. Abstract theorizing is inappropriate for them, and metaethics is alien territory for their readers and viewers. However, these thoughtful insiders can contribute credibly to the necessary intellectual work, especially by integrating cognitive substance with the avalanche of practical dilemmas. Codification requires a reservoir of value theory and informed ethical inquiry.

Organizational discourse fired by a normative epicenter does not merely engage problems one by one. An institutional story or a prescription from ethical codes or a trenchant analysis is trivialized if used primarily to extinguish a fire or patch a rut in the company road. Moral dramas, codes, peer criticism, and principial claims—in their noble forms—actually fulfill the elusive role of establishing, through mutually formulated language, an organizational culture of integrity.

The Humanized Workplace

It would be absurd to suggest that newspapers or broadcast stations can escape internally the distrust, rivalry, and stark competitiveness that pervade a news company's external relations. Opposition between a newspaper's advertising and editorial offices is a corporate given. Animosity between reporters and time salespeople is fundamental. Nevertheless, mutuality as an alternative basis for news shop–neighborhood–city relations inevitably calls for enhanced community within the workplace.

Charles Conrad contrasts the communication climates of the traditional organization with the human-relations type of organization.[49] The former are hierarchical and task-oriented, with job-related communication normally restricted to the chain of command. Only during periods of legitimate crisis would protocol give way to expediency in temporary organizational transmissions across command lines—a situation called the Fayol bridge, after the French industrialist who devised the pyramidal organizational chart.[50] But in normal times, employees are organized in platoons not unlike military units with routinized and specialized tasks; creative activities are accomplished at the top of the organization; written policies and guidelines represent criteria by which supervisors are held accountable for their unit's quota. These are efficient, formal, bureaucratic, and predictable work cultures.

The textbook on newspaper management was written by Robert Giles, a veteran news journalist with management experience in Detroit, Akron, and Rochester, New York. His *Newsroom Management* is a compendium of management theories and journalistic applications. Giles journeys from the celebrated humanist Abraham Maslow to the simplistic yet helpful distinction between theories X and Y. But his journey is no potpourri; Giles remains committed to a pyramidal management structure. "In a newspaper company, power is centralized at the top. Information and authority flow downward," he asserts on page 1.[51] There is room, certainly, for newspaper managers to learn the grace of supportive interpersonal skills (though the personal mentor Giles describes was hardly a soft touch) and the team sense that rides like a parasite on participatory management initiatives. But theory Y–based democratic newsroom governance does not permit editors to "abdicate the role of the boss" and use a common ballot rather than their own horse sense in making the final decision (which is the only one that counts).[52]

Giles writes descriptively for the most part. His tone emerges from the heart of the profession: his own experience in the Gannett organization and as a chief executive. His accommodation of participatory styles—perhaps a reflection of surveys that reveal how valuable shared decision making is to a reporter's sense of fulfillment, perhaps a response to the reporter power movement of the late 1960s and early 1970s—is only an adjustment to the *via traditionalis,* not a rethinking of the system. Giles's book is a monument to the resilience of the top–down approach to newspaper management: the "great editor" who has a 1990s "feel" for motivation and enjoys MBWA (management by walking about). "The idea of a majority of one is played out at many newspapers when the editorial board meets,"[53] and because that's the way it is, that's the way it ought to be.

On the surface, the mentality of journalists would seem to challenge this traditional model at every desk and terminal. The journalistic mind balks at militaristic regimentation, our instincts tell us. Yet such structures are not impossible to find, and occasionally they even attain mythic status. Chicago's City News Bureau was one such organization. A. A. Dornfeld's story of the CNB is filled with the green-eyeshades mythos, wherein university-bred journalism graduates learned the other side of the craft from Dornfeld himself, described by Mike Royko as the man with the klaghorn voice and the "bulging, merciless, angry, all-knowing" eye.[54]

But such shops and legendary editors are rare today. More common are the newsrooms typified by Conrad and clarified by Giles as the kind of organization that emerged from studies in the late 1920s at Western

Electric's Hawthorne factory near Cicero, Illinois. There Harvard psychologists determined that despite poor lighting and other work-site problems, workers were more efficient and felt more positive about work if supervisors listened to their concerns and responded in ways congruent with the mutuality model advanced throughout this book. Thus the human-relations movement was born in the workplace—or, more accurately, reborn.

It is taken for granted that human relations was a *sine qua non* of preindustrial guilds, that the efficiency of mass production brought on regimentation of work and labor, and that people are not tools and machines. The human-relations type of organization recognizes that communication and mutuality are nonnegotiable elements of a viable organizational culture. Conrad's theory builds on Rensis Likert's determinants of a productive organization:

1. Work groups (with high performance goals) led by supervisors who give specific attention to the human aspects of subordinates' problems.
2. Enthusiastic encouragement at all levels to attain reasonable goals.
3. Subordinates given substantial latitude to use their own creativity to achieve goals.
4. Shared decision-making processes.[55]

Less mythos attaches to this alternative schema, but the evidence of worker satisfaction and sustained professionalism makes a strong case for the imperative of mutuality.

Other recent scholarship in industrial management highlights a concern for mutuality at the work site. William Ouchi, for example, recommends that American organizations follow the Japanese model toward more "open and trusting" relations as a way to mitigate the inefficiency of fiercely competitive individualism. Advances in science and technology have created a human blind-side, and Ouchi claims that "involved workers are the key to increased productivity."[56] Marvin Harris's diatribe against bureaucracy and oligopoly urges a "decentralized configuration" to recover the irrigated, egalitarian society that might keep the future open to democracy. His version of the call to "consensus management" implores the creation of small-scale "profit-sharing work teams" producing sufficient surplus to pay for first-rate education and care services.[57] The thrust would be toward community newspapers challenging metro dailies and low-power television cutting into network share. David Smith urges that all corporations recognize the need for continuing education and human development. "The likelihood of profitably spending one's whole working life in a job that requires a fixed set of narrowly focused skills is now approaching zero."[58] Meaningful work requires a moral vision, a recovery of teleological direction to counter the modern angst that Charles Taylor has aptly described as fractured horizons.

Departments within companies compete for personnel, resources, and often for a piece of an expanding corporate vision. A tiny department content with its intimacy is often a winter coat forgotten in summer. In both large and small media companies, significant choices remain open to reporters and editors, models of corporate integration that distinguish work environments conceived of atomistically from those contoured by mutuality.

In contrast to contractarian individualism, a mutuality model offers at least three distinctives that are amenable to every grit and strain in the hard work of news gathering. We advocate no slack in the mission of news agencies to get significant material to readers in haste, no compromise with clarity of purpose, no swing to sensitivity at the price of accuracy. This alternative also avoids knee-jerk or pragmatic responses to ethical dilemmas. Its ground is normative theory and not marketplace contrivance.

The Editor Is First Among Equals

At a conference on ethics held at the Poynter Institute in St. Petersburg, Florida, the discussion around the fabled oak table in the second-floor conference room turned to coverage of survivors' grief at airports. Would you pursue grieving relatives who, in the moments after the bad news came to them, had sought privacy and refuge in the lavatory? Several reporters insisted on sensitivity: let people have a minute alone to accommodate their harsh new circumstances. But a Miami reporter dismissed all such weeping-willow reactions. An airline accident had occurred just a month before in her city, and in the mêlée at the airport, reporters had in fact put microphones and notepads up to the tear-streaked faces of people who had just been informed. "In my shop," she said, "if the editor says go, you'd best get into the john or whatever else, like it or not." The discussion halted and the room took on the quiet of a hurricane's aftermath. What is the point of further moral inquiry if the editor plays Massah and one's job depends on raw aggression? Some reporters claimed they would not do it: charity overcometh news deadlines. "You wouldn't work long in Miami," was her reply.

Steel-jawed management of that kind eventually produces a Don Craig, age thirty-one, salary $80,000, Chicago television anchor, burned out, quit. "I want to get off this merry-go-round," he explained,

> ... stop intruding on people's lives, stop doing stories on gays, divorce, rape, and the mob to spur ratings. ... I'd like to see the day come when you just cover the news and let the chips fall where they may in terms of ratings, recognition, personal popularity, and the rest. ... I wince at the

thought of waking up when I'm fifty and finding out I've spent my whole life in a newsroom and all the cynicism and superficiality that it sometimes stands for.[59]

Miami and Chicago are only two examples and Craig is hardly represent-ative of the tens of thousands in media professions who have refused to quit. Usually one has no alternative but to follow orders, but there needs to be strategic restlessness: company loyalty with an ongoing reflectiveness that leads to stalwart action. It is reductionist to believe that all orders must be obeyed on the penalty of being fired; in reporting there is, on balance, generous room for compromise.

The editor who orders reporters into danger and grief without respect-ing their on-site judgment thwarts growth toward mutuality. Likewise, the editor who gives no direction or seems constantly preoccupied has surren-dered the possibility of the strong mutuality that makes a newsroom more than the sum of its parts. The editor in dialogue with trusted colleagues can build a news team united on goals of justice, empowerment, and care for the voiceless. This model is rare, but its congruence with the human condition—personhood-in-community—makes it a model with normative obligations.

Owners, too, best contribute to the community not by standing apart or domineering, but by serving as examples in the workplace and by choos-ing personnel wisely—in other words, by participating meaningfully in both the business and editorial operations of their news agencies. According to Philip Meyer,

> The key goal is to put the entire weight and majesty of the newspaper behind its ethical decisions and not to dilute those decisions by partitioning them off to different segments. A newspaper can never be the centrally directed monolith that the public often perceives, but the public is right in holding the newspaper as a whole responsible for what appears or fails to appear on the printed page. "That's not my department" is not an ethical response.[60]

Meyer reached this conclusion after scrutinizing the results of his exhaustive survey of newspaper personnel. He identified four types of publishers, persons to whom editors report:

First are those he calls *fixers,* owners who sometimes request favorable coverage of persons or organizations for personal or economic reasons, who sometimes have reporters perform work not directly related to news gathering, and who provide news coverage for the benefit of advertisers. Fixers and their editors tend to hold each other in low regard. Fortunately, few owners are fixers.

More owners are *politicians,* persons who sometimes behave as fixers, but who are just as likely to act in benign ways. They might suggest a

major investigation or series of articles but let the editor make the final
decision, using praise or criticism selectively to indicate what the editor
should do, being present in the newsroom, and participating in the assignment of a particular reporter to a story or a beat. Perhaps because they
are less predictable than fixers, politicians and their editors have the lowest
mutual respect of all four types.

Tradition would favor *absentees,* owners who are hardly involved in
the editorial end of the news business at all. According to editors and their
staffs, most owners fit this category. Absentees are highly sensitive to issues
of fairness and balance and issues of financial conflict. Four out of five
support codes of ethics. Because of their detachment, absentees can more
easily support strong moral rules, given that they are less familiar with the
ambiguities that reporters and their editors face.

Absentees rank second in esteem to *statesmen,* owners who do not
influence the coverage of pet persons, causes, or groups but who are actively
involved in the editorial process. Statesmen earn the respect of their editors
because they are sensitive to the nuances involved in issues of fairness and
balance. Furthermore, newsroom morale is highest for this type of publisher. As Meyer observes, "[N]ews people work for psychic income as
much as any other kind. An astute publisher realizes this and creates an
organization that supplies psychic reward in the form of shared values and
support for high ideals."[61]

The publisher of Lewiston, Idaho's *Morning Tribune* demonstrated
statesmanship qualities in the newspaper's comprehensive review of its
civic and political involvements.[62] The question was whether or not the
staff's external activities represented genuine conflicts of interest. The publisher's lengthy list of board memberships (the local bank, the area's largest
industry, for example) and good-will missions (historical society, the United
Way, and a boy's club, among a dozen others) appeared alongside those
of editors, reporters, and part-time writers.

It was an open examination of the newspaper's operation, with the
results of the survey published to inform readers of the company's commitments. The paper concluded that preventing membership in organizations altogether risks the isolation of journalists from community affairs
and presumes an artificial split between the roles of unbiased reporter and
responsible citizen. A series of concrete steps emerged in addition to alert-
ing readers: a few memberships were considered unacceptable and were
relinquished, and no one was allowed to cover the activities of their affiliations. The publisher took an additional step and filed a copy of his complete income tax return with the newsroom secretary. He could have gone
even further and resigned from local corporation boards in order to free
reporters for whatever coverage might be necessary, but at least he participated in a wholesome process that on this one issue oriented the work-

place around mutuality. George Rupp applauds such openness and vulnerability as a key to understanding work as "shared commitment."[63] Such editors live out the mutuality principle. They see themselves as first among equals, not sovereigns over contentious serfs.

The Reporter as Steward

The common rhetoric that a company is one happy family or a team is usually fatuous and coercive. A mosaic of stewardship, spheres of responsibility, a composite of caretaking units—that is collegiality of the most sophisticated sort. In a humanized workplace, reporters see themselves as trustees of public information, and they respect the particular mission of other supporting units as well.

Edgar Schein's dissection of organizational culture extends this fiduciary motif even to physical space, proximity of workers to supervisors, and deference to authority.[64] Physicians sharing floor space do much of their work in private rooms; securities specialists need privacy to conduct conversations about investment instruments with people who want their assets kept secret; automobile salespersons review offers with prospective buyers in semiprivate cubbyholes. But journalists who deal with information, public and private, sensitive and trivial, confidential and banal, do so mostly in open space, which raises some profoundly moral questions. Why in a newsroom would a reporter within easy earshot of colleagues and perhaps of an editor take a phone call from an irate citizen and succeed in generating from that brief interaction a libel suit that will cost both parties exorbitant fees and probably never result in either feeling "made whole"?

The Bezanson, Cranberg, and Soloski study of libel, introduced earlier, identifies the typical plaintiffs as citizens who have had a telephone bucketful with reporters.[65] Is a newsroom conspicuously arranged for such purposes? Is newsroom bias a result of negotiations carried on by phone from within the enclosed private professional space of a newsroom and into a large public space where the events resistant to news coverage happen? And for reporters who prize spheres of stewardship for colleagues in the enterprise, why is the secretarial space in these arrangements available to spontaneous entry by anyone—a trampling territory the symbolic equivalent of low-status work?

There is a need for inefficiency in the arrangement of newsrooms. Mutuality requires not only private space for sensitive discussions, but also the possibility of stumbling into someone else's territory for reasons having nothing to do with status or even formal business. When the brilliant Albert Kahn designed Ford's River Rouge plant, he eliminated stumble space and set up each worker as lord over a discrete manor: flow technology metic-

ulously interconnected but not overlapping. Ford wanted such an integrated network of movements that a chunk of iron ore in the northwestern
ranges would not sit still until it was parked on a street in the form of a
Model T.

But information is different. Symbols are not commodities to be
launched into cultural assembly lines with an utterly predictable product.
Real news is rarely produced efficiently, despite the forests that institutional
press releases consume each year. News gathering is not account auditing;
the journalist needs intuition, insight, serendipity, art, hunches, *Verstehen*,
and the Eureka! experience to make a story intelligible. Stewardship over
a vital domain enhances the instinct that journalists commonly cite as their
mainstay in the formidable task of collecting and publishing the day's
intelligence. Stumbling space enriches stewardship, just as the efficiency
of flow technology often inhibits it.

The workplace as spheres of stewardship extends beyond vocational
roles to gender and ethnicity. The humanized workplace is also a mosaic
of demographic pluralism. Insisting on pluralism in hiring and promotion
is obvious; deliberately building it into workplace culture is a more elusive
goal. Mumby suggests one illustration of how gender discrimination can
be attacked directly in the hiring process:

> A local corporation has a female vice-president who employs a male
> personal secretary. The secretary frequently accompanies her when she
> interviews job candidates, although the candidate is not initially aware
> who is the vice-president and who is the secretary. Any candidate who
> automatically assumes that the male is the vice-president is excluded from
> consideration for the position.[66]

Advocates of a humanized work environment, constituted as a stewardship mosaic, are scandalized by the statistics that a scant 6 percent of
the top positions in newspapers are filled by women and that only 14.5
percent of television news directors are women.[67] The subtle failures of
gender inclusion continue as well—the long-standing trick of giving women
visibility in organizational charts, for example, while in the everyday work
experience making them invisible as competent leaders and rational decision makers.[68] Advocates also refuse to be content with token inclusion
of non-Caucasian employees.[69] English-only shops—at least if rooted in
hostility to other languages—are an inhospitable and demeaning habitat
for many Hispanics and Asian-Americans.

The spheres of stewardship should also encompass age, rank, and experience. This principle applies to relatively discrete matters as encultur-
ating new employees and mentoring the less experienced. Sociologists have
identified three common needs of persons who enter a new social context—
for example, a journalism graduate in a newsroom. These needs apply to

all emotional types, from the hyperconfident to the socially retiring. More-over, the needs vary and intersect at each stage in an employee's career within an organization.

First is the need for a viable identity, a congruence between expectations and achievements, a midrange between engulfment by the group and es-trangement from it. The new reporter wants to be "Tribunish" without changing her surname to *Tribune*. She wants to hear the desk editor yell her name with as much energy and exasperation as he does the name of the senior city hall reporter, without confusing the names. She wants per-sonhood in community, not personhood under community. The new mem-ber also needs power, a reflection of the common need to feel independent from the group and able to contribute uniquely and conspicuously to it. Professionals, even while engaged in teamwork among peers, need to be a central gear, an indispensable head, a nucleus of some considerable value to the group. Finally, the new member needs intimacy, an inwardly felt acceptance beyond the basic need for identity, an affirmation of the person herself apart from the variables of day-to-day job performance.[70]

In the strange confluence of human needs, these are the precise vari-ables that the press in its news and entertainment role should afford its sources, readers, and viewers. Now the same variables show up as needs in the news organization itself; but, sadly, the news organization often overlooks or disregards them.

One of the classic stories of investigative journalism is the rambunctious Watergate investigation by then–*Washington Post* reporters Bob Wood-ward and Carl Bernstein—their dark encounters with Deep Throat, their questionable quizzing of grand jurors, their last-minute confirmations be-fore deadline. Much of their drama and appeal had to do with their com-plementary styles, the "wing man" arrangement that assures powerful and obstinate news sources that two reporters multiply infinitely the resistance to compromise and corruption. A generation of journalists has been influ-enced by this Watergate team.

Ironically, broadcasters have used the team notion reasonably well. Morning news is a competitive market, and in all cases teams of two or three battle for the wake-up audience. Kouric and Gumble, Lunden and Gibson, Smith and Zahn vie for viewers and celebrity-interview junkies who need a fix on the world before breakfast. While evening network news still proffers solo anchors, local TV news is nearly always an anchor team of two or more—strength in numbers. Mutuality in a news organization favors teamwork and promotes mentoring.

A favorite dilemma discussed among journalists is whether and how much an individual would intervene in the news-gathering efforts of another reporter or photographer. On a stakeout of a private residence, from the vantage point of the sidewalk, one observes a news photographer skulking around the house searching for a through-the-window shot. Under what conditions should the photographer's presence be challenged? What if she works at a rival paper? At your paper? Experienced photographer on the prowl or new shutterbug trying for the front page? Acquaintance or unknown? Most journalists will readily explain why they would or would not scout the windows of a private residence, but few are comfortable with imposing their moral insight on someone else's news-gathering methods. To do so might appear self-righteous.

Leadership finds many styles, but mentoring requires an affirmative corporate commitment to mutuality and depends on the personal perspective of the mentor as consummate teacher, eager that others learn and advance beyond the learning. Individuals can and have become mentors to fulfill personal goals of passing along investigative or interviewing skills. Corporations, however, operating in a universe where service to others is the end and profitability a means, cannot shirk the duty to intensify collegial training with specific mentoring programs—everyone a learner, everyone a teacher—and cannot evade the inevitable institutional overlap and inefficiency that such a commitment entails. Police departments do not send academy graduates into gang neighborhoods alone with a nightstick and a handgun. Plumbers' unions do not drop off an apprentice at a new construction site with a pipe wrench and a soldering gun. Given the fundamental cultural importance of language and the intrinsic dilemmas attached to truthtelling, news organizations committed to their democratic role ought to be mentoring at every level of the operation—generating talk, groping for consensus, resisting authoritarianism, articulating moral options, and affirming ethical imperatives.

Such mentoring would do more than address the quandaries of reporting; it would speak to the process of enculturation, too. When is subordination required? When is independent action mandatory? At what point does mentor–apprentice become peer–colleague? How do written codes within the profession at large affect the personal dynamic of moral learning by mentor? How can creativity and spontaneity challenge dusty truisms and still maintain respect for the process by which new truisms will generate tradition? A normative process of corporate change in terms of stewardship spheres—one that avoids Nietzschean power struggles and yet responds to changing patterns of social power—is built on the same principles of mutuality that ought to animate the press and broadcast news in its public-service role. Mentoring is the process by which news gathering is examined, refined, improved, and confirmed.

The mutuality model needs the widest possible range of emotional styles. Journalists are rarely artists, seldom timid, never phlegmatic. But persons in community need complementary styles for prosperity and strength. Mutuality may require expansion of some of the emotional ranges currently underrepresented, not for the sake of social presence only, but more for the purpose of genuine encounter. As Elizabeth Beverly and Richard Fox argue in their critique of liberalism:

> The path forward . . . is to make cultural pluralism a risky venture—risking actually being molded by new perspectives. Tolerance and respect for other cultures are necessary liberal virtues, but they are not sufficient. . . . [T]he quest for equality doesn't end when formerly outcast groups finally become visible or gain a degree of legitimacy. The quest continues in the struggle to listen actively to new voices, to permit them to shape our thinking.[71]

A well-oiled news operation with balanced psychographic profiles, or one that reduces the spectrum of passions represented by professional journalists to fit within prescribed parameters, should be anathema. Such channeling produces clones, not persons in strong community. Mutuality is served not by sameness, but by coordinated responses to common problems.

Put to radical use, mentoring would cut across traditional walls that separate units of responsibility. Could a reporter be truly mentored by an advertising salesperson? Under current mythologies of corporate cultures, such a reporter would be tainted. As in the case of testifying before a grand jury about an anonymous source, who could tell the extent of compromise? But in a more radical vein, under compelling assumptions that the advertising department has its own distinctive forms of mutuality in which to foster democratic stewardship, the reporter-cum-seller does not jettison integrity as much as expand integrity into new and—to the corporation surely—vital arenas.

A tradition of mentoring would gradually relieve the news reporter on the sidewalk of agonizing over whether and how to approach the skulking photographer under the window. Pervasive reluctance to intervene would now be all the testimony needed for an argument that active mentoring, supported by the corporation and fundamental to the practice of the profession, is an obligatory outgrowth of the ontological recovery of person-in-community. Reporters should care enough to shout, at least to inquire, and in doing so they must have widely understood obligations of access to the moral imaginations of their peers.

At a recent convention of newspaper publishers, the president of a Midwest newspaper company described how he develops his staff, the people who report to him. Because there is no textbook, no credit course that turns out students ready to discharge the responsibilities of top management, the executive relies on mentoring. He chooses and teaches his staff, and is doing so now to his eventual successor. Inherent in this executive's commitment is foreclosure to private decision making: he can never keep a blunder to himself; he cannot self-justify his actions; someone else is always trooping through his mind, second-guessing, quizzing about implications, tracing latent biases. Such is the price of working in strong community: one's professional skin must at the same time be capillary-thin and artery-tough, transparent and vulnerable, yet willing to abide by the consequences of difficult choices. The same investment in training should operate at all levels of the press.

Mutuality Seeks Connection

Reinhold Niebuhr reminded us that the civil rights movement would have failed as a nonviolent revolution apart from widely dispersed and narrowly cooperative communities of interest. Because a national coalition including Catholics and Jews prevailed against sectional and individualistic interests—southern Protestantism—the desperation of a racial minority was "transmuted . . . into that wonderful combination of hope and despair which has been the motive power of all rebellions against injustice."[72] Niebuhr saw the 1954 *Brown* decision as a turning point in the struggle, although he understood the crucial role of the press, having served the Commission on Freedom of the Press as an active debater.

Niebuhr also knew the difficulty of maintaining the fragile coalitions that kept the movement from bogging down in the internal warfare of SNCC versus CORE, SCLC versus NAACP, Washington march versus local voter-registration drives. Niebuhr's writings inspired Martin Luther King, Jr., during his studies at Crozier Seminary, and in the early 1960s he described himself as roused from retirement by the challenge of changing a nation's racial attitudes. But it was the press—broadcast and magazine primarily—that put this aging moral philosopher back into the center of social controversy, repaying a debt, as it were, for Niebuhr's active work on press freedom and responsibility two decades earlier. And Niebuhr's mediated pronouncements on civil rights were a telling reminder that wisdom is as quickly found beyond editorial boardrooms as inside them. The point is obvious: that the press serves well which recognizes it does not serve alone.

When a news operation seeks civic transformation through political literacy, it does not achieve these goals in isolation. Countless intermediate agencies have their pitch in the game of public justice. News companies can sift wheat from chaff, separate quackery and quibble, and move disputants closer to consensus. But in the process, the news company is obliged to be open to the moving presence of its readers and constituents.

Here mutuality may seem most vulnerable to the charge that evisceration of independence is to a newspaper or broadcast station what pollution is to a wilderness bay. An editor too entangled with boycott groups or business interests becomes a public-relations toady. But mutuality has sufficient models of success to allay these fears: the eleven-year record of the National News Council, the ongoing press council in Minnesota, and the provocatively public work of the Office of Communication of the United Church of Christ.

Paul Ansah of the University of Ghana turns democratic political theory full force against the Fourth Estate concept of the press in his apologia for the development model. Arguing on behalf of closer ties between government and media, he asks, "Who is better qualified to articulate and pursue the public interest? Is it the elected government having the people's mandate or a minority of unelected persons who happen to have the financial resources . . . to communicate with the people? Does press freedom belong to the people in general or to publishers and editors?"[73] If the people invest trust in elected leaders to mobilize the country for economic trade, mass education, medical-delivery systems, and agriculture, is it not feasible also to regard the means of mobilization as a social service vital to a people's future?

Against capitalistic pressures, Ansah's appeal—that press power ought to be vested in coalitions of people—begins to ring true. Traditional liberal theory has created an adversarial press to check the excesses of state power. Heavily capitalized American media companies fear little when the state gripes or an advertiser complains. However, in Ghana, Niger, Sierra Leone, Nigeria, and other states immediate to Ansah's sphere, capitalized strength is unknown. Mutuality neither sits idle in the face of cooptation nor erects chain-link intransigence in the face of responsible appeal from outside the newsroom.

In summary, journalism requires a humanized workplace in order to nurture itself as a vocation. The occupational environment must be commensurate with mutuality—understood as servant leadership, spheres of stewardship, and a welcoming disposition toward the public voice. But these are only glimmers in the contemporary labyrinth of reporting. It is formidable, for example, to weave these three facets of mutuality into a framework for the international beat. Newspaper readers overwhelmingly prefer local news. Usually broadcast news can take us to more distant sites, an advantage of the visual medium. Charitable Americans might feign interest in and concern for the subjects of foreign governments—notably in times of extreme crisis—but bridges, roads, and schools draw a larger audience than barrios and piazzas. Foreign correspondents must find news relevant to the entertainment and business interests of their paying readers and viewers. Communitarian journalism is no guarantee that readers will rush to newsstands for stories on impoverished Latin peasants or fragile Amazonian ecologies. Most news organizations realize that quite the opposite is true. Except for war, assassinations, or unusual natural disasters, foreign news is last to sell papers and expand audience share.

Of all journalists, foreign correspondents are most vulnerable to what Emile Durkheim called *anomie,* a condition reflecting "the relaxation of social bonds, a sort of collective anesthesia, or social malaise, just as individual sadness, when chronic, in its way reflects the poor organic state of the individual."[74] Mutual dependence and "sufficiently prolonged" contact suppress *anomie,* but "if some opaque environment is interposed, then only stimuli of a certain intensity can be communicated from one organ to another. Relations, being rare, are not repeated enough to be determined; each time there ensues new groping."[75]

Schein traces *anomie* in organizations to a lack of consensus on how individuals ought to relate "in order to make the group safe and comfortable."[76] What is the dominant paradigm of work, for example? Is productivity paramount, or caring for one's children? Are management meetings consensual or antagonistic? May innovations be kicked around with the boss, or is the procedure highly formalized, with reporting techniques and hierarchies intact? A news shop committed to protecting its own and rejecting outside influence (as is typical among certified professions) can be alien ground to reporters socialized into more community-responsive (sometimes mistakenly called wimpish) modes of news gathering. But *anomie* can occur whenever dominant trends are subverted and predictability obscured. The feature film *The Year of Living Dangerously* illustrates the difficulty of a journalist's adjustment to the unusual, the non-Western, the bizarre. Only after Guy Hamilton meets a British consulate worker and feelings of *anomie* dissolve does he begin to file genuine news. His Indonesian photographer-partner tried to show Guy the depth of the culture, but failed.

Perhaps because foreign news is the most expensive to collect, perhaps because of a tradition of roving and revelry that traces from Henry Stanley to Carleton Beals, perhaps because readers reflect a nurtured ethnocentrism that news agencies cannot afford to ignore, the foreign assignment has usually been undertaken by reporters with a strong sense of individualism and an inbred suspicion of community encumbrances. Would the news read or look different if the organization of foreign news took on communitarian appearances?

Consider the options. If mutuality defines the human condition and persons are known in relationship, a foreign news team takes over where the correspondent once ventured. Bureaus, not lone reporters, become the rule. Since a plurality of cultures is an operative assumption, nationals who are able to represent fully the culture's diversity become integrated into the process of news gathering. Neil Sheehan makes this point dramatically in his account of Vietnam War coverage.[77] Early in that intervention, when John Kennedy and later Lyndon Johnson were attempting to stall communist advance in Southeast Asia by propping up a comic-opera government in Saigon, press coverage was largely controlled by military spokesmen and U.S. political operatives. Sheehan, his colleague David Halberstam, and others were shielded from field advisers and from life in the hamlets, where corrupt Saigon officials were handing the war to Viet Minh cadre with inhumane "free-fire zones" and forced relocation from countryside to prefab squalor. Sheehan credits John Vann, a lieutenant colonel whose clear view of the war's eventual outcome met with deaf ears in military headquarters, but ready ears among journalists eager to break through the prevailing narrative. (Not entirely eager, perhaps; the press was often timid in those early years, mindful of public fallout and political repercussions if headlines directly challenged Pentagon press releases.) Vann talked, introduced Sheehan and others to farmers and corporals and hamlet chiefs, showed photographers the effects of free fire (a strategy of revenge against villages that had harbored Viet Cong patrols), and began to reveal the extent of corruption among South Vietnamese officers. The result was the demise of Vann's military career and a new sense of urgency and illumination in Sheehan's reporting.

And what a social upheaval these press accounts helped to foment! One can only imagine what changes would have been wrought had the U.S. press sent to Vietnam correspondents as daring as the intrepid Vann—reporters who knew Dienbienphu and understood the roots of Ngo Dinh Diem's psychotic distrust of the Buddhist monks, journalists who could tell the story of the Vietnamese rice farmer threatened and terrorized by both sides, protected by none. As it was, careful and dangerous reporting eventually shattered stereotypes of "gooks" in straw helmets and righteous Western democrats in Saigon. The press had learned a hard lesson in foreign reportage.

Concerns over cultural imperialism and ethnocentrism are the constant nemesis of the foreign staff, but raised to the level of self-consciousness and dialogue, their sting is reduced and their impact on bias controlled. Development programs for foreign correspondents are expanded to include formal study in literature, the arts, and philosophy as well as political science and economics, typical mainstays of foreign reportage. Foreign bureaus begin to produce sections, not merely stories, in the newspaper. Broadcast segments and occasional specials expand cross-cultural learning on television beyond the Cousteau group and National Geographic expeditions, valuable as they are. American television viewers begin to dismantle distinctions between "our news" and "their news" as communities of interest grow beyond language and color differences. Marshall McLuhan's global village loses its common-consciousness mythology as its dimensions become clearer in real relationships between heretofore unacquainted persons. Mutuality pushes toward such change. Then a network hires an Indonesian journalist for its New York production staff to show us the news of ourselves through different lenses, and the cycle of discovery begins again.

Institutional Infrastructure

The first major theorist of modern organization was the German political economist and sociologist Max Weber. He considered bureaucratic coordination of the political, economic, and sociological realms the distinctive mark of the modern era. He understood power and authority in terms of a formalized matrix: organizational instruments mobilize resources and technical expertise into measurable increments of productivity ordered by administrative regulations. For Karl Marx, power is always rooted in economic relations. Weber agreed that in modern capitalism, economic power is a predominant form. But the source of power, he contended, is an empirical question that cannot be answered by Marx's dogmatic emphasis on one explicit source. Technology is a locus of power, for example; and in addition to the relations of production, Weber recognized group status or expert power under certain structural and historical circumstances.[78]

Weber recognized bureaucratic systems as technically superior to feudalism, military authority, or handicraft. However, he also fretted continually about the stultifying dysfunctions of bureaucracy. In a cynical mood he predicted that a bureaucratized legal system will become "a vending machine into which pleadings are inserted together with the fee and which then disgorges the judgment together with the reasons mechanically derived from the Code."[79] Weber worried that unprecedented bureaucratic efficiency would turn large-scale organizations into iron cages rather than paradises. In Weber's tradition, Robert Michels argues that bureaucratic mechanisms follow "the iron law of oligarchy," in which democratic participation declines in inverse proportion to expanding and streamlining the structures.[80]

Although this chapter concentrates on the common features of all organizations regardless of their age, demographics, or size, Weber's concern for the infrastructure in macro bureaucracies warrants particular attention. The bureaucratization of the mass media since the 1890s has been catapulted forward by monumental economic capital, supertechnologies, and coteries of experts, leading in our day to a bewildering array of media monopolies, multinationals, conglomerates, oligopolies, cross-media ownership, chains, and interlocking directorates.

The Hutchins Commission warned as early as 1947 that the press was becoming a concentrated, industrialized, big-business enterprise impervious to its social responsibility. Current trends suggest that by the year 2000, a handful of corporations will control all the significant Western mass media—newspapers, wire services, broadcasting networks, and data-transmission facilities. Stanley Cunningham concludes that the situation in Canada is even worse than in Rupert Murdoch's Australia and England or in the United States. Two companies, Southam and Thomson Newspapers, account for 60 percent of the circulation of the English-language dailies, making media concentration in Canada the highest among industrial democracies.[81]

Media ownership concentrated among a minuscule number of corporate bodies does not necessarily mean that a few powerful owners will directly intervene in the democratic process. Nor is the problem limited to the particular behavior of a media group; the Donrey chain is known for high profits and low-quality newspapers, but Knight-Ridder won seven Pulitzers in one year and is not imprisoned by stockholders. The issue is rooted in Weberian bureaucracy—in the stifling, homogenizing manner in which information is disseminated and in the erosion of our epistemic values toward corporate efficiency rather than civic transformation. As Sheldon Wolin complains, America's primary institutions, including the mass media, "have become antidemocratic in spirit, design, and operation . . . elitist and managerial."[82] They have become closed, autonomous systems, largely impervious to public influence.

Bigness per se may not be the root of reportorial evils, but the issues are certainly more complicated than concluding dispassionately that "any risk of anticompetitive behavior . . . must be balanced by the greater efficiency benefits of large size that chain operations can realize."[83] Gone are the days of local newspapers competing with one another for the attention of the citizenry. Nine out of ten cities now rely on only one daily paper, and chances are that this paper is part of a chain or conglomerate. As a result, newspapers are both bigger and smaller than they appear.

They are bigger in that they belong to an organization of which any one newspaper is but a small unit. Gannett, for instance, owns almost ninety newspapers with a total circulation of more than 6 million per day. It also owns eighteen radio stations, eight television stations, and the second largest billboard-advertising firm in the United States. Its devotion is divided between the cities it serves—Detroit or Des Moines or Louisville—and the dispersed shareholders who train their eyes to the profits reported on the New York Stock Exchange. Newspapers owned and operated locally are free to plow their profits back into their local news operations; by necessity, newspapers operated from afar serve two masters: their stocks and their trade. Chains are less likely to reinvest the lion's share of their profits, given the corporate salaries to be paid, stock dividends to be distributed, and other media to be acquired. When asked whether Gannett was pronounced "GANnett" or "GanNETT," former company chairman Allen Neuharth said that the accent was on the net. Underscoring that point is Gannett's policy of transferring all bank deposits above operating expenses to its headquarters every night.[84]

How a chain invests its capital is only one way that it affects local communities. Reporters and editors who work for chains are affected also. Not only are they socialized into the firm at least as much as they are into the doctrines of the local paper, but they also move more often than their colleagues who work for independent news organizations. Promotion in a chain newspaper typically entails relocating to another city, whereas promotion in an independent newspaper means taking on greater responsibility in the same community's newspaper. More disturbing is the likelihood that promotion in a chain is more of a business decision than a professional one. Editors who do not meet the profit quotas of their quarterly "Progress Plans" are likely to be replaced by editors more willing to substitute features for more expensive hard news, to charge maximum advertising and subscription rates, and to busy themselves with the cosmetics of design and layout.[85]

The threat to news posed by newspaper chains and media conglomerates surpasses the direct effects that Wall Street may have on local news outlets. It also involves telling readers and viewers what they should think about, formally called agenda setting.

Ben Bagdikian often refers to a survey by the American Society of Newspaper Editors which discovered that one out of three editors who works for a newspaper chain does not feel free to report news that is damaging to the parent firm.[86] This research has ominous implications for the millions of viewers who watch NBC News. NBC is owned by RCA, which in turn is owned by General Electric, which, among other things, is an important defense contractor. On a smaller scale, for every feature story that a television station broadcasts, a potential hard-news story is not covered. Diversity of perspective narrows and public access vanishes as news operations package information for middle-class consumers, eighteen to forty-nine years old. Corporate ownership and local monopolies raise disturbing questions regarding who decides what is and is not reported and whose interest is served.

The bureaucratization of mass media has been fueled by capitalist materialism, but economics is not the sole explanation. Economic power must be understood in concert with a spiraling technological sophistication. An unending wave of innovations during the twentieth century has made technology one of the media's defining features at present. Yale sociologist Charles Perrow exemplifies an important school of organizational sociologists who argue convincingly that "technology is a better basis for comparing organizations than the several schemes that now exist. . . . In the interests of efficiency, organizations wittingly or unwittingly attempt to maximize the congruence between their technology and their structure."[87] The news industry's technological sophistication, in other words, needs careful deconstruction. An uncritical adaptation to media technologies has made them nearly determinative in our notions of newsworthiness—the cameras and gadgets driving reporters to sound bites and to visually powerful events that themselves begin to determine what is newsworthy.

Newsroom mechanization also results in centralizing authority by standardizing the work flow: "Faced with a universe of uncertainty . . . news organizations have strained toward regularization of their technology. In so doing, they have constructed systems capable of recognizing only selected inputs, processes that are highly routinized, and products that . . . are standardized and bland."[88] Technology's vexatious power intimately links administration and authority. Organizational control takes on an abstract, impersonal regularity in heavily computerized and electronically edited journalism. Decision making is not typically a naked force wielded by mean-spirited executives. The control apparatus in technologically superior news operations is subtly comprehensive; it becomes hidden away in operational boxes that seem mysterious and outside personal influence. Power is administered in daily doses that are sinister because they seem innocuous.

In this fashion, Weber's worry about bureaucratization as a locus of power has come to roost in the news industry. Because technocratic systems recast authority and control in terms of impersonal rules, specialized expertise is moved to the organization's center. "The data systems analyst, the marketing specialist, the labor negotiator, the management theorist, and the public relations expert are necessary ingredients in the modern corporate success formula."[89] Whereas traditional professions have been bound, in principle, to a public-service altruism, the technocratic professions have been created with the explicit aim of marshalling expertise to facilitate bureaucratic efficiency.

Thus James Ottoway, chairperson of the Ottoway newspaper group, repeatedly warns against the invasion of investment bankers into American newspapers. He argues that media enterprises then talk too much about asset values and return on investment; he insists that they publish newspapers rather than run banks. Time Inc.'s $13 billion acquisition of Warner Communications was initiated by a report from stock analysts that Time's growth would be limited to 6 percent annually. The Time-Warner combination was hailed as a business match made in heaven, but in actuality it was driven by lawyers, accountants, international financiers, judges, bond dealers, and MBAs. Henry Luce III of Time Inc.'s board of directors and former editor-in-chief Hedley Donovan objected to the deal. They complained bitterly that Time's historic journalistic commitment and news-editorial independence had not been factored into the merger calculus.

In this age of bureaucratic and transnational media organizations, it is understandable that a growing number of managers have degrees in business or law rather than journalism or communication. Furthermore, more and more executives are chosen on the basis of merit rather than family ties. These changes have the advantage of opening positions to nonwhite persons who traditionally were excluded from management, but they also have the unfortunate consequence of signaling an emphasis on the business of publishing over the content of publishing.[90]

But this is an essay on organizational accountability, on institutionalizing communitarian ethics. What makes bureaucratization a moral issue, not restricted to political remedies and economic models? As Cunningham has argued, Hegel's transitional principle demonstrates how the quantitative graduates into a qualitative change. This metamorphosis is not merely empirical; it involves a moral alteration as well.[91] In Hegel's words:

> There enters a point in this quantitative alteration at which the quality is changed and the quantum shows itself as specifying, so that the altered quantitative relation is converted into a measure, and thus into a new quality, a new something. . . . In the moral sphere, in so far as it is considered under the categories of being, there occurs the same transition from quantity into quality and different qualities appear to be based on a difference of magnitude. It is through more and less that the measure of frivolity or thoughtlessness is exceeded and something quite different comes about, namely crime, and thus right becomes wrong and virtue vice.[92]

When "a certain state of affairs graduates to a certain degree of amplitude" and a new critical mass is achieved, individual action no longer defines accountability. The ethical problems are murkier when there is wholesale misdirection or systemic disorder; but Hegel's transitional dialectic indicates that ethical principles apply nonetheless.[93] Displacing perspicacity with profits as the raison d'être of news does more than transform information into a commodity or endanger freedom of expression; given Hegel's principle of transition, this magnum alteration of ends is also injustice—a massive violation of human innocence.

In terms of organizational accountability, emancipatory narrative and a humanized workplace remain constituent features of macro organizations. The twentieth century's relentless bureaucratization has expanded into a qualitatively new situation, but that does not mean that organizations can abrogate the imperatives that apply to all institutions. Giant corporations create a battlefield of distinct proportions that demand attention in their own terms; however, institutional ethics limited exclusively to concentrated ownership or technological prowess or bloated profession-alism fails to recognize that the principle of amplitude entails a pre-or nonbureaucratized domain as well.

Appropriate alternatives to bureaucratized media must be found while si-multaneously etching norms into organizational discourse and transforming the workplace into a mosaic of stewardship. Public broadcasting, for exam-ple, warrants vastly more resources and significance than it has ever received since first chartered by Congress. National Public Radio's "All Things Con-sidered" and PBS's "The MacNeil/Lehrer NewsHour," "Washington Week in Review," and "Frontline" are high-quality programming. Alistair Cooke's "America" series opened up history with stunning precision.

Even critical acclaim has not released public broadcasting from its fi-nancial juggernaut. The broadcast industry spends $3 billion a year on programming, while only $44 million in federal funds are

> grudgingly earmarked for alternative productions which attempt to reflect the wider horizons of human affairs. The time has come to liberate public radio and television from the gatekeepers and give it to the public. When Congress established public broadcasting in 1967, it tied the system to White House political oversight and the institutional begging bowl, and failed to provide a way to fund it on a sensible, long-range basis. Now, as public broadcasting prepares to make yet another trek to the Office of Management and Budget and Congress for its triennial fix, its appropri-ations request should be accompanied by a plan for fiscal independence.[94]

Regrettably, its limited resources and small audience prevent PBS from truly competing with commercial broadcasters. If PBS should join the major Western democracies and give free air time to presidential candidates during a campaign and expand serious political programming, the enter-tainment-oriented networks would not necessarily be overwhelmed or shamed into abandoning soundbites. Says Patricia Aufderheide, a noted PBS observer, "most viewers respect PBS in the same way that people like Sunday School."[95]

Although entrenched patterns are difficult to alter, new technologies provide unusual opportunity for innovation in ownership. City and county governments in California and Colorado have experimented with computer bulletin boards as channels of political activity and underreported news. Detailed information about government affairs is made available through modems and computers, including election business and referenda. Fiber-optic, third-generation cable provides another opportunity for institutional reform. Distribution networks need not be organized according to ability to pay in the open marketplace of supply and demand. Municipal own-ership, a city-sponsored public corporation, or a regional governmental authority could enable impartial distribution regardless of geographic lo-cation or income. As with the postal service, schools, and public libraries, a need conception of justice insists on equal access to this new technology rather than using it to provide an added convenience for those already information-rich.[96]

Democratized media are a trend worldwide. Even in the face of comprehensive mass-media fortresses, oppositional forms—audio cassettes, photocopiers, facsimile transmissions, and local small-group assemblies— challenge the hegemony of guns and autocrats worldwide. Independent film companies, underground presses, people's radio, and popular theater provide an alternative media system from below. They are rivers of hope in the desert of technological culture. In the vernacular tongue, they nurture communities that are going for efficiency's jugular. These local settings, emancipated from an insidious adaptation, are the incubators of nonviolent civic transformation.[97]

Despite TV Globo's virtual monopoly in Brazil, for example, video cassettes have provided an alternative communication system from the ground up, allowing backyard groups to use them as a tool for social change. Labor unions have found video particularly helpful in sharing ideas and strategies from one chapter to another. The Metalworkers Union of São Bernardo has initiated a training project called Workers' TV. Since political repression makes democratic opposition extremely difficult, the diffusion of video among indigenous bodies gives them a voice outside government control. In Brazil today, about a hundred such groups are "active in video, spread throughout the country, in both rural and urban areas. They are linked to unions, neighborhood and cultural associations, organizations that support the grass-roots movements, or the church, or they are independent."[98]

These radical shifts in the size and shape of the technologies themselves are vital links in a technological infrastructure built to desacralize streamlined power pragmatism. Meanwhile, enlightened regulation and taxation policies could encourage decentralization, diversity, and economic democracy in bureaucratized media. To promote greater community service, one could imagine, for example, federal limits on the scope of communications enterprises. A newspaper company might be restricted to owning a certain number of newspapers and forbidden from owning non-news businesses. Such a policy would encourage companies to invest more heavily in the papers they own and to promote more employees locally. However much this policy would serve local communities, it is a populist's daydream, given the current relaxation of antitrust sentiments in the federal government.

A more realistic proposal is for local news staffs to choose their own editors. Whatever the office politics involved—and however uncomfortable—this reform would encourage local commitment and perhaps offer greater resistance to encroaching business customs. Communitarian values would favor a policy of local control and some version of democracy in the newsroom. As Bagdikian concludes: "The object of reform is not to silence voices but to multiply them, not to foreclose ideas but to awaken them. For it is in diversity and openness that the genius of the United States can flower."[99] If Western media were to develop a healthy mixture of corporate and public channels, technologically sophisticated and participatory systems, large-scale companies committed to news and independent producers, they could become the model and envy of democratic societies everywhere.

Conclusion

In a speech to the first Congress of Sociology meeting in Frankfurt in 1910, Max Weber argued for studying the news-production process rather than the content of the message. He identified newspaper trusts, advertising influence, and source constraints, for example, as dangerous liabilities; therefore, "we cannot be satisfied with an examination of the product at hand."[100] Weber recognized that, like the proverbial iceberg, seven-eighths of news production lies beneath the surface. But not until Warren Breed's groundbreaking research, "Social Control in the Newsroom," was the news media's bureaucratic organization studied systematically.[101]

Organizational dynamics are currently recognized as inherent in how we define reporting, in how we barter news as a commodity for sale and frame it within mainstream values. However, within the general patterns of production, news units differ—some superficially and others substantially. "Just as each paper . . . has a particular organizational framework, sense of news and readership, so each will develop a regular and characteristic mode of address."[102] Unless production processes are radically reformed, in other words, no transparent differences will appear in news content itself.

The branches of an old tree in our neighborhood hang close to the ground and kill off the grass underneath. Each spring, the neighbors plant and water new grass and keep a thin stand alive until the tree's thick leaves in the summer block out the sunlight and emaciate it. Instead of persisting in this futile struggle, the neighbors could trim the branches ten feet high, welcome the sun, and let the grass grow luxuriantly. By analogy, an empowering news, shaped by justice and covenant, will occur only as occasional fragments on the social landscape unless there is a fundamental restructuring of the organizational culture within which news is constituted. If news reporting is to redirect its mission toward civic transformation, nurturing institutional integrity in terms of communitarian ethics is indispensable.

6

Normative Pluralism

In an ancient fable, a dragon is urgently summoned to defend the king's castle. It pulls together its mighty frame and draws deep inside for a torrent of fire to scorch the attackers. Nothing happens. The flames in its stomach have died. At the moment of challenge, the dragon is little more than a puffing hulk with its fire gone out.

Today, when the demands are most intense, the great communications enterprise rouses itself for battle. Ethics committees crop up in professional associations. Alarmists point to opinion polls that show plummeting press credibility, and they demand more responsible performance. Books, magazines, and television series are urging professional virtue, decency, prima facie duties, and compassion. The dragon is rumbling, heaving, puffing. But the fire flickers and fades. At the critical moment, when one should see roaring flames, the blaze inside sputters out.

What we mean is that the long-burning fires of normative thinking are nearly extinguished. Just when a definitive axiology is most needed for confronting the rage outside, its fundamental inspiration is falling away. Principial foundations built in a secure Newtonian world with more settled meanings have crumbled, the Enlightenment view of rational being assaulted by Freud, its static universe destroyed by Darwin, and its epistemologies forever stunted by Heisenberg's uncertainty principle and Karl Popper's falsification criterion. The stakes have escalated, the whirlwind is here, and we confront the storm with the very concept of norms in a problematic state.

Given the contemporary climate, this book's normative model needs justification. Communitarian ethics stands over against such nonnormative approaches as descriptive ethics cataloging practitioner morality, metaethics, and ethics in the analytic tradition. Normative theory can demystify questionable recourses while setting an appropriate direction; it enables critical thinking while empowering the formulation of policy. But gaining this intellectual leverage still leaves us with urgent philosophical questions about normativity.

Certainly, our communitarian model must be defended against those ethicists who treat norms as unproblematic; but it must be articulated as well against positions that are antinormative. As Hans Jonas writes, "The very same movement which put us in possession of the powers we now have to be regulated by norms—the movement of modern knowledge called science—has by a necessary complementarity eroded the foundations from which norms are derived; it has destroyed the very idea of norm as such."[1]

In the spirit of Jonas, postmodernism has mounted an encompassing attack on normative appeals. Prominent theorists of the postmodern represent different views of modernity's demise. Jean-François Lyotard's rejection of grand narratives is at odds with Frederic Jameson's cultural logic of late capitalism. And neither focuses on Jean Baudrillard's posthistorical simulacrum.[2] However, they speak in concert against totalizing conditions of knowledge: metaphysics, universal reason, ethical systems, correspondence views of truth, and essentialist theories of human nature. There are major paradoxes in postmodern theories and practices, but together they constitute what "can be called a postmodern problematics: a set of basic issues that have been created by the various discourses of postmodernism, issues that were not particularly problematic before but certainly are now."[3]

Generally speaking, professional ethics has demonstrated little concern about the status of normativity, facing neither the broader challenges of philosophical ethics nor the postmodern problematic. But this lack of interest stems from a profound misunderstanding of the nature of applied ethics. We cannot uncritically assume that ethical theory is to media ethics as theoretical physics is to engineering or as microbiology is to medical practice. The connections between pure and applied ethics are normally construed in these one-dimensional terms—first theory and then application to professional conundrums. That dualistic view highlights the field-specific problems of such professional subcultures as journalism, medicine, and law while obscuring the normative underpinnings of ethical theories. Plato has convinced us apparently that if B depends on A for its existence, then B is inferior, and that generic knowledge is superior to particular knowledge.[4] However, recent philosophy of social science has demonstrated that the *theoria*–praxis relationship is not linear but dialectical and immensely complicated. For example, Florian Znaniecki's influential conception of theory, labeled "analytic induction," insists on generalizing from the data by abstraction rather than employing an inductive strategy based on counting instances. Znaniecki opposes causal explanations as well because they assume that the formal purpose of lawlike statements is prediction and control.[5] In slightly modified versions, "grounded theory" and "disciplined abstractions" likewise integrate existential location with conceptual categories, emphasizing the integrative and interpretive character of theorizing without jettisoning natural settings.[6] Whether by minting special metaphors or creating analogies or using direct expressions, analytic induction maps out seminal taxonomies while insightfully unveiling the inner character of complex cultures. Theoretical precision is crucial. If too vague, our conceptual gateways hinder our encounter with salient issues; and if wrongly formulated, they oversimplify or obstruct relevant problems.

To be theoretically interesting, professional ethics must still benefit more persuasively from these contemporary insights contradicting Plato. A sophisticated version is interested in concrete moral judgments; but it emphasizes ethical theory as well, with both components dialectically unified. In order to test imaginatively in advance some of the difficult choices that professionals confront, our communitarian model makes normative claims about classes of conduct, judging them as right or wrong. Rather than a practitioner's decision making as the unit of analysis, states of affairs and institutional cultures can be praised or blamed in terms of the dialogic norm.

Our approach engages in the intellectual enterprise that Stephen Toulmin identifies as practical philosophy: "From Aristotle's *Nicomachean Ethics,* by way of Cicero's *De Officiis,* and right up to the Renaissance," philosophy included "diagnostics and due process, case ethics and rhetoric, topics and poetics."[7] Only when the shift to theory-centered philosophy occurred in the seventeenth century were such practical spheres as the timely, the oral, the local, and the particular set aside. Philosophy's primary agenda of abstract principles since then has left us with the puzzling redundancy "normative ethics" and the label "applied philosophy" for what formerly encompassed philosophy itself. We join Toulmin in reentering practical concerns as the legitimate domain of formal philosophy itself. In fact, for him the primary locus of ethics has already moved from the study to the bedside, to criminal courts, engineering labs, factories, the newsroom, and ethnic street corners. As they did historically, many moral philosophers are now fashioning their analysis within the conditions of contemporary struggle. Obviously, restoring philosophy "in this practical sense as a contribution to the resolution of quandaries that face us . . . with high stakes"[8] entails a commitment to norms.

Communitarian ethics establishes civic transformation as the press's goal and reorients the media's organizational culture around the principle of mutuality. Unlike approaches that are accommodationist and given to palliatives, this perspective is emancipatory in character. It participates in the profound contemporary debates over praxis, Regis Debray calling it "a revolution in the revolution—a comprehensive recasting of ideas about social transformation and how it is achieved."[9] As a virginal political idea, communitarian democracy joins community institutions—bonded through historical memory and culture—with power; thus it subverts centralized power of every variety. The people's power is the radical, the square root of all power, . . . the root term out of which the entire political vocabulary is ramified. Democracy is radical politics in the same way that faith was once called "radical grace," acetic acid "radical vinegar," and granite "the universally radical rock". . . . Its motion is not lateral toward the edge (as with "left") but straight down to the source.[10]

In this sense, communitarian democracy is not just a social hypothesis, but a normative condition.

Communitarian democrats agree with those social philosophies which oppose institutions that limit power to the few. However, they do not believe that after solving the problem we can safely abandon the emancipatory struggle and obliterate the organizations and traditions by which it has been sustained. Communitarian democracy understands that participatory justice sometimes takes root within social structures protected by authoritarianism and unilateral definitions of reality; often these structures can be changed only by a steady, consensual redistribution of social power. Merely being resistant per se is insufficient; harsh rhetoric does not in itself provide a blueprint for sociopolitical change. Radical collectivist theories, on balance, have developed a stirring critique of injustice, but have failed to construct an ethical discourse on which to ground their vision of society. And because the approach outlined in the previous chapters is epistemologically self-conscious about its transformative character, its normative claims need to be established. On what grounds, in other words, can the communitarian vision be justified over against competing views? Thus we define our task as advocating a specific normative framework while also defending the notion of normativity in itself.

"The field of applied ethics is often accused of living on borrowed conceptual capital."[11] In our case, we cannot draw on the resources of professional ethics for a discourse about or justification regarding norms. However, for an adequate professional ethics in general and for our model in particular, normativity is one ingredient that needs far greater conceptual clarity at present. We treat it here, in Herbert Blumer's terminology, as a sensitizing concept.[12] We believe that communitarian media ethics is a rich laboratory for articulating a justifiable notion of normativity and for demonstrating that norms are the catalyst to advance further professional ethics as a whole.

The Technical Artifice

Unique to our own time is technology on a worldwide scale, with today's two most powerful tools in fundamental contradiction. On the one hand, information technologies have created international communication networks that potentially involve us all in one another's business. On the other hand, their opposite, nuclear weapons, threaten the human race with annihilation. Our fragile planet has the technological sophistication dialectically to destroy all humanity while simultaneously binding all nations into a worldwide information system. Since global destruction is imminently possible, our scholarship in ethics needs an urgency about it unlike any of our previous theorizing. Also, our principial claims must henceforth embrace the needs of the entire human race within their purview.

In 1945, nuclear technology was born, in principle able to vaporize the planet. In 1957, *Sputnik:* but not merely a satellite fired from the Soviet Union in secret—the whole world watched. As Marshall McLuhan noted, humankind was bound together for the first time, and it was done electronically. While news of Lincoln's assassination took months to reach the London streets, Russian technology was now paraded instantly before an admiring world. And in November 1963 we participated as one globe in President Kennedy's funeral. Television, radio, and satellites gathered us around the casket with all the emotion and ceremony of a family burial. The procession down Pennsylvania Avenue occurred on Main Street, the Universe.

Since those heady days, we have loaded the skies with satellites of information and military surveillance. Global technology is built in counterpoint; the two options stand in conjugant relationship. We are confident that increased information will facilitate global understanding. And when we curb the nuclear arms race, we believe we have put these two technologies on the proper trajectory. The one recedes as the other expands. Open information unfettered internationally and destructive technology restrained politically—that at least yields a working formula for sustaining the planet at this auspicious moment of human history, although we realize that the connections between improved information and decreased danger are porous at best.

This relationship in sanitized form is the San Andreas fault line on which our technological civilization rests. But the problem must be stated in slightly more complicated terms.

Jacques Ellul's "La Technique"

Jacques Ellul contends that the technological phenomenon is decisive (though not exclusive) in defining twentieth-century culture. As an explanatory element, he argues, it plays the part of capital in Marx's interpretation of the nineteenth century. That does not mean that technology has the same function as capital or that the capitalist system is a thing of the past. It still exists, but capital no longer fulfills the role Marx claimed for it. Whereas work produces value for Marx, technology is the determining factor in highly industrialized societies. Technology creates value at present and is not peculiar to capitalism. The characters have changed. We can no longer divide society into capitalists and workers: the phenomenon is completely different and more abstract. We now have technological systems on one side and all humanity on the other—the former driven by necessity and the latter demanding freedom. Ellul concludes that we must read the world in which we live not in terms of political–economic structures, but in terms of technology.[13] Although this analysis privileges the industrial order, even the three-quarters of the world that is still nontechnological actually finds itself defined within technological parameters.

In terms of our bipolar model, global technologies of communication and extinction have given our age its peculiar resonance; but the fundamental issue is the technological artifice within these boundaries that now defines the human habitat. The twentieth century has entered a technological arena. Technology is not merely one more territory for philosophers and sociologists to investigate, but a new foundation for understanding the self, human institutions, and ultimate reality.

In Ellul's terms, humanity is in a total crisis, triggered by entering a previously unknown environment. The transition to a technological society is for Ellul more fundamental than anything the human race has experienced over the last 5,000 years.

> The creation of the technological environment . . . is progressively effacing the two previous environments. Of course, nature and society still exist. But they are without power—they no longer decide our future. There are still earthquakes, volcanic eruptions, and hurricanes. But humanity is no longer helpless when faced with such disasters. It has the technical means to respond, and it is only due to lack of will, of political decision, and of a global mobilization of means that the scourge spreads. We can act, but we do not, and this is why nature is always menacingly present as an environment that is subordinate and no longer basic.
>
> The same applies to society. It remains as a secondary environment. We still have politicians and police and an administrative organization. But each of these has to have technological gadgets that make it more efficient and active. It has not yet been appreciated that this entry of technology means control over all the persons involved, all the powers, all the decisions and changes, and that technology imposes its own law on the different social organizations, disturbing fundamentally what is thought to be permanent (for example, the family), and making politics totally futile. Nevertheless, it will be said, politicians make the decisions. But politicians can decide only what is technologically feasible. All decisions are dictated by the necessity of technological growth.[14]

A society is technological, Ellul argues, not because of its machines, but from the pursuit of machineness in every area of human endeavor.

Mechanistic techniques are applied not just to nature, but also to social organizations and to our analysis of personhood. A technological society with global parameters separates itself from previous ones—including industrial civilizations—"through its historical consciousness that society is not fixed and given with the order of nature, but is an artificial human creation."[15] In this sense, for Ellul, finding an orientation in a technological civilization is in essence a religious problem. Unable to establish a meaningful life outside the artifical ambience of a technological culture, human beings place their ultimate hope in it. Seeing no other source of security and failing to recognize the illusoriness of their technical freedom, they become slaves to the exacting determinations of efficiency.

Whereas previous social orders operated with a triad—humans/tools/nature—in technological societies nature recedes and humans perceive themselves as living in a technical artifice. We have become aware that fundamentally we exist not in nature but in culture. "Man does not any longer live in a natural environment but rather in a milieu composed of the products of his technology. . . . He can no longer take any significant action without technological intermediation. Technology constitutes an engulfing universe for man, who finds himself in it as in a cocoon."[16] Thus Biosphere, the artifical environment in Arizona, replicates those elements of the natural world that humans are unwilling to give up. Yet rain forests and garden plots can be expected to recede quickly as efficiency dictates other spatial needs. The willingness to experiment with social structures at this point in time probably cannot withstand the mesmerizing effect of the technical artifice over the long term.

Although cultures are always symbolic worlds of mediated meaning, our symbolic formations are now dominated by technological structures. Ellul notes, "We are in touch with nature or the social group by means of communications: television, cinema, telephone or photography. These instruments . . . form a screen of means around all of us."[17] In Jean Baudrillard's terms, industrial society has become a world of simulated images and intensified sensations. The proliferation of information technologies has shifted modernity's orientation from production to reproduction, from economic and political institutions to hyperreality, where "everything becomes immediately transparent, visible, exposed in the raw and inexorable light of communication."[18] All aspects of life, even the most private and sacred, become miniaturized circuits, a realm of terror in which humans exist as "terminals of multiple networks."[19] In what Baudrillard calls "the precession of the simulacra," we create cybernetic models to organize reality, but in actuality a reversal occurs and reality arises from them instead.[20] "The real is produced from miniaturized units, from matrices, memory banks and command modules."[21] We float anchorless in a sea of electronic fantasy images. "The masses have become the black hole into which all meaning simply disappears."[22]

Ellul astutely integrates this glittering mediascope into his sociology of technology as a whole. In his framework, communications media represent the meaning-edge of the technological system, the arena in which the latter's soul is most clearly exposed. Although exhibiting the structural elements of all technical artifacts, the media's particular identity as a technology inheres in their function as bearers of symbols. Information technologies thus incarnate the properties of technology while serving as the agent for interpreting the meaning of the very phenomenon they embody. Communication systems are the "innermost, and most elusive manifestation" of human technological activity.[23] All artifacts communicate meaning in an important sense, but media instruments do so exclusively. They sketch out our world for us, organize our conversations, determine our decisions, and influence our self-identity with a technological cadence, massaging into our souls a mechanical rhythm and predisposition. A technicized mystique permeates the media system just as categorically as it does all other contemporary institutions. An ethic of efficiency appears everywhere, fully as important to communication engineers researching a channel capacity of 1 billion bits per second as to wheat farmers and napalm companies.

We have entered a new moral posture, designed "to bring human behavior into harmony with the technicized world, to set up a new scale of values in terms of 'la technique.' "[24] Moral values are thus precluded, since technicism and judgments about rightness or wrongness are mutually exclusive. "La technique" acts tyrannically as "a spiritual guillotine, decapitating other values, depriving them of social power."[25] A civilization engrossed in means eliminates all moral obstructions to its ascendancy, as "in ancient days men put out the eyes of nightingales in order to make them sing better."[26] The technical artifice so characterizes contemporary life that moral judgment lies ruined with it; in fact, it veritably thrives on the ashes of human morality. A civilization overcome by means converges on itself relentlessly until all necessities for moral decision are obviated; an alternative center of interest becomes inconceivable. A technicized morality replaces qualitative oughts—moral goods—with averages and probabilities mathematically computed.

Information, from Ellul's perspective, does not exist in our modern age because the responsible agency has been incapacitated by technics. In fact, the media prevent increasing administrative organization "from being felt as too oppressive and to persuade men to submit with good grace."[27] The media participate in the efficiency motif, subtly encouraging the citizenry to accept the mechanized constraints that steal their freedom.

For Ellul, the communication system is immune to morality as it spreads the technicized animus throughout public life. In the face of these perilous trends—so obvious to those who know history—where is the resistance, the prophetic word from within media ethics itself? Committed to individual autonomy, we shrivel our understanding of responsibility to code enforcement, shield laws, accuracy, fewer freebies, and other ephemeralities. Meanwhile, the rhetoric of technological efficiency prospers uncritically, with each faster and more complicated mode of transmitting information trumpeted as a revolutionary development.

Technology as Augmentative

Scholars typically call for improved transmission under the assumption that the unfettered flow of information will automatically improve democratic life.[28] Ultimate triumph is almost invariably sought in more streamlined methods, faster computer banks, complex multivariate scales, and electronic consoles of unlimited news and entertainment. Moral purpose is sacrificed to technological excellence. Once printing technology was invented, a process was set in motion for constantly increasing its capacity, speeding its production, and refining it organizationally. Obeying the same autonomous development, electronics is expanded from transatlantic cable to communication satellites, from seven television channels to thirty, from specialized companies to multinational conglomerates. Beguiled by machine productivity, we do not recognize this self-augmenting process as alien to moral imperatives.

On Wall Street's Black Monday in October 1987, computer technology played the material role in the stock market's free fall toward oblivion. While such dramatic collapses are complicated phenomena, Wall Street's computer-driven system at crucial points was no longer subject to human direction. The technology took its own direction, automatically "program trading" in accelerating response to the market's fall, impervious to all frenzied attempts to redirect or stop it. This incident serves as an analogue of our concern for the technological imperative in the mass media. When we define news as whatever reporters do, the imperative is driving us forward. Whenever new technologies are assessed and implemented according to efficiency criteria, we set the stage for media capabilities to determine what happens, independent of ethical principles.

Over the centuries, in Western scholarship at least, ethicists could take divine-command theories seriously[29] or, at a minimum, presume various versions of Platonic absolutes. Even as these beliefs unraveled in the nineteenth century, the immutability of nature, which took care of itself and demonstrated physical permanence, made norms of semi-enduring status at least imaginable. In other words, all previous ethics reckoned only with noncumulative phenomena, directly or in the background. Morality could conceivably be the property of all, living as humanity did on terra firma before the face of an Eternal Being, or at least with a first principle that ordered the vacillations of everyday affairs. But as Ellul, Ivan Illich, and others have demonstrated, a technological age is cumulative, expanding, augmentative. We attempt to form a new order of world understanding through communications, as we simultaneously augment an artifice in which traditional ethical principles carry little resonance.

Thus we face a conundrum. Global realities demand global communications. The human race cannot be stitched together satisfactorily by politics or transnational economics. Information is a social necessity for the modern planet's existence; but by expanding it, thickening its content, and speeding its transmission, we are undermining a normative base that—given the complexities of a global technological civilization—is more necessary now than ever. Whatever we gain in expanded information, we lose in ethics. We are increasingly trapped in Kurt Vonnegut, Jr.'s dilemma—as he reaches into his repertoire of commitments, wisdom, and intelligence, he comes up empty-handed precisely at the moment he needed them most.

It is foolish for media ethics to offer a quick fix or hide under fancy rhetoric. But we can still work the normativity domain as an act of conscience, driven by the need to articulate a normative discourse for professional ethics in a complicated age in which technology's efficiency breeds a climate of amorality. The stubborn issue of normativity lies beneath the rhetoric of human solidarity and international cooperation. Recovering that notion is the catalyst for an authoritative communication ethics in a global context. A debate in professional ethics over the nature of norms is the open door through which can enter a brawny, long-range ethics commensurate with the extent of contemporary technological power.

Purposive Nature

Paradoxically, as those of us in communications seek a world of informed decision making, we build in the process one that is sanitized of moral imperatives. Because efficiency and morality are polar opposites, our discourse in a technological age does not smoothly accommodate normativity. But casting the problem in terms of an artifice discontinuous from nature itself indicates the origins of a solution. Providentially, open spaces still exist in the pointillist canvas called our technological civilization. Certainly scientific naturalism, built on a subject–object dichotomy and defining the natural order as inert matter-in-motion, has had disastrous consequences. However, even though the task of reconstruction is nearly intractable, the strategy for reviving norms is not a direct assault on the artifice. Instead we should radically change our concepts of nature within those tiny interstices where physical reality continues as our habitat.

Hans Jonas

Hans Jonas's seminal work, *The Imperative of Responsibility,* illustrates how a recovery of norms can be embedded in the natural world. He provocatively turns to a philosophy of nature "to bridge the alleged chasm between a scientifically ascertainable 'is' and a morally binding 'ought.' "[30] The result is an ontological ground for responsibility that is universal in scope and self-evident regardless of ideology. Nature, defined to include the biosphere as a whole and in its parts, has a moral claim on humanity for its own sake and in its own right. The philosophical foundation for human action is reverence for terrestrial life, for the organic whole, for the natural—that is, the realm outside human artifice.

But our categorical obligation to preserve nature raises profound questions about natural reality with which the West has struggled since the Greeks and the East since Confucius. Jonas's primary concern is to demonstrate that not just humanity's continued existence matters, but nature's survival as a whole. He fulfills that concern by enriching our understanding of nature, by demonstrating that nature is purposive. Although it is ordinarily assumed in the West that humans alone are conscious and purposeful and nature is spiritless, Jonas insists that we consider the negative consequences when this dualism is overwrought. In his perspective, purpose is embedded de facto in animate nature, and its purposiveness is "evident in bringing forth life. Nature evinces at least one determinate purpose—life itself."[31]

Thus Jonas concludes Chapter 3: "Showing the immanence of purpose in nature, . . . with the gaining of this premise, the decisive battle for ethical theory has already been won."[32] The alleged chasm between "is" and "ought" has been bridged, at least in principle. Axiology has become a part of ontology. Purpose as such has its own accreditation within being and therefore entails responsible action for its own sake. The agent's duty to preserve nature is to be understood as similar in kind to parental responsibility for their children. It is obligation "independent of prior assent or choice; irrevocable, and not given to alteration of its terms by the participants."[33] When new life appears, the forebears do not debate their relationship to it as though the offspring were a neutral entity and their responsibility a matter of tabulating the options. The parents' duty to their children is an archetype of the natural accountability that Jonas thus establishes—an a priori ought, objectively grounded, that is timeless and nonnegotiable. Human responsibility regarding natural existence contributes the possibility of intrinsic imperatives to our cultural framework. It demonstrates the legitimacy of concluding that responsibility for humans can be cosmic, primordial, and irrespective of human roles or contracts. Responsibility for the continued existence of the earth is a duty held in common that shapes all other collective and individual obligations.

Through the preservation of life as the ground for human responsibility, Jonas has established normative discourse to help contradict the assumption of the present age that metaphysical truths do not exist and that no "ought" can be derived from "being." Jonas, on our reading, seeks to correct debilitating dichotomies in Western cosmology; others give his argument a monistic inflection, as though it undergirds animism and pantheism. But neither interpretation overturns the primary issue. Irrespective of belief in God, position on justice, naturalistic fervor, or political power, humans acknowledge at least this one imperative. One's only escape is the absurd antinomianism that nothingness is ontologically prior to existence.

History as a Normed Process

Purposive nature with the procreator's responsibility as an archetype is a first-level approximation. For our discourse in professional ethics, it establishes the possibility that normative claims are conceivable. One student, upon hearing the word "norm," responded: "Izad." He made up a nonsense word indicating how "norm" sounds to him. It is to Izad persons that Jonas addresses himself. But the content of norms must still be made explicit—in our case in terms of the social order, since communitarian ethics entails a particular social theory. If responsibility for new life becomes both form and content, we have only established survival as a principle. In our reconstruction, Jonas gives normativity a taken-for-granted character and thereby enables us to catapult beyond survival to a stringent version of universal human dignity in terms of dialogic communitarianism.

Our perspective embeds normed phenomena within culture and history. This intellectual strategy shifts transcendental criteria from a metaphysical, vertical, punctiliar plane to the horizon of community, world, and being, but transcendental norms they remain nonetheless.[34] In this view, cultures are sets of symbols that organize the human kingdom and are therefore ipso facto evaluative. "Norms and values are not something a culture has, but something it is."[35] Societies are embodiments of institutions, practices, and structures recognized internally as legitimate. Indeed, society is inconceivable without allegiance to a web of ordering relations. As Charles Taylor insists, a culture's continued existence depends on identifying and defending its normative base.

> Societies destroy themselves when they violate the conditions of legitimacy which they themselves tend to posit and inculcate. What we need to get

> clearer, therefore, is the family of conceptions of the good life, the notions
> of what it is to be human, which have grown up with modern society and
> have framed the identity of contemporary people. . . . For these will define
> the terms in which institutions, practices, disciplines, and structures will
> be recognized as legitimate or marked out as illegitimate.[36]

Taylor is correct. When we "cease to believe in the norms governing our
social life, . . . we are threatened with a kind of anomie" resulting from "a
crisis of allegiance to our society."[37]

Such a framing of our human identity can be rooted only in an ethics
of universal solidarity, one grounded in our being as humans and therefore
not restricted to the generations now living. Those of us engaged in ethical
theory beyond parochialism ought to aim at articulating a nonrelativistic
ethics in which "human beings have certain inescapable claims on one
another which cannot be renounced except at the cost of their humanity."[38]
As Helmut Peukert states it, our minimum goal must be

> a world in which human beings can find ways of living together which
> enable every individual to work out his or her own lifestyle based on
> recognition and respect of others, and to do so ultimately with a universal
> perspective not confined to small groups or nations. . . . Universal soli-
> darity is thus the basic principle of ethics and can be shown to be the
> normative core of all human communication.[39]

Refusing to confront normative issues on every level weakens the
agenda of our universal humanness. On the other hand, when the historical
process is

> normed by a network of fundamental calls or proto-norms (such as justice
> and mercy, stewardship and equality, health and consistency) the tem-
> porality and contingency of the process will not threaten, undermine, or
> defuse the permanent character of the proto-norms. . . . The specific and
> relative forms that norms of love and justice take in our lives are possible
> only in terms of a conditioning order for justice and love. A form *of* is
> possible only in terms of a conditioning order *for* that guarantees identity
> and continuity in the changing forms.[40]

How can we legitimately appeal to the supreme value of human life,
to an affirmation of unmitigated human dignity, without accepting a network of primal norms—justice, compassion, reciprocity, stewardship—that
are nonnegotiable? Everything else comes and goes, both ideologies and
the cultures they sustain. If temporality exhausts our intellectual vistas,
how can we justify an ethics of human mutuality in the face of anarchy,
dialecticism, or equivocation? Without norms that are more than contingent, we cannot finally condemn oppression and dehumanization except
on the grounds of personal prejudice or emotional makeup.[41] Basil Mitchell
maintains that the cultural ethos can be decisive only when it is not con-

sidered exclusive. Determinate human beings are not dissolved in a sea of cultural history.[42]

Absent a defensible conception of the good, praxis will be vitiated by arbitrariness. In fact, without a commitment to norms, emancipation is radically jeopardized by moral agnosticism. George Orwell underscored this truth in his classic essay, "Revenge Is Sour." Revolutions born of revenge are futile, self-destructive. Successful revolts are normed by conciliation and peace; machine-gunning a tyrant destroys the revenger's legitimacy. Edmund Burke observed that guillotines for decapitating the old nobility confuse revenge with justice; in his estimation, arbitrary, spiteful retaliation savages a revolutionary vision and fills our vista with gallows instead of hope.[43] Paul Greenberg is correct; when no distinctive norms separate the two sides,

> history is but a contest for abitrary power. . . . That is why the French Revolution proved a new birth not of freedom but of tyranny. That is why the execution of the Ceausescus in Romania is bad news. The Romanians didn't execute just two tyrants when they killed the Ceausescus after a secret trial. They struck down the rule of law; they ignored the need for public accountability; they gave way to pressure and bloodlust. . . . Revenge lays a foundation only for counter-revenge.[44]

The debate centers, of course, on one's philosophy of culture. Paul Tillich is correct when he says that traditional ethics must give way to a theory of culture. We advocate a cultural history with an anthropological bearing, a philosophy of culture centered on the radically human and with universals as the problematic. But we recognize that a theory of culture privileging the human rests on unresolved arguments. If, for example, humans maintain one another only in culture, how is it logically possible for those who themselves are constituted by culture to explain fully the process by which they are enabled to do the explaining? It is an old dilemma in new clothes: Can a theory of something contain itself? As semiotics has taught us, there is not the self and language because one is ultimately inextricable from the other, the first but a manifestation of the second. While engaging in language, we construct a vision of life. As we comprehend culture and its catalytic agent, communication, we thereby make ontological claims about human being.

But that very conundrum contends for history as a normed process. To establish a social ethics of transformation is necessarily to articulate an understanding of human being. And any such attribution, no matter how unintended, carries with it our moral complicity, since beingness is conditioned by our language concerning it. Culture encapsulates what humanity values; but, when undeveloped, that assertion remains only an equivocation. As far as we currently know, no society has ever declared open hunting season on humans—decreeing, for example, that up to three may be shot during October. All humans create life under the presumption of responsibility for those conceived. As a sign of our distinctive human-ness, we generate symbolic patterns along the boundaries between moral norms and actual behavior, the deepest self and our collective roles, the intentional and the inevitable.[45] All healthy humans begin uttering novel sentences with similar complexity when approximately two years old. In *Totem and Taboo,* Sigmund Freud contends that social orders without exception establish taboo boundaries even as they lift up motivational ideals for emulation. Aristotle proved that the law of noncontradiction is a uni-versal condition of intelligence, precluding everywhere the proverbial square circle and married bachelor. Given our generic human existence in a common universe, we can at least speak of universal category areas, such as basic beliefs: "belief in one's own existence, belief in a real world external to one's consciousness, belief in some ultimate reality that I cannot push around but must reckon with in the final analysis."[46]

Likewise, the sacredness of human dignity is empirically verifiable as a universal principle across cultures; as such, it integrates ethical theory and praxis, serving thereby as an archetype of social transformation. And understanding history as a complex arena of universal solidarity and proto-norms entails a strong versus weak definition of human dignity. Rather than a minimal condemnation of indignities or wishful declarations about "the possibilities of this intelligent animal," in our framework,

> human dignity is the respect-worthiness imputed to humankind by reason of its privileged ontological status as creator, maintainer, and destroyer of worlds. Each self shares in this essential dignity (that is, is recognized as a moral entity) insofar as it partakes (whether by conscious intention or not) in world building or world destroying actions. Thus human dignity does not rest on intention, moral merit, or subjective definitions of self-interest. It rests on the fact that we are, in this fundamental way that is beyond our intention, human. We are moral agents. . . . To assert dignity is both to acknowledge the factuality of human creative agency and to accept responsibility for its use.[47]

Nature of Norms

In order to appreciate fully a dynamic understanding of norms and to free it from conventional skepticism, this formulation must be wrenched from propositional knowledge. Deeply embedded in the general understanding of norms is a basic misconception—that norms are

> archetypes or models . . . which serve us as templates for guiding perfor-mance. . . . On this view, what we do when we follow a norm is reproduce

it, produce a replica of it in some particular context of thought or action. Following a norm requires just this, is strictly limited to this, and is logically violated if in employing the norm violations are produced in it.[48]

Gordon W. Allport labeled this the ball-and-chain conception, as though action is an automatic, unthinking response to normative stimuli.[49] However, the penchant to reflect on norms with highly abstract deductivist procedures obscures their profoundly concrete character. History as a normed process recasts the issues away from the perplexities and confusions which presume that norms are first certified rationally and then effected mechanically.

As a replacement for "applicatory," Frederick Will uses Charles Peirce's term "ampliative" to describe the process of amplification, construction, analysis, and discernment involved in the development of norms. Thus, in the classic example, one readily repays a loan under ordinary circumstances, but one refuses to return a pistol when its owner demands it in a drunken rage. The refusal does not violate the morality of paying one's debts, but indicates that a sense of propriety—learned by experience and catechesis—is internal to the normative process. Norms are cultural equipment and not simply conceptual schemes. Certainly, they involve conscious reflection and intellectual discovery, but as a form of appropriate action they must be maintained, reconstructed, and defended as well. "Implicit in the norms we follow in the more or less routine guidance of thought and action are ideals, models, visions of life that, aborning, are resources for both the reinforcement and refashioning of these norms themselves."[50]

If norms are distorted as abstract entities, they become effectively immune to criticism or confrontation with explicit evils. Restricting the normative process to the application of deep categorical presuppositions is also excessively atomistic, rather than recognizing normative action as largely communal. "Grasp of the social character of the broad norms of thought and action . . . [is] among the sorest needs in modern philosophy. For the natural tendency of a modern philosophical mind and personality is individualistic."[51]

Thomas Nagel documents those phenomena suspended outside the human persona, compelling epiphanic moments not grounded a priori. "Truth manifests itself and we recognize its rightness"; the power of truth is authenticated by its own disclosure.[52] Nagel reiterates the genuineness of our knowing the world subjectively, but contends that we take up simultaneously a conception of the world existing independently of ourselves. His *View from Nowhere* is a "deliberate effort to juxtapose the internal and external or subjective and objective views at full strength."[53] In a genuine sense, reality exists objectively outside our description of it, or, stated more precisely, through a transcendental impulse we form an overriding conception of the world with us in it. We are contained within history and cannot create ourselves from scratch. But we "think of reality as a set of concentric circles, progressively revealed as we detach gradually from the contingencies of the self"; thus humans consider it worthwhile to bring their values and beliefs "under the influence of an impersonal standpoint," even without proof that this external vista is not illusory.[54] Over against relativism, ethical skepticism, and antirealism, the critical point is that an independent reality exists; it is from nowhere in particular and "natural to regard life and the world in this way."[55] To seek its origin is philosophically uninteresting.

A classic story from India reiterates Nagel's argument: "An Englishman, having been told that the world rested on a platform which rested on the back of an elephant which rested in turn on the back of a turtle, asked: what did the turtle rest on? Another turtle. And that turtle? 'Ah, Sahib, after that it is turtles all the way down.' "[56] As we probe beyond the hard surfaces of life, we cut through the platform and elephant layers to turtles—the normative patterns that order our social configurations into meaningful wholes. Uncertainties about the turtles' origin, their precise shape, and how deep they run do not abrogate their reality. Using an analogue to norms, the earth's continued existence is a truth of compelling power, regardless of any agnosticism about its origins.

In a post-Newtonian, counter-Enlightenment age, norms can only be recovered culturally. They are apprehended only *in locis,* yet universal proto-norms beyond region and language are essential to maintaining human societies and preventing anticultural directions in our indigenous institutions. In *The Responsible Self,* H. Richard Niebuhr defines myth as that linguistic form which combines personal and impersonal knowing: "Deep in our minds is the myth, the interpretative pattern of the metahistory, within which all our histories and biographies are enacted."[57] Norms can guide concrete action because they have this mythic generality. To believe otherwise is a patently false subjectivism contradicted by the self-referentiality argument. Master norms are of the first order, conceptually speaking, yet human beings enter them through that second-order reality known as ethnicity, geography, and history. "Nonnegotiable primal norms are experienced only in terms of specific second order ideological embodiments."[58] Note, for example, how the norm of truthtelling takes narrative form in three political controversies.

Czechoslovakia's president Vaçlav Havel, a playwright who spent five years in jail as a dissident, declared in his first speech to Parliament:

> I assume you have not named me to this office so that I, too, should lie
> to you. For forty years you have heard from my predecessors the same

thing: how many more millions of tons of steel we have produced, how we are all happy, how we believe in our government. We have become morally ill because we are used to saying one thing and thinking another.[59]

The Media Resource Center at the University of Natal in South Africa struggles in theory and production with the role of video and film in social change. Given the power of the South African Broadcast Company, a discriminatory state educational apparatus, and government control by censorship, the center realizes that there is more to oppositional media than their message. But in developing a holistic strategy for challenging South Africa's apartheid ideology, the motivation is the liberating power of authentic communication. Thus the grass-roots organizations in black townships and the media studies units at the University of Natal insist on production that "goes all the way down," on "rigorous procedures for oral and archival documentation," and on a democratic educational process in which raw footage is given "community scrutiny."[60]

During the Iran-Contra hearings, Lieutenant Colonel Oliver North portrayed himself as a scrappy patriot serving in the public interest. Apparently a broad spectrum of Americans accepted those heroic terms, and then President Ronald Reagan was noticeably relieved that North did not serve time in jail. But North's lies to Major General Richard Secord and his lies covering up the arm sales to Iran and profits to the Nicaraguan Contras did not escape an array of disillusioned commentators and statesmen. Through the rhetorical fog emerged a clear-headed understanding of truth as central to a nation's identity, and North's subsequent judicial vindication does not invalidate that insight. From this perspective, North was as dangerous to the social welfare as a rapist roaming the streets. Reagan's presidency, in fact, was seen to hinge on the veracity of his own account; the public may tolerate incompetence and bad judgment, but deception would damage his credibility beyond repair.[61]

In each of these three cases, truthtelling emerges with the cultural inflection of the second order. But all appeal in their own terms to a cross-cultural principle of veracity; none limits truthtelling to technical accuracy, but understands it more as trustworthiness. When Havel concluded that integrity was essential for Czechoslovakia to "become once again a spiritual crossroads of Europe," he reflected the first order, speaking a language that resonates with that of the Film and Allied Workers Organization in South Africa and with the critics of Reagan's foreign policy.

We distinguish between the first and second orders as with a window-pane—knowing that there is a decisive break, yet both realms are transparent to each other as well. In other words, humans "commonly and fortunately think concretely of concrete things, organically of things which in their relations with each other form organic wholes."[62] And necessarily these mental processes often occur simultaneously without being diluted; for example, one ordinarily considers activities of the local police force in terms of elementary principles of political justice. The only break with logic is to think organically of particulars and concretely of universals. Symbols are the constituent units of language that connect the two orders by making the invisible perceptible *and* by opening up reality to the deepest levels of the soul.[63] Symbols illuminate their referents so as to make them transparent; they permit us to express levels of reality that otherwise remain hidden.[64]

In April 1989, one of the authors joined twenty-five other ethicists from around the globe in Geneva at the United Nations. We debated the 1948 Human Rights Declaration—that ingenious appeal to universal human dignity which has survived for more than forty years with surprising resilience. The delegates worked to solidify it ethically and conceptually for a new worldwide thrust, each participant arrogant enough to speak for an entire nation.

Six months later, at Laguna de Bay outside Manila, this same author toured a harbor in a small fishing boat, observing how international fisheries had fenced off the productive areas for themselves and destroyed for Filipino fishermen the subsistence that had kept them from starving to death. Through the Calariz Multi-Media Project, these fishermen were gaining a voice as a Fish-Workers' Association, producing pamphlets, drawing cartoons, holding town meetings, shooting eight-minute videos—hoping to gain a hearing in Manila, where they had had no access before. As they presented their case in a small room of a cement-block building, the Geneva debates were repeated in miniature. The Calariz fishermen appealed for minimal justice, defying those who stole not only their fish but their rights and dignity as well. It became unmistakable that—alongside the chocolate waters of Laguna de Bay rather than the splashing fountains of Geneva, in a temporary structure rather than the marble Palace of the Nations, in the wooden fishing boats of Asia rather than the chauffered limousines of Europe, in the broken English of October 14 rather than the streamlined electronic translations of April 14—proto-norms were being fashioned incarnate in history.

Necessity of Norms

Yet without a universal, international commitment there is no opportunity to protect the environment or prevent economic bankruptcy or control dizzying population growth or reduce the weapons of global destruction. Those who plead for preserving local cultures and those envisioning a global information order are both right.[65] In fact, these parallel movements are interconnected in a way that makes folklore from the ground up the *sine qua non* for universal norms rooted in human solidarity. Therefore, although the sinews of high technology bind us together of necessity, an impassioned commitment to cultural diversity must be nurtured as well. In the absence of empowering indigenous groups, an elitist, paternalistic, power-driven system is created at odds with the very social ethics we construct in its name.

At his Guildhall lecture in London shortly after the Tiananmen Square massacre Ronald Reagan used this upheaval in China and its vicious repression to celebrate freedom: "You cannot massacre an idea," he said. "You cannot run tanks over hope. You cannot riddle people's yearning with bullets." Reagan was undoubtedly correct. But then he ignored the paradox as he doomed tyranny through the communications revolution: "The biggest of Big Brothers is helpless against the technology of the information age," he insisted. "Electronic beams blow through the Iron Curtain as if it were lace."[66] Not so. Even in open societies, local histories resist intrusion from an anonymous messenger. Until the symbols resonate from the ground up, the free flow of information remains alien and amorphous. For all our sophistication in constructing a new world information order between New York and Mexico City, London and New Delhi, Paris and Caracas, our deepest concerns ought to be intracultural, in the villages between Bangkok and the remote subcultures in the mountains, among the burgeoning ethnic diversity in the United States. Transformative action is impossible unless people groups are subjective participants, rather than a leader's object.

In the current debates over international development, one observes a profound disillusionment with established strategies that emphasize economic growth and technology through increasingly centralized distribution of resources. One response has been a convergence of emphases on participation, a major concern for such agencies as ILO, UNESCO, WHO, and FAO. But this form of participation is actually "mobilizing." Mobilization reflects an underlying ideology that seeks to activate the rural sector in order to make it more "modern" and the untutored masses to make them more "responsive." Essentially, in this form of so-called participation the basic decisions have already been made, and government bureaucracy as agent of implementation invites the people to endorse and collaborate with the political elite. In this sense, those whom we glibly call experts are actually oppressors. Urban administrators and planners design projects, with scanty attention to the vast populations that are considered primitive and, in a paternalistic way, need to be educated out of their ignorance. The SITE experiments in India are a classic example of what Paulo Freire calls the banking model, even though innocuous in content (agriculture and medicine, for example). The central government, in effect, declared that it had the golden resources and would dispense its riches to penniless creditors in the villages on the bank's terms, keeping its customers forever indebted.[67]

A sophisticated normative model redefines participation as an empowering process through which people create a space for themselves. Orthodox approaches tend to marginalize the poor. A perspective grounded in history as a normed process seeks countervailing power to the existing structure from below among those in continuous deprivation; it therefore articulates a plan of transformative action that is truly by the people. High-level negotiations over spectrum space and satellite orbits ignore the masses who live outside the political centers and seem oblivious to the flourishing of democratized media in the last decade. A communitarian ethics joins the outrage against the evils of transnational corporations, the abject failure of five-year economic plans, and the obscenity of regimes maintained only by military might. No one receives the primary attention when power is reinvented around participation by the disenfranchised, who insist on their own custody of social change, on defining for themselves both the problems and the solutions rather than being manipulated toward predetermined ends. A normative focus on empowerment awakens our appreciation of internal colonization, manifest in the subordination of particular regions to the capital, of rural to urban areas, of poor people to rich patrons, of sharecroppers to landowners, and of women to men.

The view of history as a normed process assumes that cultural divergence does not preclude ethical convergence. In fact, moral responsibility entails that the two be integrated appropriately. It is an argument developed by Dietrich Bonhoeffer, whose career as a resistance pastor and ethicist set him in the middle of this century's textbook case of prima facie evil, the Third Reich. Yet, even in this context, Bonhoeffer agonized over the difficulty of responsible moral choice. His *Ethics* was written (but never completed) in the years 1940 to 1943 while Bonhoeffer was employed as a member of General Wilhelm Canaris's SS Abwehr, Munich office, ostensibly to spy on ecclesiastical leaders in Europe. But Bonhoeffer was a double agent, part of the Canaris plot to negotiate a truce with the Allies and assassinate Hitler. He had already come under Gestapo suspicion for operating a resistance seminary at Finkenwalde. He had already broken with European Protestants over their failure to speak out for German Jews (Kristallnacht galvanized Bonhoeffer but frightened even his Confessing Church colleagues, those who had refused the oath of allegiance to Hitler). He had already been banned from teaching at the University of Berlin; had already chosen to return to Germany after only a month in New York City, a trip arranged by Reinhold Niebuhr and others to be his escape from the Nazis; had already fallen in love with Maria von Wedemeyer; and, before the last of the essays that were to be his magnum opus, had already been arrested and charged with subversion.

Bonhoeffer's ethics challenges us to keep penultimate concerns from becoming ultimate. Freedom and patriotism, for example, become demonic when elevated to supremacy. Cut loose from the ultimate, our penultimate concerns are merely self-serving; substituted for the ultimate domain, they become a strident claim at the expense of another's dignity, a plea for justice now transformed into an abrogation of other moral imperatives. Bonhoeffer dismissed abstract questions about the good, spurned moral theorizing detached from lived experience, repudiated theologizing that sought no more than ideals, proofs, and arguments. For Bonhoeffer, the good was to be found not in timeless theory, but in responding to the struggle of one's era, in costly discipleship to the God who was incarnate in time. Abstracted moralism, theorizing about choice apart from the experience of choice, was as impossible to Bonhoeffer as cheap grace.[68]

World-View Pluralism

Communitarianism rejects the Enlightenment's individualistic rationalism. As Richard Rorty recognizes, it also contradicts pragmatism's presumption that liberal institutions can survive the collapse of their philosophical justification. Communitarians insist that political institutions are no better than the social and anthropological theories they incorporate.[69] Michael Sandel, for instance, believes that political philosophy must account for "the nature of the moral subject," which is "in some sense necessary, noncontingent and prior to any particular experience."[70]

However, Rorty contends that "liberal democracy can get along without philosophical presuppositions." In his terms, fleshing out and justifying its theoretical base do not have the central importance that communitarians claim. "As citizens and as social theorists, we can be as indifferent to philosophical disagreements about the nature of the self as Jefferson was to theological differences about the nature of God." Thomas Jefferson thus established American liberal politics by making respectable the idea that "politics can be separated from beliefs about matters of ultimate importance."[71]

And in that tradition, John Rawls articulates a conception of justice that avoids "claims about the essential nature and identity of persons. . . . As a practical political matter no general moral conception can provide the basis for a public conception of justice in a modern democratic society."[72] In contrast to the assumption that human beings "have a natural center that philosophical inquiry can locate and illuminate," Rorty opts for the self "as a historical contingency all the way through." In his view, humans are "centerless networks of beliefs and desires" whose "vocabularies and opinions are determined by historical circumstances. . . . Reflective equilibrium is all we need try for—there is no natural order of justification of beliefs, no predestined outline for argument to trace."[73] Philosophers must "decry the very notion of having a view, while avoiding having a view about having views." Formal reflective thought is "but an activity or pursuit better seen as another way of coping."[74]

In contrast to democracy with a naked center, history as a normed process assumes Archimedian points around which the social order revolves. At least in terms of a symbolic theory of communication, how could it be otherwise? If we are cultural beings who organize life and provide it significance (at least on the immediate plane), then our patterns of life in space and time are inherently value-centered. Symbolic constructions constitute the human kingdom by organizing reality and directing the ends of societal practice. Assuming that culture is the container of our generative symbolic capacity, the constituent parts of such containers are a society's values. These variables that define outlook and life-style are ipso facto evaluative. A naked-center social order is congenitally implausible. With standards recognized as intrinsic to symbolic environments, the only option available is putting content into the normative, asking what authentic social existence involves, articulating the appropriate use of language, and specifying the ends that political entities should serve.

It should be obvious, however, that our normative communitarian model is a reconstructive strategy discontinuous from the Cartesian procedure of incorrigible first premises established as conceptually unique. We are not foundationalists, and we share the skepticism in post-Newtonian cosmology for unconditioned First Philosophy. We agree with Rorty and his circle that foundationalism has powerfully distorted Western—particularly Anglo-American—philosophy. However, Rorty's disclaimers are directed against deductivist epistemology and do not disavow normative discourse constituted in culture. His challenge—that philosophy "continue the conversation" rather than aim at "discovering truth"—establishes a fundamental break with the mathematical mindset;[75] but it seriously obscures the ampliative process of implementing and reconstituting norms. Our starting point is not ontological a prioris separated from life, but the conditions for understanding articulated by Max Weber—that is, our capacity as cultural beings to take a deliberative attitude toward the world. From the perspective of a feminist theory that eschews abstractions, Seyla Benhabib coins the label "interactive universalism" to identify this perspective. She argues for a moral framework that values the diversity of human beliefs without endorsing all our differences as ethically significant.[76]

To contradict normative theory on the grounds that it presumes an outmoded rationalism is to misconstrue its nature profoundly. Jeffrey Stout uses a telling analogue to indicate that some moral claims can be accepted as true without presuming their correspondence to transcendental givens. There is no "moral Esperanto" universally spoken and floating free of particular traditions. But there is "moral pidgin," simplified speech for strangers, never substituted for the richness of native languages but workable under duress. And over time, pidgin can develop into "moral creole," discourse "well suited to the needs of a time and place" and subtle enough for intimate communication among friends.[77] So important, in fact, are these historically contingent moral languages that the failure to cultivate them effectively—within religious communities, for example—results in the triumph of abstract styles of moral reasoning such as Enlightenment foundationalism.

Tacit Knowledge

Our normative communitarianism is not a deductivist program, but an embodiment of what Michael Polanyi called tacit knowledge.[78] This philosopher and chemist at Oxford and Manchester demonstrated conclusively that the foundations of our knowing are deeply interiorized; as we integrate particulars, we do not understand them externally but make value judgments regarding them. Focal awareness of data requires operating within a framework. Polanyi sets himself in the tradition of Wilhelm Dilthey, who had postulated a century earlier that genuine understanding (*Verstehen*) is indwelling or empathy. When scientists discover new knowledge and accept these discoveries as true, they become committed to them and thereby embody them in their beliefs. Originality breeds a context of values, although it breeds them tacitly.

All our knowledge cannot be formalized; the positivists have been fundamentally mistaken for a century now in believing that "since particulars are more tangible, their knowledge offers a true conception of things."[79] Any series of explicit operations presupposes a fund of inexplicit knowing. Biological experimentation on frogs, for example, is impossible unless this organic matter is first identified informally from our tacit knowledge of animal frogness. "The skill of a driver cannot be replaced by a thorough schooling in the theory of the motorcar; the knowledge I have of my own body differs altogether from the knowledge of its physiology; and the rules of rhyming and prosody do not tell me what a poem told me, without any knowledge of its rules."[80]

Tacit knowledge is not merely an imperfect version of its explicit counterpart. Accounting for intention and commitment is not like alchemy, awaiting the liberation of chemistry. In fact, tacit thought is indispensable to all knowing and "the ultimate mental power by which all explicit knowledge is endowed with meaning."[81] Eliminating the personal dimension would destroy knowledge of all kinds, both scientific and everyday. "By concentrating attention on his fingers, a pianist can temporarily paralyze his movement."[82] Thus Polanyi answers the *Meno*'s paradox, in which Plato made solving problems an absurdity: either you know what you are looking for and then no problem exists, or you do not know what you are looking for and therefore will not recognize it should you discover it. Tacit knowledge, however, intimates something hidden which may yet become manifest. Copernicans passionately maintained a heliocentric cosmology for 140 years before Newton could document it computationally.

As Polanyi summarizes his argument, "Thought can only live on ground which we adopt in the service of a reality to which we submit."[83] Identifying norms that are broad and deep involves more than ingenious deductive techniques. A normative model is a complex architecture developed by James Olthuis, for example, as a hermeneutics of ultimacy: "In experiencing a conceptual system as valid, we also tacitly experience our reliance on the ultimate which is the ground on which the system rests. It is our dependence on this ultimate which makes comprehension possible. Any cognition of a particular thing occurs in a framework whose ultimate horizon is the reality of this ultimate."[84] Interpretation is a constituent feature of our humanness, and this cognitive capacity, grounded in an ultimate, is directed and ordered toward the ultimate. Furthermore, "manifestations or revelations of the ultimate can be received and recognized by humans only in faith."[85] Although thinking begins with core beliefs received as revelation, human knowing is not thereby restricted. "In fact, faith commitment is the very condition through which human cognition reveals its intelligibility."[86] Through rational argumentation our vision of life is elaborated and defended, but reason does not provide an independent proof of its validity.

The reality of ultimate concerns for enabling normative discourse involves a particular form of pluralism. Admittedly, there is no uniform understanding of a richer pluralism to replace the centerless privatistic species which dominates at present. Advocates of other alternatives debate their cohering center. In one case, a pluralistic society is characterized by multiple associations; that is, a plurality of social structures (family, church, school, government, business, press, courts) coexists, each with its own integrity, identity, and rights. In a second case, multiple ethnic cultures are the reference point; in Randolph Bourne's classic description, pluralism refers to the richly woven fabric of native cultures—a federation of various races in contrast to an insipid, melting-pot nationalism, which insists on the assimilation of subcultures "into a tasteless, colorless fluid of uniformity."[87] In a third case, pluralism means confessional diversity, pluralistic cultures disavowing state religion and guaranteeing the survival of an array of ideologies, philosophies of life, and beliefs.

Importance of World Views

Defining history as a normed process entails the latter understanding of pluralism. It concludes that what might be called world-view pluralism is the axis of communitarian democracy. Eliminating world views under the guise of achieving a nondescript consensus is phony. Thinking is presuppositional, so our social vision will always be value-driven. "To demand 'neutral discourse' in public life . . . should be recognized as a way of coercing people to speak publicly in someone else's language and thus never to be true to their own."[88] In fact, since Antonio Gramsci we have realized that political action is actually a manifestation of our world views, and that only in world views is there human consciousness. Through world views, humans are organized into social blocs, and, conversely, world views are never individually generated but express communal life.[89] Since world views are inescapable, the only salient issue is whether the ultimate commitments they reflect are life-affirming or not.

As world views are lobbied within the public sphere, some agreements will emerge that form a common good. Richard John Neuhaus correctly insists on a more proactive stance here: because we hold our world views within a sociopolitical arena, we have a responsibility to make truly public the course we favor and to demonstrate the way it advances our common citizenship.[90] Among contending paradigms, some meet the community test but many do not. The press monitors these world-view debates and evaluates them in terms of their contribution to communitarian values. The question is whether they help build a civic philosophy and thereby demonstrate a transformative intent. Certainly, uncompromising authoritarian claims are threatening to a democracy; but the real enemy is an empty, shallow, unfed pluralism that neglects or trivializes serious political issues and matters of moral substance.[91] The opposite of "milk-toast civility" is not "public nastiness"; principled pluralism "strengthens debate" rather than stifling it.[92] Even if there are clashes over world views at their deepest level, this fact does not preclude their frequent similarity at crucial points as well.[93] Contrary to "G. K. Chesterton's wisecrack that tolerance is the virtue of people who do not believe anything, . . . tolerance is only a virtue in people who do believe something."[94] Freedom of conscience is meaningless jargon except to those with a developed conscience themselves. World-view pluralism thus serves as an antidote to what Stanley Hauerwas calls the murky void lurking at the heart of individualistic liberalism.[95]

Lesslie Newbigin argues for a normative pluralism in which contending paradigms deal with their claims and disagreements in public. From the perspective of forty years in India, he asks his Christian audiences: How may one legitimately argue for "absolute truth"? Not from the vantage point of abstracted foundationalism, since no one has a platform by which to speak supraculturally. Responsible pluralism never retreats to a privatized sphere in which personal well-being or transcultural certitude is the final appeal. Following Polanyi, Newbigin insists that all truth claims must be made "with universal intent." Mutuality is the context in which one may rightly say both "This I believe" and "This is to be believed." Indeed, neither statement is legitimate without the other.[96] Rather than presuming with contemporary liberalism that proper procedures can substitute for substantive morality, world-view pluralism results in deeply held norms being nurtured toward common causes within the public square.

World views are pretheoretical, consisting of "interpretive schemes, moral maxims, and collections of traditional wisdom."[97] They are culturally shared outlooks on life, a set of basic beliefs about human destiny. And often they are most clearly communicated in the public arena through religious language. H. Richard Niebuhr, for example, challenges us to recover and refashion religious word forms in order to amplify our deepest humanness. Typically, the root metaphors that shape our world views must be manifested in sacred symbols in order for values, feeling, and history to be recast toward integrity. As religious words—ordinarily in the first person—open up the divine–human relationship, our visions of life are nurtured toward moral rectitude. Only the language of ultimates has the potency to transform into maturity those "small seeds of integrity" common to our species's distinctiveness.[98]

Recognizing the role of religious discourse as a vehicle for communicating world views does not mean that we ought to see more ecclesiastical news in the press rather than only a religion page or two on Saturday. After all, goes the typical argument, more people attend a church in one Sunday than attend all National Football League games in an entire season. Nor, we are told, is the minister, priest, or rabbi as buffoon fair treatment in prime-time entertainment. We are reminded that few journalists could handle something as simple as Jimmy Carter's born-again language, so they resorted to covering his Sunday-school class in Plains, Georgia. Certainly, reporting on religion, institutionally and sociologically, merits upgrading in quantity and scope.[99] But entering world-view narratives into the public arena is more enigmatic than that. The challenge is to disclose the dimension of ultimacy in ordinary experience. Martin Luther King, Jr., was not only a black leader, but a religious hero as well.[100]

Glenn Tinder's "Can We Be Good Without God?" in the *Atlantic Monthly* at least offers a case study of how world views—in this instance,

Judeo-Christian theism—can make their way in the body politic. Tinder's purpose is not traditional apologetics, but a struggle in the open over the Judeo-Christian paradox that the human race is simultaneously exalted and morally degraded. In unaffected language, he argues for "the double insight that the evil are not beyond the reach of divine mercy nor the good beyond the need for it."[101] Insiders will legitimately reject his glorifying the individual, but it is a finely crafted attempt to make sense of contemporary political struggles in terms of the faith commitments that underlie them.

Human reality is structured by ideas. In Heidegger's profound sense, we live in the house of language. Our presuppositions are the grid through which we view the world and act upon it. As we participate in the common task of generating a normative discourse, we contribute to the first-order domain of proto-norms and thereby make possible a meaningful second-order entrée to this arena. We never encounter universal truth pure, but attending this territory gives us continuity over space and across time. At least phenomenologically speaking, public debate over norms enables us to turn a conundrum into an inspiration, and to reconceive a paradox into a mandate for transformative action.

KPFA-FM in Berkeley, California, is the oldest community radio station in the United States. Its purpose is left-wing alternative daily news. New social movements, such as feminist, immigrant, antinuclear, and Chicano, have combined with labor unions and socialist political blocs to depend on KPFA-FM as an ally in oppositional politics. In her participant-observation study of this broadcast enterprise, Nina Eliasoph documented the power of the economic and organizational infrastructure, the influence of political ideologies, and the obvious importance of news routines and conventions. In the process, her research pointed to the dramatic significance of world views: "If tomorrow the government offered unconditional funding to all news organs, with no editorial caveats, the news content would probably not change as dramatically as the ownership theories imply. Dominant worldviews would still probably prevail."[102] A large percentage of KPFA's audience is politically active and well informed; listeners tune in the news more than any other program at the station. But Eliasoph's study indicated that if basic conceptual categories about politics, society, and culture are blurred, the news becomes unintelligible. "Oppositional news only makes sense when the audience already has some inkling of a theory with which to interpret the scattered daily crises. The problem is not [with the] news; the problem is that there is little else in the empty American public sphere."[103]

Normative pluralism means that our version of communitarian ethics would be advocated openly within professional ethics, but not made exclusive. Within the public sphere, communitarianism explicitly argues against individualistic and pragmatic liberalism on the grounds that democratic ideals cannot survive without a cohering center. In the process, communitarianism contributes to democracy's core an understanding of those proto-norms without which other forms of pluralism—such as ethnic diversity—cannot be responsibly achieved.

Contemporary Debates

Meanwhile, under the aegis of normative pluralism we offer an alternative to radical theories that are deconstructive without being clearly transformative. Cultural neo-Marxists, for example, call for oppositional readings of the dominant ideology's semantic domain.[104] To detotalize the preferred code and retotalize it within an alternative framework is a politically significant moment that resists the hegemony of a historical bloc in Gramsci's sense. Critical ethics, in this view, begins "by asserting itself as a mapping of the power inscribed in (networks of) practices";[105] or, as Paul Patton declares, "We are already trapped, in thought as in reality, in the web of power. Hence the real question is one of tactics."[106] Power is the definitive feature of concrete historical practice, and our scholarly purpose is to "resist and transform the existing structures of power."[107]

The conscious aim of humanistic Marxism is not description but reformation. "The interventionist commitment is avowed and straightforward."[108] This is a normative project, but without appealing to formal categories of right or wrong. "For critical theorists, there is no absolute Truth, no absolute right or wrong, good or bad, moral duty or responsibility. But critical theorists do not posit a relativism either, where any action is fundamentally as good, as moral, or as responsible as any other."[109] In Stuart Hall's eloquent plea, it is "Marxism without final guarantees." No particular outcomes are predicted, only a call to struggle "under the open horizon of Marxist theorizing—determinacy [setting limits, establishing parameters] without guaranteed closures."[110] The destination is "not so straightforward; . . . when the precise nature of [a] just society is discussed at all, it remains somewhat elusive."[111]

But communitarian ethics asks, By what criterion ought one choose a process as final instead of theological or scientific certitudes? Why Hall's determinacy instead of an unending series of significations, as the poststructuralists predicate? In the debates between cultural studies and postmodernism, why should one not side with the latter's attempt to vitiate ethics and undercut politics? Defending privileged categories or strategies entails norms by which such privilege is established. Granted, most cultural theorists advocate social justice; but how can they establish a rationale for it other than the arbitrary choice of self-appointed elites?[112] A justified defense of any critically powerful ethics, we believe, entails a philosophically rigorous normative center—in our case, personhood-in-community.

In debates with German critical theory, communitarian democracy avoids both the rationalist and the distributive fallacies. As Adorno and Horkheimer recognized at the early stages of the Frankfurt School, Marxist social theories tend toward the distributive fallacy by presuming that humanity as one empirical subject can be represented by one particular group. And what in the perspectives of other critical theorists—Walter Benjamin, Ernest Bloch, and Herbert Marcuse—precludes the distributive fallacy of assuming that one strategic human position in the social structure represents the whole? What guarantees within their normative claims that the revolutionary working class, or a persecuted minority, or religious sects— by a faulty logic of substitution—are not made universal?[113] Herbert Marcuse's impassioned search for a revolutionary force illustrates the conundrum: Is it the student movement on campus, the National Liberation Front in Vietnam, Castro's Cuba? Marcuse worked the radical circles in fashion at the time, and located a panoply of protesters with only one continuity—conflict with the political establishment.

It is Habermas's extraordinary contribution to critical theory to confront the distributive fallacy while continuing to insist on an emancipatory goal. He unapologetically endorses the tradition of Benjamin, Bloch, and Marcuse in their resisting reformism without fulfillment. But he locates nothing in their work that precludes them from the distributive fallacy of assuming that one strategic human position in the social structure represents the whole. Habermas seeks to prevent the distasteful revolution designed and imposed by a cadre of well-intentioned elites. He makes it inescapable that normative claims regarding happiness, messianic ideals, and purposive culture must themselves be grounded in a universal norm if the fallacy of distribution is to be overcome. He appeals to universal pragmatics and an ideal speech situation for putting under judgment all systems of power— violent or benign—that pronounce their own self-styled revolution. Instead of inquiring, in the Kantian tradition, What do individual moral agents claim as universal maxims for all? Habermas asks, What norms would members of an ideal communication community agree represent their mutual interests?[114] "The procedural model of an argumentative praxis (Habermas calls them 'practical discourses') replaces the silent thought-experiment enjoined by the Kantian universalizability test."[115]

In his normative project, Habermas endorses with Kantian ethics the central role of reason, though not presupposing the Kantian a priori of duty. Habermas increasingly puts reason and eudaemonia in dialectical tension, thus not demeaning the validity of normative sentences or ignoring questions about the integrity of values. However, Habermas's protestations to the contrary, his cognitivist ethics falls prey to the rationalist fallacy in which reason determines both the genesis and the conclusion. He constructs a self-determining circle founded on a metanarrative. He thereby hands to socal ethics a two-edged sword—exorcising our frequent capitulation to elitism, while piquing us to escape the rationalist fallacy as well. Thus the heavy agenda of this chapter recommends itself—constructing a social ethics as transformative in character as critical theory's, yet unmarred by either of the Frankfurt fallacies. By reconstituting norms in disjunction from Enlightenment foundationalism and with universal solidarity as epicenter, communitarian ethics escapes the rationalist fallacy, on the one hand, and the distributive fallacy, on the other.[116]

Conclusion

Normative pluralism is a coherent alternative to Alasdair MacIntyre's conclusion that our choices—at least in the West—are reduced to Aristotle and Nietzsche.[117] While recognizing a decisive though not exclusive cultural ethos, the framework outlined above draws close connections between moral practice and the human constitution, thereby gaining more critical leverage than MacIntyre considers possible.

Cataclysmic discourse has failed the test of realism, while realism has lacked radicality. Meanwhile, we specialize in the ethics of health spas and the three-martini lunch, for example, without a prophetic word on malnutrition worldwide. Or we are driven by apocalyptic fears from nuclear war and ozone layers, with no outright concern for distributive justice in the middle range. In contrast, communitarian ethics has the special attraction of integrating ontological claims with an actionable transformative strategy.

In his provocative work on classical culture, Charles Cochrane identifies Augustine of Hippo as "the first citizen of the modern world."[118] This towering figure among distinguished thinkers constructed a searing critique of the foundations of Western civilization. His discourse on the will, for instance, stands as a precursor of Nietzsche's will to power and confronts Michel Foucault's contentless will at the center of a technological society. So penetrating was Augustine's refusal of the classical conception of dialectical reason that Arthur Kroker and David Cook credit him with setting the standard for cultural critique until today.[119] In contrast to postmodernism's rupture, and against nothingness as the totalizing word, this "Columbus of the modern experience" fashioned a normative domain by reconceiving substance as characterized by an ultimate commitment.[120] He integrated will and truth as twin principles—that is, redefining truth as reason radiated by love. Two kinds of love ultimately govern human community—either *caritas* (*agape*) or *cupiditas* (self-interest). We are governed not by autonomous rationality, but by what we love most with our whole heart as whole persons. The Augustinian tradition subverts contemporary discourse while retaining a constructive ambience that links being and history. By reclaiming normativity for professional ethics as a whole and formulating a transformative communitarian ethics of news, we seek to reenact that legacy.

NOTES

Chapter 1

1. Commission on Freedom of the Press, *A Free and Responsible Press* (Chicago: University of Chicago Press, 1947), p. 21.

2. C. Wright Mills, *The Sociological Imagination* (New York: Oxford University Press, 1959), p. 50.

3. James W. Carey, "The Dark Continent of American Journalism," in *Reading the News,* ed. Robert K. Manoff and Michael Schudson (New York: Pantheon Books, 1986), p. 180.

4. German historian Leopold von Ranke (1795–1886), addressing his concerns that history had become moralistic and instrumental, urged historians to return to sources, data, and archives so that historical scholarship could simply show "what actually happened" ("Preface to *Histories of the Latin and Germanic Nations from 1494 to 1514,*" in *The Varieties of History,* ed. Fritz Stern [New York: World, 1956], p. 55).

5. Clifford Geertz, *The Interpretation of Cultures* (New York: Basic Books, 1973), p. 3.

6. International Commission for the Study of Communication Problems, *Many Voices, One World: Communication and Society Today and Tomorrow* (London: Kogan Page, 1980).

7. Adapted from Ronald Sider, *Rich Christians in an Age of Hunger* (Downers Grove, Ill.: InterVarsity Press, 1979), pp. 203–4.

8. This tradition insists that ethics engage problems of institutional and public morality from a "realistic" and at the same time "prophetic" posture, rather than from a personal and private plain. See Mark Fackler, "Reinhold Niebuhr's Contribution to Social Responsibility Theory" (Paper presented at the Speech Communication Association annual conference, Boston, November 1987); also John P. Ferré, "Communication Ethics and the Political Realism of Reinhold Niebuhr," *Communication Quarterly* 38, no. 3 (Summer 1990): 218–25. For an overview of theocentric ethics, see James M. Gustafson, *Ethics from a Theocentric Perspective,* 2 vols. (Chicago: University of Chicago Press, 1981, 1984).

9. "Man-the-answerer" as a root metaphor is most fully developed in H. Richard Niebuhr's Robertson and Earl lectures, published posthumously as *The Responsible Self* (New York: Harper & Row, 1963), Introduction by James M. Gustafson, pp. 6–41.

10. Walter Lippmann, "The Scholar in a Troubled World," *Atlantic Monthly,* August 1932, pp. 148–52.

Chapter 2

1. See Max Horkheimer and Theodor W. Adorno, *Dialectic of Enlightenment* (New York: Seabury Press, 1972).

2. Newspapers, pamphlets, and periodicals played a central role in disseminating eighteenth-century ideas rapidly and widely—rights, freedom of expression, individualism, and so forth. For an account of the press's role in propagating Englightenment thinking in France, see Jeremy D. Popkin, *Revolutionary News: The Press in France 1789–1799* (Durham, N.C.: Duke University Press, 1990). Jeffrey A. Smith argues that American journalists self-consciously participated in promoting Enlightenment thought ("The Enticements of Change and America's Enlightenment Journalism" [Paper presented at a Library of Congress symposium, Publishing and Readership in Revolutionary France and America, Washington, D.C., 2 May 1989]). David Jaffee's research indicates that rural areas were also included ("The Village Enlightenment in New England, 1760–1820," *William and Mary Quarterly* 47 [July 1990]: 327–46).

3. Galileo Galilei, *Discoveries and Opinions of Galileo,* trans. Stillman Drake (Garden City, N.Y.: Doubleday, 1957), pp. 238–39.

4. E. J. Dijksterhuis, *Mechanization of the World Picture* (New York: Oxford University Press, 1964), sec. 4.

5. Cited by Charles Hummel, "Newton," *Christian History,* Issue 30 (n.d.): 38.

6. Ibid.

7. Lewis Mumford, *The Myth of the Machine*, vol. 1: *Pentagon of Power* (New York: Harcourt Brace Jovanovich, 1970), pp. 57–76.

8. Ernst Cassirer, *The Philosophy of the Enlightenment* (Princeton, N.J.: Princeton University Press, 1951), p. 6.

9. René Descartes, "Rules for the Direction of the Mind," in *Philosophical Essays,* trans. L. J. Lafleur (Indianapolis: Bobbs-Merrill, 1964), pp. 163, 173.

10. E. F. Schumacher, *Guide for the Perplexed* (New York: Harper & Row, 1977), pp. 8–13.

11. Charles Taylor, *Sources of the Self: The Making of the Modern Identity* (Cambridge, Mass.: Harvard University Press, 1989), p. 158.

12. Jean Jacques Rousseau, *Emile* (London: Dent, 1961), p. 350.

13. Jacques Derrida's *Of Grammatology* (Baltimore: Johns Hopkins University Press, 1980) is a semiotics of writing, focused primarily on the contrast between written and oral traditions. Two-thirds of *Of Grammatology* is devoted to Rousseau's attitudes toward writing. Derrida, informed by Rousseau, recognizes the abuses and dangers that inhere in writing. He emphasizes Rousseau's *Essay on the Origins of Language,* for example, in which writing entails servitude and absence (*Of Grammatology,* p. 168). For the Enlightenment generally, writing is seen as progress, necessary because of increased social necessity. Derrida notes that Rousseau, however, understood "progress as regression" (p. 171), since writing entrenched the dominance of reason and easily led to misconceptions in the absence of the author. However, in constructing his argument that writing during the formative eighteenth century was a tool of exploitation rather than of liberation, Derrida argues against the presumption, held since De Saussure, that speech is basic and writing a representation. On this question, we consider Derrida mistaken.

14. Isaiah Berlin, *Four Essays on Liberty* (New York: Oxford University Press, 1969), p. lix.

15. Leibniz introduced the term "monad" in 1696; he developed the doctrine during his residence in Vienna under Prince Eugene (in material that was published posthumously in 1714) (Gottfried Wilhelm Leibniz, *The Monadology and Other Philosophical Writings,* trans. R. Latta [New York: Oxford University Press, 1925]).

16. Robert N. Bellah, Richard Madsen, William M. Sullivan, Ann Swidler, and Steven Tipton, *Habits of the Heart: Individualism and Commitment in American Life* (Berkeley and Los Angeles: University of California Press, 1985), p. vii.

17. Ibid., p. 303.

18. Thomas Luckmann, *The Invisible Religion* (New York: Macmillan, 1967), p. 109.

19. Christopher Lasch, *The Culture of Narcissism: American Life in an Age of Diminishing Expectations* (New York: Warner Books, 1983), p. 10.

20. Ibid., p. 53.

21. Ibid., p. 11.

22. Alasdair MacIntyre, *After Virtue* (Notre Dame, Ind.: University of Notre Dame Press, 1981), p. 245; see also MacIntyre, *Whose Justice? Which Rationality?* (Notre Dame, Ind.: University of Notre Dame Press, 1986).

23. William L. Rivers, Jay Jensen, and Theodore Peterson, *The Mass Media and Modern Society,* 2d ed. (San Francisco: Rinehart Press, 1971), p. 69.

24. Fred S. Siebert, Theodore Peterson, and Wilbur Schramm, *Four Theories of the Press* (Urbana: University of Illinois Press, 1956), p. 44.

25. Thomas Jefferson, Letter to M. Coray, 31 October 1823, in *Thomas Jefferson on Democracy,* ed. Saul K. Padover (New York: New American Library, 1939), p. 164.

26. Harry Girvetz, *From Wealth to Welfare* (Stanford, Calif.: Stanford University Press, 1950), p. 23.

27. Berlin, *Four Essays on Liberty,* p. lvi.

28. Ibid., p. xlvii.

29. Taylor, *Sources of the Self,* p. 375.

30. Berlin, *Four Essays on Liberty,* p. liv.

31. Ibid., p. 165.

32. Taylor, *Sources of the Self,* p. 390.

33. Felix Frankfurter, *Pennekamp* v. *Florida,* 328 US. 331 (1946).

34. Siebert, Peterson, and Schramm, *Four Theories of the Press,* p. 76.

35. Commission on Freedom of the Press, *A Free and Responsible Press* (Chicago: University of Chicago Press, 1947), p. 131.

36. Siebert, Peterson, and Schramm, *Four Theories of the Press,* p. 73.

37. Richard Harwood, "Defending the Indefensible," *Editor & Publisher,* 10 August 1991, p. 3.

38. Larry Luxner, "Press Freedom in the Arab World," *Editor & Publisher,* 10 August 1991, p. 14.

39. For a summary, see David Held, *Models of Democracy* (Stanford, Calif.: Stanford University Press, 1987), pp. 243–54.

40. Robert Nozick, *Anarchy, State and Utopia* (Oxford: Basil Blackwell, 1974).

41. Frederich A. Hayek, *The Road to Serfdom* (London: Routledge and Kegan

Paul, 1976), pp. 62–3; see also Hayek, *Law, Legislation and Liberty,* vol. 3 (London: Routledge and Kegan Paul, 1982).

42. Nozick, *Anarchy, State and Utopia,* p. 310.

43. In a seminal historical and philosophical analysis, Gregory T. Wuliger argues that different interpretations of libertarian press theory have implied different moral universes. Each of the three dominant ways of understanding libertarian press theory—as a definition, an observation, and a universal—entails its own ethical dynamic, and one that is logically incompatible with the other two. His paper came to our attention too late to be incorporated fully into this chapter. We focus here on the press's overriding commitment to individual autonomy, whereas Wuliger centers on truth and falsehood in libertarianism. We do share the premise that press theory brings with it a moral universe. Wuliger's scholarship enriches that presumption and accounts for the disagreements over journalistic standards that arise among those generally committed to the same intellectual tradition ("The Moral Universes of Libertarian Press Theory," *Critical Studies in Mass Communication* 8, no. 2 [June 1991]: 152–67).

44. Paul F. Douglass, *The Newspaper and Responsibility* (Cincinnati: Cafton Press, 1929).

45. Albert F. Henning, *Ethics and Practices in Journalism* (New York: Long and Smith, 1932), p. 17, cf. p. 22.

46. William Futhey Gibbons, *Newspaper Ethics: A Discussion of Good Practice for Journalists* (Ann Arbor, Mich.: Edwards Bros., 1926), pp. 7–8.

47. Richard Hofstader, *The Progressive Movement 1900–1915* (Englewood Cliffs, N.J.: Prentice-Hall, 1963), pp. 1–15; Hofstadter, *The Age of Reform* (New York: Vintage, 1955), pp. 4–59.

48. Nelson A. Crawford, *The Ethics of Journalism* (New York: Knopf, 1924), p. 26.

49. Leon Nelson Flint, "What Shall the Ethics of Journalism Cover?" *Editor & Publisher,* 15 April 1922, p. 32. Juan José Tablada echoes this ideal in his ringing address to the First Pan American Congress of Journalists: "Newspaper Ethics: A Spanish-American View," *Journalism Bulletin* 3, no. 2 (June 1926): 1–5.

50. Gibbons, *Newspaper Ethics,* p. ii.

51. Ibid., p. 7.

52. Ibid., p. 100. Believing that "democracies are what newspapers make them," Victor S. Yarros of Chicago's Hull House wrote a compelling essay making the identical argument: "Journalism, Ethics, and Common Sense," *International Journal of Ethics* 32 (July 1932): 410–19.

53. Wilson Carey McWilliams, *The Idea of Fraternity in America* (Berkeley and Los Angeles: University of California Press, 1973), esp. chaps. 14–18.

54. John Dewey, *The Public and Its Problems* (1927; Chicago: Swallow Press, 1954), esp. chaps. 4 and 5.

55. Grove Hiram Patterson, "Social Responsibilities of the American Newspaper" (Eighteenth Address, Don R. Mellet Memorial Fund, New York University, School of Commerce, Accounts, and Finance, Department of Journalism, 12 March 1948), pp. 5–14.

56. James W. Carey, "The Communications Revolution and the Professional Communicator," *Sociological Review Monograph* 13 (January 1969): 23–38.

57. For an examination of the social and intellectual background of the Hutchins Commission report, see Mark Fackler, "The Hutchins Commissioners and the Crisis in Democratic Theory" (Ph.D. diss., University of Illinois–Urbana, 1982). The only biography of Hutchins (which does not deal with press ethics or the commission) is Harry Ashmore, *Unseasonable Truths: The Life of Robert Maynard Hutchins* (Boston: Little, Brown, 1989).

58. Frank McCulloch, quoted in M. L. Stein, "Stop the Sophistication," *Editor & Publisher,* 15 June 1991, p. 16.

59. Theodore B. Peterson, "Social Responsibility Since the Hutchins Commission" (Unpublished paper, College of Communications, University of Illinois–Urbana, 1987), pp. 1–44.

60. See David W. Miller, *George Herbert Mead: Self, Language and the World* (Austin: University of Texas Press, 1973), chap. 15.

61. Frank McCulloch, ed. *Drawing the Line* (Washington D.C.: American Society of Newspaper Editors, 1984).

62. Louis Hodges, "Review of *The Virtuous Journalist," Journal of Mass Media Ethics* 3, no. 1 (1988): 100–1.

63. Stephen Klaidman and Tom L. Beauchamp, *The Virtuous Journalist* (New York: Oxford University Press, 1987), p. 20.

64. John C. Merrill, *The Imperative of Freedom: A Philosophy of Journalistic Autonomy* (New York: Hastings House, 1974; New York: Freedom House, 1990), p. xi.

65. Ibid.

66. John C. Merrill, *The Dialectic in Journalism: Toward a Responsible Use of Press Freedom* (Baton Rouge: Louisiana State University Press, 1989), p. 7.

67. Ibid.

68. Ibid., p. 198.

69. Ibid., pp. 12, 15, 25; also see Merrill, *Existential Journalism* (New York: Hastings House, 1977).

70. Edmund Lambeth, *Committed Journalism: An Ethic for the Profession*, 2d ed. (Bloomington: Indiana University Press, 1992), p. 56.

71. Ibid.

72. Thomas M. Scanlon, "Freedom of Expression and Categories of Expression," *University of Pittsburgh Law Review* 40 (Summer 1979): 533. For elaboration, see Scanlon, "Content Regulation Reconsidered," in *Democracy and the Mass Media,* ed. Judith Lichtenberg (Cambridge: Cambridge University Press, 1990), pp. 331–54.

73. Scanlon, "Freedom of Expression," p. 534.

74. Thomas M. Scanlon, "A Theory of Freedom of Expression," *Philosophy and Public Affairs* 1, no. 2 (Winter 1972): 205.

75. Ibid., p. 204. See also Glenn Tinder, "Freedom of Expression, the Strange Imperative," *The Yale Review* 69, no. 2 (December 1979): 161–76.

76. Scanlon, "Freedom of Expression," p. 536.

77. Joseph Schumpeter, *Capitalism, Socialism and Democracy* (London: Allen & Unwin, 1976).

78. Patrick W. Hamlett, "Science, Technology, and Liberal Democratic Theory," *Technology in Society* 6, no. 3 (1984): 259.

79. Daniel Callahan, "Autonomy: A Moral Good, Not a Moral Obsession," *The Hastings Center Report,* October 1984, p. 42.

80. David Tracy, *Plurality and Ambiguity: Hermeneutics, Religion, Hope* (San Francisco: Harper & Row, 1987), p. 16.

81. Michel Foucault, *The Order of Things: An Archaeology of the Human Sciences* (1966; New York: Vintage, 1973), p. 387. We consider it our intellectual task to reconstitute the self and the social in Chapter 3 without appealing to the essentialist discourse of the classical period, Foucault's label for the mid-seventeenth to nearly the end of the eighteenth century. Taking that challenge seriously does not entail our endorsing the apocalyptic philosophy of history that Foucault's work represents. It is beyond our purpose to engage Foucault's work scholastically; we do not address either the archeology or genealogy phase in its complexity. Foucault himself has recognized that his early preoccupation with language and epistemology is a limited project (*Power/Knowledge* [New York: Pantheon Books, 1980], p. 127). Foucault's late work on sexuality (*The History of Sexuality,* vol. 1 [New York: Random House, 1978]) indicates a shift in interest to questions of subjectivity rather than merely "cutting it loose from its moorings in bourgeois individualism," in the words of Andreas Huyssen ("Mapping the Post-modern," *New German Critique* 33 [1984]: 44). We read Foucault existentially, an approach articulated by Michael Hyde in "Foucault, Derrida, and the Ethics of Rhetoric: An Existentialist Reading of Two Poststructuralists" (Paper presented at the Speech Communication Association annual conference, Chicago, November 1990). Although he prefers to be taken at face value, is not Foucault's project broader than he is willing to admit? Is he not making use of his own authenticity—on the way and constantly agitated as it is—to "speak a rhetoric" (Hyde, "Foucault, Derrida, and the Ethics of Rhetoric," p. 32) that others have the responsibility to reconstruct themselves (ibid., pp. 20–24, 30–32).

82. John Macmurray, *The Form of the Personal,* vol. 1: *The Self as Agent,* (London: Faber & Faber, 1961), p. 33.

83. For further exploration of Hegel's social philosophy, we recommend Charles Taylor's two studies: *Hegel* (Cambridge: Cambridge University Press, 1975), and *Hegel and Modern Society* (Cambridge: Cambridge University Press, 1979).

84. Marx distinguishes between abstract and concrete individuality. Abstract individuality is the alienated form of personhood in capitalist societies; concrete individuality can be achieved only within socialism. Marx's critique of bourgeois individuality as a decadent epiphenomenon in capitalism does not entail a denial of individuation as such. However, social theorists since Max Weber have noted the absence of a redemptive passage in Marx from distorted individuality to his concrete version.

85. For a historical and philosophical analysis of the distinctiveness of communitarian political theory (in Crawford B. Macpherson and Carole Pateman, for example), see Held, *Models of Democracy,* pp. 254–64; Seyla Benhabib discusses communitarian philosophies in "Autonomy, Modernity and Community: An Exchange Between Communitarianism and Social Theory," in *Zwischenbetrachtungen im Prozess der Aufkläring,* ed. A. Honneth, T. A. McCarthy, C. Offe, and A. Wellmer (Frankfurt: Suhrkamp, 1988), pp. 373–95; Robert Thigpen and Lyle

Downing also provide an overview of the debate in "Liberalism and the Communitarian Critique," *American Journal of Political Science* 31 (1987): 637–55. Communitarianism is developed in such representative works as Alasdair MacIntyre, *After Virtue* and *Whose Justice? Which Rationality?;* Michael J. Sandel, *Liberalism and the Limits of Justice* (Cambridge: Cambridge University Press, 1982); Charles Taylor, *Philosophy and the Human Sciences: Philosophical Papers,* vol. 2 (Cambridge: Cambridge University Press, 1985); Roberto M. Unger, *Politics: A Work in Constructive Social Theory,* 3 vols. (Cambridge: Cambridge University Press, 1988); Michael Walzer, *Spheres of Justice: A Defense of Pluralism and Equality* (New York: Basic Books, 1983) and *Interpretation and Social Criticism* (Cambridge, Mass.: Harvard University Press, 1987); and Bernard Williams, *Moral Luck* (Cambridge: Cambridge University Press, 1981) and *Ethics and the Limits of Philosophy* (London: Fontana Press, 1982).

86. Michael J. Sandel, "Morality and the Liberal Ideal," *The New Republic,* 7 May 1984, p. 17.

87. Callahan, "Autonomy," p. 42.

88. Amy Gutmann, "Communitarian Critics of Liberalism," *Philosophy and Public Affairs* 14, no. 3 (Summer 1985): 311.

89. Chantal Mouffe, "Rawls: Political Philosophy Without Politics," in *Universalism vs. Communitarianism: Contemporary Debates in Ethics,* ed. David Rasmussen (Cambridge, Mass.: MIT Press, 1990), p. 222. See also Callahan, "Autonomy," pp. 40–42.

90. Refer to Williams, *Ethics and the Limits of Philosophy*, pp. 1–21.

91. Michael J. Sandel, "Introduction," to *Liberalism and Its Critics,* ed. Michael J. Sandel (New York: New York University Press, 1984), pp. 1–13.

92. Seyla Benhabib, "Afterword: Communicative Ethics and Current Controversies in Practical Philosophy," in *The Communicative Ethics Controversy,* ed. Seyla Benhabib and Fred Dallmayr (Cambridge, Mass.: MIT Press, 1990), p. 332.

93. Mary Ann Glendon, *Rights Talk: The Impoverishment of Political Discourse* (New York: Free Press, 1991), p. 9.

94. Sara M. Evans and Harry C. Boyte, "Schools for Action: Radical Uses of Social Space," *Democracy* 2, no. 4 (Fall 1982): 55.

95. Ibid.

96. Jeff Lustig, "Community and Social Class," *Democracy* 1, no. 2 (April 1981): 101–2.

97. Evans and Boyte, "Schools for Action," p. 56.

98. C. A. Bowers, *Elements of a Post-Liberal Theory of Education* (New York: Teachers College Press, 1987), p. 133.

99. Sandel, "Morality and the Liberal Ideal," p. 17.

100. Ibid.

101. The communal nature of moral agency becomes apparent when one traces the failed attempts since the eighteenth century of the arrogant and presumptuous "imperial self" to arrive at universal, binding truths on its own. See Robert Solomon, *Continental Philosophy Since 1750: The Rise and Fall of the Self* (New York: Oxford University Press, 1988), p. 4.

102. Benhabib, "Afterword," p. 332.

103. David Mapel concludes that political theorists mistakenly seek conceptual

purity in the debate between liberalism and communitarianism. In his view, theoretical frameworks are limited; many important issues can be resolved only by
politics (*Social Justice Reconsidered: The Problem of Appropriate Precision in a
Theory of Justice* [Urbana: University of Illinois Press, 1989], pp. 128–45). Our
volume takes Mapel's conclusion seriously; it moves beyond a refinement of communitarianism per se to elaborate this framework in terms of the press's mission
and rationale.

104. Hans Jonas, *The Imperative of Responsibility: In Search of an Ethics for
the Technological Age* (Chicago: University of Chicago Press, 1984), pp. 1–17.

Chapter 3

1. Don Fry, "The Shocking Pictures of Sage: Two Newspapers, Two Answers," *Washington Journalism Review*, April 1988, p. 37.

2. Ibid., p. 41.

3. "A Story of Hope, a Story of Courage, the Story of Sage," *Albuquerque
Tribune*, 16 October 1987, p. F2.

4. Fry, "Shocking Pictures of Sage," p. 38.

5. Charles Taylor, *Sources of the Self: The Making of the Modern Identity*
(Cambridge, Mass.: Harvard University Press, 1989), pp. 3–8.

6. Ibid., pp. 111–14.

7. John C. Merrill, "Three Theories of Press Responsibility and the Advantages of Pluralistic Individualism," in *Responsible Journalism*, ed. Deni Elliott
(Beverly Hills, Calif.: Sage, 1986), p. 49.

8. David Shaw, "Abortion Bias Seeps into News," *Los Angeles Times*, 1
July 1990, p. 1.

9. Norman E. Bowie, "Applied Philosophy—Its Meaning and Justification,"
Applied Philosophy 1 (Spring 1982): 1–18.

10. Paul Tillich, *Love, Power, and Justice* (New York: Oxford University
Press, 1954). On page vi, he describes his work as an "ontological analysis" of
three concepts and introduces phrases such as "the ontological question" (p. 18),
"an ontology of love" (p. 24), and "the ontological unity of justice, power, and
love" (p. 67).

11. John Rawls, *A Theory of Justice* (Cambridge, Mass.: Harvard University
Press, 1971), pp. 136–42.

12. Thomas S. Kuhn, *The Structure of Scientific Revolutions*, 2d ed. (Chicago:
University of Chicago Press, 1970).

13. Tillich, *Love, Power, and Justice*, p. 24.

14. Deni Elliott, "All Is Not Relative: Essential Shared Values of the Press,"
Journal of Mass Media Ethics 3, no. 1 (1988): 29.

15. We recognize that not all who call themselves journalists are independent
of government bureaucracy and other power bases that invariably call into question
the perspective and ideology of a given news report. As we develop the argument
here, we advocate neither an antiseptic approach to the journalist as bearer of true
truth (Walter Lippmann's ideal) nor a view of the journalist as agent of the state
or corporation. In the West, we wish to keep the distinction sharp between reporter

and public relations specialist; in developing countries we recognize that advocacy journalism is often a norm from which the adversarial voice must emerge responsibly and often at great personal cost, as George Krimsky pointed out in "Understanding the Foreign Journalist," *Editor & Publisher,* 18 May 1991, pp. 60, 62.

16. What many journalists forgot was the other half of the story, that of Donna Rice, told with uncommon insight (including insight from Rice herself) in Hampden H. Smith III, "Donna Rice to the Press: 'I Lost Everything,' " *Journal of Mass Media Ethics* 5 (1990): 151–67.

17. Clifford G. Christians, Kim B. Rotzoll, and Mark Fackler, *Media Ethics: Cases and Moral Reasoning,* 3d ed. (New York: Longman, 1991), p. 143.

18. Elliott, "All Is Not Relative," p. 30.

19. Thomas W. Cooper, *Communication Ethics and Global Change* (New York: Longman, 1989), chap. 2.

20. Taylor, *Sources of the Self,* p. 10.

21. Herbert J. Gans, *Deciding What's News: A Study of CBS Evening News, NBC Nightly News, Newsweek and Time* (New York: Vintage, 1979), pp. 40–69.

22. Hadley Arkes, *First Things: An Inquiry into the First Principles of Morals and Justice* (Princeton, N.J.: Princeton University Press, 1986).

23. Richard A. Posner, *The Economics of Justice* (Cambridge, Mass.: Harvard University Press, 1981), p. 88.

24. Arthur J. Dyck, *On Human Care: An Introduction to Ethics* (Nashville, Tenn.: Abingdon, 1977), p. 127.

25. It is interesting to note, with respect to Lincoln's moral education, the following observations from *Washington Post* columnist Joseph Alsop, quoted in Hunter Lewis, *A Question of Values* (New York: Harper & Row, 1990), p. 75:

> Lincoln's texts . . . were first of all the Bible and Shakespeare. . . . He not infrequently recited the [Bible] or the great soliloquies, sometimes in the course of important policy discussions, and on a five-hour boat trip to City Point, after Appomattox . . . passed the time for his companions with Shakespeare readings. It is interesting trying to imagine a similar journey by water with one of our last three presidents. After the Bible and Shakespeare, history was his main study. As a young man in New Salem, he read the whole of Gibbon and all of Rollin's history of the world . . . with . . . much space devoted to . . . Greek and Roman history.
>
> The first point that strikes you about the foregoing [list] of books [is that what] Lincoln read and learned is neither read, nor learned, nor even taught in any normal American school or university today. . . . I do not suppose as many as one university student in a thousand has ever, read so much as a chapter of the Bible in the . . . noble . . . King James version, and I fear the same ratio of ignorance prevails among American university professors. . . . Lincoln, *per contra,* went through life without the slightest acquaintance with the social sciences, in happy ignorance of the brand of English favored by the Modern Language Association. . . . If all of us learned to [think and] express ourselves as Lincoln did—by all but getting the King James version by heart—we might even have the cure for the gummy tide of jargon and pseudoscientific pretentiousness which is spreading . . . today.

26. Edward A. Purcell, *The Crisis of Democratic Theory: Scientific Naturalism and the Problem of Value* (Lexington; University of Kentucky Press, 1973), p. 202.

27. Richard Rorty, *Contingency, Irony, and Solidarity* (Cambridge: Cambridge University Press, 1989).

28. On this point, Henry Stob, writing from a Reformed Christian perspective, circumscribes ethics as the appraised, voluntary conduct of persons, excluding from its province acts of providence, deeds of the coerced or insane, behaviors of the innocents (children, animals, the culturally ignorant) ("Ethics: An Account of Its Subject Matter," in *Ethical Reflections: Essays on Moral Themes* [Grand Rapids, Mich.: Eerdmans, 1978], pp. 7–27).

29. At precisely this point Posner beats a hasty retreat from utilitarianism based on wealth maximization, insisting on consent as necessary to moral efficiency. Apart from consent, slavery is justified when "A's labor is worth more to B than to A," assuming that the costs of physical coercion are lower than the costs of administering contracts (Posner, *Economics of Justice*, p. 102).

30. Dyck, *On Human Care*, pp. 122–3.

31. Elliott, "All Is Not Relative," p. 31.

32. Robert K. Fullinwider, "The Menace of Moral Relativism," *Report from the Center for Philosophy and Public Policy* 7 (Spring/Summer 1987): 14.

33. Max Scheler, *The Nature of Sympathy*, trans. P. Heath (Hamden, Conn.: Archon Books, 1973), pp. 8–36. For a description of feeling-states, see Scheler, *Formalism in Ethics and Non-Formal Ethics of Values*, trans. M. Frings and R. Funk (Evanston, Ill.: Northwestern University Press, 1973), pp. 253–64. As with all Scheler's genuine contributions to sociology and social psychology, his concept of "fellow-feeling" must be disconnected from the aristocratic spirit of his work overall.

34. Max Scheler, *Problems of a Sociology of Knowledge*, trans. M. Frings (1960; London: Routledge and Kegan Paul, 1980), p. 17, also pp. 33–63.

35. Hans Jonas, *The Imperative of Responsibility: In Search of an Ethics for the Technological Age* (Chicago: University of Chicago Press, 1984), p. 35.

36. Alfred Schutz, *The Phenomenology of the Social World* (1932; Evanston, Ill.: Northwestern University Press, 1967), chap. 2. For a similar argument—that the relational is a constitutive feature of humanness—applied to epistemology, see Eduardo Nicole, *Los principios de la ciencia* (Mexico City: Fundo de Cultura Económica, 1965), chap. 1. Obviously, reconstructing selfhood from social structure is not an innocent process. Erving Goffman shows how inmates are defined in terms of the asylum's self-practices. Harold Garfinkel's Agnes cannot escape the consequences of historically situated gender practices. Michel Foucault's imprisoned are rendered powerless.

37. Martin Buber, *I and Thou*, 2d ed., trans. R. G. Smith (New York: Scribner's, 1958), pp. 69, 60.

38. Ibid., p. 3.

39. Michael Theunissen argues that Buber's relational self is distinct from the subjectivity of Continental existentialism, in *The Other: Studies in the Social Ontology of Husserl, Heidegger, Sartre, and Buber*, trans. C. Macann (Cambridge, Mass.: MIT press, 1984). The subjective sphere of Husserl and Sartre, for example, "stands in no relation to a Thou and is not a member of a We" (p. 20; see also p. 276). "According to Heidegger the self can only come to itself in a voluntary separation from the other self; according to Buber, it has its being solely in the relation" (p. 284). Lawrence Grossberg demonstrates how subjectivity ought to be debated in broad theoretical terms, "namely, the general critique of the transcen-

dental status of experience in philosophy and its associated philosophies of the subject and meaning" ("The Ideology of Communication: Post-structuralism and the Limits of Communication," *Man and World* 15 [1982]: 93). Theunissen's work contributes to that philosophical project.

40. Martin Buber, *The Knowledge of Man: Selected Essays,* trans. M. Friedman and R. G. Smith (New York: Harper & Row, 1965), p. 71.

41. Buber, *I and Thou,* p. 102.

42. For an answer to postmodern critics who insist on a more radical alternative than Buber's I–Itness, see Steven Kepnes, *Buber's Hermeneutic Philosophy and Narrative Theology* (Bloomington: Indiana University Press, 1991), chap. 6. Kepnes argues that Buber's interactional self stands between modernity's autonomous self and poststructuralism's decentered self, entrapped by neither and filling up the space left by both. In other words, posthumanism's fragmented self challenges Enlightenment individualism, but Buber's social ontology challenges both. Buber joins the contemporary critique of atomistic selfhood while offering an alternative model.

43. Buber, *I and Thou,* p. 45. For Buber, otherness as the vehicle to personhood ultimately finds its true source in the eternal other, God. "The extended lines of relations meet in the eternal Thou. Every particular Thou is a glimpse through to the eternal Thou" (p. 75). For him, the core of personhood cannot be touched by secularized social science, but in realistic and credible ways only by religious discourse.

44. Frank G. Kirkpatrick, *Community: A Trinity of Models* (Washington, D.C.: Georgetown University Press, 1986), p. 145.

45. John Macmurray, *The Form of the Personal,* vol. 1: *The Self as Agent;* vol. 2: *Persons in Relation* (London: Faber & Faber, 1961). Macmurray focuses on the dualisms of classical philosophy. As he writes: "The point of view adopted by Western philosophy is that of the self in its moment of reflection, when its activity is directed toward acquirement of knowledge. The Self is self-isolated from the world which it knows. . . . My purpose has been to challenge these presuppositions" (vol. 1, p. 11). He thus participates in the contemporary attacks on a transcendental subject, transparent to itself and isolated from the determinations of society and history. In addition to his familiarity with Buber and Marx, Macmurray demonstrates an acquaintance with sociologists who affirm the social nature of the self (such as George Herbert Mead and Charles Cooley) and with such philosophers as Josiah Royce, Maurice Merleau-Ponty, and Alfred North Whitehead, who set a dynamic self in a social matrix. Kirkpatrick provides a useful summary of Macmurray's work in *Community,* pp. 146–220. For a description of the broader context, see Paul Ricoeur's defense of the timeliness of philosophical debates on anthropology in "The Antinomy of Human Reality and the Problem of Philosophical Anthropology," in *Readings in Existential Phenomenology,* ed. Nathaniel Lawrence and Daniel O'Connor (Englewood Cliffs, N.J.: Prentice-Hall, 1967).

46. Macmurray, *Self as Agent,* p. 38.

47. Ibid., p. 85.

48. Kirkpatrick, *Community,* p. 163.

49. Macmurray, *Self as Agent,* p. 87.

50. John Macmurray, *Conditions of Freedom* (Atlantic Highlands, N.J.: Humanities Press, 1978), pp. 17–18.

51. Macmurray, *Persons in Relation,* pp. 48–60.

52. Ibid., p. 119.

53. Taylor, *Sources of the Self,* p. 134.

54. Ibid, pp. 127–37.

55. Ibid., p. 112.

56. Kirkpatrick, *Community,* p. 198.

57. John Macmurray, *The Clue to History* (London: Student Christian Movement Press, 1938), pp. 94, 100; for Macmurray's definition of the supreme personal other as a universal agent, see *Persons in Relation,* p. 164.

58. J. B. Lotz, "Person and Ontology," *Philosophy Today* 7 (Winter 1963): 279, 294.

59. Dyck, *On Human Care,* p. 144.

60. Stuart Ewen, *All Consuming Images: The Politics of Style in Contemporary Culture* (New York: Basic Books, 1988), p. 14.

61. Justice Blackmun wrote: "Consumers' interest in the free flow of commercial information may be as keen as, if not keener by far than, interest in the day's most urgent political debate" (*Virginia State Board of Pharmacy* v. *Virginia Citizens' Consumer Council, Inc.,* 425 U.S. 748 [1976].

62. Michael Schudson, "The Profession of Journalism in the United States," in *The Professions in American History,* ed. Nathan O. Hatch (Notre Dame, Ind.: University of Notre Dame Press, 1988), p. 157.

63. Paul Tournier, *The Meaning of Persons,* trans. E. Hudson (New York: Harper & Row, 1957), chaps. 1, 3, 7.

64. Richard P. Hiskes, *Community Without Coercion* (Newark: University of Delaware Press, 1982), p. 21.

65. Gary Gumpert, *Talking Tombstones & Other Tales of the Media Age* (New York: Oxford University Press, 1987), p. 168.

66. Wendell Berry, *What Are People For?* (San Francisco: North Point Press, 1990), pp. 154, 158, 77.

67. See Flannery O'Connor, *The Complete Stories* (New York: Farrar, Straus & Giroux, 1980). Her story "Good Country People" describes the petty deceit that betrays simplistic rural gullibility, wrenching from the people their deepest convictions, leaving some unchanged in their blinding stubbornness, particularly the deceiver herself. The two chronic country folk are named Freeman and Hopewell, and they do not change.

68. Berry, *What Are People For?* p. 86.

69. Ibid.

70. Derek McKiernan, "Television and the Dialectic of Community," *Media Development* 36 (1989): 33.

71. George Gerbner, "A New Environmental Movement on Community and Culture," *Media Development* 37 (April 1990): 13.

72. Berry, *What Are People For?* p. 200.

73. Pitirim A. Sorokin (1889–1968) established the Harvard Research Center in Creative Altruism and later, in the mid–1950s, the Research Society in Creative Altruism. His findings on altruism are reported in *Forms and Techniques of Al-*

truistic and Spiritual Growth (Boston: Beacon Press, 1954) and in *The Ways and Power of Love* (Boston: Beacon Press, 1954). See also Joseph A. Matter, *Love, Altruism, and World Crisis: The Challenge of Pitirim Sorokin* (Chicago: Nelson-Hall, 1974).

74. Taylor, *Sources of the Self,* p. 516.

75. Kirkpatrick, *Community,* pp. 1–12.

76. Rorty, *Contingency, Irony, and Solidarity.*

77. Michael Emery and Edwin Emery, *The Press and America: An Interpretive History of the Mass Media,* 6th ed. (Englewood Cliffs, N.J.: Prentice-Hall, 1988), p. 205.

78. Timothy W. Gleason, *The Watchdog Concept: The Press and the Courts in Nineteenth-Century America* (Ames: Iowa State University Press, 1989).

79. Martin Linsky, "Practicing Responsible Journalism: Press Impact," in *Responsible Journalism,* ed. Deni Elliott (Beverly Hills, Calif.: Sage, 1986), p. 149.

80. Randall P. Bezanson, Gilbert Cranberg, and John Soloski, *Libel Law and the Press: Myth and Reality* (New York: Free Press, 1987), p. 30.

81. Ibid., p. 35.

82. David Margolick, "Rape Victim Steps Out of 'Unidentified' Shadow to Let Paper Tell Story," *Louisville Courier-Journal,* 25 March 1990, p. A14.

83. Diane Aprile, "Breaking the Silence," *The Courier-Journal Magazine,* 24 February 1991, pp. 4–9.

84. John C. Bennett, *Christianity and Our World* (New York: Association Press, 1936), p. 38.

85. We explicitly reject the reductionist theory that markets define mutuality, that notions of justice are fundamentally expressions of contract, that utilitarian motives undergird the movement from atomism through organicism to mutuality, as though pragmatism were the fire in a great Hegelian steam engine. Arkes clearly sees that morality can explain contracts, but not vice versa (*First Things,* p. 18), although Posner advances an impressive argument for justice as fair economic play. Taylor has shown that the history of the notion of self is much richer than the heuristic potential of pragmatism to solve the riddles that selfhood creates. Our argument here extends the implications of Taylor's history to the press: that marketing is merely a means in the service of community, wherein persons explore their lives and establish their commitments. Profit is not the press's purpose or final appeal, as the subsequent argument will show.

86. Arkes, *First Things,* p. 124.

87. John P. Ferré, "The Dubious Heritage of Media Ethics: Cause-and-Effect Criticism in the 1890s," *American Journalism* 5, no. 4 (1988): 191–203.

88. "Foes to New Journalism," *New York Times,* 30 March 1897, p. 12.

89. Attorney General's Commission on Pornography, *Final Report,* 2 vols. (Washington, D.C.: Government Printing Office, 1986), pp. 901–1035.

90. A summary of this project is in Shearon Lowrey and Melvin L. DeFleur, *Milestones in Mass Communications Research,* 2d ed. (New York: Longman, 1988), pp. 365–67.

91. For an introduction to virtue ethics and a comprehensive bibliography, see Richard L. Johannesen, "Virtue Ethics, Character, and Political Communication,"

in *Ethical Dimensions of Political Communication,* ed. Robert E. Denton, Jr. (New York: Praeger, 1991), pp. 69–90.

92. Wendell Berry, *Remembering* (San Francisco: North Point Press, 1988), p. 60.

93. *The Front Page,* United Artists, 1931.

94. R. Melvin Keiser, *Recovering the Personal: Religious Language and the Post-Critical Quest of H. Richard Niebuhr* (Atlanta: Scholars Press, 1988), pp. 16–17, 36.

95. H. Richard Niebuhr, *The Responsible Self* (New York: Harper & Row, 1963), pp. 152, 160.

96. Ibid., pp. 59, 61, 106–7, 153.

97. Dyck, *On Human Care,* p. 160.

98. Karen Lebacqz, *Professional Ethics: Power and Paradox* (Nashville, Tenn.: Abingdon, 1985), p. 30.

99. Tom Goldstein, *The News at Any Cost: How Journalists Compromise Their Ethics to Shape the News* (New York: Simon and Schuster, 1985), pp. 29–30.

Chapter 4

1. Samuel Ringgold, Letter Ward to Henry Bibb, 16 October 1851, in *The Black Abolitionist Papers,* vol. 2: *Canada, 1830–1865,* ed. C. Peter Ripley, Roy E. Finkenbine, Paul A. Cimbala, and Michael F. Hembree (Chapel Hill: University of North Carolina Press, 1986), p. 179.

2. For a definitive, historically detailed account of this cooptation, see Richard A. Schwarzlose, "The Marketplace of Ideas: A Measure of Free Expression," *Journalism Monographs* 118 (December 1989): 1–41.

3. Mobil advertisement, "The Myth of the Open Airwaves," *Time,* 19 September 1983, p. 4. James S. Ettema sets the Mobil campaign within the context of a *Harper's* symposium on truth, and he indicates how the reality of multiple stories has generated the critique of news as ideology ("Journalism in the 'Post-Factual Age,' " *Critical Studies in Mass Communication* 4, no. 1 [March 1987]: 82–86).

4. Jürgen Habermas, *The Structural Transformation of the Public Sphere* (Cambridge, Mass.: MIT Press, 1989), pp. 171–88. For an elaboration of Habermas in the context of democratic political theory, see Theodore L. Glasser, "Communication and the Cultivation of Citizenship," *Communication* 12, no. 4 (1991): 235–48.

5. James W. Carey, "The Press and the Public Discourse," *The Center Magazine,* March/April 1987, pp. 5, 14.

6. John Pauly, "Interesting the Public: A Brief History of the Newsreading Movement," *Communication* 12, no. 4 (1991): 286.

7. Carey, "Press and the Public Discourse," p. 14.

8. Daniel Boorstin, *The Americans,* vol. 2: *The Democratic Experience* (New York: Vintage, 1973), p. 33. Even the courts assisted in suppressing the news of the infamous Johnson County war.

9. Carey, "Press and the Public Discourse," p. 14.

10. This summary follows Jay Rosen's description and analysis, "Making Journalism More Public," *Communication* 12, no. 4 (1991): 267–84. For relevant back-

ground documents, see Rosen's bibliography (pp. 282–84). "Columbus Beyond 2000" is available as a reprint from the *Columbus Ledger-Enquirer,* 29 May–5 June, 1988.

11. Rosen, "Making Journalism More Public," p. 271.

12. Ibid., pp. 272–75.

13. H. Richard Niebuhr describes his intention in *The Responsible Self* (New York: Harper & Row, 1963) as exploring "the nature and role of symbolic forms" (p. 151).

14. H. Richard Niebuhr, *The Meaning of Revelation* (New York: Macmillan, 1941), p. 96; see also p. 17.

15. Niebuhr, *Responsible Self,* pp. 64–65, 93–95.

16. John Locke, *An Essay Concerning Human Understanding* (1690; Oxford: Clarendon Press, 1894), vol. 1, p. 478. All of Book III is devoted to the problem of communication.

17. Ibid., p. 408.

18. Ibid. John Durham Peters has clarified the Lockean dilemma most precisely in "John Locke, the Individual, and the Origin of Communication," *Quarterly Journal of Speech* 75, no. 4 (November 1989): 387–99.

19. Fred S. Siebert, Theodore Peterson, and Wilbur Schramm, *Four Theories of the Press* (Urbana: University of Illinois Press, 1956), pp. 40–41.

20. Thomas Jefferson, *The Writings of Thomas Jefferson,* ed. Andrew A. Lipscomb (Washington, D.C.: Thomas Jefferson Memorial Association, 1904), vol. 11, pp. 32–33.

21. Obviously, praxis has been a complicated issue in social theory since Marx. While this discussion of the press's *telos* benefits from that literature, it does not make claims about the nuances. For an overview, see Richard J. Bernstein, *Praxis and Action: Contemporary Philosophies of Human Activity* (Philadelphia: University of Pennsylvania Press, 1971).

22. First developed systematically in Noam Chomsky's indictment of Vietnam policy, *American Power and the New Mandarins* (New York: Random House, 1969), and elaborated subsequently in a spate of books on language and politics, ideology and power.

23. Rosen, "Making Journalism More Public," pp. 274–75.

24. Upton Sinclair, Thorstein Veblen, Russell Jaccoby, James Carey, Allan Bloom, and others have centered their attention on the modern university, not permitting professors to teach classes, conduct research, and matriculate students in isolation from the contemporary confusion about our educational mission. That illustrates our identical concern for the press. Richard Rorty's aggressive project in philosophy—redirecting it from its Enlightenment moorings to a new prophetic mission—is similar to what ethics scholarship should accomplish for the press.

25. Oriana Fallaci, *Interview with History,* trans. J. Shepley (New York: Liveright, 1976), p. 11.

26. These three motifs reflect Paul Tillich's typology in *Love, Power, and Justice* (New York: Oxford University Press, 1954). J. Mark Thomas weaves together these concepts and Tillich's philosophy of culture in order to describe Tillich's social ethics (*Ethics and Technoculture* [Lanham, Md.: University Press of America, 1987], chap. 3).

27. Hy Steirman, "The Publisher's Responsibility," in *The Responsibility of the Press,* ed. Gerald Gross (New York: Fleet, 1966), pp. 250, 253.

28. Paul Tillich, *Morality and Beyond* (New York: Harper & Row, 1963), p. 20.

29. Ibid., p. 38.

30. Elizabeth O'Connor, *The New Community* (New York: Harper & Row, 1976), p. 100.

31. For elaboration, see Clifford G. Christians, "Reporting and the Oppressed," in *Responsible Journalism,* ed. Deni Elliott (Beverly Hills, Calif.: Sage, 1986), pp. 109–30.

32. William Ernest Hocking, "Freedom of the Press: A Summary Statement of Principle," in Commission on Freedom of the Press, *A Free and Responsible Press* (Chicago: University of Chicago Press, 1947), p. 117.

33. Recent research among Trappists suggests that their silence was not pure: the urge to speak evaded formal prohibitions via sign language. See Frank Cianco, *Voices of Silence: Lives of the Trappists Today* (New York: Paragon, 1991).

34. Leroy S. Rouner, *Within Human Experience: The Philosophy of William Ernest Hocking* (Cambridge, Mass.: Harvard University Press, 1969), p. 322. Rouner's most recent writing on Hocking is "Selfhood, Nature, and Society: Ernest Hocking's Metaphysics of Community," in *On Community,* Boston University Studies in Philosophy and Religion, vol. 12, ed. Leroy S. Rouner (Notre Dame, Ind.: University of Notre Dame Press, 1991), pp. 76–90.

35. William Ernest Hocking, "The Crisis of Our Time," *University of Chicago Roundtable,* no. 353, 24 December 1944.

36. William Ernest Hocking, *The Lasting Elements of Individualism* (New Haven, Conn.: Yale University Press, 1937), p. 135.

37. William Ernest Hocking, "The Future of Liberalism," *Journal of Philosophy* 32 (25 April 1935): 243.

38. Hocking, "Freedom of the Press," p. 112.

39. Max Lerner, *Ideas Are Weapons* (New York: Viking, 1939), p. 10; John Milton, *Areopagitica: A Speech for the Liberty of Unlicensed Printing* (1644; Boston: Beacon Press, 1951), p. 5.

40. Hocking, "Freedom of the Press," p. 113.

41. Lovejoy's promise of silence comes from a report of the meeting written by Governor Thomas Ford. According to the governor, Lovejoy pledged "not to mingle the question of slavery with discussions in his paper." Assured that the new publisher shared their economic visions, the leaders of Alton collected money to replace the press destroyed earlier on their docks (Thomas Ford, *A History of Illinois* [Chicago: S. C. Griggs, 1854], pp. 234–35, cited in John Gill, "Lovejoy's Pledge of Silence," *Bulletin of the Missouri Historical Society,* January 1958, p. 172).

42. From the record of Thomas Dimmock, who interviewed people present at the meeting (Gill, "Lovejoy's Pledge of Silence," p. 177). Gill also suggests that Ford's record may be tainted by threats from Attorney General Usher Linder to expose corruption in the Ford administration. After the murder, Linder prosecuted Lovejoy's defenders for riotous behavior, and is suspected himself of helping to organize the mob that fired at Lovejoy on November 7.

43. Margaret Jones Patterson and Robert H. Russell, *Behind the Lines: Case Studies in Investigative Reporting* (New York: Columbia University Press, 1986), pp. 203–64.

44. Benjamin Barber, *Strong Democracy: Participatory Politics for a New Age* (Berkeley and Los Angeles: University of California Press, 1984); see especially chap. 8, "Citizenship and Participation." David Protess and his colleagues at Northwestern University demonstrate that the historic purpose of investigative reporting is social change. Using actual cases, they examine the relationship between muckraking and policymaking. They outline strategies for constructively influencing citizen agendas and enabling political reform (David L. Protess, Fay Lomax Cook, Jack Doppelt, James Ettema, Margaret Gordon, Donna Leff, and Peter Miller, *The Journalism of Outrage: Investigative Reporting and Agenda Building in America* (New York: Guilford, 1991).

45. Reinhold Niebuhr, *Moral Man and Immoral Society: A Study in Ethics and Politics* (New York: Scribners, 1932), pp. 250–51.

46. Nicholas Wolterstorff, *Until Justice and Peace Embrace* (Grand Rapids, Mich.: Eerdmans, 1983), p. 69. For a sociological and theological account that integrates justice with *shalom,* see pp. 69–72.

47. Isaiah 32:16.

48. Cooley and Tönnies provide the classic account of these hierarchies. Charles Horton Cooley elaborates on peer influence in *Human Nature and the Social Order* (New York: Schocken Books, 1964); Ferdinand Tönnies's well-known analysis is in *Community and Society (Gemeinschaft und Gesellschaft),* trans. C. P. Loomis (East Lansing: Michigan State University Press, 1957).

49. Robert Nisbet, "The Present Age and the State of Community," *Chronicles,* June 1988, pp. 11–18; Boorstin, *Americans,* vol. 2: *Democratic Experience,* p. 248.

50. The term comes from a much-disputed article by Philip Weiss, "Invasion of the Gannettoids," *New Republic,* 2 February 1987, pp. 18–22.

51. Day's story has been ably told in a biography by Nancy L. Roberts, *Dorothy Day and the* Catholic Worker (Albany: State University of New York Press, 1984).

52. Ibid., p. 37.

53. Dorothy Day, "Catholic Worker Appeal," *Catholic Worker,* May 1944, p. 8, quoted in Roberts, *Dorothy Day,* p. 41.

54. Dorothy Day, "Fall Appeal 1977," Dorothy Day–*Catholic Worker* Collection, Memorial Library Archives at Marquette University, Milwaukee, Wisconsin; quoted in Roberts, *Dorothy Day,* p. 42.

55. For a discussion of media stereotyping in comic book publishing, see the classic study by Fredric Wertham, *Seduction of the Innocent* (New York: Rinehart, 1954).

56. "Street Saint," *Time,* 15 December 1980, p. 74.

57. Jacques Ellul, *The Political Illusion,* trans. K. Kellen (New York: Knopf, 1967), p. 222.

58. "Born Again Catholic Workers: A Conversation Between Jeff Dietrich and Katherine Temple," *The Ellul Studies Forum* 7 (July 1991): 7–9.

59. Paul Ramsay introduced covenant into professional ethics; it became the

centerpiece of Robert Veatch's theory of medical ethics. William F. May develops the covenantal model most comprehensively in "Code and Covenant or Contract and Philanthropy: Alternative Bases for Professional Ethics," in *Ethics in Medicine: Historical Perspectives and Contemporary Concerns,* ed. Stanely J. Reiser, Arthur J. Dyck, and William J. Curran (Cambridge, Mass.: MIT Press, 1977), pp. 65–76.

60. Invasion of privacy was the ground on which Judge Harry Kalus, affirmed by the Supreme Judicial Court of Massachusetts, banned *Titicut Follies* from public viewing. The courts found that inmate Jim, shown being led naked from his cell and struck by guards en route to the barber, was a victim of the invasion. Wiseman contends that only inmates who had granted consent were shown in the film. Political turf battles surround the ban on the film, and it remains the only work that an American court currently restricts for reasons other than obscenity or national security.

61. Paulo Freire, *Pedagogy of the Oppressed* (New York: Seabury Press, 1970), p. 57.

62. William A. Henry III, "Beyond the Melting Pot," *Time,* 9 April 1990, p. 28.

63. Ibid., p. 29.

64. Richard John Neuhaus, *The Naked Public Square* (Grand Rapids, Mich.: Eerdmans, 1984), pp. 3–19.

65. Commission on Freedom of the Press, *Free and Responsible Press,* p. 27.

66. Claude Lévi-Strauss, *The Savage Mind* (Chicago: University of Chicago Press, 1966), pp. 4–5.

67. Freire, *Pedagogy of the Oppressed,* chap. 3.

68. Alice Frazer Evans, Robert A. Evans, and William B. Kennedy, *Pedagogies for the Non-Poor* (Maryknoll, N.Y.: Orbis Books, 1987), p. 229.

69. Freire, *Pedagogy of the Oppressed,* p. 63.

70. Enoch Waters, *American Diary: A Personal History of the Black Press* (Chicago: Path Press, 1987), p. 252.

71. A brilliant case study of the Japanese relocation is included in Peter Irons, *The Courage of Their Convictions: Sixteen Americans Who Fought Their Way to the Supreme Court* (New York: Penguin Books, 1990), pp. 37–62. A content analysis of editorials in three newspapers indicates that the press served as a government publicist rather than a watchdog (Lloyd Chiasson, "Japanese-American Relocation During World War II: A Study of California Editorial Reactions," *Journalism Quarterly* 68, no. 1/2 [Spring/Summer 1991]: 263–68).

72. Michael Walzer, *Spheres of Justice: A Defense of Pluralism and Equality* (New York: Basic Books, 1983), p. 32.

73. Robert N. Bellah, Richard Madsen, William M. Sullivan, Ann Swindler, and Steven Tipton, *Habits of the Heart: Individualism and Commitment in American Life* (Berkeley and Los Angeles: University of California Press, 1985), pp. 3–26. See also Robert N. Bellah, Richard Madsen, William M. Sullivan, Ann Swindler, and Steven Tipton, *The Good Society* (New York: Knopf, 1991).

74. Carey, "Press and the Public Discourse," pp. 4–16.

75. Walt Harrington, "In Ricky's Wake," *The Washington Post Magazine,* 7 June 1987, pp. 15–21, 42–45.

76. Ibid., pp. 20, 14.

77. Ibid., p. 43.

78. M. Scott Peck, *People of the Lie: The Hope for Healing Human Evil* (New York: Simon and Schuster, 1983).

79. M. Scott Peck, *The Different Drum: Community Making and Peace* (New York: Touchstone Books, 1988).

80. Roger Rosenblatt, "Journalism and the Larger Truth," *Time,* 2 July 1984, p. 88.

81. Quoted in Michael Moss, "The Poverty Story," *Columbia Journalism Review* 26, no. 2 (July/August 1987): 43.

82. For seminal work on the ethics of representation across human communication as a whole, see Wayne Booth, *The Company We Keep: An Ethics of Fiction* (Berkeley and Los Angeles: University of California Press, 1988). For an attempt in mass communications, see *Image Ethics: The Moral Rights of Subjects in Photographs, Film, and Television,* eds. Larry Gross, John S. Katz, and Jay Ruby (New York: Oxford University Press, 1988), esp. Larry Gross, John Stuart Katz, and Jay Ruby, "Introduction: A Moral Pause" (pp. 3–33), and Larry Gross, "The Ethics of (Mis)representation" (pp. 188–202).

83. Nancy Hicks Maynard, "The Journalist as Storyteller," *Gannett Center Journal* 2, no. 2 (Spring 1988): 80–81. Emphasis added.

84. For the most detailed account, see Walter R. Fisher, *Human Communication as Narration: Toward a Philosophy of Reason, Value, and Action* (Columbia: University of South Carolina Press, 1987). Helpful summaries are included in Fisher, "Narrativity and Community," in *Proceedings of the Conference on Narrativity and Community,* ed. Michael Casey (Malibu, Calif.: Conference on Christianity and Communication, 1991), chap. 1, pp. 1–34; "The Narrative Paradigm: In the Beginning," *Journal of Communication* 35, no. 4 (Autumn 1985): 74–89; and "Narration as a Human Communication Paradigm: The Case of Public Moral Argument," *Communication Monographs* 51 (March 1984):1–22.

85. Renato Rosaldo, *Culture and Truth: The Remaking of Social Analysis* (Boston: Beacon Press, 1989), p. 20.

86. Ibid., pp. 129–30.

87. Michael Traber, "Narrativity and Community: A Cultural Studies Approach," in *Proceedings of the Conference on Narrativity and Community,* ed. Michael Casey (Malibu, Calif.: Conference on Christianity and Communication, 1991), chap. 4, p. 1.

88. This summary is based on Bernard Murchland's synopsis, "Hannah Arendt as Public Thinker," *The Civic Arts Review* 2, no. 4 (Fall 1989): 9–11. For additional biographical details, see Bernard Murchland, "The Thinking Citizen: A Conversation with Elizabeth Minnich," *The Civic Arts Review* 2, no. 1 (Winter 1989): 4–9. Seyla Benhabib, Suzanne Jacobitti, and B. Honig summarize Arendt's argument in a compilation of three essays: "Arendt, Politics, and the Self," *Political Theory* 16, no. 1 (February 1988): 29–98; see also Seyla Benhabib, "Hannah Arendt und die erlösende Kraft des Erzählens," in *Zivilisationsbruch: Denken nach Auschwitz,* ed. Dan Diner (Frankfurt am Main: Fischer Taschenbuch Verlag, 1988), pp. 150–74. For a critical response, see Jürgen Habermas, "Hannah Arendt's Communications Concept of Power," *Social Research* 44, no. 1 (Spring 1977): 3–24.

89. Glasser, "Communication and the Cultivation of Citizenship," pp. 235–36. Glasser integrates Arendt's work into a pathbreaking analysis of the current debates in democratic political philosophy. He is the first communications scholar to bring Arendt into our understanding of the narrative paradigm.

90. The examples in this paragraph are elaborated in Traber, "Narrativity and Community." Traber distinguishes foundational stories, parables, and pseudo-stories, and sets narrative within the context of ritual. See Hayden White, "The Value of Narrativity in the Representation of Reality," *Critical Inquiry* 7, no. 1 (1980): 5–27.

91. Alasdair MacIntyre, *After Virtue* (Notre Dame, Ind.: University of Notre Dame Press, 1981), p. 245.

92. Stanley Hauerwas, *A Community of Character* (Notre Dame, Ind.: University of Notre Dame Press, 1981), pp. 1–4. See also Hauerwas, *Truthfulness and Tragedy* (Notre Dame, Ind.: University of Notre Dame Press, 1977); (with L. Gregory Jones) *Why Narrative? Readings in Narrative Theology* (Grand Rapids, Mich.: Eerdmans, 1989); and *Naming the Silences: God, Medicine, and the Problem of Suffering* (Grand Rapids, Mich.: Eerdmans, 1990).

93. George Gerbner, "Telling Stories: The State, Problems, and Tasks of the Art" (Paper presented at the Institute of Communications Research fortieth anniversary, University of Illinois–Urbana, 19 March 1988), p. 6. See George Gerbner, Larry Gross, Michael Morgan, and Nancy Signorielli, "Living with Television: The Dynamics of the Cultivation Process," in *Perspectives on Media Effects,* ed. Jennings Bryant and Dolf Zillman (Hillsdale, N.J.: Erlbaum, 1986), pp. 17–40.

94. Argued persuasively by Hans-Georg Gadamer, *Reason in the Age of Science,* trans. F. G. Lawrence (Cambridge, Mass.: MIT Press, 1981), pp. 58 ff.

95. John Dewey, *Problems of Men* (Totowa, N.J.: Littlefield Adams, 1958), p. 35; similarly stated in Dewey, *The Public and Its Problems* (1927; Chicago: Swallow Press, 1954), p. 207.

96. Fisher, "Narrativity and Community," p. 22. Fisher elaborates on this thesis in terms of Buber, Dewey, Hauerwas, and Gadamer; he includes an extensive bibliography (pp. 1–34).

97. Seyla Benhabib, "Afterword: Communicative Ethics and Current Controversies in Practical Philosophy," in *The Communicative Ethics Controversy,* ed. Seyla Benhabib and Fred Dallmayr (Cambridge, Mass.: MIT Press, 1990), p. 331.

98. Ibid., pp. 331, 336.

99. Ibid., p. 339.

100. Hauerwas, *Community of Character,* p. 3.

101. Mary E. Mander, "Narrative Dimensions of the News: Omniscience, Prophecy, and Morality," *Communication* 10, no. 1 (1987): 54, 59. Mander analyzes news narrative in terms of classic literary theory. Her case studies are drawn from news stories about battles in World Wars I and II; these occasions for "rendering events in far-flung places," where "journalists are all-knowing" (p. 62) compared with their audiences, provide a rich context for examining precisely how reporters translate "events in the order of existence . . . into the order of narrative" (p. 54).

102. John Hartley, *Understanding News* (London: Methuen, 1982), p. 15; see pp. 75–86 for elaboration. This section of Chapter 4 benefits directly from Matthew

Paul McAllister, "Medicalization in the News Media: A Comparison of AIDS Coverage in Three Newspapers" (Ph.D. diss., University of Illinois–Urbana, 1990), pp. 224–25.

103. Paula A. Treichler, "AIDS, Homophobia, and Biomedical Discourse: An Epidemic of Signification," *Cultural Studies* 1, no. 4 (1987): 263.

104. Hartley, *Understanding News,* p. 15.

105. Ethicists are contributing substantially to narrative theory. This section of Chapter 4 is shaped primarily by literary and social theory; it focuses largely on the implications for professional morality (*Sittlichkeit*) when news is defined as social narrative. In Chapter 6, the ethical justification for our normative communitarianism will be developed in contrast to competing versions of discourse ethics such as Jürgen Habermas's cognitive rationalism ("Discourse Ethics: Notes on a Program of Philosophical Justification," in *Moral Consciousness and Communicative Action,* trans. C. Lenhardt and S. W. Nicholsen [Cambridge, Mass.: MIT Press, 1990], pp. 43–115). Fred Dallmayr is correct that a "justification program" appropriate to discursive ethics must deal with a "logical trilemma"—demonstrating how it avoids infinite regress, a *petitio principii,* and dogmatic acceptance of a first axiom ("Introduction," in *The Communicative Ethics Controversy,* ed. Seyla Benhabib and Fred Dallmayr [Cambridge, Mass.: MIT Press, 1990], pp. 5–10).

106. Richard Rorty, *Philosophy and the Mirror of Nature* (Princeton, N.J.: Princeton University Press, 1979), pp. 365–94.

107. David L. Eason, "On Journalistic Authority: The Janet Cooke Scandal," *Critical Studies in Mass Communication* 3, no. 4 (December 1986): 438.

108. Ibid., p. 434.

109. Rilla Dean Mills, "Newspaper Ethics: A Qualitative Study," *Journalism Quarterly* 60, no. 4 (Winter 1983): 589–94; Mills uses qualitative measures. For a review of the literature and relevant research, see Philip Meyer, *Ethical Journalism* (New York: Longman, 1987), chap. 4.

110. Rosaldo, *Culture and Truth,* p. 169.

111. Ibid., p. 224.

112. Rorty, *Philosophy and the Mirror of Nature,* p. 10.

113. Dietrich Bonhoeffer, *Ethics,* trans. N. H. Smith (New York: Macmillan, 1955), chap. 5.

114. For an initial attempt to define journalism in terms of truth, see Wesley G. Pippert, *An Ethics of News: A Reporter's Search for Truth* (Washington, D.C.: Georgetown University Press, 1989), p. 11.

115. Anthony Giddens, *Central Problems in Social Theory* (Berkeley and Los Angeles: University of California Press, 1979), p. 73. Ettema and Glasser's research indicates that investigative reporting—in contrast to the objectivism of daily journalism—receives its rationale from what Bonhoeffer calls "discernment" and Giddens, "discursive penetration." They use Michael Schudson's term "mature subjectivity" for the investigative process of weighing evidence and justifying conclusions (James S. Ettema and Theodore L. Glasser, "On the Epistemology of Investigative Journalism," *Communication* 8, no. 2 [1985]: 183–206).

116. Kevin M. Carragee, "Defining Solidarity: Themes and Omissions in Coverage of the Solidarity Trade Union Movement by ABC News," *Journalism Monographs* 119 (February 1990): 42.

117. "Qualitative studies" is shorthand for the counter-Enlightenment alternative. It is known by a variety of labels in different countries: *les sciences humaine, Geisteswissenschaften,* critical theory, interpretive social science, cultural hermeneutics, interpretive interactionism, cultural studies, naturalistic inquiry, humanistic sociology, phenomenology, and anthropological ethnography.

118. For an introduction to the literature, logic, and methodology of qualitative research applied to mass communications, see John Pauly, "A Beginner's Guide to Doing Qualitative Research in Mass Communication," *Journalism Monographs* 125 (February 1991): 1–29; see also Kevin M. Carragee, "Interpretive Media Study and Interpretive Social Science," *Critical Studies in Mass Communication* 7, no. 2 (June 1990): 81–96. For criteria by which to evaluate competent use of these strategies, see Clifford G. Christians and James W. Carey, "The Logic and Aims of Qualitative Research," in *Research Methods in Mass Communication,* 2d ed., ed. Guido H. Stempel III and Bruce H. Westley (Englewood Cliffs, N.J.: Prentice-Hall, 1989), pp. 354–74. For an assessment of the ways in which qualitative material should be presented, see Robert S. Fortner and Clifford G. Christians, "Separating Wheat from Chaff in Qualitative Studies," in *Research Methods in Mass Communication,* ed. Stempel and Westley, pp. 375–87; see also Harry F. Wolcott, *Writing Up Qualitative Research* (Newbury Park, Calif.: Sage, 1990).

119. For a review of this genre, from classical life-history strategies to postmodernism, see Norman K. Denzin, *Interpretive Biography* (Newbury Park, Calif.: Sage, 1989).

120. Richard Critchfield, "The Village Voice of Richard Critchfield: Bringing the Third World to the Fourth Estate," *Washington Journalism Review,* October 1985, pp. 30, 34.

121. Richard Critchfield, *Shahhat: An Egyptian* (Syracuse, N.Y.: Syracuse University Press, 1978); *Villages* (Garden City, N.Y.: Anchor Books, 1983); and *The Golden Bowl Be Broken: Peasant Life in Four Cultures* (Bloomington: Indiana University Press, 1988).

122. Critchfield, "Village Voice of Richard Critchfield," pp. 28, 34.

123. Jacques Derrida, "Deconstruction and the Other," in *Dialogues with Contemporary Continental Thinkers: The Phenomenological Heritage,* ed. R. Kearney (Manchester: Manchester University Press, 1984), p. 120.

124. Richard Rorty, *Contingency, Irony, and Solidarity* (Cambridge: Cambridge University Press, 1989), p. 53.

125. As with Michel Foucault in Chapter 2, we read Derrida existentially, as Hyde recommends. Even though selves are built from the discourse of others, Derrida insists on the task of relentlessly uncovering the symbolic forms that keep modern power intact. Derrida can be said to "speak a rhetoric" and to "affirm his own authenticity," which in the process enables others to reconstruct authentic rhetorics as well (Michael Hyde, "Foucault, Derrida, and the Ethics of Rhetoric: An Existential Reading of Two Poststructuralists" [Paper presented at the Speech Communication Association annual conference, Chicago, November 1990], pp. 25–32).

Chapter 5

1. Claude-Jean Bertrand, "Media Ethics in Perspective," *Journal of Mass Media Ethics* 2, no. 1 (Fall/Winter 1986–87): 20. Also see Bertrand, "La Responsabilité sociale de la presse," *Presse-Actualité,* April 1978, pp. 56–63, and "Como mejorar los medios de communicación y por que," *Nuestro Tiempo,* June 1988, pp. 110–23.

2. Bertrand, "Media Ethics in Perspective," pp. 20, 18.

3. Ibid., p. 19.

4. The history of alternative and minority media is introduced in John Downing, *Radical Media: The Political Experience of Alternative Communication* (Boston: South End Press, 1984), and David Armstrong, *A Trumpet to Arts: Alternative Media in America* (Boston: Houghton Mifflin, 1981).

5. John Milton, *Areopagitica: A Speech for the Liberty of Unlicensed Printing* (1644; Boston: Beacon Press, 1951), p. 61.

6. *Abrams* v. *United States,* 250 U.S. 616 (1919).

7. Eberhard Bethage, "Editor's Preface," in Dietrich Bonhoeffer, *Ethics* (London: SCM Press, 1955), p. xii.

8. "Alliance with Nature's Government," *Time,* 19 March 1990, pp. 76–77.

9. Adrienne Rich, *On Lies, Secrets, and Silence* (New York: Norton, 1979), p. 34.

10. Charles Taylor, *Sources of the Self: The Making of the Modern Identity* (Cambridge, Mass.: Harvard University Press, 1989), p. 18.

11. Thomas Donaldson, *Corporations and Morality* (Englewood Cliffs, N.J.: Prentice-Hall, 1982), p. 1.

12. Peter French, "The Corporation as a Moral Person," *American Philosophical Quarterly* 16 (1979): 207. For historical background, see Frederick Pollock and F. W. Maitland, "Corporation and Person," in *Anthropology and Early Law,* ed. Lawrence Krader (New York: New York University Press, 1965), pp. 300–36.

13. Donaldson, *Corporations and Morality,* p. 23.

14. Kenneth E. Goodpaster and John B. Matthews, Jr., "Can a Corporation Have a Conscience?" *Harvard Business Review* 60 (January/February 1982): 132–41.

15. For elaboration, see Donaldson, *Corporations and Morality,* chap. 2.

16. Chief Justice John Marshall initiated this definition in 1819: "A corporation is an artificial being, invisible, intangible, and existing only in the contemplation of law. Being the mere creation of law, it possesses only those properties which the charter of its creation confers upon it, either expressly, or as incidental to its very existence" (*Dartmouth College* v. *Woodward,* 4 Wheat. 518.636 [1819]).

17. Milton Friedman, "The Social Responsibility of Business Is to Increase Its Profits," *The New York Times Magazine,* 13 September 1970, pp. 32–33, 122–26. See also Friedman, *Capitalism and Freedom* (Chicago: University of Chicago Press, 1962). Friedman's sharp separation between ethics and economics actually reflects nineteenth-century Social Darwinism more than Adam Smith's *Wealth of Nations.* Contrary to popular opinion about his "invisible hand" and laissez-faire strategies, Smith was suspicious of commercial motives and never championed the pursuit of

profit with the blanket endorsement of a Milton Friedman (Donaldson, *Corporations and Morality,* pp. 62–66, 68–69).

18. Charles Dickinson, *Rumor Has It* (New York: Morrow, 1991).

19. Goodpaster and Matthews, "Can a Corporation Have a Conscience?" p. 140.

20. Systems theory in the 1960s and 1970s introduced an interactive framework, thereby making communication more dynamic and processual than the static, point-to-point stimulus–response conception. However, this contribution to organizational theory continued to interpret communication as the transmission of information, and its sophisticated models were otherwise functionalist in character.

21. The political-economy literature contradicts functionalism in parallel terms and constructs a powerful paradigm by articulating material conditions. However, the focus of this chapter on institutional accountability is not served as directly by this approach as by the value-embeddedness of organizational-culture theory. Also, the political-economic perspective privileges capitalist corporations, and we are concerned in the current North American mix of public and private media to problematize institutions generally. Business organizations thus form an important subunit, but the theoretical axis here is organizational culture. We cast the crucial infrastructure question into cultural terms through Weber's bureaucratization and Hegel's transitional principle, a formulation that allows us more emphasis on technology than is characteristic of political-economy approaches and that indicates precisely what specific moral issues are faced by mega-institutions. However, in contrast to functionalism, both the organizational-culture and the political-economy perspectives are critical paradigms that turn away from managerial control orientations and toward worker eudaemonia.

22. Dennis K. Mumby, *Communication and Power in Organizations: Discourse, Ideology, and Domination* (Norwood, N.J.: Ablex, 1988), p. 5. In Chapter 1, Mumby summarizes why organizational culture has become "a major theoretical rallying point": the continuing impact of Max Weber's writings on bureaucracy, the rediscovery of the American symbolic tradition, disaffection among mainline organizational theorists, the impact of European intellectuals (Heidegger, Schutz, Gadamer, Habermas), and the influence of organizational-communication theorists such as Deetz, Pondy, Morgan, Frost, and Dandridge.

23. Linda Smircich and Marta B. Calás, "Organizational Culture: An Assessment," in *Handbook of Organizational Communication: An Interdisciplinary Perspective,* ed. Frederic M. Jablin Linda L. Putnam, Karlene H. Roberts, and Lyman W. Porter (Beverly Hills, Calif.: Sage, 1987), p. 231. Italics in original.

24. Linda Smircich, "Concepts of Culture and Organizational Analysis," *Administrative Science Quarterly* 28 (1983): 347–50.

25. Clifford Geertz, *Local Knowledge* (New York: Basic Books, 1983), pp. 22–23.

26. J. Martin, "Can Organizational Culture Be Managed?" in *Organizational Culture,* ed. Peter Frost, Gareth Morgan, and Thomas Dandridge (Beverly Hills, Calif.: Sage, 1985), pp. 95–98.

27. Ibid. Martin labels this camp "cultural pragmatism."

28. Mumby, *Communication and Power in Organizations,* pp. 20, 22. The im-

portance of Mumby's framework is evident throughout this section of Chapter 5.

29. Quoted in Karl E. Weick, *The Social Psychology of Organizing*, 2d ed. (Reading, Mass.: Addison-Wesley, 1979), p. 1. In a more serious version, see Richard White's *Inventing Australia* (London: Allen & Unwin, 1981), in which he argues that there was never an Australia waiting to be uncovered; national identity is an invention.

30. John B. Thompson, *Studies in the Theory of Ideology* (Berkeley and Los Angeles: University of California Press, 1984), p. 10.

31. Stuart Hall, "Signification, Representation, Ideology: Althusser and the Post-Structuralist Debates," *Critical Studies in Mass Communication* 2, no. 2 (June 1985): 103. Italics in original.

32. Mumby, *Communication and Power in Organizations*, pp. 108–9.

33. Hayden White, "The Value of Narrativity in the Representation of Reality," *Critical Inquiry* 7 (1980), p. 24.

34. All quotes in this paragraph are from Dan Dorfman, "Inside the Scandal at Columbia Pictures," *New York*, 16 January 1978, pp. 1–9. For a book-length treatment of this case, see David McClintick, *Indecent Exposure: A True Story of Hollywood and Wall Street* (New York: Morrow, 1982).

35. Paul Ricoeur, *Interpretation Theory: Discourse and the Surplus of Meaning* (Fort Worth: Texas Christian University Press, 1976), pp. 45–57.

36. For interpretive details on the Watson story, see Mumby, *Communication and Power in Organizations*, pp. 115–25.

37. M. Cash Mathews, *Strategic Intervention in Organizations: Resolving Ethical Dilemmas* (Newbury Park, Calif.: Sage, 1988), p. 137.

38. Taylor, *Sources of the Self*, pp. 30–32.

39. Ibid., pp. 135–36.

40. Karen Lebacqz, *Professional Ethics: Power and Paradox* (Nashville, Tenn.: Abingdon, 1985), p. 24.

41. Lawrence Kohlberg, *The Philosophy of Moral Development: Moral Stages and the Idea of Justice* (San Francisco: Harper & Row, 1981); Carol Gilligan, *In a Different Voice: Psychological Theory and Women's Development* (Cambridge, Mass.: Harvard University Press, 1982).

42. Highlights from the 521 issues of *In fact* are included in George Seldes, *Even the Gods Can't Change History: The Facts Speak for Themselves* (Secaucus, N.J.: Lyle Stuart, 1976), pp. 326–35. Seldes lists several stories never covered adequately; for example, "The documentation on the relationship of tobacco to diseases and death was suppressed throughout the *In fact* decade and until recently" (p. 12). Challenging the contemporary press to more muckraking and investigative reporting, he concludes, "The mass media as a whole have never served the public interest," although it is good news that "a few of the most powerful newspapers" recently have become some of the "best newspapers" (p. 12).

43. Collected as Abbott Joseph Liebling, *The Press*, rev. ed. (New York: Ballantine Books, 1964). For a rich collection of the best in media criticism over 100 years, see Tom Goldstein, ed., *Killing the Messenger* (New York: Columbia University Press, 1989).

44. Ron Dorfman, "Present at the Creation," *Quill* 76, no. 7. (July/August 1988): 11.

45. For a more complete list and historical summary, see James R. Bennett, "Media Critics Survive 'Active and Unafraid,' " *St. Louis Journalism Review* 21, no. 140 (October 1991): 12.

46. Charles L. Klotzer, "Journalism Reviews: Their Role, Impact and Limitations," *St. Louis Journalism Review* 21, no. 140 (October 1991): 10–11. This section benefits directly from Klotzer's analysis.

47. David H. Weaver and G. Cleveland Wilhoit, *The American Journalist: A Portrait of U.S. News People and Their Work,* 2d ed. (Bloomington: Indiana University Press, 1991), p. 110.

48. For elaboration, see J. Martin and M. E. Powers, "Truth or Corporate Propaganda: The Value of a Good War Story," in *Organizational Symbolism,* ed. Louis R. Pondy, Peter J. Frost, Gareth Morgan, and Thomas C. Dandridge (Greenwich, Conn.: JAI Press, 1983), pp. 93–107.

49. Charles Conrad, *Strategic Organizational Communication: Cultures, Situations, and Adaptations* (New York: Holt, Rinehart and Winston, 1985), pp. 1–98.

50. Ibid., p. 35. Henri Fayol's major contributions were fourteen principles that summarized his approach to effective management. Robert Giles provides those principles in *Newsroom Management: A Guide to Theory and Practice* (Detroit: Media Management Books, 1990), pp. 5–6.

51. Giles, *Newsroom Management*, p. 1.

52. Ibid., p. 233.

53. Ibid.

54. Mike Royko, Introduction to A. A. Dornfeld, *Hello Sweetheart, Get Me Rewrite* (Chicago: Academy Chicago, 1983), p. ix.

55. Conrad, *Strategic Organizational Communication,* pp. 81–82, originally reported in Rensis Likert, *New Patterns of Management* (New York: McGraw-Hill, 1961).

56. William G. Ouchi, *Theory Z* (Reading, Mass.: Addison-Wesley, 1981), p. 4.

57. Marvin Harris, *America Now* (New York: Simon and Schuster, 1981), p. 181.

58. David H. Smith, "Work, Community and the Corporation" (Paper presented at the Poynter Center for the Study of Ethics and American Institutions, Indiana University, Bloomington, February 1989), p. 28.

59. Joel Weisman, "The Don Craig Story," *Quill,* October 1978, p. 24.

60. Philip Meyer, *Ethical Journalism* (New York: Longman, 1987), p. 115.

61. Ibid., p. 109.

62. For details on this case, see Cassandra Tate, "Conflict of Interest: A Newspaper's Report on Itself," *Columbia Journalism Review* 17, no. 2 (July/August 1978): 44–48.

63. George Rupp, "Communities of Collaboration: Shared Commitments/Common Tasks," in *On Community,* ed. Leroy S. Rouner (Notre Dame, Ind.: University of Notre Dame Press, 1991), pp. 192–208.

64. Edgar H. Schein, *Organizational Culture and Leadership* (San Francisco: Jossey-Bass, 1985), p. 14.

65. Randall P. Bezanson, Gilbert Cranberg, and John Soloski, *Libel Law and the Press: Myth and Reality* (New York: Free Press, 1987), pp. 19–40.

66. Mumby, *Communication and Power in Organizations,* p. 106.

67. Jean Gaddy Wilson, "Women in the Newspaper Business," *Presstime,* October 1986, pp. 31–37; Vernon A. Stone, "Minority Men Shoot ENG, Women Take Advancement Tracks," *Communicator,* August 1988, pp. 10–14. For an overview of the statistical data, see Weaver and Wilhoit, *American Journalist,* chap. 7, "Women Journalists." A sample book-length treatment of gender issues including, but extending beyond, institutional matters is Ramona R. Rush and Donna Allen, eds., *Communications at the Crossroads: The Gender Gap Connection* (Norwood, N.J.: Ablex, 1989). Linda Steiner provides a state-of-the-art review of the literature and issues in feminist communication ethics. Rather than pursue a purified feminism with special moral status, she contends that the feminist project already has a politically and morally ambitious agenda, such as that represented in the works cited above (Steiner, "Feminist Theorizing and Communication Ethics," *Communication* 12, no. 3 [1991]: 157–73).

68. Such problems have been most closely monitored since 1972 by *Media Report to Women;* this monthly is published by Donna Allen, President of the Women's Institute for Freedom of the Press, 3306 Ross Place, N.W., Washington, D.C. 20008.

69. Twenty years after the Kerner Commission's report, research indicates that the role of people of color in the press has been strengthened only marginally. For a status report and evaluation, see "Kerner Plus Twenty Special Issue," *Mass Comm Review* 15, nos. 2–3 (1988): 2–68. Of the six articles included, four deal with organizational structure and policy (pp. 3–44). See also Carolyn A. Stroman, Bishetta D. Merritt, and Paula W. Matabane, "Twenty Years After Kerner: The Portrayal of African Americans on Primetime Television," *The Howard Journal of Communications* 2, no. 1 (Winter 1989–90): 44–56. For a comprehensive history of African-Americans in all mass media (including cinema, music, advertising, and entertainment radio), see Jannette L. Dates and William Barlow, eds., *Split Image: African Americans in the Mass Media* (Washington, D.C.: Howard University Press, 1990); a bibliographical essay is included on pp. 473–74.

70. Schein, *Organizational Culture and Leadership,* p. 150. See W. Schutz, *FIRO: A Three-Dimensional Theory of Interpersonal Behavior* (New York: Holt, Rinehart and Winston, 1958), and J. E. McGrath, *Groups: Interaction and Performance* (Englewood Cliffs, N.J.: Prentice-Hall, 1984).

71. Elizabeth Beverly Fox and Richard Wightman Fox, "Liberals Must Confront the Conservative Argument: Teaching Humanities Means Teaching about Values," *The Chronicle of Higher Education,* 1 November 1989, p. A52.

72. Reinhold Niebuhr, *Man's Nature and His Communities* (New York: Scribner's, 1965), pp. 102–3.

73. Paul A. V. Ansah, "Media Ownership and Accountability: An African Perspective" (Paper presented at the International Communication Association annual conference, Honolulu, Hawaii, May 1985). Also see Ansah, "In Search of

a Role for the African Media in the Democratic Process," *African Media Review* 2, no. 2 (1988): 1–16.

74. Emile Durkheim, *Suicide: A Study in Sociology,* trans. J. Spaulding and G. Simpson (1897; New York: Free Press, 1951), p. 391.

75. Emile Durkheim, *The Division of Labor in Society,* trans. G. Simpson (1893; New York: Free Press, 1933), p. 368.

76. Schein, *Organizational Culture and Leadership,* p. 104.

77. Neil Sheehan, *A Bright Shining Lie: John Paul Vann and America in Vietnam* (New York: Random House, 1988).

78. Max Weber, *From Max Weber: Essays in Sociology,* trans. and ed. H. H. Gerth and C. Wright Mills (New York: Oxford University Press, 1946), pp. 180–84, 196–203.

79. Quoted in Richard Bendix, *Max Weber, an Intellectual Portrait* (Garden City, N.Y.: Doubleday, 1960), p. 421.

80. Robert Michels, *Political Parties: A Sociological Study of Oligarchical Tendencies of Modern Democracy,* trans. E. and C. Paul (1908; New York: Free Press, 1949), p. 32.

81. Stanley Cunningham, "Between Moral Theory and Utterance: The Need for Heuristic Principles in Communication Ethics" (Paper presented at the National Communication Ethics Conference, Kellogg Education Center, Gull Lake, Michigan, June 1990), p. 12.

82. Sheldon Wolin, "Why Democracy?" *Democracy* 1, no. 1 (January 1981): 3.

83. David Waterman, "A New Look at Media Chains and Groups," *Journal of Broadcasting and Electronic Media* 35, no. 2 (Spring 1991): 175. For a collaborative attempt by thirty researchers over three years to document and assess the status and impact of media ownership trends, see Robert Picard, Maxwell McCombs, James Winter, and Stephen Lacy, eds., *Press Concentration and Monopoly: New Perspectives on Newspaper Ownership and Operation* (Norwood, N.J.: Ablex, 1988).

84. Ben Bagdikian, *The Media Monopoly,* 3d ed. (Boston: Beacon Press, 1990), p. 85.

85. Ibid., pp. 78–83.

86. Ibid., p. 30.

87. Charles Perrow, "A Framework for the Comparative Analysis of Organizations," *American Sociological Review* 32 (April 1967): 195; Charles Perrow, *Organizational Analysis: A Sociological View* (Belmont, Calif.: Brooks/Cole, 1970), p. 80. Perrow served as a member of the President's Commission to Investigate the Three Mile Island Incident. In his *Normal Accidents* (New York: Basic Books, 1984), he argues that the structure of high-technology organizations and their decision-making processes coalesce and virtually guarantee that disasters (such as Three Mile Island, Chernobyl, *Challenger,* Bhopal, and *Exxon Valdez*) will recur frequently. See also Perrow, *Complex Organizations,* 3d ed. (New York: Random House, 1987).

88. James Bissland, "The Mechanical Journalist: Implications of Considering Media Organizations as Technological Systems," *Journal of Communication Inquiry* 2, no. 1 (Summer 1976): 38.

89. Donaldson, *Corporations and Morality,* p. 113.

90. Ellis Cose, "The New Generation of Newspaper Giants," *Gannett Center Journal* 3 (Winter 1989): 110–22.

91. Cunningham, "Between Moral Theory and Utterance," pp. 10–15.

92. Georg F. W. Hegel, *Science of Logic I,* trans. A. V. Miller (London: Allen & Unwin, 1969), pp. 367, 371.

93. Cunningham, "Between Moral Theory and Utterance," p. 11.

94. Jerry M. Landay, "Paying for Public Broadcasting: Set the System Free," *Chicago Tribune,* 1 August 1990, sec. 1, p. 11. Landay recommends a tax on the profits of commercial stations, networks, and cable providers or a spectrum fee on the natural monopolies of frequency and cable franchises. In addition, he asserts that the public should pay an excise tax on TV sets or an annual licensing fee for each TV set, as in Great Britain.

95. Dick Polman, "PBS Considers Free Air Time for Politicians," *Chicago Tribune,* 9 July 1990, sec. 1, p. 5. See also Patricia Aufderheide, "Public Television and the Public Sphere," *Critical Studies in Mass Communication* 8, no. 2 (June 1991): 168–83.

96. Clifford G. Christians and Leon Hammond, "Social Justice and a Community Information Utility," *Communication* 9 (1986): 127–49.

97. Majid Tehranian's *Technologies of Power: Information Machines and Democratic Prospects* (Norwood, N.J.: Ablex, 1991) also applauds miniaturization and describes a number of examples in which technology enhances democratic possibilities (pp. 87–92, 212–39).

98. Regina Festa and Luiz Santoro, "Policies from Below—Alternative Video in Brazil," *Media Development* 1 (1987): 28. Penina M. Mlama argues that an inattention to grass-roots media excludes women who have little access to mass media in developing countries ("Culture, Women and the Media," in *Communication and Culture: African Perspectives,* ed. S. T. Kwame Boafo (Nairobi, Kenya: Africa Church Information Service, 1989), pp. 11–18.

99. Bagdikian, *Media Monopoly,* p. 237.

100. Max Weber, "Towards a Sociology of the Press," *Journal of Communication* 26, no. 3 (1976): 100 (the article is taken from a speech delivered at the First Congress of Sociologists, Frankfurt, Germany, 1910. Translated by Hanno Hardt). For a summary of the scholarship on news production that has emerged in this tradition, see Matthew P. McAllister, "Medicalization in the News Media: A Comparison of AIDS Coverage in Three Newspapers" (Ph.D. diss., University of Illinois–Urbana, 1990), chap. 2.

101. Warren Breed, "Social Control in the Newsroom: A Functional Analysis," *Social Forces* 33, no. 4 (1955): 326–35.

102. Stuart Hall, Chas Critcher, Tony Jefferson, John Clarke, and Brian Roberts, *Policing the Crisis: Mugging, the State, and Law and Order* (New York: Holmes and Meier, 1978), p. 83.

Chapter 6

1. Hans Jonas, *The Imperative of Responsibility: In Search of an Ethics for the Technological Age* (Chicago: University of Chicago Press, 1984), p. 22.

2. Douglas Kellner, for example, concludes, "Against Lyotard, Jameson employs the form of a grand narrative . . . which interprets as the cultural logic of capital rather than as a code word for a new (post) historical condition—as do Lyotard and Baudrillard. . . . Obviously Jameson wishes to preserve Marxism as the Master Narrative" ("Postmodernism as Social Theory: Some Challenges and Problems," *Theory, Culture and Society* 5, nos. 2–3 [June 1988]: 262). For elaboration and bibliography, see Stanley Aronowitz and Henry A. Giroux, *Postmodern Education: Politics, Culture, and Social Criticism* (Minneapolis: University of Minnesota Press, 1991), pp. 60–86. For a systematic historical and theoretical introduction to Lyotard, Jameson, and Baudrillard—as well as Foucault, Deleuze, Laclau, and Mouffe—see Stephen Best and Douglas Kellner, *Postmodern Theory: Critical Interrogations* (New York: Guilford, 1991).

3. Linda Hutcheon, "A Postmodern Problematics," in *Ethics/Aesthetics: Post-Modern Positions,* ed. Robert Merrill (Washington, D.C.: Maisonneuve Press, 1988), p. 5, quoted in Aronowitz and Giroux, *Postmodern Education,* p. 67.

4. Norman E. Bowie, "Applied Philosophy—Its Meaning and Justification," *Applied Philosophy* 1 (Spring 1982): 1–18.

5. Florian Znaniecki, *The Method of Sociology* (New York: Holt, Rinehart and Winston, 1935); Znaniecki, *Cultural Sciences* (Urbana: University of Illinois Press, 1952).

6. Barney C. Glazer and Anselm L. Strauss, *The Discovery of Grounded Theory* (Chicago: Aldine, 1967); John Lofland, *Doing Social Life* (New York: John Wiley, 1976), chap. 5. For elaboration, see Alfred Schutz, "Concepts and Theory Formation in the Social Sciences," *Journal of Philosophy* 51 (1954): 257–73.

7. Stephen Toulmin, "The Recovery of Practical Philosophy," *The American Scholar,* Summer 1988, pp. 338, 341.

8. Ibid., p. 352.

9. Jeff Lustig, "Community and Social Class," *Democracy* 1, no. 2 (April 1981): 96.

10. Charles Douglas Lummis, "The Radicalism of Democracy," *Democracy* 2, no. 4 (Fall 1982): 12–13.

11. David Fisher, "Applied Ethics in Postmodern Perspective," *Philosophy in Context* 17 (1987): 61.

12. In contrast to the definitive concepts of scientific naturalism, and consistent with his roots in Chicago-school symbolic interactionism, Herbert Blumer argued for expressions with prophetic density that illuminate the phenomena themselves from within. ("What Is Wrong with Social Theory?" *American Sociological Review* 19 [1954]: 3–10).

13. Fredric Jameson considers "the technology of contemporary society" to be a "network of power and control" representing "the third stage of capitalism"; examining today's sprawling global technological networks, he believes, gives one a "privileged representational shorthand" of multinational capitalism itself ("Postmodernism, or the Cultural Logic of Late Capitalism," *New Left Review* 146 [1984]: 79–80). Jameson concludes that "advanced capitalist countries today are a field of discursive heterogeneity without a norm" (p. 67), and Ellul reaches a similar conclusion that technological societies are amoral. However, we consider Ellul's way of accounting for Marxist social theory to be superior. Ellul's formulation likewise

connects technology and culture, but it enables us to see the remarkable similarities among all advanced technological societies, capitalist and socialist. In the process, Ellul focuses the issues more fruitfully on the oppressive rupture between technology's efficiency and human freedom.

14. Jacques Ellul, *What I Believe,* trans. G. W. Bromiley (London: Marshall Morgan and Scott, 1989), pp. 134–35.

15. Darrell J. Fasching, "Theology, Technology and Transcendence: Reflections on Bernard Lonergan and Jacques Ellul" (Unpublished paper, University of South Florida, Tampa, n.d.).

16. Jacques Ellul, "Symbolic Function, Technology and Society," *Journal of Social and Biological Structures,* October 1978, p. 216. Jean Baudrillard uses the robot to represent this stage of industrialism. Whereas analogue and orientation are possible in the era of "clocklike man," when efficiency finally dominates, technology is no longer "turned toward a resemblance with man, to whom it no longer bears comparison"; no basis remains for "interrogat[ing] appearance," since the only truth is "mechanical efficiency." In the new order of signs that arises, "the problem of their uniqueness, of their origin, is no longer a matter of concern; their origin is technique" (Baudrillard, *Simulations,* trans. P. Foss, P. Patton, and P. Beichtman [New York: Semiotext(e), 1983], pp. 94, 96).

17. Ellul, *What I Believe,* p. 135.

18. Baudrillard, *Simulations,* pp. 21–22.

19. Ibid., p. 16.

20. Ibid., p. 32.

21. Ibid., p. 3.

22. Aronowitz and Giroux, *Postmodern Education,* p. 66. We agree with these authors' generally constructive treatment of Baudrillard, although we argue that Ellul integrates media spectacle more satisfactorily into his philosophy of technology as a whole. We concur also with Aronowitz and Giroux's reluctant conclusion, following Kellner: "Baudrillard's society of simulations . . . translates less into a provocative analysis of the changing contours and features of the age than it does into a nihilism that undermines its own radical intent" (ibid.).

23. Jacques Ellul, *Propaganda,* trans. K. Kellen and J. Lerner (New York: Knopf, 1969), p. xvii.

24. Jacques Ellul, *To Will and to Do,* trans. C. E. Hopkin (Philadelphia: Pilgrim Press, 1969), p. 184.

25. Donald W. Shriver, "Man and His Machines: Four Angels of Vision," *Technology and Culture* 13 (October 1972): 537.

26. Jacques Ellul, *The Presence of the Kingdom,* trans. O. Wyon (1948; New York: Seabury Press, 1967), p. 75.

27. Ellul, *Propaganda,* p. xviii. Ellul commonly uses "information" as the opposite of "propaganda," as in "Information and Propaganda."

28. Clifford G. Christians, "Jacques Ellul and Democracy's 'Vital Information' Premise," *Journalism Monographs* 45 (August 1976): 5–14. John M. Staudenmaier develops this thesis in terms of technological systems as a whole. A commitment to the rhetoric of technological progress erodes our capacity for the common good. He contradicts various versions of autonomous technological determinism as themselves abetting this misconstrued rhetoric (Staudenmaier, "U.S. Technological

Style and the Atrophy of Civic Commitment," in *Beyond Individualism: Toward a Retrieval of Moral Discourse in America,* ed. Donald L. Gelpi [Notre Dame, Ind.: University of Notre Dame Press, 1989], pp. 120–225). Anura Goonasekera's research charts a new path for examining the impact of technological development on the dissolution of the self. It focuses on the changing patterns of social density (Durkheim called it moral or dynamic density) as nonindustrial countries experience technological growth (Goonasekera, "Communication, Culture and the Growth of the Individual Self in Third World Societies," *Asian Journal of Communication* 1, no. 1 [1990]: 34–52).

29. For a recent, responsible presentation of divine-command theory, we recommend Richard J. Mouw, *The God Who Commands: A Study in Divine Command Ethics* (Notre Dame, Ind.: University of Notre Dame Press, 1990).

30. Jonas, *Imperative of Responsibility,* p. x.

31. Ibid., pp. 71, 74.

32. Ibid., p. 78.

33. Ibid., p. 95.

34. Alasdair MacIntyre argues for a similar understanding of history as a normed process; his "embodied rational enquiry" is likewise contra-Enlightenment (*Whose Justice? Which Rationality?* [Notre Dame, Ind.: University of Notre Dame Press, 1986], pp. 6–9).

35. Henry McDonald, *The Normative Basis of Culture: A Philosophical Inquiry* (Baton Rouge: Louisiana State University Press, 1986), p. 3.

36. Charles Taylor, "Growth, Legitimacy and the Modern Identity," *Praxis International* (1981): 111.

37. Ibid., p. 120.

38. Helmut Peukert, "Universal Solidarity as Goal of Communication," *Media Development* 28, no. 4 (1981): 11. See also Peukert, "Fundamental Theology and Communicative Praxis as the Ethics of Universal Solidarity," *Conrad Grebel Review* 3 (Winter 1985): 41–65.

39. Peukert, "Universal Solidarity as Goal of Communication," p. 10.

40. James H. Olthuis, "Evolutionary Dialectics and Segundo's *Liberation of Theology,*" *Calvin Theological Journal* 21, no. 1 (April 1986): 93.

41. Ibid., p. 93.

42. Basil Mitchell, *Morality: Religious and Secular* (Oxford: Clarendon Press, 1980). For elaboration, see Peter J. Mehl, "In the Twilight of Modernity: MacIntyre vs. Mitchell on Human Nature, Cultural Context, and Ethical Ideals" (Unpublished paper, University of Chicago, 1986), p. 3.

43. Edmund Burke, *Reflections on the Revolution in France* (London: Dent, 1910), pp. 131–36, 164–68.

44. Paul Greenberg, "Revenge Is Sour," *Chicago Tribune,* 3 January 1990, sec. 1, p. 11; Greenberg elaborates on Orwell and Burke.

45. In constructing such boundaries, humans establish moral codes to orient their cultures and guide behavior. See Robert Wuthnow, *Meaning and Moral Order: Explorations in Cultural Analysis* (Berkeley and Los Angeles: University of California Press, 1987), pp. 71–75.

46. Arthur F. Holmes, *Contours of a World View* (Grand Rapids, Mich.: Eerdmans, 1983), p. 48.

47. Manfred Stanley, *The Technological Conscience: Survival and Dignity in an Age of Expertise* (Chicago: University of Chicago Press, 1978), pp. 69–70.

48. Frederick L. Will, *Beyond Deduction: Ampliative Aspects of Philosophical Reflection* (New York: Routledge, 1987), p. 9.

49. Gordon W. Allport, "Dewey's Individual and Social Psychology," in *The Philosophy of John Dewey,* ed. Paul Arthur Schlipp (Evanston, Ill.: Northwestern University Press, 1939), pp. 263–90.

50. Will, *Beyond Deduction,* p. 90.

51. Ibid., p. 35. Feminist theory is contributing substantially to our understanding of mutuality, caring, and community. However, in a sympathetic but agonizing critique, Elizabeth Fox-Genovese concludes that feminism has not adequately acknowledged the influence of individualism on its arguments and commitments. Feminism's campaigns for social justice, for example, typically insist on the rights of individuals over the good of the community (Fox-Genovese, *Feminism Without Illusions: A Critique of Individualism* [Chapel Hill: University of North Carolina Press, 1991]).

52. David Tracy, *Plurality and Ambiguity: Hermeneutics, Religion, Hope* (San Francisco, Harper & Row, 1987), p. 28.

53. Thomas Nagel, *The View from Nowhere* (New York: Oxford University Press, 1986), p. 4.

54. Ibid., p. 5.

55. Ibid., p. 7.

56. Clifford Geertz, "Thick Description," in *The Interpretation of Cultures* (New York: Basic Books, 1973), pp. 28–29.

57. H. Richard Niebuhr, *The Responsible Self* (New York: Harper & Row, 1963), p. 106.

58. Olthuis, "Evolutionary Dialectics," p. 87.

59. "Czechoslovak Leader Announces Amnesty," *Chicago Tribune,* Chicago Tribune Wires, 2 January 1990, sec. 1, p. 1.

60. Costas Criticos, "Film and Video as a Catalyst for Change in South Africa," *Media Resource Center Working Papers* (University of Natal, Durban, South Africa), no. 2 (October 1989): 1–4. Keyan Tomaselli, Director of Contemporary Cultural Studies at the University of Natal, is editor of the media studies journal *Critical Arts* and author of *The Cinema of Apartheid: Race and Class in South African Film* (Chicago: Lake View Press, 1990).

61. North's memoirs, prepared by publishers under intense secrecy and finally introduced in a *Time* magazine excerpt, underscores the call to truth that even the duty-only North feels is his ultimate obligation to the public. See Oliver L. North, *Under Fire: An American Story* (San Francisco: HarperCollins/Zondervan, 1991). No author should be pilloried for attempting to recover his honor; critics who dismiss *Under Fire* as vainglory or market hype fail to understand the nature of the public dialogue of which North himself is a part. Fixing on the genesis of deception in this bizarre international case now becomes the province of biographers and third-party investigators. Who lied, when, and to what extent remains the primal question.

62. Will, *Beyond Deduction,* p. 142.

63. For a comprehensive treatment of Tillich's symbolic theory, see Carolyn

C. Deile, "Paul Tillich's Philosophy of Communication" (Ph.D. diss., University of Illinois–Urbana, 1971), and William L. Rowe, *Religious Symbols and God: A Philosophical Study of Tillich's Theology* (Chicago: University of Chicago Press, 1968).

64. While not specifically developed as a contradiction of Jean François Lyotard, the symbolic theory represented here provides an alternative to his declaration that all metanarratives have ended (*The Post-Modern Condition: A Report of Knowledge,* trans. G. Bennington and B. Massumi, [Minneapolis: University of Minnesota Press, 1988]). Lyotard argues appropriately that the meta-narratives that have undergirded the modern age—positivism, Marxism, and humanism, for example—no longer unify and inspire, they have been exposed as language games with no status as ontological truth (pp. xxiv, 37–41). Moreover, he is undoubtedly correct that Habermas's modernist attempt at consensus is "outmoded and suspect" (p. 66). But our understanding of first and second orders transparent to each other requires us to reject Lyotard's claim that locally determined linguistic rules are a postmodern condition only. In all human knowledge—ancient, modern, and postmodern—narratives are appropriated locally, but at the same time they can be understood holistically even though these two levels are not typically commensurate. The reality of conflictual, locally determined language games and the current crisis of grand narratives certainly stifles the Enlightenment's attempt to give standardized scientific knowledge a place of privilege. However, Lyotard's critique does not preclude our integration of the particular and universal in terms of what we call normative pluralism. His analysis has not adequately distinguished between relativistic perspectives assuming no center and pluralistic viewpoints on a common center that no one language interprets fully.

65. Social ethicists ought to develop the same skill that Clifford Geertz claims is essential for modern anthropology: "a continuous dialectical tracking between the most local of local detail and the most global of global structure in such a way as to bring them into simultaneous view" ("From the Native's Point of View: On the Nature of Anthropological Understanding," in *Local Knowledge* [New York: Basic Books, 1983], p. 69).

66. David Broder, "On Technology, Tyranny and the Information Age," *Chicago Tribune,* 19 June 1989, sec. 1, p. 13.

67. Pradip Chakravarty, "Development and Communication: Ideas of Freire" (Unpublished paper, University of Illinois–Urbana, Fall 1986), pp. 1–21.

68. See Geffrey B. Kelly and F. Burton Nelson, eds., *A Testament of Freedom: The Essential Writings of Dietrich Bonhoeffer* (San Francisco: HarperCollins, 1990). An accessible review of Bonhoeffer's life and times is in *Christian History* 10, no. 4, Issue 32 (n.d.). For a collection of eighteen academic papers that also attempt to reconnect norms and cultural diversity, see Sander Griffioen and Jan Verhoogt, eds., *Norm and Context in the Social Sciences* (Lanham, Md.: University Press of America, 1990). The purpose of this volume is identical to Bonhoeffer's: constructing an alternative to the Enlightenment's search for universal laws of human behavior, on the one hand, and to a phenomenological pluralism rejecting universals, on the other.

69. Richard Rorty, "The Priority of Democracy to Philosophy," in *The Virginia*

Statute for Religious Freedom, ed. Merrill D. Peterson and Robert C. Vaughn (New York: Cambridge University Press, 1988), pp. 259–61.

70. Michael J. Sandel, *Liberalism and the Limits of Justice* (Cambridge: Cambridge University Press, 1982), p. 49.

71. Rorty, "Priority of Democracy to Philosophy," pp. 263, 257.

72. John Rawls, "Justice as Fairness: Political Not Metaphysical," *Philosophy and Public Affairs* 14 (1985): 223, 225.

73. Rorty, "Priority of Democracy to Philosophy," pp. 262, 267, 269, 271.

74. Richard Rorty, *Philosophy and the Mirror of Nature* (Princeton, N.J.: Princeton University Press, 1979), pp. 371, 356.

75. Ibid., p. 373.

76. Seyla Benhabib, "The Generalized and the Concrete Other," in *Feminism as Critique: Essays in the Politics of Gender in Late-Capitalist Societies,* ed. Seyla Benhabib and Drucilla Cornell (Minneapolis: University of Minnesota Press, 1987), pp. 77–95.

77. Jeffrey Stout, *Ethics After Babel: The Languages of Morals and Their Discontents* (Boston: Beacon Press, 1988), chap. 3. For a thoughtful introduction to Stout's attempt to escape the dilemma of choosing either foundationalism or relativism, see Allen D. Verhey, "Review of *The Flight from Authority* and *Ethics After Babel,*" *Calvin Theological Journal* 25, no. 2 (November 1990): 262–66.

78. For a summary of H. Richard Niebuhr's dependence on Polanyi's epistemology, see R. Melvin Keiser, *Recovering the Personal: Religious Language and the Post-Critical Quest of H. Richard Niebubr* (Atlanta: Scholars Press, 1988), pp. 49–54.

79. Michael Polanyi, *The Tacit Dimension* (Garden City, N.Y.: Doubleday, 1966), p. 19. For an accessible, general introduction to Polanyi's epistemology, see his Lindsay Memorial Lectures, *The Study of Man* (Chicago: University of Chicago Press, 1959), pp. 11–70.

80. Polanyi, *Jacit Dimension,* p. 20.

81. Ibid., p. 60.

82. Ibid., p. 18.

83. Ibid., p. xi.

84. James H. Olthuis, *A Hermeneutics of Ultimacy: Peril or Promise?* (Lanham, Md.: University Press of America, 1987), p. 13.

85. Ibid.

86. Ibid., p. 15.

87. Randolph Bourne, "Transnational America," in *History of a Literary Radical and Other Essays* (New York: Huebsch, 1920), p. 278.

88. Os Guinness, "Tribespeople, Idiots or Citizens?" (Paper presented at the Conference on Evangelical Affirmations, Deerfield, Illinois, May 1989), p. 10.

89. Chantal Mouffe, "Hegemony and Ideology in Gramsci," in *Gramsci and Marxist Theory,* ed. Chantal Mouffe (London: Routledge and Kegan Paul, 1979), pp. 181–86, 191–92.

90. Richard John Neuhaus, *The Naked Public Square* (Grand Rapids, Mich.: Eerdmans, 1984), chap. 2.

91. William Lee Miller, "Religious Liberty and American Pluralism" (Paper

presented at the Conference on Conflicts in the Public Square: Religion Versus Secularism, Chicago, November 1986), p. 8.

92. Guinness, "Tribespeople, Idiots or Citizens?" p. 22.

93. For an articulation of the nature of world views, see Brian J. Walsh, "Theology and Modernity: A Study in the Thought of Langdon Gilkey" (Ph.D. diss., McGill University, Montreal, 1987), chap. 2.

94. Miller, "Religious Liberty and American Pluralism," p. 14.

95. Stanley Hauerwas, *A Community of Character* (Notre Dame, Ind.: University of Notre Dame Press, 1981), chap. 4.

96. Lesslie Newbigin, *The Gospel in a Pluralist Society* (Grand Rapids, Mich.: Eerdmans, 1989), chap. 5.

97. Peter Berger, *The Sacred Canopy* (Garden City, N.Y.: Doubleday, 1969), p. 21. Clifford Geertz provides the standard definition of a world view in cultural anthropology: "The picture of the way things in sheer actuality are [a people's] concept of nature, of self, of society. It contains their most comprehending ideas of order" (*Interpretation of Cultures,* p. 127).

98. Niebuhr, *Responsible Self,* p. 139; for elaboration, see Keiser, *Recovering the Personal,* chap. 7, "Speaking and Being Transformed: The Logic of Religious Discourse." Obviously, the religious dimension here is intended in David Tracy's sense, not as a separate human activity but in terms of what he calls its "limit-character." The religious dimension, in other words, "discloses a reality which functions as a final, now gracious, now frightening, now trustworthy, now absurd, always uncontrollable limit of the very meaning of existence itself" (Tracy, *Blessed Rage for Order* [New York: Seabury Press, 1975], p. 108).

99. For a recent review of the interaction between the media and religion, see Benjamin J. Hubbard, ed., *Reporting Religion: Facts & Faith* (Sonoma, Calif.: Polebridge Press, 1990). Part I focuses on the problems of the religion writer in the secular press (pp. 1–57), and Part II examines media use by Protestants, Catholics, and Jews (pp. 59–139). Part III pushes beyond this standard institutional treatment to explore such questions as religion's role in media reform (pp. 145–58) and religion's general concern for press fairness (pp. 159–76). We support such efforts to enhance religion reporting, and we see particular promise in examining the issues illustrated in Part III. However, world-view pluralism centers on a deeper domain: the spiritual dimension of our humanity, numinous world views beyond the commonplace, aesthetic, and scientific. We are asking the press to represent the underlying spiritual domain which cultures and social institutions reflect.

100. Miller, "Religious Liberty and American Pluralism," p. 9. For the theoretical argument that human life is most clearly understood as *Homo religiosus,* see Langdon Gilkey, *Naming the Whirlwind: The Renewal of God Language* (Indianapolis: Bobbs-Merrill, 1969), and *Reaping the Whirlwind: A Christian Interpretation of History* (New York: Seabury Press, 1976), part I.

101. Glenn Tinder, "Can We Be Good Without God? On the Political Meaning of Christianity," *Atlantic Monthly,* December 1989, pp. 69–85.

102. Nina Eliasoph, "Routines and the Making of Oppositional News," *Critical Studies in Mass Communication* 5, no. 4 (December 1988): 315.

103. Ibid., p. 332.

104. Stuart Hall, "Encoding/Decoding," in *Culture, Media, Language,* ed.

Stuart Hall, Dorothy Hobson, and Andrew Lowe (London: Hutchinson, 1980), pp. 128–38.

105. Jennifer Daryl Slack, "Critical Strategies for a Non-normative Ethics" (Paper presented at the International Communication Association annual conference, Honolulu, Hawaii, May 1985), p. 11.

106. Paul Patton, "Notes for a Glossary," *Ideology and Consciousness* 8 (1981): 46.

107. Lawrence Grossberg, "It's a Sin: Politics, Postmodernity and the Popular," in *It's a Sin: Essays on Postmodernism, Politics and Culture,* ed. V. Spate (Sydney, Australia: Power Publications, 1988), p. 22.

108. Jennifer Daryl Slack and Laurie Anne Whitt, "Ethics and Cultural Studies," in *Cultural Studies,* ed. Lawrence Grossberg, Cary Nelson, and Paula Treichler (New York: Routledge, 1992), p. 572.

109. Slack, "Critical Strategies for a Non-normative Ethics," p. 10.

110. Stuart Hall, "The Problem of Ideology—Marxism Without Guarantees," in *Marx One Hundred Years On,* ed. Betty Matthews (London: Lawrence and Wishart, 1983), p. 84.

111. Slack and Whitt, "Ethics and Cultural Studies," p. 572.

112. For the first major attempt to provide such a basis, see ibid., pp. 571–92. Slack and Whitt argue for locating ultimate values "in ecosystems rather than in the individuals who compromise them. The ecosystem replaces the individual as the fundamental moral datum" (p. 572).

113. Seyla Benhabib, *Critique, Norm and Utopia: A Study of the Foundations of Critical Theory* (New York: Columbia University Press, 1986), p. 328. An earlier version of Chapter 8.3 was published as "The Utopian Dimension in Communicative Ethics," *New German Critique* 35 (Spring/Summer 1985): 83–96. See also John Torpey, "Ethics and Critical Theory: From Horkheimer to Habermas," *Telos* 19, no. 3 (Fall 1986): 68–84.

114. For the historical location of Jürgen Habermas's discourse ethics in the history of ideas and theoretical elaboration, see his collection of essays: *Moral Consciousness and Communicative Action,* trans. C. Lenhardt and S. W. Nicholsen (Cambridge, Mass.: MIT Press, 1990). Originally published as *Moralbewusstsein und kommunikatives Handeln* (Frankfurt am Main: Suhrkamp Verlag, 1983).

115. Seyla Benhabib, "Afterword: Communicative Ethics and Current Controversies in Practical Philosophy," in *The Communicative Ethics Controversy,* ed. Seyla Benhabib and Fred Dallmayr (Cambridge, Mass.: MIT Press, 1990), p. 331.

116. World-view pluralism entails a deeper confrontation, of course, than do theories of professional ethics. Existentialist humanism, scientific naturalism, Marxism, liberal humanitarianism, and Judeo-Christian theism are all important contemporary world views, for example. World views are perspectival; they cohere around a pretheoretical beginning, a world picture (*Weltbild,* as the German philosopher Wilhelm Dilthey called it, "the ultimate" as noted above). In that sense, they are more similar to Michel Foucault's episteme then to Thomas Kuhn's paradigm. In the latter, Darwin constituted a paradigm revolution. For Foucault, the unquestioned givens that reside beneath Darwinian theory are consonant with traditional biological thinking—what are considered facts, purpose of science, typologies of life forms, historical progress, and so forth (*The Order of Things* [New

York: Vintage, 1973], p. xii). The Darwin example is introduced in Foucault's *The Archaeology of Knowledge* (New York: Harper & Row, 1976), p. 224.

World views function like a gearbox between an engine and the wheels, between theories and their application. However, in adequate world views this unifying perspective is always elaborated theologically and philosophically. Thus debates over their intellectual credibility and practical sufficiency involve long-term confrontations of the highest theoretical magnitude over metaphysics, cosmology, epistemology, anthropology, and axiology. While this book leaves those disputes unargued, confessional pluralism encourages such disputations without seeking hegemony for any one paradigm. Even within world views pluralism is inescapable, since all options themselves appear historically in a variety of compelling formulations. Those who are articulate about their world views recognize that the latter are, at best, only partial and conditioned representations of the truth.

117. Alasdair MacIntyre, *After Virtue* (Notre Dame, Ind.: University of Notre Dame Press, 1981), chap. 18.

118. Charles Norris Cochrane, "The Latin Spirit in Literature," *University of Toronto Quarterly* 2, no. 3 (1932–33): 338. For elaboration, see Cochrane, *Christianity and Classical Culture: A Study of Thought and Action from Augustus to Augustine* (Oxford: Oxford University Press, 1940).

119. Arthur Kroker and David Cook, *The Postmodern Scene: Excremental Culture and Hyper-Aesthetics* (New York: St. Martin's, 1986), chap. 3.

120. Ibid., p. 37.

BIBLIOGRAPHY

Allport, Gordon W. "Dewey's Individual and Social Psychology." In *The Philosophy of John Dewey,* edited by Paul Arthur Schlipp, pp. 263–90. Evanston, Ill.: Northwestern University Press, 1939.

Ansah, Paul A. V. "In Search of a Role for the African Media in the Democratic Process." *African Media Review* 2, no. 2 (1988): 1–16.

———. "Media Ownership and Accountability: An African Perspective." Paper presented at the International Communication Association annual conference, Honolulu, Hawaii, May 1985.

Aprile, Diane. "Breaking the Silence." *The Courier-Journal Magazine,* 24 February 1991, pp. 4–9.

Arkes, Hadley. *First Things: An Inquiry into the First Principles of Morals and Justice.* Princeton, N.J.: Princeton University Press, 1986.

Armstrong, David. *A Trumpet to Arts: Alternative Media in America.* Boston: Houghton Mifflin, 1981.

Aronowitz, Stanley, and Henry A. Giroux. *Postmodern Education: Politics, Culture, and Social Criticism.* Minneapolis: University of Minnesota Press, 1991.

Ashmore, Harry. *Unseasonable Truths: The Life of Robert Maynard Hutchins.* Boston: Little, Brown, 1989.

Attorney General's Commission on Pornography. *Final Report.* 2 vols. Washington, D.C.: Government Printing Office, 1986.

Aufderheide, Patricia. "Public Television and the Public Sphere." *Critical Studies in Mass Communication* 8, no. 2 (June 1991): 168–83.

Bagdikian, Ben. *The Media Monopoly.* 3d ed. Boston: Beacon Press, 1990.

Barber, Benjamin. *Strong Democracy: Participatory Politics for a New Age.* Berkeley and Los Angeles: University of California Press, 1984.

Baudrillard, Jean. *Simulations.* Translated by P. Foss, P. Patton, and P. Beichtman. New York: Semiotext(e), 1983.

Bellah, Robert N., Richard Madsen, William M. Sullivan, Ann Swidler, and Steven Tipton. *The Good Society.* New York: Knopf, 1991.

———. *Habits of the Heart: Individualism and Commitment in American Life.* Berkeley and Los Angeles: University of California Press, 1985.

Bendix, Richard. *Max Weber, An Intellectual Portrait.* Garden City, N.Y.: Doubleday, 1960.

Benhabib, Seyla. "Afterword: Communicative Ethics and Current Controversies in Practical Philosophy." In *The Communicative Ethics Controversy,* edited by Seyla Benhabib and Fred Dallmayr, pp. 330–64. Cambridge, Mass.: MIT Press, 1990.

———. "Autonomy, Modernity and Community: An Exchange Between Communitarianism and Social Theory." In *Zwischenbetrachtungen im Prozess der Aufkläring,* edited by A. Honneth, T. A. McCarthy, C. Offe, and A. Wellmer, pp. 373–95. Frankfurt: Suhrkamp, 1988.

————. *Critique, Norm and Utopia: A Study of the Foundations of Critical Theory.* New York: Columbia University Press, 1986.

————. "The Generalized and the Concrete Other." In *Feminism as Critique: Essays in the Politics of Gender in Late-Capitalist Societies,* edited by Seyla Benhabib and Drucilla Cornell, pp. 77–95. Minneapolis: University of Minnesota Press, 1987.

————. "Hannah Arendt und die erlösende Kraft des Erzählens." In *Zivilisationsbruch: Denken nach Auschwitz,* edited by Dan Diner, pp. 150–174. Frankfurt am Main, Germany: Fischer Taschenbuch Verlag, 1988.

————. "The Utopian Dimension in Communicative Ethics." *New German Critique* 35 (Spring/Summer 1985): 83–96.

Benhabib, Seyla, and Fred Dallmayr, eds. *The Communicative Ethics Controversy.* Cambridge, Mass.: MIT Press, 1990.

Benhabib, Seyla, Suzanne Jacobitti, and B. Honig. "Arendt, Politics, and the Self." *Political Theory* 16, no. 1 (February 1988): 29–98.

Bennett, James R. "Media Critics Survive 'Active and Unafraid.' " *St. Louis Journalism Review* 21, no. 140 (October 1991): 12.

Bennett, John C. *Christianity and Our World.* New York: Association Press, 1936.

Berger, Peter. *The Sacred Canopy.* Garden City, N.Y.: Doubleday, 1969.

Berlin, Isaiah. *Four Essays on Liberty.* New York: Oxford University Press, 1969.

Bernstein, Richard J. *Praxis and Action: Contemporary Philosophies of Human Activity.* Philadelphia: University of Pennsylvania Press, 1971.

Berry, Wendell. *Remembering.* San Francisco: North Point Press, 1988.

————. *What Are People For?* San Francisco: North Point Press, 1990.

Bertrand, Claude-Jean. "Como mejorar los medios de communicación y por que." *Nuestro Tiempo,* June 1988, pp. 110–23.

————. "Media Ethics in Perspective." *Journal of Mass Media Ethics* 2, no. 1 (Fall/Winter 1986–87): 17–22.

————. "La Responsabilité sociale de la presse." *Presse-Actualité,* April 1978, pp. 56–63.

Best, Stephen, and Douglas Kellner. *Postmodern Theory: Critical Interrogations.* New York: Guilford, 1991.

Bethage, Eberhard. "Editor's Preface." In Dietrich Bonhoeffer, *Ethics.* London: SCM Press, 1955.

Bezanson, Randall P., Gilbert Cranberg, and John Soloski. *Libel Law and the Press: Myth and Reality.* New York: Free Press, 1987.

Bissland, James. "The Mechanical Journalist: Implications of Considering Media Organizations as Technological Systems." *Journal of Communication Inquiry* 2, no. 1 (Summer 1976): 29–40.

Blumer, Herbert. "What Is Wrong with Social Theory?" *American Sociological Review* 19 (1954): 3–10.

Bonhoeffer, Dietrich. *Ethics.* Translated by N. H. Smith. New York: Macmillan, 1955.

Boorstin, Daniel. *The Americans.* Vol. 2: *The Democratic Experience.* New York: Vintage, 1973.

Booth, Wayne. *The Company We Keep: An Ethics of Fiction.* Berkeley and Los Angeles: University of California Press, 1988.

"Born Again Catholic Workers: A Conversation Between Jeff Dietrich and Katherine Temple." *The Ellul Studies Forum* 7 (July 1991): 7–9.

Bourne, Randolph. *History of a Literary Radical and Other Essays.* New York: Huebsch, 1920.

Bowers, C. A. *Elements of a Post-Liberal Theory of Education.* New York: Teachers College Press, 1987.

Bowie, Norman E. "Applied Philosophy—Its Meaning and Justification." *Applied Philosophy* 1 (Spring 1982): 1–18.

Breed, Warren. "Social Control in the Newsroom: A Functional Analysis." *Social Forces* 33, no. 4 (1955): 326–35.

Broder, David. "On Technology, Tyranny and the Information Age." *Chicago Tribune,* 19 June 1989, sec. 1, p. 13.

Buber, Martin. *I and Thou.* 2d ed. Translated by R. G. Smith. New York: Scribner's, 1958.

———. *The Knowledge of Man: Selected Essays.* Translated by M. Friedman and R. G. Smith. New York: Harper & Row, 1965.

Burke, Edmund. *Reflections on the Revolution in France.* London: Dent, 1910.

Callahan, Daniel. "Autonomy: A Moral Good, Not a Moral Obsession." *The Hastings Center Report,* October 1984, p. 42.

Carey, James W. "The Communications Revolution and the Professional Communicator." *Sociological Review Monograph* 13 (January 1969): 23–38.

———. "The Dark Continent of American Journalism." In *Reading the News,* edited by Robert K. Manoff and Michael Schudson, pp. 146–96. New York: Pantheon Books, 1986.

———. "The Press and the Public Discourse." *The Center Magazine,* March/April 1987, pp. 4–16.

Carragee, Kevin M. "Defining Solidarity: Themes and Omissions in Coverage of the Solidarity Trade Union Movement by ABC News." *Journalism Monographs* 119 (February 1990): 1–30.

———. "Interpretive Media Study and Interpretive Social Science." *Critical Studies in Mass Communication* 7, no. 2 (June 1990): 81–96.

Cassirer, Ernst. *The Philosophy of the Enlightenment.* Princeton, N.J.: Princeton University Press, 1951.

Chakravarty, Pradip. "Development and Communication: Ideas of Freire." Unpublished paper, University of Illinois–Urbana, Fall 1986.

Chiasson, Lloyd. "Japanese-American Relocation During World War II: A Study of California Editorial Reactions." *Journalism Quarterly* 68, no. 1/2 (Spring/Summer 1991): 263–68.

Chomsky, Noam. *American Power and the New Mandarins.* New York: Random House, 1969.

Christians, Clifford G. "Jacques Ellul and Democracy's 'Vital Information' Premise." *Journalism Monographs* 45 (August 1976): 1–38.

———. "Reporting and the Oppressed." In *Responsible Journalism,* edited by Deni Elliott, pp. 109–30. Beverly Hills, Calif.: Sage, 1986.

Christians, Clifford G., and James W. Carey. "The Logic and Aims of Qualitative

Research." In *Research Methods in Mass Communication*. 2d ed., edited by Guido H. Stempel III and Bruce H. Westley, pp. 354–74. Englewood Cliffs, N.J.: Prentice-Hall, 1989.

Christians, Clifford G., Kim B. Rotzoll, and Mark Fackler. *Media Ethics: Cases and Moral Reasoning*. 3d ed. New York: Longman, 1991.

Christians, Clifford G., and Leon Hammond. "Social Justice and a Community Information Utility." *Communication* 9 (1986): 127–49.

Cianco, Frank. *Voices of Silence: Lives of the Trappists Today*. New York: Paragon, 1991.

Cochrane, Charles Norris. *Christianity and Classical Culture: A Study of Thought and Action from Augustus to Augustine*. Oxford: Oxford University Press, 1940.

———. "The Latin Spirit in Literature." *University of Toronto Quarterly* 2, no. 3 (1932–33): 315–38.

Commission on Freedom of the Press. *A Free and Responsible Press*. Chicago: University of Chicago Press, 1947.

Conrad, Charles. *Strategic Organizational Communication: Cultures, Situations, and Adaptations*. New York: Holt, Rinehart and Winston, 1985.

Cooley, Charles Horton. *Human Nature and the Social Order*. New York: Schocken Books, 1964.

Cooper, Thomas W. *Communication Ethics and Global Change*. New York: Longman, 1989.

Cose, Ellis. "The New Generation of Newspaper Giants." *Gannett Center Journal* 3 (Winter 1989): 110–22.

Crawford, Nelson A. *The Ethics of Journalism*. New York: Knopf, 1924.

Critchfield, Richard. *The Golden Bowl Be Broken: Peasant Life in Four Cultures*. Bloomington: Indiana University Press, 1988.

———. *Shahhat: An Egyptian*. Syracuse, N.Y.: Syracuse University Press, 1978.

———. "The Village Voice of Richard Critchfield: Bringing the Third World to the Fourth Estate." *Washington Journalism Review*, October 1985, pp. 26–30.

———. *Villages*. Garden City, N.Y.: Anchor Books, 1983.

Criticos, Costas. "Film and Video as a Catalyst for Change in South Africa." *Media Resource Center Working Papers* (University of Natal, Durban, South Africa), no. 2 (October 1989): 1–4.

Cunningham, Stanley. "Between Moral Theory and Utterance: The Need for Heuristic Principles in Communication Ethics." Paper presented at the National Communication Ethics Conference, Kellogg Education Center, Gull Lake, Michigan, June 1990.

"Czechoslovak Leader Announces Amnesty." *Chicago Tribune*. Chicago Tribune Wires, 2 January 1990, sec. 1, p. 1.

Dates, Jannette L., and William Barlow, eds. *Split Image: African Americans in the Mass Media*. Washington, D.C.: Howard University Press, 1990.

Day, Dorothy. "Catholic Worker Appeal." *Catholic Worker*, May 1944, p. 8.

———. "Fall Appeal 1977." The Dorothy Day–*Catholic Worker* Collection, Memorial Library Archives at Marquette University, Milwaukee, Wisconsin.

Deile, Carolyn C. "Paul Tillich's Philosophy of Communication." Ph.D. diss., University of Illinois–Urbana, 1971.

Denzin, Norman K. *Interpretive Biography.* Newbury Park, Calif.: Sage, 1989.

Derrida, Jacques. "Deconstruction and the Other." In *Dialogues with Contemporary Continental Thinkers: The Phenomenological Heritage,* edited by R. Kearney, p. 120. Manchester: Manchester University Press, 1984.

———. *Of Grammatology.* Baltimore: Johns Hopkins University Press, 1980.

Descartes, René. "Rules for the Direction of the Mind." In *Philosophical Essays,* pp. 147–236. Translated by L. J. Lafleur. Indianapolis: Bobbs-Merrill, 1964.

Dewey, John. *Problems of Men.* Totowa, N.J.: Littlefield Adams, 1958.

———. *The Public and Its Problems.* 1927. Chicago: Swallow Press, 1954.

Dickinson, Charles. *Rumor Has It.* New York: Morrow, 1991.

Dijksterhuis, E. J. *Mechanization of the World Picture.* New York: Oxford University Press, 1964.

Donaldson, Thomas. *Corporations and Morality.* Englewood Cliffs, N.J.: Prentice-Hall, 1982.

Dorfman, Dan. "Inside the Scandal at Columbia Pictures." *New York,* 16 January 1978, pp. 1–9.

Dorfman, Ron. "Present at the Creation." *Quill* 76, no. 7 (July/August 1988): 10–12.

Douglass, Paul F. *The Newspaper and Responsibility.* Cincinnati: Cafton Press, 1929.

Downing, John. *Radical Media: The Political Experience of Alternative Communication.* Boston: South End Press, 1984.

Durkheim, Emile. *The Division of Labor in Society.* Translated by G. Simpson. 1893. New York: Free Press, [1893] 1933.

———. *Suicide: A Study in Sociology.* Translated by J. Spaulding and G. Simpson. 1897. New York: Free Press, 1951.

Dyck, Arthur J. *On Human Care: An Introduction to Ethics.* Nashville, Tenn.: Abingdon, 1977.

Eason, David L. "On Journalistic Authority: The Janet Cooke Scandal." *Critical Studies in Mass Communication* 3, no. 4 (December 1986): 429–47.

Eliasoph, Nina. "Routines and the Making of Oppositional News." *Critical Studies in Mass Communication* 5, no. 4 (December 1988): 313–34.

Elliott, Deni. "All Is Not Relative: Essential Shared Values of the Press." *Journal of Mass Media Ethics* 3, no. 1 (1988): 28–32.

Ellul, Jacques. *The Political Illusion.* Translated by K. Kellen. New York: Knopf, 1967.

———. *The Presence of the Kingdom.* Translated by O. Wyon. 1948. New York: Seabury Press, 1967.

———. *Propaganda.* Translated by K. Kellen and J. Lerner. New York: Knopf, 1969.

———. "Symbolic Function, Technology and Society." *Journal of Social and Biological Structures,* October 1978, pp. 207–18.

———. *To Will and to Do.* Translated by C. E. Hopkin. Philadelphia: Pilgrim Press, 1969.

————. *What I Believe.* Translated by G. W. Bromiley. London: Marshall Morgan and Scott, 1989.

Emery, Michael, and Edwin Emery. *The Press and America: An Interpretive History of the Mass Media.* 6th ed. Englewood Cliffs, N.J.: Prentice-Hall, 1988.

Ettema, James S. "Journalism in the 'Post-Factual Age.' " *Critical Studies in Mass Communication* 4, no. 1 (March 1987): 82–86.

Ettema, James S., and Theodore L. Glasser. "On the Epistemology of Investigative Journalism." *Communication* 8, no. 2 (1985): 183–206.

Evans, Alice Frazer, Robert A. Evans, and William B. Kennedy. *Pedagogies for the Non-Poor.* Maryknoll, N.Y.: Orbis Books, 1987.

Evans, Sara M., and Harry C. Boyte. *Free Spaces: The Sources of Democratic Change in America.* Chicago: University of Chicago Press, 1992.

————. "School for Action: Radical Uses of Social Space." *Democracy* 2, no. 4 (Fall 1982): 55–65.

Ewen, Stuart. *All Consuming Images: The Politics of Style in Contemporary Culture.* New York: Basic Books, 1988.

Fallaci, Oriana. *Interview with History.* Translated by J. Shepley. New York: Liveright, 1976.

Fasching, Darrell J. "Theology, Technology and Transcendence: Reflections on Bernard Lonergan and Jacques Ellul." Unpublished paper, University of South Florida, Tampa, n.d.

Ferré, John P. "Communication Ethics and the Political Realism of Reinhold Niebuhr." *Communication Quarterly* 38, no. 3 (Summer 1990): 218–25.

————. "The Dubious Heritage of Media Ethics: Cause-and-Effect Criticism in the 1890s." *American Journalism* 5, no. 4 (1988): 191–203.

Festa, Regina, and Luiz Santoro. "Policies from Below—Alternative Video in Brazil." *Media Development* 1 (1987): 27–30.

Fink, Conrad C. *Media Ethics: In the Newsroon and Beyond.* New York: McGraw-Hill, 1988.

Fisher, David. "Applied Ethics in Postmodern Perspective." *Philosophy in Context* 17 (1987): 61–72.

Fisher, Walter R. *Human Communication as Narration: Toward a Philosophy of Reason, Value, and Action.* Columbia: University of South Carolina Press, 1987.

————. "Narration as a Human Communication Paradigm: The Case of Public Moral Argument." *Communication Monographs* 51 (March 1984): 1–22.

————. "The Narrative Paradigm: In the Beginning." *Journal of Communication* 35, no. 4 (Autumn 1985): 74–89.

————. "Narrativity and Community." In *Proceedings of the Conference on Narrativity and Community,* edited by Michael Casey, pp. 1–34. Malibu, Calif.: Conference on Christianity and Communication, 1991.

Flint, Leon Nelson. *The Conscience of the Newspaper.* New York: Appleton, 1925.

————. "What Shall the Ethics of Journalism Cover?" *Editor & Publisher,* 15 April 1922, pp. 5, 32–33.

"Foes to New Journalism." *New York Times,* 30 March 1897, p. 12.

Ford, Thomas. *A History of Illinois.* Chicago: S. C. Griggs, 1854.

Fortner, Robert S., and Clifford G. Christians. "Separating Wheat from Chaff in

Qualitative Studies." In *Research Methods in Mass Communication.* 2d ed. Edited by Guido H. Stempel III and Bruce H. Westley, pp. 375–87. Englewood Cliffs, N.J.: Prentice-Hall, 1989.

Foucault, Michel. *The Archaeology of Knowledge.* New York: Harper & Row, 1976.

———. *The History of Sexuality.* Vol. 1. New York: Random House, 1978.

———. *The Order of Things: An Archaeology of the Human Sciences.* 1966. New York: Vintage, 1973.

———. *Power/Knowledge.* New York: Pantheon Books, 1980.

Fox, Elizabeth Beverly, and Richard Wrightman Fox. "Liberals Must Confront the Conservative Argument: Teaching Humanities Means Teaching about Values." *The Chronicle of Higher Education,* 1 November 1989, p. A52.

Fox-Genovese, Elizabeth. *Feminism Without Illusions: A Critique of Individualism.* Chapel Hill: University of North Carolina Press, 1991.

Freire, Paulo. *Pedagogy of the Oppressed.* New York: Seabury Press, 1970.

French, Peter. "The Corporation as a Moral Person." *American Philosophical Quarterly* 16 (1979): 207–15.

Freud, Sigmund. *Totem and Taboo.* Translated by James Strachey. New York: Norton, 1952.

Friedman, Milton. *Capitalism and Freedom.* Chicago: University of Chicago Press, 1962.

———. "The Social Responsibility of Business Is to Increase Its Profits." *The New York Times Magazine,* 13 September 1970, pp. 32–33, 122–26.

Fry, Don. "The Shocking Pictures of Sage: Two Newspapers, Two Answers." *Washington Journalism Review,* April 1988, pp. 35–41.

Fullinwider, Robert K. "The Menace of Moral Relativism." *Report from the Center for Philosophy and Public Policy* 7 (Spring/Summer 1987): 12–14.

Gadamer, Hans-Georg. *Reason in the Age of Science.* Translated by F. G. Lawrence. Cambridge, Mass.: MIT Press, 1981.

Galilei, Galileo. *Discoveries and Opinions of Galileo.* Translated by Stillman Drake. Garden City, N.Y.: Doubleday, 1957.

Gans, Herbert J. *Deciding What's News: A Study of CBS Evening News, NBC Nightly News, Newsweek and Time.* New York: Vintage, 1979.

Geertz, Clifford. *The Interpretation of Cultures.* New York: Basic Books, 1973.

———. *Local Knowledge.* New York: Basic Books, 1983.

Gerbner, George. "A New Environmental Movement on Community and Culture." *Media Development* 37 (April 1990): 13.

———. "Telling Stories: The State, Problems, and Tasks of the Art." Paper presented at the Institute of Communications Research fortieth anniversary, University of Illinois–Urbana, 19 March 1988, pp. 6–9.

Gerbner, George, Larry Gross, Michael Morgan, and Nancy Signorielli. "Living with Television: The Dynamics of the Cultivation Process." In *Perspectives on Media Effects,* edited by Jennings Bryant and Dolf Zillman, pp. 17–40. Hillsdale, N.J.: Erlbaum, 1986.

Gibbons, William Futhey. *Newspaper Ethics: A Discussion of Good Practice for Journalists.* Ann Arbor, Mich.: Edwards Bros., 1926.

Giddens, Anthony. *Central Problems in Social Theory.* Berkeley and Los Angeles: University of California Press, 1979.

Giles, Robert. *Newsroom Management: A Guide to Theory and Practice.* Detroit: Media Management Books, 1990.

Gilkey, Langdon. *Naming the Whirlwind: The Renewal of God Language.* Indianapolis: Bobbs-Merrill, 1969.

————. *Reaping the Whirlwind: A Christian Interpretation of History.* New York: Seabury Press, 1976.

Gill, John. "Lovejoy's Pledge of Silence." *Bulletin of the Missouri Historical Society,* January 1958, pp. 167–77.

Gilliam, Dorothy Butler. "Harnessing the Assets of a Multicultural Future." *Media Studies Journal* 5, no. 4 (Fall 1991): 127–35.

Gilligan, Carol. *In A Different Voice: Psychological Theory and Women's Development.* Cambridge, Mass.: Harvard University Press, 1982.

Girvetz, Harry. *From Wealth to Welfare.* Stanford, Calif.: Stanford University Press, 1950.

Glasser, Theodore L. "Communication and the Cultivation of Citizenship." *Communication* 12, no. 4 (1991): 235–48.

Glazer, Barney C., and Anselm L. Strauss. *The Discovery of Grounded Theory.* Chicago: Aldine, 1967.

Gleason, Timothy W. *The Watchdog Concept: The Press and the Courts in Nineteenth-Century America.* Ames: Iowa State University Press, 1989.

Glendon, Mary Ann. *Rights Talk: The Impoverishment of Political Discourse.* New York: Free Press, 1991.

Goldstein, Tom, ed. *Killing the Messenger.* New York: Columbia University Press, 1989.

————. *The News at Any Cost: How Journalists Compromise Their Ethics to Shape the News.* New York: Simon and Schuster, 1985.

Goodpaster, Kenneth E., and John B. Matthews, Jr. "Can a Corporation Have a Conscience?" *Harvard Business Review* 60 (January/February 1982): 132–41.

Goodwin, H, Eugene. *Groping for Ethics in Journalism.* 2d ed. Ames: Iowa State University Press, 1987.

Goonasekera, Anura. "Communication, Culture and the Growth of the Individual Self in Third World Societies." *Asian Journal of Communication* 1, no. 1 (1990): 34–52.

Greenberg, Paul. "Revenge Is Sour." *Chicago Tribune,* 3 January 1990, sec. 1, p. 11.

Griffioen, Sander, and Jan Verhoogt, eds. *Norm and Context in the Social Sciences.* Lanham, Md.: University Press of America, 1990.

Gross, Larry, John Katz, and Jay Ruby. *Image Ethics: The Moral Rights of Subjects in Photographs, Film, and Television.* New York: Oxford University Press, 1988.

Grossberg, Lawrence. "The Ideology of Communication: Post-structuralism and the Limits of Communication." *Man and World* 15 (1982): 83–101.

————. "It's a Sin: Politics, Postmodernity and the Popular." In *It's a Sin: Essays* on *Postmodernism, Politics and Culture.* edited by V. Spate, pp. 6–71. Sydney, Australia: Power Publications, 1988.

Guinness, Os. "Tribespeople, Idiots or Citizens?" Paper presented at the Conference on Evangelical Affirmations, Deerfield, Illinois, May 1989.

Gumpert, Gary. *Talking Tombstones & Other Tales of the Media Age.* New York: Oxford University Press, 1987.

Gustafson, James M. *Ethics from a Theocentric Perspective.* 2 vols. Chicago: University of Chicago Press, 1981, 1984.

Gutmann, Amy. "Communitarian Critics of Liberalism." *Philosophy and Public Affairs* 14, no. 3 (Summer 1985): 308–22.

Habermas, Jürgen. "Hannah Arendt's Communications Concept of Power." *Social Research* 44, no. 1 (Spring 1977): 3–24.

———. *Moral Consciousness and Communicative Action.* Translated by C. Lenhardt and S. W. Nicholsen. Cambridge, Mass.: MIT Press, 1990.

———. *The Structural Transformation of the Public Sphere.* Cambridge, Mass.: MIT Press, 1989.

Hall, Stuart. "Encoding/Decoding." In *Culture, Media, Language,* edited by Stuart Hall, Dorothy Hobson, and Andrew Lowe, pp. 128–38. London: Hutchinson, 1980.

———. "The Problem of Ideology—Marxism Without Guarantees." In *Marx One Hundred Years On,* edited by Betty Matthews, pp. 57–86. London: Lawrence and Wishart, 1983.

———. "Signification, Representation, Ideology: Althusser and the Post-Structuralist Debates." *Critical Studies in Mass Communication* 2, no. 2 (June 1985): 91–114.

Hall, Stuart, Chas Critcher, Tony Jefferson, John Clarke, and Brian Roberts. *Policing the Crisis: Mugging, the State, and Law and Order.* New York: Holmes and Meier, 1978.

Hamlett, Patrick W. "Science, Technology, and Liberal Democratic Theory." *Technology in Society* 6, no. 3 (1984): 249–62.

Harrington, Walt. "In Ricky's Wake." *The Washington Post Magazine,* 7 June 1987, pp. 15–21, 42–45.

Harris, Marvin. *America Now.* New York: Simon and Schuster, 1981.

Hartley, John. *Understanding News.* London: Methuen, 1982.

Harwood, Richard. "Defending the Indefensible." *Editor & Publisher,* 10 August 1991, p. 3.

Hauerwas, Stanley. *A Community of Character.* Notre Dame, Ind.: University of Notre Dame Press, 1981.

———. *Naming the Silences: God, Medicine, and the Problem of Suffering.* Grand Rapids, Mich.: Eerdmans, 1990.

———. *Truthfulness and Tragedy.* Notre Dame, Ind.: University of Notre Dame Press, 1977.

Hauerwas, Stanley, and L. Gregory Jones. *Why Narrative? Readings in Narrative Theology.* Grand Rapids, Mich.: Eerdmans, 1989.

Hayek, Friedrich A. *Law, Legislation and Liberty.* Vol. 3. London: Routledge and Kegan Paul, 1982.

———. *The Road to Serfdom.* London: Routledge and Kegan Paul, 1976.

Hegel, Georg F. W. *Science of Logic I.* Translated by A. V. Miller. London: Allen & Unwin, 1969.

Held, David. *Models of Democracy.* Stanford, Calif.: Stanford University Press, 1987.

Heller, Agnes. *General Ethics.* Oxford: Basil Blackwell, 1988

Henning, Albert F. *Ethics and Practices in Journalism.* New York: Long and Smith, 1932.

Henry, William A., III. "Beyond the Melting Pot." *Time,* 9 April 1990, pp. 28–31.

Hiskes, Richard P. *Community Without Coercion.* Newark: University of Delaware Press, 1982.

Hocking, William Ernest. "The Crisis of Our Time." *University of Chicago Round-table,* no. 353, 24 December 1944.

———. "The Future of Liberalism." *Journal of Philosophy* 32 (25 April 1935): 225–47.

———. *The Lasting Elements of Individualism.* New Haven, Conn.: Yale University Press, 1937.

Hodges, Louis. "Review of *The Virtuous Journalist.*" *Journal of Mass Media Ethics* 3, no. 1 (1988): 100–101.

Hofstader, Richard. *The Age of Reform.* New York: Vintage, 1955.

———. *The Progressive Movement 1900–1915.* Englewood Cliffs, N.J.: Prentice-Hall, 1963.

Holmes, Arthur F. *Contours of a World View.* Grand Rapids, Mich.: Eerdmans, 1983.

Horkheimer, Max, and Theodor W. Adorno. *Dialectic of Enlightenment.* New York: Seabury Press, 1972.

Hubbard, Benjamin J., ed. *Reporting Religion: Facts & Faith.* Sonoma, Calif.: Polebridge Press, 1990.

Hulteng, John L. *The Messenger's Motives: Ethical Problems of the Mass Media.* 2d ed. Englewood Cliffs, N.J.: Prentice-Hall, 1985.

Hummel, Charles. "Newton." *Christian History,* Issue 30 (n.d).

Hutcheon, Linda. "A Postmodern Problematics." In *Ethics/Aesthetics: Post-Modern Positions,* edited by Robert Merrill, pp. 1–10. Washington, D.C.: Maisonneuve Press, 1988.

Huyssen, Andreas. "Mapping the Postmodern," *New German Critique* 33 (1984): 5–52.

Hyde, Michael. "Foucault, Derrida, and the Ethics of Rhetoric: An Existentialist Reading of Two Poststructuralists." Paper presented at the Speech Communication Association annual conference, Chicago, November 1990.

International Commission for the Study of Communication Problems. *Many Voices, One World: Communication and Society Today and Tomorrow.* London: Kogan Page, 1980.

Irons, Peter. *The Courage of Their Convictions: Sixteen Americans Who Fought Their Way to the Supreme Court.* New York: Penguin Books, 1990.

Isaacs, Norman E. *Untended Gates: The Mismanaged Press.* New York: Columbia University Press, 1988.

Jaffee, David. "The Village Enlightenment in New England, 1760–1820." *William and Mary Quarterly* 47 (July 1990): 327–46.

Jameson, Fredric. "Postmodernism, or the Cultural Logic of Late Capitalism." *New Left Review* 146 (1984): 53–92.

Janis, Irving. *Groupthink: Psychological Studies of Policy Decisions*. 2d ed. Boston: Houghton Mifflin, 1982.

Jefferson, Thomas. Letter to M. Coray, 31 October 1823. In *Thomas Jefferson on Democracy,* edited by Saul K. Padover, p. 164. New York: New American Library, 1939.

————. *The Writings of Thomas Jefferson*. Vol. 11. Edited by Andrew A. Lipscomb. Washington, D.C.: Thomas Jefferson Memorial Association, 1904.

Johannesen, Richard L. "Virtue Ethics, Character, and Political Communication." In *Ethical Dimensions of Political Communication,* edited by Robert E. Denton, Jr., pp. 69–90. New York: Praeger, 1991.

Jonas, Hans. *The Imperative of Responsibility: In Search of an Ethics for the Technological Age*. Chicago: University of Chicago Press, 1984.

Keiser, R. Melvin. *Recovering the Personal: Religious Language and the Post-Critical Quest of H. Richard Niebuhr*. Atlanta: Scholars Press, 1988.

Kellner, Douglas. "Postmodernism as Social Theory: Some Challenges and Problems." *Theory, Culture and Society* 5, nos. 2–3 (June 1988): 239–69.

Kelly, Geffrey B., and F. Burton Nelson, eds. *A Testament of Freedom: The Essential Writings of Dietrich Bonhoeffer*. San Francisco: HarperCollins, 1990.

Kepnes, Steven. *Buber's Hermeneutic Philosophy and Narrative Theology*. Bloomington: Indiana University Press, 1991.

"Kerner Plus Twenty Special Issue." *Mass Comm Review* 15, nos. 2–3 (1988): 2–68.

Kirkpatrick, Frank G. *Community: A Trinity of Models*. Washington, D.C.: Georgetown University Press, 1986.

Klaidman, Stephen, and Tom L. Beauchamp. *The Virtuous Journalist*. New York: Oxford University Press, 1987.

Klotzer, Charles L. "Journalism Reviews: Their Role, Impact and Limitations." *St. Louis Journalism Review* 21, no. 140 (October 1991): 10–11.

Kohlberg, Lawrence. *The Philosophy of Moral Development: Moral Stages and the Idea of Justice*. San Francisco: Harper & Row, 1981.

Krimsky, George. "Understanding the Foreign Journalist." *Editor & Publisher,* 18 May 1991, pp. 60, 62.

Kroker, Arthur, and David Cook. *The Postmodern Scene: Excremental Culture and Hyper-Aesthetics*. New York: St. Martin's, 1986.

Kuhn, Thomas S. *The Structure of Scientific Revolutions*. 2d ed. Chicago: University of Chicago Press, 1970.

Lambeth, Edmund B. *Committed Journalism: An Ethic for the Profession*. 2d ed. Bloomington: Indiana University Press, 1992.

Landay, Jerry M. "Paying for Public Broadcasting: Set the System Free." *Chicago Tribune,* 1 August 1990, sec. 1, p. 11.

Lasch, Christopher. *The Culture of Narcissism: American Life in an Age of Diminishing Expectations*. New York: Warner Books, 1983.

Lebacqz, Karen. *Professional Ethics: Power and Paradox.* Nashville, Tenn.: Abingdon, 1985.

Leibniz, Gottfried Wilhelm. *The Monadology and Other Philosophical Writings.* Translated by R. Latta. New York: Oxford University Press, 1925.

Lerner, Max. *Ideas Are Weapons.* New York: Viking, 1939.

Lévi-Strauss, Claude. *The Savage Mind.* Chicago: University of Chicago Press, 1966.

Lewis, Hunter. *A Question of Values.* New York: Harper & Row, 1990.

Liebling, Abbott Joseph. *The Press.* Rev. ed. New York: Ballantine Books, 1964.

Likert, Rensis. *New Patterns of Management.* New York: McGraw-Hill, 1961.

Linsky, Martin. "Practicing Responsible Journalism: Press Impact." In *Responsible Journalism,* edited by Deni Elliott, pp. 133–50. Beverly Hills, Calif.: Sage, 1986.

Lippmann, Walter. "The Scholar in a Troubled World." *Atlantic Monthly,* August 1932, pp. 148–52.

Locke, John. *An Essay Concerning Human Understanding.* Vol. 1. 1690. Oxford: Clarendon Press, 1894.

Lofland, John. *Doing Social Life.* New York: Wiley, 1976.

Lotz, J. B. "Person and Ontology," *Philosophy Today* 7 (Winter 1963): 294–97.

Lowrey, Shearon, and Melvin L. DeFleur. *Milestones in Mass Communications Research.* 2d ed. New York: Longman, 1988.

Luckmann, Thomas. *The Invisible Religion.* New York: Macmillan, 1967.

Lummis, Charles Douglas. "The Radicalism of Democracy." *Democracy* 2, no. 4 (Fall 1982): 9–16.

Lustig, Jeff. "Community and Social Class." *Democracy* 1, no. 2 (April 1981): 96–111.

Luxner, Larry. "Press Freedom in the Arab World." *Editor & Publisher,* 10 August 1991, p. 14.

Lyotard, Jean François. *The Post-Modern Condition: A Report of Knowledge.* Translated by G. Bennington and B. Massumi. Minneapolis: University of Minnesota Press, 1988.

MacIntyre, Alasdair. *After Virtue.* Notre Dame, Ind.: University of Notre Dame Press, 1981.

———.*Three Rival Versions of Moral Enquiry.* Notre Dame, Ind.: Notre Dame University Press, 1990.

———. *Whose Justice? Which Rationality?* Notre Dame, Ind.: University of Notre Dame Press, 1986.

Macmurray, John. *The Clue to History.* London: Student Christian Movement Press, 1938.

———.*Conditions of Freedom.* Atlantic Highlands, N.J.: Humanities Press, 1978.

———. *The Form of the Personal.* Vol. 1: *The Self as Agent.* London: Faber & Faber, 1961.

———. *The Form of the Personal.* Vol. 2: *Persons in Relation.* London: Faber & Faber, 1961.

Mander, Mary E. "Narrative Dimensions of the News: Omniscience, Prophecy, and Morality." *Communication* 10, no. 1. (1987): 51–70.

Mapel, David. *Social Justice Reconsidered: The Problem of Appropriate Precision in a Theory of Justice.* Urbana: University of Illinois Press, 1989.

Margolick, David. "Rape Victim Steps Out of 'Unidentified' Shadow to Let Paper Tell Story." *Louisville Courier-Journal,* 25 March 1990, p. A14.

Martin, J. "Can Organizational Culture Be Managed?" In *Organizational Culture,* edited by Peter Frost, Larry Moore, Meryl Louis, Craig Lundberg, and Joanne Martin, pp. 95–98. Beverly Hills, Calif.: Sage, 1985.

Martin, J., and M. E. Powers. "Truth or Corporate Propaganda: The Value of a Good War Story." In *Organizational Symbolism,* edited by Louis R. Pondy, Peter J. Frost, Gareth Morgan, and Thomas C. Dandridge, pp. 93–107. Greenwich, Conn.: JAI Press, 1983.

Mathews, M. Cash. *Strategic Intervention in Organizations: Resolving Ethical Dilemmas.* Newbury Park, Calif.: Sage, 1988.

Matter, Joseph A. *Love, Altruism, and World Crisis: The Challenge of Pitirim Sorokin.* Chicago: Nelson-Hall, 1974.

May, William F. "Code and Covenant or Contract and Philanthropy: Alternative Bases for Professional Ethics." In *Ethics in Medicine: Historical Perspectives and Contemporary Concerns,* edited by Stanley J. Reiser, Arthur J. Dyck, and William J. Curran, pp. 65–76. Cambridge, Mass.: MIT Press, 1977.

Maynard, Nancy Hicks. "The Journalist as Storyteller." *Gannett Center Journal* 2, no. 2 (Spring 1988): 78–84.

McAllister, Matthew P. "Medicalization in the News Media: A Comparison of AIDS Coverage in Three Newspapers." Ph.D. diss., University of Illinois–Urbana, 1990.

McClintick, David. *Indecent Exposure: A True Story of Hollywood and Wall Street.* New York: Morrow, 1982.

McCulloch, Frank, ed. *Drawing the Line.* Washington, D.C.: American Society of Newspaper Editors, 1984.

McDonald, Henry. *The Normative Basis of Culture: A Philosophical Inquiry.* Baton Rouge: Louisiana State University Press, 1986.

McGrath, J. E. *Groups: Interaction and Performance.* Englewood Cliffs, N.J.: Prentice-Hall, 1984.

McKiernan, Derek. "Television and the Dialectic of Community." *Media Development* 36 (1989): 33–36.

McWilliams, Wilson Carey. *The Idea of Fraternity in America.* Berkeley and Los Angeles: University of California Press, 1973.

Mehl, Peter J. "In the Twilight of Modernity: MacIntyre vs. Mitchell on Human Nature, Cultural Context, and Ethical Ideals." Unpublished paper, University of Chicago, 1986.

Merrill, John C. *The Dialectic in Journalism: Toward a Responsible Use of Press Freedom.* Baton Rouge: Louisiana State University Press, 1989.

———. *Existential Journalism.* New York: Hastings House, 1977.

———. *The Imperative of Freedom: A Philosophy of Journalistic Autonomy.* New York: Hastings House, 1974; New York: Freedom House, 1990.

———. "Three Theories of Press Responsibility and the Advantages of Pluralistic Individualism." In *Responsible Journalism,* edited by Deni Elliott, pp. 47–59. Beverly Hills, Calif.: Sage, 1986.

Meyer, Philip. *Ethical Journalism.* New York: Longman, 1987.

Michels, Robert. *Political Parties: A Sociological Study of Oligarchical Tendencies of Modern Democracy.* Translated by E. and C. Paul. 1908. New York: Free Press, 1949.

Miller, David W. *George Herbert Mead: Self, Language and the World.* Austin: University of Texas Press, 1973.

Miller, William Lee. "Religious Liberty and American Pluralism." Paper presented at the Conference on Conflicts in the Public Square: Religion Versus Secularism, Chicago, November 1986.

Mills, C. Wright. *The Sociological Imagination.* New York: Oxford University Press, 1959.

Mills, Rilla Dean. "Newspaper Ethics: A Qualitative Study." *Journalism Quarterly* 60, no. 4 (Winter 1983): 589–94.

Milton, John. *Areopagitica: A Speech for the Liberty of Unlicensed Printing.* 1644. Boston: Beacon Press, 1951.

Mitchell, Basil. *Morality: Religious and Secular.* Oxford: Clarendon Press, 1980.

Mlama, Penina M. "Culture, Women and the Media." In *Communication and Culture: African Perspectives,* edited by S. T. Kwame Boafo, pp. 11–18. Nairobi, Kenya: Africa Church Service, 1989.

Moss, Michael. "The Poverty Story." *Columbia Journalism Review* 26, no. 2 (July/ August 1987): 43–54.

Mouffe, Chantal. "Hegemony and Ideology in Gramsci." In *Gramsci and Marxist Theory,* edited by Chantal Mouffe, pp. 168–203. London: Routledge and Kegan Paul, 1979.

———. "Rawls: Political Philosophy Without Politics." In *Universalism vs. Communitarianism: Contemporary Debates in Ethics,* edited by David Rasmussen, pp. 217–35. Cambridge, Mass.: MIT Press, 1990.

Mouw, Richard J. *The God Who Commands: A Study in Divine Command Ethics.* Notre Dame, Ind.: University of Notre Dame Press, 1990.

Mumby, Dennis K. *Communication and Power in Organizations: Discourse, Ideology, and Domination.* Norwood, N.J.: Ablex, 1988.

Mumford, Lewis. *The Myth of the Machine.* Vol. 2: *Pentagon of Power.* New York: Harcourt Brace Jovanovich, 1970.

Murchland, Bernard. "Hannah Arendt as Public Thinker." *The Civic Arts Review* 2, no. 4 (Fall 1989): 9–11.

———. "The Thinking Citizen: A Conversation with Elizabeth Minnich." *The Civic Arts Review* 2, no. 1 (Winter 1989): 4–9.

Nagel, Thomas. *The View from Nowhere.* New York: Oxford University Press, 1986.

Neuhaus, Richard John. *The Naked Public Square.* Grand Rapids, Mich.: Eerdmans, 1984.

Newbigin, Lesslie. *The Gospel in a Pluralist Society.* Grand Rapids, Mich.: Eerdmans, 1989.

Nicole, Eduardo. *Los principios de la ciencia.* Mexico City: Fundo de Cultura Económica, 1965.

Niebuhr, H. Richard. *The Meaning of Revelation.* New York: Macmillan, 1941.

———. *The Responsible Self.* New York: Harper & Row, 1963.

Niebuhr, Reinhold. *Man's Nature and His Communities.* New York: Scribner's, 1965, pp. 102–3.

———. *Moral Man and Immoral Society: A Study in Ethics and Politics.* New York: Scribner's, 1932.

Nisbet, Robert. "The Present Age and the State of Community." *Chronicles,* June 1988, pp. 11–18.

North, Oliver L. *Under Fire: An American Story.* San Francisco: HarperCollins/ Zondervan, 1991.

Nozick, Robert. *Anarchy, State and Utopia.* Oxford: Basil Blackwell, 1974.

O'Connor, Flannery. *The Complete Stories.* New York: Farrar, Straus & Giroux, 1980.

O'Connor, Elizabeth. *The New Community.* New York: Harper & Row, 1976.

Olthuis, James H. "An Ethics of Compassion: Ethics in a Post-Modernist Age." In *What Right Does Ethics Have,* edited by Sander Griffeon, pp. 125–46. Amsterdam: Free University Press, 1990.

———."Evolutionary Dialectics and Segundo's *Liberation of Theology.*" *Calvin Theological Journal* 21, no. 1 (April 1986): 79–93.

———. *A Hermeneutics of Ultimacy: Peril or Promise?* Lanham, Md.: University Press of America, 1987.

Ouchi, William G. *Theory Z.* Reading, Mass.: Addison-Wesley, 1981.

Patterson, Grove Hiram. "Social Responsibilities of the American Newspaper." Eighteenth Address, Don R. Mellet Memorial Fund. New York University, School of Commerce, Accounts, and Finance, Department of Journalism, 12 March 1948, pp. 5–14.

Patterson, Margaret Jones, and Robert H. Russell. *Behind the Lines: Case Studies in Investigative Reporting.* New York: Columbia University Press, 1986.

Patton, Paul. "Notes for a Glossary." *Ideology and Consciousness* 8 (1981): 44–48.

Pauly, John. "A Beginner's Guide to Doing Qualitative Research in Mass Communication." *Journalism Monographs* 125 (February 1991): 1–29.

———. "Interesting the Public: A Brief History of the Newsreading Movement." *Communication* 12, no. 4 (1991): 286–97.

Peck, M. Scott. *The Different Drum: Community Making and Peace.* New York: Touchstone Books, 1988.

———. *People of the Lie: The Hope for Healing Human Evil.* New York: Simon and Schuster, 1983.

Peck, William J., ed. *New Studies in Bonhoeffer's Ethics.* Toronto: Edwin Mellen Press, 1987.

Perrow, Charles. *Complex Organizations.* 3d ed. New York: Random House, 1987.

———. "A Framework for the Comparative Analysis of Organizations." *American Sociological Review* 32 (April 1967): 194–208.

———. *Normal Accidents.* New York: Basic Books, 1984.

———. *Organizational Analysis: A Sociological View.* Belmont, Calif.: Brooks/ Cole, 1970.

Peters, John Durham. "John Locke, the Individual, and the Origin of Communication." *Quarterly Journal of Speech* 75, no. 4 (November 1989): 387–99.

Peterson, Theodore B. "Social Responsibility Since the Hutchins Commission."

Unpublished paper, College of Communications, University of Illinois–Urbana, 1987, pp. 1–44.

Peukert, Helmut. "Fundamental Theology and Communicative Praxis as the Ethics of Universal Solidarity." *Conrad Grebel Review* 3 (Winter 1985): 41–65.

———. "Universal Solidarity as Goal of Communication." *Media Development* 28, no. 4 (1981): 10–12.

Picard, Robert, Maxwell McCombs, James Winter, and Stephen Lacy, eds. *Press Concentration and Monopoly: New Perspectives on Newspaper Ownership and Operation.* Norwood, N.J.: Ablex, 1988.

Pippert, Wesley G. *An Ethics of News: A Reporter's Search for Truth.* Washington, D.C.: Georgetown University Press, 1989.

Polanyi, Michael. *The Study of Man.* Chicago: University of Chicago Press, 1959.

———. *The Tacit Dimension.* Garden City, N.Y.: Doubleday, 1966.

Pollock, Frederick, and F. W. Maitland. "Corporation and Person." In *Anthropology and Early Law,* edited by Lawrence Krader, pp. 300–36. New York: New York University Press, 1965.

Polman, Dick. "PBS Considers Free Air Time for Politicians." *Chicago Tribune,* 9 July 1990, sec. 1, p. 5.

Popkin, Jeremy D. *Revolutionary News: The Press in France 1789–1799.* Durham, N.C.: Duke University Press, 1990.

Posner, Richard A. *The Economics of Justice.* Cambridge, Mass.: Harvard University Press, 1981.

Protess, David, Fay Lomax Cook, Jack Doppelt, James Ettema, Margaret Gordon, Donna Leff, and Peter Miller. *The Journalism of Outrage: Investigative Reporting and Agenda Building in America.* New York: Guilford, 1991.

Purcell, Edward A. *The Crisis of Democratic Theory: Scientific Naturalism and the Problem of Value.* Lexington: University of Kentucky Press, 1973.

Ranke, Leopold von. "Preface to *Histories of Romance and Germanic Nations from 1494 to 1514.*" In *The Varieties of History,* edited by Fritz Stern, pp. 54–62. New York: World, 1956.

Rawls, John. "Justice as Fairness: Political Not Metaphysical." *Philosophy and Public Affairs* 14 (1985): 223–52.

———. *A Theory of Justice.* Cambridge, Mass.: Harvard University Press, 1971.

Rich, Adrienne. *On Lies, Secrets, and Silence.* New York: Norton, 1979.

Ricoeur, Paul. "The Antinomy of Human Reality and the Problem of Philosophical Anthropology." In *Readings in Existential Phenomenology,* edited by Nathaniel Lawrence and Daniel O'Connor, pp. 390–401. Englewood Cliffs, N.J.: Prentice-Hall, 1967.

———. *Fallible Man.* 2d ed. Translated by Charles A. Kelbley. New York: Fordham University Press, 1986.

———. *Interpretation Theory: Discourse and the Surplus of Meaning.* Fort Worth: Texas Christian University Press, 1976.

Ripley, C. Peter, Roy E. Finkenbine, and Paul A. Cimbala, eds. *The Black Abolitionist Papers.* Vol. 2: *Canada, 1830–1865.* Chapel Hill: University of North Carolina Press, 1986.

Rivers, William L., Jay Jensen, and Theodore Peterson. *The Mass Media and Modern Society.* 2d ed. San Francisco: Rinehart, 1971.

Rivers, William L., and Cleve Mathews. *Ethics for the Media*. Old Tappan, N.J.: Prentice-Hall, 1988.

Rivers, William L., Wilbur Schramm, and Clifford Christians. *Responsibility in Mass Communication*. 3d ed. New York: Harper & Row, 1980.

Roberts, Nancy L. *Dorothy Day and the Catholic Worker*. Albany: State University of New York Press, 1984.

Rorty, Richard. *Contingency, Irony, and Solidarity*. Cambridge: Cambridge University Press, 1989.

———. *Philosophy and the Mirror of Nature*. Princeton, N.J.: Princeton University Press, 1979.

———. "The Priority of Democracy to Philosophy." In *The Virginia Statute for Religious Freedom,* edited by Merrill D. Peterson and Robert C. Vaughn, pp. 257–82. New York: Cambridge University Press, 1988.

Rosaldo, Renato. *Culture and Truth: The Remaking of Social Analysis*. Boston: Beacon Press, 1989.

Rosen, Jay. "Making Journalism More Public." *Communication* 12, no. 4 (1991): 267–84.

Rosenblatt, Roger. "Journalism and the Larger Truth." *Time,* 2 July 1984, p. 88.

Rouner, Leroy S. "Selfhood, Nature, and Society: Ernest Hocking's Metaphysics of Community." In *On Community,* edited by Leroy S. Rouner, pp. 76–90. Notre Dame, Ind.: University of Notre Dame Press, 1991.

———. *Within Human Experience: The Philosophy of William Ernest Hocking*. Cambridge, Mass.: Harvard University Press, 1969.

Rousseau, Jean Jacques. *Emile*. London: Dent 1961.

Rowe, William L. *Religious Symbols and God: A Philosophical Study of Tillich's Theology*. Chicago: University of Chicago Press, 1968.

Royko, Mike. Introduction to A. A. Dornfeld, *Hello Sweetheart, Get Me Rewrite: The Story of the City News Bureau of Chicago*. Chicago: Academy Chicago Publishers, 1983.

Rupp, George. "Communities of Collaboration: Shared Commitments/Common Tasks." In *On Community,* edited by Leroy S. Rouner, pp. 192–208. Notre Dame, Ind.: University of Notre Dame Press, 1991.

Rush, Ramona R., and Donna Allen, eds. *Communications at the Crossroads: The Gender Gap Connection*. Norwood, N.J.: Ablex, 1989.

Sandel, Michael J. *Liberalism and the Limits of Justice*. Cambridge: Cambridge University Press, 1982.

———. "Morality and the Liberal Ideal." *The New Republic,* 7 May 1984, pp. 15–17.

———, ed. *Liberalism and Its Critics*. New York: New York University Press, 1984.

Scanlon, Thomas M., Jr. "Content Regulation Reconsidered." In *Democracy and the Mass Media,* edited by Judith Lichtenberg, pp. 331–54. Cambridge: Cambridge University Press, 1991.

———. "Freedom of Expression and Categories of Expression." *University of Pittsburgh Law Review* 40 (Summer 1979): 519–50.

———. "A Theory of Freedom of Expression." *Philosophy and Public Affairs* 1, no. 2 (Winter 1972): 204–26.

Schein, Edgar H. *Organizational Culture and Leadership.* San Francisco: Jossey-Bass, 1985.

Scheler, Max. *Formalism in Ethics and Non-Formal Ethics of Values.* Translated by M. Frings and R. Funk. Evanston, Ill.: Northwestern University Press, 1973.

———. *The Nature of Sympathy.* Translated by P. Heath. Hamden, Conn.: Archon Books, 1973.

———. *Problems of a Sociology of Knowledge.* Translated by M. Frings. 1960. London: Routledge and Kegan Paul, 1980.

Schudson, Michael. "The Profession of Journalism in the United States." In *The Professions in American History,* edited Nathan O. Hatch, pp. 145–61. Notre Dame, Ind.: University of Notre Dame Press, 1988.

Schumacher, E. F. *Guide for the Perplexed.* New York: Harper & Row, 1977.

Schumpeter, Joseph. *Capitalism, Socialism and Democracy.* London: Allen & Unwin, 1976.

Schutz, Alfred. "Concepts and Theory Formation in the Social Sciences." *Journal of Philosophy* 51 (1954): 257–73.

———. *The Phenomenology of the Social World.* 1932. Evanston, Ill.: Northwestern University Press, 1967.

Schutz, W. *FIRO: A Three-Dimensional Theory of Interpersonal Behavior.* New York: Holt, Rinehart and Winston, 1958.

Schwarzlose, Richard A. "The Marketplace of Ideas: A Measure of Free Expression." *Journalism Monographs* 118 (December 1989): 1–41.

Seldes, George. *Even the Gods Can't Change History: The Facts Speak for Themselves.* Secaucus, N.J.: Lyle Stuart, 1976.

Shaw, David. "Abortion Bias Seeps into News." *Los Angeles Times,* 1 July 1990, p. 1.

Sheehan, Neil. *A Bright Shining Lie: John Paul Vann and America in Vietnam.* New York: Random House, 1988.

Shriver, Donald W. "Man and His Machines: Four Angels of Vision." *Technology and Culture* 13 (October 1972): 531–55.

Sider, Ronald. *Rich Christians in an Age of Hunger.* Downers Grove, Ill.: InterVarsity Press, 1979.

Siebert, Fred S., Theodore Peterson, and Wilbur Schramm. *Four Theories of the Press.* Urbana: University of Illinois Press, 1956.

Slack, Jennifer Daryl. "Critical Strategies for a Non-normative Ethics." Paper presented at International Communication Association annual conference, Honolulu, Hawaii, May 1985.

Slack, Jennifer Daryl, and Laurie Anne Whitt. "Ethics and Cultural Studies." In *Cultural Studies,* edited by Lawrence Grossberg, Cary Nelson, and Paula Treichler, pp. 571–92. New York: Routledge, 1992.

Smircich, Linda. "Concepts of Culture and Organizational Analysis." *Administrative Science Quarterly* 28 (1983): 347–50.

Smircich, Linda, and Marta B. Calás. "Organizational Culture: An Assessment." In *Handbook of Organizational Communication: An Interdisciplinary Perspective,* edited by Frederic M. Jablin, Linda L. Putnam, Karlene H. Roberts, and Lyman W. Porter, pp. 228–63. Beverly Hills, Calif.: Sage, 1987.

Smith, David H. "Work, Community and the Corporation." Paper presented at the Poynter Center for the Study of Ethics and American Institutions, Indiana University, Bloomington, February 1989.

Smith, Hampden H., III. "Donna Rice to the Press: 'I Lost Everything.' " *Journal of Mass Media Ethics* 5 (1990):151–67.

Smith, Jeffrey A. "The Enticements of Change and America's Enlightenment Journalism." Paper presented at a Library of Congress symposium, Publishing and Readership in Revolutionary France and America, Washington, D.C., 2 May 1989.

Solomon, Robert. *Continental Philosophy Since 1750: The Rise and Fall of the Self.* New York: Oxford University Press, 1988.

Sorokin, Pitirim A. *Forms and Techniques of Altruistic and Spiritual Growth.* Boston: Beacon Press, 1954.

———. *The Ways and Power of Love.* Boston: Beacon Press, 1954.

Stanley, Manfred. *The Technological Conscience: Survival and Dignity in an Age of Expertise.* Chicago: University of Chicago Press, 1978.

Staudenmaier, John M. "U.S. Technological Style and the Atrophy of Civic Commitment." In *Beyond Individualism: Toward a Retrieval of Moral Discourse in America,* edited by Donald L. Gelpi, pp. 120–56. Notre Dame, Ind.: University of Notre Dame Press, 1989.

Stein, M. L. "Stop the Sophistication." *Editor & Publisher,* 15 June 1991, p. 16.

Steiner, Linda. "Feminist Theorizing and Communication Ethics." *Communication* 12, no. 3 (1991): 157–73.

Steirman, Hy. "The Publisher's Responsibility." In *The Responsibility of the Press,* edited by Gerald Gross, pp. 249–57. New York: Fleet, 1966.

Stob, Henry. "Ethics: An Account of Its Subject Matter." In *Ethical Reflections: Essays on Moral Themes.* Grand Rapids, Mich.: Eerdmans, 1978.

Stone, Vernon A. "Minority Men Shoot ENG, Women Take Advancement Tracks." *Communicator,* August 1988, pp. 10–14.

"A Story of Hope, A Story of Courage, the Story of Sage." *Albuquerque Tribune,* 16 October 1987, pp. F2–F11.

Stout, Jeffrey. *Ethics After Babel: The Languages of Morals and Their Discontents.* Boston: Beacon Press, 1988.

Stroman, Carolyn A., Bishetta D. Merritt, and Paula W. Matabane. "Twenty Years After Kerner: The Portrayal of African Americans on Primetime Television." *The Howard Journal of Communications* 2, no. 1 (Winter 1989–90): 44–56.

Swain, Bruce M. *Reporters' Ethics.* Ames: Iowa State University Press, 1978.

Tablada, Juan José. "Newspaper Ethics: A Spanish-American View." *Journalism Bulletin* 3, no. 2 (June 1926): 1–5.

Tate, Cassandra. "Conflict of Interest: A Newspaper's Report on Itself." *Columbia Journalism Review* 17, no. 2 (July/August 1978): 44–48.

Taylor, Charles. "Growth, Legitimacy and the Modern Identity." *Praxis International* (1981):111.

———. *Hegel.* Cambridge: Cambridge University Press, 1975.

———. *Hegel and Modern Society.* Cambridge: Cambridge University Press, 1979.

———. *Philosophy and the Human Sciences: Philosophical Papers.* Vol. 2. Cambridge: Cambridge University Press, 1985.

————. *Sources of the Self: The Making of the Modern Identity.* Cambridge, Mass.: Harvard University Press, 1989.

Tehranian, Majid. *Technologies of Power: Information Machines and Democratic Prospects.* Norwood, N.J.: Ablex, 1990.

Theunissen, Michael. *The Other: Studies in the Social Ontology of Husserl, Heidegger, Sartre, and Buber.* Translated by C. Macann. Cambridge, Mass.: MIT Press, 1984.

Thigpen, Robert, and Lyle Downing. "Liberalism and the Communitarian Critique." *American Journal of Political Science* 31 (1987):637–55.

Thomas, J. Mark. *Ethics and Technoculture.* Lanham, Md.: University Press of America, 1987.

Thompson, John B. *Studies in the Theory of Ideology.* Berkeley and Los Angeles: University of California Press, 1984.

Tillich, Paul. *Love, Power, and Justice.* New York: Oxford University Press, 1954.

————. *Morality and Beyond.* New York: Harper & Row, 1963.

Tinder, Glenn. "Can We Be Good Without God? On the Political Meaning of Christianity." *Atlantic Monthly,* December 1989, pp. 69–85.

————. "Freedom of Expression, the Strange Imperative." *The Yale Review* 69, no. 2 (December 1979):161–76.

Tomaselli, Keyan. *The Cinema of Apartheid: Race and Class in South African Film.* Chicago: Lake View Press, 1990.

Tönnies, Ferdinand. *Community and Society (Gemeinschaft und Gesellschaft).* Translated by C. P. Loomis. East Lansing: Michigan State University Press, 1957.

Torpey, John. "Ethics and Critical Theory: From Horkheimer to Habermas." *Telos* 19, no. 3 (Fall 1986):68–84.

Toulmin, Stephen. "The Recovery of Practical Philosophy." *The American Scholar,* Summer 1988, pp. 337–52.

Tournier, Paul. *The Meaning of Persons.* Translated by E. Hudson. New York: Harper & Row, 1957.

Traber, Michael. "Narrativity and Community: A Cultural Studies Approach." In *Proceedings of the Conference on Narrativity and Community,* edited by Michael Casey, chap. 4. Malibu, Calif.: Conference on Christianity and Communication, 1991.

Tracy, David. *Blessed Rage for Order.* New York: Seabury Press, 1975.

————. *Plurality and Ambiguity: Hermeneutics, Religion, Hope.* San Francisco: Harper & Row, 1987.

Treichler, Paula A. "AIDS, Homophobia, and Biomedical Discourse: An Epidemic of Signification." *Cultural Studies* 1, no. 4 (1987):263–305.

Unger, Roberto M. *Politics: A Work in Constructive Social Theory.* 3 vols. Cambridge: Cambridge University Press, 1988.

Verhey, Allen D. "Review of *The Flight from Authority* and *Ethics After Babel.*" *Calvin Theological Journal* 25, no. 2 (November 1990): 262–66.

Walsh, Brian J. "Theology and Modernity: A Study in the Thought of Langdon Gilkey." Ph.D. diss., McGill University, Montreal, 1987.

Walzer, Michael. *Interpretation and Social Criticism.* Cambridge, Mass.: Harvard University Press, 1987.

———. *Spheres of Justice: A Defense of Pluralism and Equality.* New York: Basic Books, 1983.

Waterman, David. "A New Look at Media Chains and Groups." *Journal of Broadcasting and Electronic Media* 35, no. 2 (Spring 1991): 167–78.

Waters, Enoch. *American Diary: A Personal History of the Black Press.* Chicago: Path Press, 1987.

Weaver, David H., and G. Cleveland Wilhoit. *The American Journalist: A Portrait of U.S. News People and Their Work.* 2d ed. Bloomington: Indiana University Press, 1991.

Weber, Max. *From Max Weber: Essays in Sociology.* Translated and edited by H. H. Gerth and C. Wright Mills. New York: Oxford University Press, 1946.

———. "Towards a Sociology of the Press." Translated by Hanno Hardt. *Journal of Communication* 26, no. 3 (1976): 96–101. Speech delivered at the First Congress of Sociologists, Frankfurt, Germany, 1910.

Weick, Karl E. *The Social Psychology of Organizing.* 2d ed. Reading, Mass.: Addison-Wesley, 1979.

Weisman, Joel. "The Don Craig Story." *Quill,* October 1978, pp. 24–26.

Weiss, Philip. "Invasion of the Gannettoids." *New Republic,* 2 February 1987, pp. 18–22.

Wertham, Fredric. *Seduction of the Innocent.* New York: Rinehart, 1954.

White, Hayden. "The Value of Narrativity in the Representation of Reality." *Critical Inquiry* 7, no. 1 (1980): 5–27.

White, Richard. *Inventing Australia.* London: Allen & Unwin, 1981.

Will, Frederick L. *Beyond Deduction: Ampliative Aspects of Philosophical Reflection.* New York: Routledge, 1987.

Williams, Bernard. *Ethics and the Limits of Philosophy.* London: Fontana Press, 1982.

———. *Moral Luck.* Cambridge: Cambridge University Press, 1981.

Wilson, Jean Gaddy. "Women in the Newspaper Business." *Presstime,* October 1986, pp. 31–37.

Wolcott, Harry F. *Writing Up Qualitative Research.* Newbury Park, Calif.: Sage, 1990.

Wolin, Sheldon. "Why Democracy?" *Democracy* 1, no. 1 (January 1981): 3–5.

Wolterstorff, Nicholas. *Until Justice and Peace Embrace.* Grand Rapids, Mich.: Eerdmans, 1983.

Wuliger, Gregory T. "The Moral Universes of Libertarian Press Theory." *Critical Studies in Mass Communication* 8, no. 2 (June 1991): 152–67.

Wuthnow, Robert. *Meaning and Moral Order: Explorations in Cultural Analysis.* Berkeley and Los Angeles: University of California Press, 1987.

Wyschogrod, Edith. *Saints and Postmodernism.* Chicago: University of Chicago Press, 1990.

Yarros, Victor S. "Journalism, Ethics, and Common Sense." *International Journal of Ethics* 32 (July 1932): 410–19.

Znaniecki, Florian. *Cultural Sciences.* Urbana: University of Illinois Press, 1952.

———. *The Method of Sociology.* New York: Holt, Rinehart and Winston, 1935.

INDEX